The Quaker Family in Colonial America

The Quaker Family in Colonial America

A Portrait of the Society of Friends

J. WILLIAM FROST

VASSAR COLLEGE

ST. MARTIN'S PRESS   NEW YORK

To Susan and James

Library of Congress Catalog Card Number: 72–95835

Manufactured in the United States of America.
For information write: St. Martin's Press, Inc., 175 Fifth Avenue, New York, N.Y. 10010

AFFILIATED PUBLISHERS: Macmillan Limited, London—also at Bombay, Calcutta, Madras, and Melbourne.

Acknowledgments

I was fortunate to be able to do my research in libraries whose staffs were friendly, knowledgeable, and efficient. The work was greatly aided by the presence of librarians such as Sylvia Stevens at Friends' House, London; Frederick Tolles, Eleanor Mayer, Betty MacPherson, and Jane Thorson at Friends' Historical Library, Swarthmore; Edwin Bronner, Betty Tritle, Francis Barnet, and Alice Whittelsey at the Quaker Collection at Haverford; Conrad Wilson and Peter Parker at the Historical Society of Pennsylvania; Thomas Adams, Mrs. Joseph Hardy, Samuel Hough, and Donald Farren at the John Carter Brown Library; Mary Hogenauer of Westtown School; and Alice Allen of the Department of Records of Philadelphia Yearly Meeting. With particular pleasure I acknowledge the kindness of Dorothy Gilbert Thorne in opening the Guilford College Quaker Collection on a weekend, of Edward Milligan in bringing books from the library to my flat in London, of Dorothy Harris in investigating multitudinous queries, of Thyra Jane Foster in making special trips to the John Carter Brown library on the chance that I might need materials, and of Albert Klyberg in letting me work evenings in the Rhode Island Historical Society during the last week I could spend in Providence. Henry J. Cadbury suggested that I live at Pendle Hill when I was working in Philadelphia, and he made arrangements accordingly. This Quaker retreat in a bucolic setting has an excellent library accessible at any hour every day. The Vassar College librarians spent great amounts of time obtaining books or films and checking obscure references.

Grants from the University of Wisconsin, the John Carter Brown Library, and Vassar College made possible the research for this book. Portions of Chapter 1 previously appeared in *Church History* and sections of Chapter 4 in *Quaker History*, and they are reprinted with the permission of those publications. I owe a special debt to David Lovejoy, who first suggested the topic and provided continuing encouragement and criticism of my endeavors on this project. At various stages the manuscript was read by Max Savelle, Stanley Katz, Mildred Campbell, Henry J. Cadbury, Donald Olsen, and Sydney James. These historians saved me from many errors and provided excellent suggestions for improvements. I also profited from conversations with scholars who happened to be working in a library at the same time I was there. Nancy Schrom, Josefa Rosenberger, and Vicki Metzel did valuable work as student assistants. My wife deserves special mention for having read and reread each chapter for content and style and for having endured my periodic absences for research and my endless discussions of the Quaker family.

J. W. F.

Contents

Introduction 1
1. The Dry Bones of Quaker Theology 10
2. The Quest for Holiness 30
3. The Nature of Christian Discipline 48
4. Childhood: As the Twig Is Bent 64
5. "A Guarded, Religious, and Useful Education" 93
6. Quaker School Life 108
7. Youth: The Age of Temptation 133
8. Choosing a Wife 150
9. Quaker Marriage Customs 172
10. The Quaker Style of Life 187
11. Conclusions 217
Appendices 221
Bibliography 228
Index 246

Abbreviations

BFHA	*Bulletin of Friends' Historical Society* (Philadelphia)
DR	Philadelphia Yearly Meeting Department of Records
FH	Friends' House, London
FHL	Friends' Historical Library, Swarthmore College
HSP	Historical Society of Pennsylvania
JFHA	*Journal of Friends' Historical Society* (London)
LC	Library Company of Philadelphia
Min	Minutes
MM	Monthly Meeting
NHS	Newport Historical Society
PMHB	*Pennsylvania Magazine of History and Biography*
PP	Pemberton Papers
QC	Quaker Collection, Haverford College
QH	Quaker History
YM	Yearly Meeting

In quotations, capitalization and italics remain in their original form, but archaic spelling and punctuation have been modernized.

Introduction

The easiest way of becoming acquainted with the modes of thinking, the rules of conduct, and the prevailing manners of any people, is to examine what sort of education they give their children; how they treat them at home, and what they are taught in their places of public worship.

Crèvecoeur, Letters from an American Farmer

The most basic institution in early America was the family, and yet historians are just beginning to understand the family's importance in education, religion, work, and government. Knowledge of the Quaker family structure is useful for the insights it provides about that religious group and for the information which, when added to the demographic work being done on particular localities, will contribute to conclusions about the changing nature and distinctive patterns of family life in early America.[1] We may soon discover whether there are characteristics common to most American families or if one must deal with selected groups defined on the basis of religion, class, or region. Colonial Friends could be merchants or artisans, city or country dwellers, wealthy or poverty stricken, educated or barely literate, but to treat them as primarily sectionally divided and economically diverse would distort the central importance of religion in shaping their lives. To be a Quaker meant to share certain values about the family. Since the Society of Friends was never a purely American denomination, and since colonial Quakers retained close contacts with Friends in the British Isles, one ought not to treat American Quakers in isolation. Wherever they lived, all Quakers held essentially the same beliefs.

A crucial problem in the study of the Quakers' attitudes toward the family is the definition of what was unique about those attitudes and what was similar to the rest of the culture to which they belonged. The dilemma of Friends—like that of all Christians—was how to reform society while keeping aloof from worldly ways. Quakers were normally interested in political theories only when their religious ideas had social consequences. Many of their beliefs about the rearing of children, the functions of the school, the position of women, and ethical practices in business they shared with most eighteenth-century Protestants. Perry Miller has written that 90 percent of the ideas of the "Puritan culture" were held by "all Englishmen."[2] A similar estimate would hold if applied to the relationship between Quakers and New England Puritans. One should not, of course, denigrate the significance of the other 10 percent, since Quaker beliefs included such concepts as pacifism, religious toleration, and a rejection of the sacraments.

American Friends did not differ from their neighbors in farming techniques, arrangements of rooms in houses, or types of implements used in cooking. A geographical rather than a religious framework serves as a more efficient method of describing material artifacts. While quantification has provided useful information on many facets of family life, the problems discussed here cannot be placed into numerical categories. Ideas about children, views of courtship, and the impact of religious values upon behavior patterns can be best dealt with through literary sources. The impressionistic nature of the evidence used in this study may disturb those who believe that history should be a social science. The techniques used by modern sociologists and anthropologists suggest new problems but cannot add solid information to fragmentary records. Asking the traditional types of questions of the sources remains the most effective method of determining the ideas that govern behavior.

In dealing with an organization formed and maintained for religious or theological purposes, one must examine its beliefs. All historians assume a relationship between activities and thought but rarely intimate how the two are juxtaposed. The physical environment conditions the mind, but ideas shape the material culture. This issue becomes central to the social and intellectual history of a denomination whose very existence depended upon its unique combination of thought and behavior patterns. In all cultures, parents (or their functional equivalents) and the larger social groupings combine in order to support, educate, and control the children. Since the parents have the task of integrating the children into the social milieu, what they, as members of the religious body, consider most important will appear prominently in the theories of how the children are reared.

This book combines church history with social history and is based on the premise that to understand the meeting, one needs to know the family. Conversely, to comprehend the family one must study the meeting. In a sectarian community, religious concerns, which cut across regional or class divisions, cannot be separated from the daily life of adult or child. The meeting's admonitions to children can be best understood when joined to an awareness of what was expected from mature members. Disciplines listed what was demanded of adults, as parents and as members, and proper child-rearing practices were as important to the faith as right business dealings or correct theology. Quakerism endured through the interaction of the family, the school, and the meeting. Since there were few outsiders converted in the eighteenth century, the survival of the meeting depended upon the nurturing of the faith within the family.

Quakers and Puritans were products of the religious turmoil of the seventeenth century, and both groups wrote voluminously about the practice of piety and published enough about family relations to enable one to determine their general beliefs. There was a fundamental difference in the influence of these two religious movements. The Puritans dominated Massachusetts and Connecticut, generally excluded all other religious groups, and could legislate observance of their beliefs for the entire society in those areas. Even after toleration was decreed, a state church existed and the overwhelming majority of the people adhered to it. In contrast, the only colony that the Quakers controlled for any length of time was Pennsylvania, and even there they promoted religious toleration. By 1700 Friends were a minority in Philadelphia and by 1730 (at the latest) a minority in the province. After the 1730s Quaker political power was founded upon an alliance with non-Quaker German settlers, and after 1756 there was never a Quaker majority in the assembly. While the Friends were powerful enough in Pennsylvania to ensure that provincial legislation was acceptable to them, one cannot assume that either the laws or local jurisprudence necessarily reflected Quaker ideas about government and society. Friends in the assembly made certain that their religious practices were respected, but they never required others to follow their customs. Before 1700 Friends may have constituted a majority of the population of West Jersey and Rhode Island, and in the eighteenth-century they retained substantial political power due to bloc voting, but their legislative demands were normally restricted to insuring their ability to practice their religious testimonies without hindrance.[3]

II

This book is about the Quaker family in Colonial America from 1672, when George Fox toured America, until the American Revolution. In matters of family structure and social history there are no definite beginnings and endings, and I have used materials from as early as 1650 and as late as 1815. I have defined a Quaker as a person who considered himself a member of the Society of Friends and who was esteemed as such by the Society; this meant that he was under the supervision of the meeting. A religious leader like Anne Hutchinson, whose ideas were similar to those of early Quakers, has been excluded since she never had any relationships with the formal body of Friends.[4]

Quakerism was a lay religion with no professional religious leaders or paid clergy. The only time a Friend received compensation for his services was when he worked as a traveling preacher; then the yearly meeting paid his expenses. The ministry was composed of individuals deemed to have been given by the Holy Spirit the gift of speaking in the meeting. The elders (men and women who watched over the ministers and congregation) were not officially recognized as such until the eighteenth century, but certain individuals had carried on their essential functions of advising and rebuking ministers and laymen long before 1700.[5] A third group of men and women were termed overseers. These persons, often the most substantial farmers or merchants in the community, acted as trustees for church property, supervised the funds of the meeting, and served as arbitrators in disputes between members. Ministers, elders, and overseers provided most of the leadership at meetings and watched over the conduct of the entire membership.

The organization of the society was pyramidal. At the base was the local meeting with its worshipping congregation. In this regard, the popular picture of a plain-garbed group sitting silently in an unornamented room is correct. Such mundane affairs as seeing that the meeting house was cleaned, firewood provided, and broken glass repaired were entrusted to preparative meetings. Most large local meetings were preceded by preparatory meetings, which could settle minor offenses and appoint overseers to report any violations of the discipline to the monthly meeting.

The level at which most of the work of the church was conducted was the monthly meeting, which was composed of all the local meetings in a township or small geographical area; men and women met in separate monthly meetings normally held at the same time. Any Friend in good standing could attend and speak at these business meetings, but the opinions of "weighty" members—ministers, elders, overseers—carried the most influence in arriving at a "sense of the meeting." All decisions were made by the entire body, with the clerk ascertaining the will of the group; such procedures as voting and majority rule were never used. Many activites of the meeting were entrusted to small committees, again consisting primarily of weighty Friends. The monthly meeting regulated marriages, controlled funds, gave charity, supervised the schools, disciplined or disowned anyone guilty of a moral offense, and sent reports to the quarterly meetings.

The quarterly meetings, normally composed of all the monthly meetings in a particular county, were attended by delegates from each monthly meeting. Quarterly meetings were a half-way point between the monthly and yearly meetings. Any problem too large for a local meeting to solve was referred to the quarterly meeting, which could settle the matter or place it on the agenda of the yearly meeting. The epistles from the yearly meeting were read and questions answered about the state of local meetings. In England the quarterly meetings sent written reports of the doings of the monthly meetings to the yearly meeting, but in America oral reports were often used, and the practice of giving written answers to specific queries was not general until 1755. There were special quarterly meetings for ministers and elders designed to aid them in overseeing the congregation. Both types of quarterly meetings usually began with a period of silence and worship after which business was discussed.

Delegations from the quarterly meetings attended the yearly meetings. In the colonies there were six yearly meetings: Pennsylvania and New Jersey (usually termed Philadelphia), New York, Maryland (or Baltimore), Virginia, North Carolina, and New England. (See appendix A for the number of meetings in each yearly meeting.) In Great Britain there were yearly meetings in London and Ireland. (At various times there were special yearly meetings and half-year's meetings held in America and England; these were generally occasions for worship and no administrative business took place.) The yearly meetings occupied several days; several thousand people attended the largest, such as those at Philadelphia or Newport. In theory, any decision reached by the yearly meeting on any matter was binding upon all quarterly and monthly meetings within its jurisdiction. A controversial matter was apt to be appealed from the monthly or quarterly meetings to the yearly meeting, and if a consensus could not be reached, the problem would be postponed until the next session. During the year, Friends might write to London Yearly Meeting for its counsel. All yearly meetings were autonomous, but the two most powerful meetings were London and Philadelphia, and London was first among equals. Philadelphia attempted to exercise similar influence in America but enjoyed only sporadic success.

The yearly meetings were in close contact with each other. London Yearly Meeting distributed printed epistles every year to all quarterly and monthly meetings in England and to every yearly and many quarterly and monthly meetings in America.[6] Most yearly meetings received a second letter which might contain answers to specific problems faced by that meeting. The yearly meetings in America sent out epistles to London and to their own monthly meetings, but they did not always send letters to each other. In 1714, when Philadelphia Yearly Meeting wished to consult with other American yearly meetings on the subject of slavery, it sent a message to London Friends requesting them to ask the question since it was easier for London to communicate with North Carolina and Virginia meetings than for Philadelphia to attempt to correspond directly.[7]

Friends attempted to make their organization and their religious beliefs as harmonious as possible. Since they thought that Christian revelation was the same the world over. they made a deliberate effort to make certain that their recommendations were agreed upon by most Friends. Frederick Tolles believed that "Quaker thinking on most subjects varied relatively little from place to place, so that the ideas of English and American Friends down at least to the Revolution can be regarded as practically interchangeable."[8] One can examine the epistles, or discipline, or minutes of a meeting in England, in New England, or in North Carolina and fail to determine from the contents any difference in geographical location. (See appendix B for a discussion of unity of thought in official Quaker documents.)

There were minor differences in organization. London Yearly Meeting entrusted the censorship of the press to a Morning Meeting of ministers and elders that met in London. Yearly meetings in America appointed committees to oversee publications. In 1754 American Friends persuaded their English brethren to establish a yearly meeting of ministers and elders, and in 1784 the English Friends were prevailed upon to set up a women's yearly meeting.[9] Some American meetings used the manuscript copies of the English disciplines as rules for every contingency. The agency that carried out most of the executive functions for London Yearly Meeting was the Meeting for Sufferings, so named because it was formed to deal with the problems of persecution in England. This organization, composed of the most influential Friends residing in or close to London, supervised finances, lobbied with the government, and wrote epistles to meetings all over the world. In America the first meeting for sufferings was set up by Philadelphia Yearly Meeting during the French and Indian War, and Friends were so fearful of forming a domineering oligarchy that at first its powers were subject to annual renewal. New York organized a meeting for sufferings in 1758; New England established one in 1775.

Traveling ministers helped maintain close contact among Quakers in widely separated areas. The beliefs of the Society of Friends were first spread by men and women journeying through the English countryside, and the custom continued as a missionary endeavor and as a means of perpetuating the Quaker community. English and American Friends crossed the ocean to join each other, and together they traveled to meetings along the American seaboard. The small, isolated meeting in Charleston, South Carolina, received 22 visitors between 1751 and 1786, and New England received 233 between 1672 and 1759.[10] Sometimes the travelers would pass through localities and hold single meetings; but they might stay several weeks and did not hesitate to inform their hosts of any misdoing or deviation from generally accepted procedures.

III

Friends everywhere in America had access to works of the most famous Quaker authors and to a wide variety of tracts on different aspects of the religious testimonies. The intellectual linkage in the transatlantic community was fostered by frequent epistles and the sending of published works. Friends used these books to proselytize and to form meeting libraries. Almost all the monthly meetings that regularly received copies of books formed libraries. The establishment of the Philadelphia library at the first monthly meeting held in 1682 gave evidence to the stress that Quakers placed on book collections. Rhode Island Monthly Meeting (Newport) established a library in 1679, Thirdhaven Meeting (Maryland) in 1676, and Charleston Meeting (South Carolina) by 1720 at the latest, since the meeting took an inventory of all books in its possession in that year.[11] Enough books were distributed by London and Philadelphia to the South, New York, and New England that meetings there could also have formed libraries. Quakerism was a lay religion, but the members were remarkably literate on theological issues.

Before assessing the influence of an author's work, the historian needs to distinguish between one man's opinions and the ideas of the entire religious body. When a Friend published a religious tract, he wrote on behalf of the Society. The meetings made certain that his ideas did not misrepresent the "truth." Every work written by a Quaker was first perused by a committee of weighty Friends, and these committees edited the works of such prominent Quakers as Fox, Penn, and Barclay. When the Morning Meeting in London turned down one of his papers, George Fox reacted explosively: "I was not moved to set up that meeting to make orders against the reading of my papers."[12]

Any printed work approved by the Friends should not be taken as one man's opinion—primarily because, by the time it was published, the ideas it contained had met the approbation of an entire committee designed to screen out unorthodox ideas. Any phrase or sentiment that the members did not like could be striken and whole sections rewritten. Since those appointed to these committees in the eighteenth century were usually the most devout members, and since the Friends feared innovations that might oppose the traditions handed down by the first Quaker martyrs, the contents of printed sources tend to read very much alike.

To supplement these monolithic published accounts the historian can turn to a variety of other manuscripts. George Fox instilled in the Friends a devotion for collecting and recording anything of relevance: epistles, advices, personal letters, condemnations, retractions, certificates of removal and admission, and minutes of monthly, quarterly, and yearly meetings. These show not only great similarities in procedure but also the attempts of the meetings to bridge the interstices between the theory and practice of Quakerism. The quality of such records depends upon individual clerks, whose interests differed from those of today's social historian. One can read several hundred pages of minutes and still have only a hazy notion of the personalities involved or the way the meeting actually functioned.

Other sources useful in obtaining Quaker ideas are the letters, diaries, and personal papers of Friends. The Quakers whose papers were preserved were of two types. First, there were men and women of outstanding religious qualities whose journals and letters were kept as examples of devotional literature. Second, the wealthy and influential Quakers of Philadelphia, such as the Pembertons, Logans, and Norrises, preserved much correspondence relating to politics, business, and religious matters. Court records, laws, accounts written by travelers in the colonies, and anti-Quaker tracts written by political or religious opponents help round out the portrait of Quakerism.

Even with all this information, there remain sizable omissions in our knowledge of Quakerism, particularly in its early period. The farmer who was neither devout enough to serve on meeting committees nor wicked enough to be disciplined is missing from meeting records and, unless he was engaged in trade or was very prosperous, is unlikely to have left any personal correspondence. The same gap occurs in the knowledge of very young Quaker children. There is, for example, only one document in 100 years that provides information as to when a child was toilet-trained. With such gaps in knowledge, it would be rash to attempt to use the insights of Freud or Erik Erikson. To admit ignorance of some crucial ingredients in the formative years is far better than to discuss child nurture using a twentieth-century theory of human behavior.

IV

The first portion of this book attempts to define the faith professed by Friends. The beginning chapter assesses the theological content of Quakerism by contrasting the Westminster Confession, the most definitive statement of Presbyterian and Puritan beliefs, with the most authoritative sources of Quaker thought. Chapter 2 describes the practice of piety by focusing on Christian life as it was presented in Quaker diaries and by showing the kind of worship in which Friends participated. Chapter 3 discusses the extent to which the monthly meeting was involved in the daily life of Friends by contrasting the rationale for church discipline with the way in which the meeting actually operated.

The second part (Chapters 4 through 9) analyzes the Quaker family by showing the process of growing up. What was the conception of the infant? How was the child disciplined? What was the nature of his religious life? Two chapters on education describe Quaker ideas on the role of learning, the amount of literacy, the curriculum, the daily life of the student, and changing ideas about the school. Between the time he attended school and the time he reached marriageable age, the Quaker youth experienced what twentieth-century man calls adolescence. How did Quaker parents deal with disciplinary problems during that period? How did the youth learn a trade? Adult status was formalized by marriage. How did a young man choose a girl and court her? And what role did the parents and the meeting play? Was the wife-to-be selected because of money, piety, or romantic love? What was the position of the woman in a Quaker household?

The Quaker style of living, summarized in the final chapters, links the sections on the meeting and the family. Friends could see the impact of worship, discipline, and parental guidance in the behavior of the adult. How did his religion influence the attitude of a Friend toward the physical world, money, business, poverty, morality, recreation? What were the effects of Quaker customs in dress, speech, and peace? Can one speak of a Quaker personality? What role did the Friends play in the formation of an American national character?

Notes

1 Research on family life is not a new concern of historians, but the great variety of research techniques now being used has posed again the problem of how the family functioned internally and within the context of the larger society. Recently published studies of small areas in New England are Kenneth Lockridge, *A New England Town: The First Hundred Years* (New York, 1970); Philip J. Greven, Jr., *Four Generations: Population, Land, and Family in Colonial Andover, Massachusetts* (Ithaca, N.Y., 1970); and John Demos, *A Little Commonwealth: Family Life In Plymouth Colony* (New York, 1970). These books rely on town records, laws, wills, architecture, demography, and psychology. Edmund Morgan, *The Puritan Family* (New York, 1966) provides the framework of ideas about the family in New England. Darrett Rutman, *Husbandmen of Plymouth: Farms and Villages in the Old Colony, 1620–1692* (Boston, 1967) surveys the agricultural techniques of Plymouth. David Hunt applies psychoanalysis to the rearing of Louis XIII in *Parents and Children in History* (New York, 1970); Alan Macfarlane uses anthropological methods in *The Family Life of Ralph Josselin* (Cambridge, 1970). James Lemon, *The Best Poor Man's Country* (Baltimore, 1972) provides the basic geographical information on Pennsylvania agriculture that is required to understand the economic base of the Society. Obviously many types of historical investigation will be needed in order to properly encompass the family, an institution crucial to social, economic, and religious life. This book is based largely upon meeting records and literary sources (diaries, tracts, and letters), and it emphasizes Quaker ideas about the family and correct behavior.

2 Perry Miller and Thomas H. Johnson, *The Puritans* (New York, 1963), 1: 7.

3 James Logan estimated in 1741 that Friends made up one-third of the population of Pennsylvania; in 1756 opponents alleged that Friends constituted between one-fourth and one-fifth of the population. A Quaker estimate in 1761 was that 1,027 Quaker families lived in Rhode Island and 1,146 in the rest of New England. Edmund Peckover described the attendance at New England's yearly meeting in 1743 as not less than 5,000 and in 1755 Samuel Fothergill maintained that it had the "largest attendance of any yearly meeting in the world." *PMHB* 6 (1882): 408; 10 (1886): 301: *Extracts from the Itineraries and Miscellanies of Ezra Stiles* (New Haven, 1916), pp. 92–93, 95, 106, 191; *Quaker History* 52 (1968): 2–4; Joseph Wanton, *Observations and Reflections on the Present State of the Colony of Rhode Island* (Newport, 1763), p. 4; "Account of the People in the Colony of Rhode Island," ca.1755, Broadside, Rhode Island Historical Society.

4 Rufus Jones, Isaac Sharpless, and Amelia Gummere, *The Quakers in the American Colonies* (New York, 1966), pp. 3–25.

5 Min. Philadelphia YM, 1. (7/18/1706): 111, and (7/18–22/1714): 157.

6 In 1703 London sent 12 epistles to Burlington and West Jersey, 12 to Pennsylvania, 4 to East Jersey, 20 to Maryland, 20 to Virginia, and 6 to Carolina. Yorkshire, which contained the heaviest concentration of Quakers in England, received 80. In 1758 London sent 700 copies to Pennsylvania and New Jersey, 100 to New England, and 60 to North Carolina. Min. London YM, 3 (3/24/1703): 103–105; Min. London Meeting for Sufferings, 30 (6/11/1758): 188.

7 In 1684 Philadelphia Yearly Meeting asked Friends throughout America to send delegates to a general yearly meeting. Only Rhode Island and Maryland sent representatives. In 1687 Rhode Island began sending epistles to Philadelphia. In 1705 Philadelphia decided to open a correspondence with other American yearly meetings, but it was not until 1713 that epistles were sent to Maryland and Long Island. In 1718 Virginia was added to the list. Philadelphia always kept its own meetings liberally supplied with epistles. The 1759 epistle was issued in an edition of at least 2,500 copies and the quotas for distribution to quarterly meetings by the time of the Revolution were based upon editions of

2,000 or 2,500 copies. Min. Philadelphia YM, 1 (7/24/1684): 8; (7 mo./1686): 12; (7 mo./1705): 104–105; (7/20–23/1713): 150; (7 mo./1718): 190–91; London YM, Epistles Received, 2: 173; Min. Philadelphia Meeting for Sufferings, 11/15/1759.

8 Frederick Tolles, *Meeting House and Counting House* (New York, 1963), p. ix; Thomas E. Drake, "Patterns of Influence in Anglo-American Quakerism," *JFHS*, Supplement no. 28 (Great Britain, 1958): 5–6; *PMHB* 60 (1936): 362–72.

9 John Pemberton to Israel Pemberton 6/22/1753, PP, 9: 21; John Griffith to John Pemberton 8/4/1754, 10: 22 HSP; *JFHS* 22 (1925): 82–83.

10 Min. Charleston MM, DR; "Register of names of Publick Friends that have visited New England since the year 1656," copied by John Smith, Smith Mss, LC, 4: 198; Frederick Tolles, *Quakers and the Atlantic Culture* (New York, 1960), pp. 21–35.

11 Min. Philadelphia MM, 11/3/1682, p. 1; Min. Rhode Island MM, 1/2/1679; Min. Charleston MM, 9/7/1720, p. 12; *JFHS* 11 (1914): 130–31; William Dunlap, *Quaker Education in Baltimore and Virginia Yearly Meeting* (Philadelphia, 1936), p. 297.

12 Elfrida Vipont, *The Story of Quakerism* (London, 1954), p. 99.

1 The Dry Bones of Quaker Theology

After having surveyed the barrenness of the valley in which were scattered skeletal remains, the prophet in the Book of Ezekiel was asked, "O mortal man, can these bones live?" And his reply was not an optimistic "they will live," but rather "O Lord God, thou knowest." When the historian begins to discuss the common theological assumptions and issues that perplexed seventeenth-century man, he does not know whether they can be put into a meaningful context, and he is uncertain that these "bones" can be made to live. Historian Perry Miller recently made a large American audience aware of seventeenth-century thought when he summarized the New England strands of thought in an essay entitled "The Marrow of Puritan Divinity."[1] Miller argued that theology was part of the essence, the very marrow, of Puritanism and that a copious amount of thought was devoted to it. The seriousness of the Puritan concern was witnessed by the succession of able theologians, from William Ames and Richard Baxter in the seventeenth century to Solomon Stoddard, Jonathan Edwards, and Charles Chauncy in the eighteenth.

The contrast between Quaker and Puritan theological attainment is striking. After the initial outpouring of works by the "First Publishers of Truth" and the more orderly expositions of the faith by William Penn, Robert Barclay, and George Keith—all of whom had created their most significant writings between 1664 and 1695—the Friends produced no original able thinkers for the next 100 years. Moreover, none of these men was educated at a Quaker school. William Penn, trained at Oxford, wrote many tracts defending Quaker beliefs and religious toleration, but his greatest ability lay in expressing in clear practical terms what one should do in order to be a consistent Christian. Keith and Barclay, the best systematic Quaker theologians, were from Scotland, where Friends had the least impact in the British Isles; both were extraordinarily well-educated in Calvinist (and Barclay also in Roman Catholic) schools, and both wrote voluminously to prove that the Quaker religion was the truth. Because in the 1690s George Keith became a schismatic and, after being disowned, ended as an Anglican priest, his works were neglected during the eighteenth century. Robert Barclay remained the standard-bearer for the next 150 years. His *Apology for the True Christian Divinity,* written in Latin and first issued in English in 1678, went as deeply into the mysteries of faith as Friends cared to go. The problems that he wrestled with were assumed to have been solved. The *Apology* was given to anyone interested in becoming a Quaker or to anyone thought to need enlightenment about the Society of Friends.[2] Practically every monthly meeting in England and America owned at least one copy. The book was translated into German, Dutch, French, Spanish, Danish, and Arabic; London Yearly Meeting even gave a copy to each of the ambassadors involved with the treaty of Aix-la-Chapelle. Anyone who read the *Apology* would have had to be vitally interested in Quakerism, for it is devoid of the flashes of insight or brilliance found in the works of Keith or Penn. The book was clearly written, well-organized, and provided a coherent, biblically based, and solidly argued statement of Quaker doctrine. Clearly, it is a fundamental source that must be dealt with before one can comprehend Quakerism.

The Quakers were a by-product of the religious and social upheavals called the Puritan Revolution. The clash of ideas among Presbyterian, Anglican, and Independent churches meant that, in the absence of a controlling orthodoxy, new groups could form such as the Diggers, Muggletonians, Fifth Monarchy Men, Ranters, or Quakers. Of these only the Friends have survived. The spectrum from Seeker through Ranter, Quaker, Independent, and Presbyterian to Anglican was one of extraordinarily gradual transitions. All the groups had much in common, but this did not prevent theological debate from being carried on with an intensity that has rarely been equaled. Each side claimed that the others' doctrinal perversity was endangering salvation, and each wrote as if the triumph of righteousness depended upon an answer being written to the answer of an original pamphlet long since forgotten. The present-day observer, not used to theological hairsplitting buttressed by every conceivable biblical precedent, might conclude that their similarities far outweighed any differences. And he would be right. Hugh Barbour, author of a recent study of the birth of the Friends, argued that the great bitterness of the quarrel between the Puritans and the Quakers stemmed from the closeness of the issues—that is, that the intensity was heightened because it was basically a family dispute.[3] William Penn and Charles Leslie or Francis Howgill and Richard Baxter were actually just feuding, rather than kissing, cousins.

The purpose of this chapter is to delineate Quaker theology as it developed after the Restoration in England by contrasting it with the Reformed traditions which dominated Scotland and New England and produced Nonconformity in England. The primary source for Quaker beliefs will be Robert Barclay's *Apology,* supplemented by certain works of George Fox, William Penn, and George Keith. For the Reformed tradition the most convenient expressions of doctrine are found in the Synod of Dort of 1619 and the Westminster Confession of 1653. Only a few Independents participated in the Westminster Assembly but when drawing up their own creed in the Savoy Declaration of 1658, the Congregationalists specifically endorsed the doctrines promulgated at Westminster. They differed only over church organization.[4]

II

Calvinist orthodoxy had been defined by the five doctrines of Dort, which countless students have learned through the mnemonic device of "tulip," that is, total depravity, unconditional election, limited atonement, the irresistibility of grace, and final perseverance of the saints. In short, they believed that man was totally evil and by justice condemned to hell, but that God saw fit, by His own judgment made before the world existed, to save a certain number of men. The rest were damned to hell for their sins. The grace of God that came to the saint could not be negated by man, for God's attractiveness overwhelmed the man with salvation. The true Christian, the man whom God had elected for eternal bliss, could not fall because God's judgment was never wrong. Therefore, if a man fell, he could be sure that he was not of the elect. The rigors of these doctrines had been protested by groups of more rationalistic Christians known as Socinians and Arminians; the "tulip" decrees were enunciated as a condemnation of the Arminians. The Puritans of England, whether Presbyterian or Independent, although they weakened the harshness of the system by many "neverthelesses," did not deny any of these principles, and the Westminster Confession contained them all. The nonseparating Congregationalists who settled New England mitigated the doctrines somewhat by saying that God set forth the details of his will in a covenant.[5] The individual, the church, and the state were to accept the covenant and strive to uphold it. By forcing covenant responsibility into the foreground and downplaying the nature of absolute predestination, the New Englanders were able to adopt a more persuasive program of action. But they did not at any time deny the five decrees of Dort, and to be called an Arminian was an insult long after the Great Awakening. Since the chief rivalry to Quakers in the colonies came from Presbyterians and New England Puritans, to outline their doctrines is to portray the intellectual world in which the Quakers lived.

The most basic question of every religious man was what must one do to be saved? There was general agreement about where religion ended—in union with Christ—and most concurred on the position from whence man started. No naturally virtuous good citizen listened to comfortable exhortations in Puritan or Quaker worship. He was told, quite frankly, that he was damned, that on his own he was utterly worthless—lower than the vermin of the earth. The Westminster Confession defined man as corrupted by original sin which extended to all mankind. Barclay summarized the Quaker position:

> All *Adam's* posterity (or mankind) . . . is fallen, degenerated, and dead, deprived of the sensation or feeling of this testimony or *seed of God*. . . .Man, therefore, as he is in this state can know nothing aright; yea, his thoughts and conceptions concerning God and things spiritual . . . are unprofitable both to himself and others.[6]

There were minor differences in the doctrine of how one fell. The Puritans saw man as having been born corrupt and having confirmed his depravity by sinning, while the Friends asserted that children were born innocent and remained so until they committed their inevitable act of sin. Yet children had within them an evil tendency caused by Adam's fall. The Friends' somewhat milder view of original corruption is the only basis for asserting, as certain historians of Quakerism have done, that Friends began with a positive view of mankind.[7]

Both groups also agreed upon an absolute separation between man and the divine. God was and man was, and since man had sinned there was no contact. If anything, the Quakers had a lower view of man's abilities than the Puritans, for the latter believed that man retained in his faculty of reason some of his marks of innocence, even though they had been tainted by the fall. The New England Puritans believed that God had created an orderly universe and had provided a key to its understanding in the logical system articulated by Petrus Ramus. His logic was not an empirical discipline subject to the varieties of experience; rather, it was the means through which all experience could be discovered.[8] Friends believed that logic was subject to reason and reason was corrupted. Logic, words, reason, natural experience, and conscience could in no sense give man any right understanding of anything to do with religion. The Puritans should be seen as asserting a scholastic argument in permitting reason to mingle with faith in the discussion of belief. Friends, although never affirming that revelation went contrary to reason, were more closely associated with the Tertullian stream of Christian thought, which refused to admit even the relevance of reason in spiritual matters.[9]

Barclay did not deny the role of reason in other spheres. Reason was preeminent in its field, which included all natural matter, for to "be rightly and comfortably ordered" in physical entities demanded such a faculty. Both Friends and Puritans recognized the necessity of something other than reason in religion, but with this difference: The Puritans used and defended all possible tools of man in learning about and communicating the contents of revelation; the Friends admitted only supernatural means in evaluating supernatural matters.[10]

The most famous doctrine of John Calvin was predestination, and following his death the tenet was emphasized rather than negated. If one examined unconditional election from inside the church and felt assurance that he was one of the elect, then the belief could be comforting. (Friends said it fostered spiritual pride.) But if one were not sure whether or not salvation was his and then realized that no act or deed could bring him closer to God, the doctrine could appear unbelievably harsh. This apparent capriciousness of God was the Achilles' heel of the Reformed traditions and was furiously attacked by Friends. Predestination injured God, said Barclay, by making Him "the author of sin." No matter what syllogisms or sophistry were employed, God's exercise of foreknowledge determined man's ending and this made Him responsible for evil. The Calvinists had created a monster God who delighted in the death of sinners and even willed them to eternal damnation only to "show forth his justice and power in them."[11]

Not only was God libeled but Christ was traduced, for the doctrine rendered useless His "mediation, as if he had not by his sufferings . . . removed the *wrath* of God, or purchased the love of God towards all mankind." Although Christians were supposed to believe that Jesus was the fruit of God's redeeming love, the Calvinists had made Him a curse to mankind for, instead of opening the possibility of salvation to all, He had made inevitable the damnation of a "far greater number of men." If man's fate had already been determined by an "irrevocable decree," what good could come from preaching? In fact, had Christ not really heaped coals upon the head of a poor man who was now convicted not only of Adam's sin but of his own?[12]

Limited atonement necessarily follows predestinationism, and the above critique should make clear the Quaker opposition to both. Since predestination was an attempt to exalt the sovereignty and power of God, the Quaker rebuttal should be understood as aiming to exonerate God from injuries. Humanitarian considerations played a secondary role in Quaker beliefs about the availability of heaven. They asserted *universal redemption,* or *Christ's dying for all men* but proceeded to condemn just as many people as the Puritans. But there was a difference. The Calvinists had trouble convincing outsiders of man's responsibility; by stressing covenants, the Puritans made the doctrine more palatable; the Friends, by denying predestination, transferred all responsibility to man. Since all men received a visitation of the light of God, no one could complain about the justice of God.[13] If man was damned it was because he turned thumbs down on Christ.

The key to Quakerism was the inward light of Christ. Both opponents and Friends recognized this. George Fox declared that the true Christian must necessarily "wait on God, in his Light to receive his counsel; [for] how else do Friends differ from the World."[14] Certainly the doctrine of the necessity of the Holy Spirit was not unique with Friends. The Westminster Confession stated that "our full persuasion and assurance of the infallible truth . . . is from the inward work of the Holy Spirit."[15] An emphasis upon the personal experience of grace was an important tenet among Puritans of all stances. What the Friends did was to adopt the doctrine and extend it further than any other group—while managing to control the divisive effects of individual revelation.

Since the entire religious life (which included every activity) of a Quaker was governed by his attempt to receive and act within the leadings of the Holy Spirit, one must understand what Friends thought about the light. The experience was never divorced from a Christian context. Fox proclaimed that "God hath raised up his own seed in his saints, which seed, Christ. . . ." George Whitehead, who served as the informal leader of the English Friends following Fox's death, elucidated what Fox meant: "He often mentions the seed, the life, the power of God, and the like; whereby he intends no other than what the holy scriptures testify of Christ."[16] Although George Keith, after becoming schismatic, accused American Quakers of denying the historic Jesus, the writings of Fox, Penn, Barclay, and all eighteenth-century Friends asserted the link between the historic Jesus and the Christ within. However, by emphasizing the complete dichotomy between natural and supernatural, the Quakers ended with a very docetic view of Jesus.[17] Certainly there was far more emphasis upon the ethical teachings of Christ and the inward illumination than upon the actual events in the New Testament.

The relationship of Christ within to Jesus of Nazareth and to God should have been the central problem for Quaker theology, and although Barclay and Keith wrestled with the issues, the eighteenth-century followers were satisfied with previous formulations. When one reads Fox's epistles, he can readily imagine why the Puritans accused him of making his own illuminations equal God. Theologically sophisticated Friends attempted to define more precisely what they meant by Christ within.

> For though we affirm that Christ dwells in us, yet not immediately, but mediately, as he is in that *seed,* which is *in us;* whereas he, to wit, the *Eternal Word,* which was with God, and was God, dwelt immediately in that holy man.

If the light within did not equal Christ, so also it was not pure God. In the Father was perfection, which man could not resist or touch or harm, but man did all these actions to the inward revelation.

> *We understand a spiritual, heavenly, and invisible principle, in which God, as Father, Son, and Spirit dwells;* a measure of which divine and glorious life is *in all men as a seed,* which of its own nature draws, invites, and inclines to God; and this we call *vehiculum Dei,* or the *spiritual body of Christ, the flesh and blood of Christ, which came down from heaven,* of which all the saints do feed, and are thereby nourished into eternal life.[18]

The inward light was not a subjective feeling, a mystical intuition, reason, or conscience; it was a "real *spiritual substance*" that the soul of man could "feel and apprehend."[19] Friends had a tendency to see some part of the body as an organ especially equipped to experience God—an innate supernatural receiver.[20] No Quaker ever speculated about what this faculty located in the body was. Again, notice the centrality of the fear of pollution by natural man of the light of God. God could not be received by a normal faculty because this would contaminate the light and result in confusion. Friends "solved" the problem of uncertainty in religion by making all the faith equal God; therefore, God had to have some agency within by which He could infallibly let man know His will.

Like the Puritans, Friends normally discussed their religious experiences in metaphoric terms. The most prevalent word was *light.* (Seventeenth- and eighteenth-century Friends did not use the term *inner light.*) "There is an evangelical and saving light and grace in all," or "As many as resist not this light. . . ."[21] Certainly there was ample Gospel precedent for such language. Like the New Englanders, the Quakers used the simile of the sun and its rays. Learning of God was likened to the sun beaming a light into a house and then drawing that light back to its source, the sun. As the sun attracted men by its glory, beauty, and brightness, so also was man attracted to God.[21] Stephen Crisp, in the Quaker equivalent of Bunyan's *Pilgrim's Progress,* saw himself being led through all sorts of morasses down a narrow path by the light. If he ever stopped to dispute religion or to look at the dangers from beasts or fires, he took his eyes away from the light and his feet "slipt into mires and puddles."[22] The light was a specially apt metaphor because the inward grace brought insight, knowledge, or illumination, and it conveyed the essential fact of the experience of God, which did not involve His entire essence.

The second most frequently used metaphor was *seed.* The word had been widely used by the Puritans, and the parables of the sower, the bruised seed, the mustard seed, and Abraham's seed provided the scriptural references. Puritan theologian William Perkins called the desire for God "the seed, conception, or bud" of grace which could be first planted through baptism.[23] God made a covenant with Abraham and his seed. The Puritans in the church were equivalent to Abraham; their children equaled the seed and were also included within the church. Friends defined the seed as "the heavenly, spiritual, and invisible substance and being, that is the most glorious being and principle, in which God, as Father, Son, and holy Ghost doth dwell" and "shine forth," so that man at his "highest supernatural elevation" could experience Him.[24] The Quakers used the metaphor of a seed to convey the idea of the presence of God in man from birth which did not justify unless he repented and turned from sin. At times the Quakers became almost Manichaean in discussing an innate seed of righteousness as it contended with a seed of evil. Often the metaphor was used to indicate growth. God planted his seed in all human beings, but the individual had to permit the seed to sprout and (in spite of the mixed metaphor) to bring forth fruit in its season.

> It is in and by this inward and substantial seed in our hearts as it comes to receive nourishment, and to have a birth or geniture *in* us, that we come to have those spiritual senses raised by which we are made capable of *tasting, smelling, seeing,* and *handling* the things of God.[25]

The social uses of this analogy by magistrate or parent or meeting were apparent. Before God planted the seed, man had to cultivate the soul in preparation. Then he was to prune all entangling vines or weeds of evil away from the divine seed, lest it be choked. Finally, by attending meetings and harkening to the light within, man would help the Lord nourish the seed by means of His showers of grace. Even the fact of the absence of the divine presence at certain times was explained through a metaphor about seasonal visitations. God planted only at certain seasons; so man should be prepared whenever the seed came.[26] Occasional visits were not only a convenient device to explain the intervals of barrenness in convinced Friends, but they also lent urgency to the demand placed upon the unregenerate to prepare to accept the seed. Since life was fragile and grace only infrequently present, a wise man must permit God to operate without delay. By preaching the seasonal availability of grace, Friends brought a sense of immediacy to the quest for holiness while warning of the dangers of delaying repentance.

To eighteenth-century Quakers the importance of the growth analogy was as far-reaching as the idea of covenant in Puritan thought. The Puritans used the covenant as a means of asserting man's responsibility and ability to influence events. Friends believed the inward light to be a completely God-given thing. The seed analogy enabled them to say that not only was man passive in the reception of it, but he was actively engaged in fostering its growth. All religious and social institutions had the same task. The theological justification of activity came from the Quakers' insistence that man's will was involved negatively in preparing for the seed and clearing the way for it to grow.

In spite of their extensive usage of metaphoric language, the Friends never forgot that the actual means through which the Lord operated were a mystery. Even after writing many thousands of pages in favor of their faith, the Quakers maintained that they had no systematic theology—they had only an experience of God which called the true church of Christ into being and which would nourish and sustain it until the day of judgment. The Friends obtained the truth of God in a self-authenticating experience. One who had never recognized the Lord could not know what the Quakers were discussing when they referred to the inward workings of God. In a passage that reminds one of the later gropings of Jonathan Edwards with religious language, Barclay confessed the impossibility of communicating God through words predicated upon empirical data.

> But as the description of the light of the sun, or of curious colours to a blind man, who, though of the largest capacity, cannot so well understand it by the most acute and lively description, as a child can by seeing them; so neither can the natural man, of the largest capacity, by the best words, even scriptural words, so well understand

> the *mysteries of God's Kingdom,* as the least and weakest child who tasteth them, by having them *inwardly* and *objectively* by the Spirit.[27]

When their opponents accused Friends of being arrogant and of damning them at first encounters, the Quakers answered that, by their questioning, the antagonists had shown that they did not know grace and so were ruled by the Adversary. If the Puritan had truly experienced grace, he would have become a Quaker.

The Calvinist doctrine of limited atonement and election involved the pre-Christian heathens, some of whom had been saintly, and the non-Christian nations. The Westminster Confession asserted that Christ's benefits had been given to man before the actual physical events in Palestine;[28] Christendom had inserted a "descent into hell" into the Apostle's Creed so that Christ in the three days between His death and resurrection could actually preach to those who had died previously and gone to hell. The doctrine of the inward light was thought to preserve God's justice better than predestination. How did the Quakers meet the issue of the heathen? William Penn reasoned that (1) God required of all men that they fear and obey Him; and (2) in His justice He gave them the ability to work righteousness. Since man was commanded to know God and could not do so through instinct or reason or conscience (all were tainted by the fall), then no natural means existed for people who had never heard of Christ to be saved. The Lord within provided the only source of knowledge and grace.[29]

The Friends sought to prove by empirical and historical studies that the light alone was sufficient. A few Pennsylvania Quakers and traveling ministers journeyed out to visit the Indians to discover whether they knew the essentials of religion. They learned to their satisfaction that the Indians had conceptions of God, heaven, and the necessity of doing good.[30] In *The Christian Quaker,* William Penn, by quotations from Greek and Roman poets and philosophers, proved that the inward illumination had led many of these early sages to believe in one God who revealed Himself within, to do good and assert immortality. Penn found testimonials stating that these pagans had refused to take oaths, objected to the payment of priests, and believed in simplicity. A selective exegesis of Virgil proved that the poet knew that Christ was coming and would be born of a virgin.[31] William Penn did not argue that the light had revealed everything in Scripture but that it had taught enough to save. The historical Jesus was necessary to strengthen and spread more widely the message of the possibility of salvation. George Keith, after he left the Friends, called *The Christian Quaker* "plain deism appearing with open face." Certainly the universality of the light that brought a "Gentile Divinity" deemphasized the historicity of the Gospels and the need for atonement and came very close to being deism. Penn had taken a belief held by Fox, Barclay, and even Keith and had carried it to its final conclusions.[32]

Worrying about the ancient Greeks was less important to early Quakers than convincing Englishmen of the necessity of being reborn. The belief was nearly universal in Puritan circles that no man could be a Christian unless he had experienced God. The disagreement with the Calvinists lay over the irresistibility of grace. Since God sent grace and He was all-powerful and never wrong, the Synod of Dort asserted that no man could resist His charge. The

Puritan began the experience of grace with utter quietness. Man must be absolutely passive "until, being quickened and renewed by the Holy Spirit, he is thereby enabled to answer this call, and to embrace the grace offered and conveyed in it." The exact parallel was in Barclay:

> So that the first step is not by man's working, but by his not contrary working. And we believe, that at these singular seasons of every man's visitation, . . . as man is wholly unable of himself to work with grace, neither can he move one step out of the natural condition, until the grace lay hold upon him; so it is possible for him to be passive, and not resist it, as it is possible for him to resist it.[33]

The last clause was the only difference between the Quaker and Puritan views of the first experience of grace; the Calvinist could not stop God; the Quaker could. The light of Jesus used every possible means to bring men to salvation; it *invites, calls, exhorts, and strives with every man, in order to save him.* Those who accepted it were Christians; those who rejected it were lost.[34]

When Christ first appeared, the experience was not necessarily pleasant. Since the light equaled both law and Gospel, that part of grace that man experienced depended upon his earlier condition. Man was a sinner, and pure goodness made him suffer for his sins. To experience his own weaknesses against the standard of perfection in Christ brought great turmoil. Men must first arrive at "a sense of their own *misery,* and to be sharers in the sufferings of Christ inwardly." The exorcising of sin meant the conquering of all self-will and pride or, in other words, the negation of concern for this "dunghill."[35] The Quaker had to become a pilgrim living and participating in the world and yet keeping it in due subordination. Every thought, every desire must be brought before the cross to be examined. And though one could ultimately receive infinite pleasure from religion, the first step was to deny all worldly blessings by accepting the cross of Christ. Wives, children, food, raiment had to be judged, and man had to be prepared to sacrifice them. "The great Work and Business of the *Cross* of Christ, in man, is *SELF-DENIAL.*" Self-denial did not mean abstinence, but the subservience of all physical entities to the demand of God. The process of salvation was an endless internal duel between the supremacy of the supernatural and the attractiveness of the natural.

> What, thy *Wife,* dearer to thee than thy Savior! And thy *Land* and *Oxen* preferred before thy Soul's Salvation! O beware, that thy Comforts prove no Snares first, and then Curses.[36]

Man's role was purely negative, to subordinate all evil desires within himself, for to God belonged all positive gain. Yet, because the knowledge of Christ was the greatest pleasure conceivable, the Friend had to enjoy his renunciation.

Reformed theology referred to the process of inward purging as sanctification but insisted that acceptance by God or justification came first and that internal purity was not a precondition. Barclay distinguished between past and present justification. Level one was the historic death of Jesus whereby all men were "put into a capacity of salvation" and experienced the "power . . . which was in Christ" which overcame "the evil seed wherewith we are naturally . . . leavened."[37] This stage was available universally, and so Friends tended to take it for granted. The inward Christ, and not the Christ of history, became central.

Level two was the acceptance of the grace within, "whereby we . . . know this pure and perfect redemption *in ourselves,* purifying, cleansing, and redeeming us from the power of corruption, and bringing us into unity . . . with God."[38] While the first level was a precondition, the Friend's act of justification came through the acceptance of the governance of the inward light and the purging of sin. Where Puritans said Christ died for man, the sinner, and justified him even while he was a sinner, Quakers asserted that Christ died for man, the sinner, and justification could come only when the light was in man.[39] Christ was not crucified so that God could come to sinful man. Christ was sacrificed in order that He could come and dwell within sinful man so that man would no longer be sinful and could be saved. There was no order or separation between justification and sanctification. Notice the sequence in Fox's epistle written in 1674

> And strive not for mastery, but let Christ be the master, who is in the wisdom of God, and your wisdom, and righteousness and sanctification, and justification, and you to dwell in humility and love. . . .

Richard Claridge expressed the same conclusion:

> Whosoever is justified, he is also in measure sanctified. And so far as he is sanctified, so far he is justified, and no further.[40]

If the Friends had been perfectly consistent, they would have argued that good works done by Christ saved, because otherwise the light could not cause activity. The Puritans, who reasoned that all actions were tainted, adopted the Reformation view that God accepted sinners just as they were and esteemed them because of Christ's merit. Because any involvement of works in salvation seemed to Protestant England to be a popish remnant, Barclay followed the traditional separation between faith and works. Good works "naturally follow" from the dominance of the light within just as heat always came from fire without being a cause of the flame though essential to it. So also good works did not cause, but were of "*absolute* necessity to, justification."[41]

If a man was saved, did he know it? The Calvinists said that a man elected "may in this life be certainly assured." But the Puritans in Old and New England refused to say that every saved man knew it. The Calvinists, after tentatively putting forth the possibility of assurance, drew back suddenly. Edmund S. Morgan has argued that New Englanders went through life searching for evidences of salvation because they were unsure whether or not they were saved.[42] Since the fruits of this life were seen as evidence of salvation, the Calvinist strove to succeed in order to show forth virtue. In economic terms, this is the fundamental outline of the view that holds Protestantism responsible for capitalism. The Quakers were as good capitalists in the eighteenth century as the Puritans, but they did not have a fundamental uncertainty to drive them.[43] The Friends, starting from the same premises as the Puritans—the promise of salvation and the inward evidence—argued that man could gain an "infallible" assurance of faith. Every Christian recognized God within him, was aware if he had exorcised his sins, and knew if he had permitted grace to abound.[44] George Fox, whose writings show a complete confidence that he was in the truth, greatly emphasized the doctrine of absolute assurance. When asked "whether freedom from all sin, and infallible assurance of God's will be of absolute necessity" for marriage, he replied: "To have infallible assurance [that] there is freedom from all sin, to hunger and thirst, and press after it, to witness a growth, to be sincere in heart, and faith to God in measure, is of absolute necessity." Since Friends began with a religion of experience, they naturally asserted that "we witness and know this pure and perfect redemption *in ourselves.*"[45] To have an experience and not to know it would be absurd.

Closely linked with the doctrine of knowledge of salvation was the belief that a man called by God could not fall; this was known in seventeenth-century terms as perseverance of the saints. Since the Lord chose only just men, He selected only the pure, and, although saints could stray, they must inevitably endure. Otherwise God would be subject to man's disposal and would no longer be omnipotent. The Puritan searched his life for marks of success and strove after godliness as signs of his election. Friends hedged on this doctrine. Their normal thrust was to say that no Christian was ever exempted from falling and that at any time his natural depravity could cancel out the seed of God within. If man succumbed to sin, he was neither justified nor sanctified. Of course, after a man had fallen, he could always regain his grace and sanctification by repenting and letting the seed of God grow. No matter how heinous his deeds, man was never "incapable of rising again."[46]

The Quakers could not categorically deny that some might rise above the temptation to fall without detracting from their belief in the possibility of perfection. The Westminster Confession clearly indicated that the act of justification did not stop man from sinning. The Presbyterians did not believe that acts could be pure because they did not think that man could be pure. Even the deeds of a converted and nearly sanctified man retained the effects of Adam's fall, and man's will could never be made perfect. Friends agreed that man could do no work by himself that was not corrupt, but they insisted that the light of God working in man could produce a sinless act.[47]

It logically followed that if man could do one act that was sinless, why could he not do several; in fact, why could he not lead a perfect life? Jesus said, "Be ye perfect," and He expected man to be able to fulfill the commandment. Men could subordinate themselves so to the will of God within that "to do righteousness may become so natural to regenerate souls, that in the stability of this condition they cannot sin."[48] In spite of the grammatical condition which admits of no comparisons in perfection, Friends from Fox through Barclay and Keith distinguished degrees of faultlessness. No one asserted that man could attain the perfection of God, but he could reach a "Perfection from sin, and so the first *Adam* was made perfect by Creation, and true Believers are made perfect by Redemption. . . ."[49]

Every Friend who accepted the discipline of the inward Christ and who acted directly under it was at that moment perfect; he was redeemed by Christ and was without sin. Yet as that person continually, by an exercise of will, negated his volition so that God became his will, he became "more" perfect. An early pamphlet showed this belief clearly.

> Perfection of Believers from sin had Degrees in it.
> First, To believe that Perfection is attainable, such are in measure perfect. . . .
> 2. There is a Growth, and in some more than others. . . .
> 3. There is Perfection from sin, transgression finished . . . none knoweth it but they that are in it; nor none can come into it but they that are led and guided by the Spirit of God in them.[50]

The ambiguity in perfectionist terminology was not eased by the varying usages among Friends. Fox often referred to Quakers as renewed to the first Adam, and at times he even saw them as reaching unto the second Adam.[51] If he meant that Friends' sinlessness was the same as Adam's state before the fall because Christ within purified and replaced a corrupt will, did this not make the Friend equal to Jesus? Certainly the assertion that Friends were renewed to the second Adam because Christ was purer than Adam ran the legal risk of blasphemy. (The incidents involving James Naylor show that there was a real danger.[52]) Later Quaker theologians toned down the definition of perfection. George Keith defined sinlessness as in will or intention rather than in action, since one could never be certain of the consequences of the deed. Robert Barclay saw perfection as freedom "from actual sinning, and transgressing of the law of God, and in that respect perfect." Here the state permitted growth insofar as man continued free from sin while being able to "answer what he requires of us."[53] As man improved in grace, God made increasing demands upon him; these new tasks came as he grew in understanding of God's will.

Barclay's affirmation of perfection was important not only for what he stated but also for what he omitted. He affirmed the possibility of others being perfect but weakened the whole argument by saying:

> Others may perhaps speak more certainly, of this state, as having attained to it. For myself, I shall speak modestly, as acknowledging not to have arrived at it; yet I dare not deny it, because it seems to be positively asserted by the apostle.[54]

In the eighteenth century Quakers continued to assert that man could reach perfection, but no important Friend ever claimed that he had reached it. Perfection became an eventual goal rather than a present reality.

III

In focusing upon the drama of salvation as portrayed in Quaker theology, this chapter may have fostered the wrong impression that the nature and the authority of Scripture were not issues. When Puritans and Quakers quarreled, both buttressed their assertions with lengthy biblical quotations from the Old and the New Testament. As in nearly all their theological disputes, the similarities in positions are far more striking than the differences. They agreed that the authority of Scripture rested not on man or church but on God alone. Both believed that the Bible was written under the immediate direction of the Holy Ghost and that every word in it was true.[55] Both found that there were perplexities in certain passages and agreed to interpret these verses by the spirit of the whole. Both claimed that all things necessary for salvation were perfectly clear. They could concur in the statement in the Westminster Confession that "our full persuasion of the infallible truth, and divine authority thereof, is from the inward work of the Holy Spirit."

Their real difference lay in this section of the Confession:

> The whole counsel of God, concerning all things necessary for his own glory, man's salvation, faith, and life, is either expressly set down in Scripture, or by good and necessary consequence may be deduced from Scripture: unto which nothing at any time is to be added, whether by new revelations of the Spirit, or traditions of men. Nevertheless, we acknowledge the inward illumination of the Spirit of God to be necessary for the saying and understanding of such things as are revealed in the Word. . . .[56]

Friends agreed with the wording of the last clause, beginning with "Nevertheless"; the first two clauses they vehemently opposed, particularly the phrase denying "New revelations of the Spirit." The Puritans appeared to be setting Scripture over the inward light and making it the authority in faith. For the Quakers the Bible was subordinate to the light of God within.

> They [Scriptures] are only a declaration of the *fountain,* and not the *fountain* itself, therefore they are not to be esteemed the principal ground of all truth and knowledge, nor yet the adequate primary rule of *faith and manners.*

The final arbiters for Friends were not Scriptures but the "inward *objective manifestations in the heart.*"[57] Although the Westminster Confession asserted the necessity of an "inward illumination" in order to understand the Word, the Puritans believed that this illumination was never "objective." That is, a Puritan reading the Bible was shown by God that the Bible was truth and he was confirmed in the correct interpretation. But this illumination was always only "effective"—allowing him to understand—and never "objective"—presenting new knowledge. Friends believed that the inward revelation could be objective, that God could present knowledge not in the Bible to an individual. Just as man's physical senses presented an object to the mind, so did his spiritual senses. The knowledge gained through the agency of the spiritual senses was as certain as the *a priori* mathematical truth structured by the mind alone or the *a posteriori* truth obtained from physical senses. Quakers charged that the Puritans could never know whether their "illumination" was from God or Satan since it was without content. Quaker revelation could be infallibly known because God spoke to the spiritual senses, and one could determine the origin of the clear and distinct ideas that resulted.[58]

The direct revelations of the Friends inevitably agreed with the Bible, although they were not subject to it. The Scriptures came from the light and not the light from the Scriptures, and therefore the Quakers' inward revelation was not "to be subjected to the examination, either of the outward testimony of the scriptures, or right and sound reason." For the more certain, the whole, the sum totality of the faith should not be subjected to only one part of it.[59] The Bible was words, and words could not prove falsity or truth. What was required was a verification from the source of Scripture. The Puritans also believed that God made the Scriptures true, but they did not regard this truth as requiring a new inward revelation.

The Puritans claimed that the Bible was a general rule of faith and practice.

The first clause in the disputed section of the Westminster Confession asserted that "the whole counsel of God" was either "expressly set down" or "may be deduced from Scripture." The latter phrase opened the gate for logic, and by using the system of Petrus Ramus the New Englanders built up an imposing edifice of divinity. Friends refused to "deduce" from Scripture; the light was clear and no additions of logic were necessary. The Quakers denied that the "whole counsel of God" was in the Bible. No man by reading it could learn directly his inward calling, or whether he was justified and sanctified, or called to minister, or told to pray. The Bible, in short, did not contain "the whole Mind, Will, and Counsel of God."[60] Revelation had not ceased.

The New Englanders charged the Friends with belittling Scriptures. Penn retorted. "There is a great difference between asserting that the Spirit is the Rule, and casting away and vilifying of Scripture."[61] The new revelation was in time, not in content; Quakerism was *Primitive Christianity Revived,* not a new religion. Like the Presbyterians, the Quakers found in the Bible an accurate history of the "acts of God's people in divers ages," a prophetical record of past, present, and future occurrences, and a "full and ample account of all the chief principles of doctrine of Christ."[62] For all this knowledge the Bible was indispensable.

Friends believed that the same spirit that had directed the biblical writers directed them. If the spirit had been able to inspire men to perfection in the writing of Scripture, then the spirit could also teach men the absolutely correct interpretation. The Apostle Paul was guided by the grace of God; George Fox was led by the grace of God; therefore George Fox equalled Paul. And what was true for Fox was also true for every other Christian who was directly under the command of God. Where the Puritans asserted that there had been a fullness of grace in the first century that was not duplicated in the seventeenth century, the Friends said that the light remained the same.[63] The grace that gave Paul the ability to do miracles also gave George Fox the same rights, not because of any intrinsic merit on Fox's part but because of the power of God's spirit.

Since biblical revelation and Friends' revelation were equal (in fact the same), then all Quaker practices and beliefs could be confirmed by appeal to Scripture.

> There is a sufficient testimony left to all the essentials of the Christian faith [in the Scriptures]; we do look upon them as the only fit outward judge of controversies among Christians; and that whatsoever doctrine is contrary unto their testimony, may therefore justly be rejected as false. And, for our parts, we are very willing that all doctrines and practices be tried by them; which we never refused, nor ever shall, in all controversies with our adversaries, as the judge and test.[64]

The Friends could use Scripture as a proof for their practices because the spirit was the same in all generations. The corollary, accepted by both Puritans and Friends, was that the spirit was uniform and therefore the fruits of the spirit must be the same. All the Bible had to be consistent.[65] There could be no differences in any detail in what the Bible said. If any one verse proved decisively that a practice was wrong, then that act or theological tenet should be thrown out.

The best way to demonstrate how Friends used the Bible is to examine their justifications for certain beliefs; these examples have been selected to indicate the different principles operating in each case. The most striking feature is the sheer amount of biblical precedent that could be gathered. The difficulty in reading the works of George Fox is that they were so based on Scripture that, lacking a knowledge of the verses he paraphrased, one often cannot understand what he was advocating. In the index to the *Apology* are listed 821 citations of the Bible; 165 from the Old Testament and 656 from the New Testament. Barclay's catechism contained 559 references to the New Testament and only forty to the Old. Clearly, any attempt to describe seventeenth-century Quakerism as preponderantly Hebraic or dominated by the Old Testament is false.

Certain passages were approached in a manner of absolute literalism. When Matthew has Christ say, "Swear not at all," the Friends accepted the statement and refused to utter oaths. The passages in the Sermon on the Mount in which Christians were told to love their enemies and in which peacemakers were praised made Friends refuse to be involved in war. The Old Testament precedents of holy wars so often quoted by Puritans in Old and New England were of no value because Jesus had specifically set them aside.[66] Friends, like every other religious group, did not esteem all passages equally. Although they believed in the duty of charity, they did not echo Christ's advice to the rich young ruler to "sell all that thou hast, and distribute unto the poor."

When using the Old Testament, Quakers also showed some selectivity in the choice of passages. Friends refused to bow; when opponents mentioned that Abraham bowed to the children of Heth and Lot to the two angels, Barclay argued that the practice of the patriarchs was not to be the practice of today or else polygamy would be allowed.[67] Yet, since the Old Testament was much clearer than the New Testament about forbidding mixed marriages, Friends used as a precedent the passages in Genesis where the giants became sinful because they married daughters of the earth and Jacob pleased his parents by marrying one of Isaac's kin while Esau displeased them by marrying a Hittite. (Gen. 6:1–4, 24:4, 26:35.)

Since Friends had no sacraments, the passages in the New Testament that seemed to advocate water baptism and the use of bread and wine in the Lord's supper were often debated. The Quakers' guiding principle in this type of exegesis was spirituality. The New Testament dispensation was an inward one, and the means of conveying grace were purely nonmaterial. To use any physical or formal entity, whether water, music, or liturgy, was an untruth. Certainly there were many precedents for baptism of the spirit in Scripture; for example, Acts 11:16, when Peter declared, "John truly baptized with water, but ye shall be baptized with the Holy Ghost."[68] The difficulty was that there were also verses that stated that Peter baptized with water, one of which is in the same story in Acts where Peter says, "Can anyone refuse the use of water to baptize these people when they have received the Holy Spirit just as we did." Barclay admitted that Peter used water, and he proceeded to argue that Peter's practice showed that he retained part of the old dispensation and that the early church had not purified itself of all Jewish elements. Since there were statements about baptism where water was not specified, clearly water was not an essential element. The bestowal of the holy spirit was the essential. What Quakers demanded here was a clear command saying, "Go and baptize with water." Since there was none, the fact that Peter or Philip baptized non-Jews with water was irrelevant. In asserting that water baptism was nonessential, Friends had negated their equality with the early church. They felt that the meeting was purer than primitive Christianity.[69]

Although Friends demanded clear scriptural precedent for all practices done by Puritans, they enforced beliefs that had no clear biblical basis. For example, there was nothing in either Testament demanding that the language be absolutely consistent grammatically, but all Quakers insisted that addressing a single person as "you" was a sin. The point is not that there was no defense of the Quaker's testimony but that there was no Bible verse commanding it.

The Presbyterian and the Puritan could be trapped in just as many inconsistencies as the Friends since none recognized that in attempting to let the Bible speak for itself they had imposed canons of interpretation. The Friends wanted uniformity in the Bible. They distinguished between types, figures, shadows and substance, old and new dispensation, and the example of the early church, and sometimes they negated all these in order to assert a spiritual interpretation. The Puritans used all the above as well as reason and logic. And yet the Friends took Scripture with the utmost seriousness. They refused to use words like *trinity,* or *sacrament,* or *original sin,* which were not found in the Bible. The Society of Friends issued no official doctrinal statements because the Bible was their creed. William Penn hoped that all confessions could be written in scriptural verses so that all Protestants could unite.[70] The whole superstructure of Protestant scholastic thought was denied because Friends believed it destroyed the purity of the Gospel. They saw all religious life, all personal relationships, all social institutions in terms of what the Bible said about them. Granted that they often left certain passages out of their calculations; but they obviously found many that the Puritans tended to neglect. The experience of the inward light plus the undercurrent of literalism gave Quakers the confidence that they could live Christian lives.

IV

Quaker theology began with, was structured by, and concluded with the inward light of Christ. All these words were essential. The experience was *inward* and therefore subject to no external proof. Grace was *light* and brought knowledge. And since the *inward light* was *of Christ,* the subjective illumination was equal to the revelation of God described in the New Testament. Friends' claims of authority were based on the same power that had been the sole arbiter of the apostles for the early church. Since the Quakers knew God's will and God never changed, all knowledge from God, whether in Scripture or in the writings of early Friends, had to agree. What this recapitulation illustrates is that, by placing emphasis upon one word or another, a different basic thrust was revealed. For example, if one stressed the subjective, inward spiritual element, he had an excellent weapon for attacking schooling, learning, liturgy, set forms of worship, or a hireling ministry. If he emphasized the *of Christ* and pled the sameness of revelation for all, he could claim to be orthodox and plead for the necessity of church government. By combining the *inward* and *of Christ* with the illumination of the *light,* the Quaker could claim a completely subjective, yet paradoxically objective, interpretation of Scripture which would prove Friends' religious practices to be those of the early church. In polemics against their opponents, the Quakers stressed whichever tenet was needed. Their versatility in arguing made Charles Leslie, one of the Friends' most bitter and most prolific opponents, charge:

> As it was said of *Hannibal,* that he never fought without an Ambush, so the Quakers never write without a Reserve, a double Meaning, to secure their Retreat when pinch'd from another Quarter.[71]

In spite of the frequency of disputes in the early years, Friends were repeatedly exhorted to refrain from needless theological quarrels. The dry bones of Quaker doctrine were not the essence of what the Friend was to emphasize. The test of Christianity was the pilgrimage through the world, the cultivation of the inward seed. After engaging in theology, the Quaker, like Candide, ultimately turned from speculation to the cultivation of seeds in his own garden.

Notes

1 Perry Miller, *Errand into the Wilderness* (New York, 1956), pp. 48–98.

2 Before 1800 the *Apology* was reprinted in English once in Holland, 12 times in England, 3 times in Ireland, and 5 times in America. Barclay's *Catechism and Confession of Faith* was issued in English 16 times in Great Britain and 4 times in America before 1800. In addition, the complete works of Barclay were published in 1692 and 1717–18 in England and in 1831 in America. The most recent edition is Dean Freiday, *Barclay's Apology in Modern English* (Alburtus, Pa., 1967). After the Keithan schism, Friends did not reprint any of Keith's works. The only biography is Ethyn Kirby, *George Keith* (New York, 1942). Leif Eeg-Olofsson, *The Conception of the Inner Light in Robert Barclay's Theology* (Lund, Norway, 1954) contrasts Barclay's "inner light mysticism" with the doctrines of Luther, Calvin, and Roman Catholic scholasticism, but it ignores all English theologians. David Elton Trueblood, *Robert Barclay* (New York, 1968) is a readable biography and a very favorable study of Barclay's thought. Different views as to the worth of the *Apology* appear in *Quaker Religious Thought* 7, no. 1 (Spring 1965). William I. Hull, *William Penn: A Topical Biography* (New York, 1937); C. O. Beatty, *William Penn as a Social Philosopher* (New York, 1939); and Melvin Endy, Jr., "William Penn and Early Quakerism: A Theological Study" (Ph.D. diss., Yale University, 1969) are the best works on Penn's thought. Rachel H. King, *George Fox and the Light Within 1650–1660* (Philadelphia, 1940) is the best study of the theology of Fox. Hugh Barbour, *The Quakers in Puritan England* (New Haven, Conn., 1964) relates Fox to many Quaker leaders and contrasts the entire movement to Puritanism. The Barbour and King books offer detailed analyses of only the period before 1660. William Braithwaite, *The Beginnings of Quakerism* and the *Second Period of Quakerism* (London, 1912 and 1917; revised editions prepared by Henry J. Cadbury, Cambridge, 1955 and 1961) remain the standard works on Quaker church organization, factional disputes, theology, and social ethics.

3 Barbour, *The Quakers in Puritan England,* 2: 133–59; a bibliography of the different interpretations of the origin of Friends is in *Church History* 39, no. 4 (December 1970): 504.

4 This attempt to make the Westminster Confession stand for the theology of all Puritans is an oversimplification and gives a static quality to their doctrines. But to take as normative a theologian—such as Cotton, Perkins, or Baxter—would involve an even more subjective view of what Puritan theology entailed. The Westminster Confession was at least drawn up by an assembly of divines and endorsed by both Presbyterians and Congregationalists. The complete texts of the confessions of Dort and Westminster appear in Philip Schaff, *Biblioteca Symbolica Ecclesiac Universalis: Creeds of Christiandom* (New York, 1919), 3: 580–87, 600–60.

5 The standard works on New England's covenant theology are Perry Miller, *The New England Mind: The Seventeenth Century* and *From Colony to Province* (Cambridge, Mass., 1939, and 1953); Edmund Morgan, *Visible Saints* (New York, 1963); Norman Pettit, *The Heart Prepared: Grace and Conversion in Puritan Spiritual Life* (New Haven, Conn., 1966). Two recent discussions of English religious thought before the Civil War are Charles and Katherine George, *The Protestant Mind of the English Reformation, 1570–1740* (New Jersey, 1961) and John F. H. New, *Anglican and Puritan: The Basis of Their Opposition* (Stanford, Calif., 1964).

6 Westminster Confession, Chapter 6, pp. 1–6, 615–16; Robert Barclay, *An Apology for the True Christian Divinity,* 13th ed. (Manchester, England, 1860), prop. 4, p. xi.

7 Barclay, *Apology,* p. xii; Rufus Jones, *The Later Periods of Quakerism* (London, 1921), 1: 33; Isabel Ross, *Margaret Fell: Mother of Quakerism* (London, 1949), p. 41; King, *George Fox*, pp. 41–43.

8 Edmund Morgan, *The Puritan Family* (New York, 1966), p. 22; Miller, *The New England Mind,* chapters 5–6.

9 Barclay, *Apology,* prop. 2, pg. i, 4. Eeg-Olofsson argues that Barclay used scholastic theology in *Conception of Inner Light*, pp. 73, 81.

10 Barclay, *Apology,* prop. 2, pg. iv, 8, and prop. 5 and 6, pg. xvi, 85; Robert Barclay, *Truth Triumphant* (Philadelphia, 1831), 1: 210–12, 445, 446 (Hereafter cited as *Works*).

11 Barclay, *Apology,* prop. 5 and 6, pg. iv, 64, 66.

12 Ibid., pg. 66–67.

13 Ibid., p. 68, and prop. 6 and 7, pg. xi, 78.

14 Thomas Lawrence and George Fox, *Concerning Marriage: A Letter Sent to G. F. And with it, a Copy of an Answer to a Friend's Letter Concerning Marriage* (n.p., 1663), p. 12.

15 Westminster Confession, Chapter 1, pp. 5, 603.

16 George Fox, "A Collection of Many Select Christian Epistles," *Works of George Fox* (Philadelphia, 1831), 7: 31; George Whitehead, "Preface to Epistles" (1698), in Fox, *Works,* 7: vi-vii.

17 Doceticism was an early Christian heresy closely related to Gnosticism. The docetics viewed Christ as a purely divine being and denied a mixture between the human and the divine. Friends occasionally wrote as if Christ had been a divine being who had come down from heaven and used the earthly body of Jesus. The man Jesus suffered on the cross, but the divine being inhabiting his body was incapable of physical pain. See Fox, *Works,* 7: 236; William Penn, *Works of William Penn* (London, 1726), 1: 589; Barclay, *Works,* 3: 566.

18 Barclay, *Apology,* prop. 5 and 6, pg. xiii, 80–81.

19 Ibid., pg. xiv, 81–82. The idea of a spiritual substance dates from the Middle Ages. Thomas Aquinas wrote about three kinds of substances: God or divine substance, spiritual or intellectual substances like the soul and angels, and material substances. In *Paradise Lost* Milton has an angel describe his nature as of "pure Intelligential substances." When describing the light as a "spiritual substance," Barclay may have been using this philosophical tradition to assert that the inward light was divine and yet not the pure essence of God. See Thomas Gilby, ed., *St. Thomas Aquinas: Philosophical Texts* (New York, 1952), pg. 436, 153–57; John Milton, *Paradise Lost*, in *Complete Poetry and Selected Prose* (New York, 1950), book 5, line 408.

20 In Barclay's epistemology—which he termed Cartesian—all natural ideas were formed by the outward objects imprinting "in our sensible organs a corporal motion." There were also spiritual motions; otherwise, man could have no true knowledge of God or experience his personal guidance. Since there were supernatural ideas, there must be "divine and spiritual senses" to receive the ideas. A corporal object could not convey a spiritual idea because the "less excellent cannot produce the more excellent, else the effect would exceed its cause." Barclay, *Works,* 3: 568–78. See also William Penn, *Works,* 2: 857.

21 Barclay, *Apology,* prop. 6 and 7, pg. xii, xiii.

22 Joseph Sleigh, *Good Advice and Counsel Given Forth by Joseph Sleigh of the City of Dublin, in the time of his Sickness, to his Children* (London, 1696), pp. 9–10; Stephen Crisp, *A Short History of a Long Travel, From Babylon to Bethel* (London, 1777), p. 16; Barclay, *Apology,* prop. 5 and 6, pg. xvii, xxi, 88–89, 98.

23 William Perkins, *Works* (Oxford, 1626), 1: 637–39, quoted in Pettit, *The Heart Prepared,* pp. 63–64; Morgan, *The Puritan Family,* p. 184.

24 Barclay, *Apology,* prop. 5 and 6, pg. xiv, 82; George Keith, *Immediate Revelation . . . Not Ceased* (London, 1675), p. 11.

25 Ibid., p. 82.

26 Barclay, *Apology,* prop. 5 and 6, pg. xvii, xx, 88, 92–93; idem, *Works,* 1: 365–67, and 3: 59; Keith, *Some of the Fundamental Truths of Christianity,* pp. 6–7.

27 Barclay, *Apology,* prop. 2, pg. xvi, 34.

28 Westminster Confession, Chapter 8, pp. vi, 621.

29 Penn, *Works,* 1: 586–87; Barclay,

Apology, prop. 5 and 6, pp. xi, xxvi, 77, 111–14; Barclay *Works,* 3: 104–06.

30 Sydney V. James, *A People Among Peoples: Quaker Benevolence in Eighteenth-Century America* (Cambridge, Mass., 1963), pp. 92–94. Barclay used the story of Hai Ebn Yokdan, who lived alone on an island without contacts with any other person, to show how a man without aid of Scriptures could arrive at a knowledge of God.

31 Penn, *Works,* 1: 554, 559, 562–64.

32 Penn's defenses of Christianity and Quakerism combined, somewhat ambiguously, biblical authority and confidence in natural reason and showed eighteenth-century Friends that a pious man could participate in the Enlightenment. When Keith criticized Penn for declaring that reason alone was adequate for salvation, he distorted Penn's position. The main difference between Penn and Keith was that Penn was less guarded than Keith in certain statements concerning the nature and authority of the light and its relationship to reason. Penn believed that the supernatural light that saved was "natural"; that is, it was naturally in every person. Penn, like Barclay, Keith, and Fox, did not believe that man, through his own ability, could reason his way to saving grace. In 1688 Keith asserted that God could save the Gentiles without an outward knowledge of Scripture but that the means he used remained a mystery to mankind. Keith speculated that perhaps God revealed the knowledge of Christ to the good heathen at the moment of death. Penn, *Works,* 1: 766–77; 2: 857; George Keith, *The Deism of William Penn* (London, 1699), preface; idem, *A Refutation of Three Opposers of Truth* (Philadelphia, 1690) pp. 40–44; Fox, *Works,* 3: 411.

33 Westminster Confession, chapter 10, pg. 2, 625; Barclay, *Apology,* prop. 5 and 6, pg. xvii, 88. The role of the Puritan in conversion was far more complex than the simple statement in the Westminster Confession indicated. Edmund Morgan showed the stages of religious life and Norman Pettit delineated the major disagreements over preparation for grace and where man's abilities ended and God's works began. The preaching of Puritans (and Quakers) focused on the nearness of God and the necessity for repentance. See Morgan, *Visible Saints,* pp. 66–72, 91 and Pettit, *Heart Prepared,* pp. 217–22.

34 Barclay, *Apology,* pg. xi, 77. Barclay did not deny that a few special messengers of God, like Paul, of necessity received grace because God did not allow them to resist it.

35 Penn, *Works,* 1: 566; Fox, *Works,* 8: 153; Barclay, *Works,* 1: 217.

36 Penn, *Works,* 1: 281, 286–87; Barclay, *Works,* 1: 288–89, 404.

37 Barclay, *Apology,* prop. 7, pg. iii, 124.

38 Ibid.

39 Ibid., pg. ii, vii, 121, 125–26, 131.

40 Fox, *Works,* 8: 63; Richard Claridge, *Tractatus Hierographicus; or a Treatise of the Holy Scriptures* (New York, 1893), pp. 158–59; Barclay, *Works,* 1: 164–65, and 3: 555.

41 Westminster Confession, chapter 18, pg. 1, v, 626–27; Barclay, *Apology,* prop. 7: pg. iv, 126. Barclay somewhat qualifies this prohibition of the merit of good works on pg. xii, 146.

42 Morgan, *The Puritan Family,* pp. 4–5.

43 Isabel Grubb, *Quakerism and Industry before 1800* (London, 1930), and Arthur Raistrick, *Quakers in Science and Industry* (London, 1950) concentrate on English Quakers' economic ethics. Frederick Tolles, *Meeting House and Counting House* (New York, 1963) is the standard work on American Quakers' business practices.

44 Barclay, *Apology,* prop. 7, pg. iii, 124; George Keith, *The Presbyterian and Independent Visible Churches* (Philadelphia, 1689), p. 99.

45 Lawrence and Fox, *Concerning Marriage,* pp. 10, 7; Barclay, *Apology,* prop. 7, pg. iii, 124.

46 Barclay, *Apology,* prop. 8, pp. ii, 149. George Keith stated that God's elect could not "finally fall away," though they could temporarily fall and be restored by repentance. He refused to discuss as too philosophical an issue whether there was a difference between a faith which could and could not be lost. George Keith, *A Serious Appeal to All the more Sober, Impartial, and Judicious People in New England* (Philadelphia, 1692), pp. 51–52.

47 Westminster Confession, chapter 9; pg. iv, 623–24; Penn, *Works,* 2: 781; Fox, *Works,* 7: 28.

48 Barclay, *Apology,* prop. 85, pg. ii, vii, 149, 155.

49 Ibid., p. 149. See also Lawrence and Fox, *Concerning Marriage,* p. 8; Keith, *The Presbyterian and Independent Visible Churches,* p. 108.

50 Lawrence and Fox, *Concerning Marriage,* pp. 8–9.

51 Fox, *Works,* 7: 81, 190.

52 Braithwaite, *Beginnings of Quakerism,* pp. 241–78.

53 Keith, *The Presbyterian and Independent Visible Churches,* pp. 162–64, 144–45; Barclay, *Apology,* prop. 8, pg. 148–49.

54 Barclay, *Apology,* prop. 8, pg. ii, 149.

55 Penn, *Works,* 1: 748; Barclay, *Works,* 1: 180; Keith, *Immediate Revelation,* pp. 171–72.

56 Westminster Confession, chapter 1, pg. v and vi, 603–04.

57 Barclay, *Apology,* prop. 2, p. x; prop. 3, p. xi.
58 Barclay, *Works,* 3: 66, 91–92; Keith, *Immediate Revelation,* pp. 13–14, 26–27, 37–38, 132–35, 153–54.
59 Barclay, *Apology,* prop. 2, pg. x-xi; Penn, *Works,* 1: 593-99.
60 Keith, *The Presbyterian and Independent Visible Churches,* pp. 1–4; Penn, *Works,* 2: 781–82.
61 Penn, *Works,* 1: 598 (printed incorrectly as 589).
62 Barclay, *Apology,* prop. 3, p. xi.
63 Ibid., pg. ii, 35, 38; Barclay, *Works,* 3: 293–94.
64 Barclay, *Apology,* prop. 3, pg. vi, 47.
65 Ibid.; Barclay, *Works,* 1: 443.
66 Barclay, *Apology,* prop. 15, pg. x, 343–49; prop. 20, pg. xv, 356. Barclay did not deny the lawfulness of a magistrate conducting a defensive war in a sinful world.
67 Ibid., prop. 15, pg. vi, 335.
68 Ibid., prop. 12, pg. iii, 262.
69 Ibid., prop. 7, pg. iii, iv, 262–65; Barclay, *Works,* 1: 152, 399–400, 564–65, and 3: 142. Barclay noted how even Christ observed Jewish customs that were no longer binding upon the church.
70 Penn, *Works,* pp. 746–47.
71 Charles Leslie, "The Snake in the Grass; or, Satan Transform'd into an Angel of Light," in *The Theological Works of the Reverend Mr. Charles Leslie* (London, 1721), 2: 125.

2 The Quest for Holiness

What school is more profitably instructive than the death-bed of the righteous, impressing the understanding with a convincing evidence, that they have not followed cunningly devised fables, but solid substantial truth.

A Collection of Memorials Concerning Divers Deceased Ministers (Philadelphia, 1787), pp. iii-iv.

Few outsiders joined the Society of Friends for purely intellectual reasons. It was far more likely for a person to be converted while in a meeting for worship, after recognizing the moral actions of Quakers, than during an involved study of theological tenets. Thomas Story, an educated man whose journal contains evidence of many theological disputes, recorded that, when attending his first meeting, he heard an attack on predestination

> Yet I took not much notice of it; for as I did not doubt but, like all other Sects, they might have something to say, both for their own, and against the Opinions of others; yet my Concern was much rather to know whether they were a People gathered under a Sense . . . of the Presence of GOD in their meetings.[1]

Only after experiencing in the meeting the corporate presence of the Lord, which he had known before individually, did he become a Quaker. Even Robert Barclay, certainly the prime example of a theologically oriented Friend, noted that he was persuaded to become a member not by arguments but by being "secretly reached" by the power of God in meeting.[2] When Quakers thought about their faith, they expressed their thoughts in terms used by Barclay or Fox or Penn, but to discuss the impact of religion upon them one must go to individual experiences of grace. The various journals of ministering Friends are the best sources for information on how Quakers lived their faith.

The writing of spiritual autobiographies was common among Quakers from the middle of the seventeenth until the beginning of the twentieth century. George Fox and John Woolman were the two most famous journalists, but many other ministers and some ordinary laymen recorded the progress of their devotional lives. These works were meant, much like the biographies by the Puritan Cotton Mather in the *Magnalia Christi Americana,* to be edifying entertainment and to picture the Christian way of life. The writers thought that the temptations they met and the exaltations they received should be handed down as a medium for posterity to participate in their spiritual life. Howard

H. Brinton called the diaries the "most characteristic form of Quaker composition."[3]

No systematic study of family life can be made from Quaker spiritual journals because the writers' children were usually mentioned only when they died. Although intensely introspective, these books contain almost no details of actual living. A tradition records that John Woolman once gave his uncompleted journal to a Friend to read. Upon returning the manuscript, the Quaker wondered why Woolman had never mentioned his wife. So Woolman added one sentence saying that he had married and that the Lord "was pleased to give me a well inclined Damsel."[4] Whether true or not, the story is illustrative of the way in which Friends structured their autobiographies. Thomas Story (1662–1742) was married to Ann Shippen, daughter of a mayor of Philadelphia, from 1706 until her death in 1712. Story lived in Pennsylvania from 1705 until 1709; between 1720 and 1727 he became involved in an acrimonious dispute concerning the Pennsylvania Land Company. He was also extraordinarily interested in the study of natural history.[5] Although his journal ran to nearly 500 pages, none of these personal details appeared in the work. His book contained long religious debates, but some other journals included little systematic theology.

A reader should not expect the diaries to contain objective portraits of the subjects. A late eighteenth-century English Friend, James Jenkins, wondered why Quakers "above others have been . . . given 'to build the tombs of the Prophets, and to garnish the sepulchres of the righteous?' " His answer was that to expose guilt or personal weakness would "militate against the Doctrine of *Perfection in this life.*"[6] The hagiographic character of the journals also resulted from their intended use as a preaching aid; that is, they showed lives transformed by the inward light of Christ.

Most prominent in these books were the religious exercises of the subjects. When the Friend experienced a sense of opening and could give a weighty discourse in meeting, he rejoiced, but he acquiesced in silence if there were no message from the Lord to deliver. Many journals concentrated almost exclusively on detailing the itineraries of the traveling ministers and describing states of the meetings. Since the journals were always edited by committees of Friends before publication, what they said was authoritative. And since the later writers tended to follow a format similar to that found in previous journals, a study of the general characteristics of the journals will reveal a pattern of religious development attained by the elite of Quakerdom and aimed at by the commonality.

II

The writers' childhoods received slight emphasis in these journals. Most were children of pious parents, but little attention was focused on how they were raised. Usually, early life was covered in the first 10 pages of a 200-300 page journal. Two themes were normally stressed: divine visitations and sin. The child, often before the age of 10 or 12, experienced a sense of divine providence. For example, Thomas Scattergood (1748–1814) at 6 years of age "was favored with seasons of serious thoughtfulness." Joshua Evans (1731–98) recorded that he had received favors from the Divine even in his "tender years" and had "weighty thoughts" about death, eternity, and life. These youthful visitations were never very effective, for the youngster, no matter what he thought or knew to be right, found having fun and playing games to be pleasant diversions from the serious periods of religion. Joshua Evans inclined to "folly and pranks," and Thomas Chalkley (1665–1742) "loved play exceedingly" and delighted in music, dancing, card playing and secretly indulged in "sports and games."[7]

Childhood was followed by a period of "compunction over youthful frivolity"—a time between 12 and 18 when the person was in school and then an apprentice. Today we might call this stage adolescence, but Friends had no conception of a difficult age concerned with the physical and emotional problems of maturation. As in the earlier period, the youth's moments of religious emphasis were closely followed by indulgence in the vanities of life. Thomas Story recorded his experience of

> the common Temptations among Youth. . . . And tho' was preserved from Guilt, as in the Sight of Men, yet not so before the Lord. . . . The Lust of the Flesh, and of the Eye, and the Pride of Life, had their Objects and Subjects presented: The Airs of Youth were many and potent: Strength, Activity, and Comeliness of Person were not a-wanting and had their Share; nor were natural Endowments of Mind.

Joshua Evans between 11 and 14 was tempted and joined "unsuitable company." He had a "libertine spirit" and would jest and talk lightly, speak falsely, use "you" to a single person, and even curse. David Cooper (1745–95) while a student was "much addicted to play and mirth" and had few equals either in scholarship or "mischief." He felt "two Spirits of Strife," one which inclined him to "sadness and Sorrow," resulting in his seeking solitude to weep, and the other a frivolous "endeavouring to persuade that none of my play fellows was like me, nor any body else in the world, others were lively and Merry, and I was better than they." While most of the journalists recorded how desperately sinful they were, almost all wrote that they were preserved from gross pollutions and maintained a good reputation with parents and Friends. John Woolman (1720–72) confessed, "I was not so hardy as to commit things scandalous, but to Exceed in Vanity, and promote mirth, was my chief study." John Griffith (1713–76) was afraid to tell lies (except to embellish a pleasant story), never swore an oath or uttered a curse, never departed from the plain speech, kept "much love and regard" for those whom he regarded as truly religious, and commonly attended first day meetings. Yet he was "hardened in evil" and in a "Carnal degenerate state."[8] Clearly, the theological separation before and after experiencing grace was so absolute that behavior of children was pictured in stark terms.

The next stages were the crucial ones during which the sinner was made into an expectant saint. Howard H. Brinton labeled these periods *search and conflict*, *convincement*, and *conversion*. The search and conflict consisted of a deepening of the contrast between the good the person knew and the bad he did. When he finally realized what he must do to be saved, he was convinced, and when he eventually reached unity with God he was converted. (Convincement thus defined does not reflect the eighteenth-century Friends' normal usage of the term, by which they meant the procedure that an outsider could follow to become a member of the Society.) Conversion did not necessarily mean a sudden, dramatic renascence as experienced by persons in the Wesleyan revival or the Great Awakening. Quakers rarely used the word conversion to describe what they experienced, perhaps because of its enthusiastic connotations.[9] In more traditional theological terms, what the journalists were undergoing can be described as conviction of sin and the realization of the failure of good works to save, justification, and progression toward sanctification. Since Friends always linked justification and santification as a part of the process of becoming a Christian, one should be aware that these stages were a conceptual framework and that the evolution involved a gradual shading from one state into the other. At times the religious experience could be rapid, at other times extraordinarily protracted.

As the youth became a young man, he began to worry about the course of his life. Very often this awakening was precipitated by an external event—sickness, an accident, or the death of a friend. The journalist's attention was thus keenly focused on the inevitability of his own death and his lack of religion. He therefore set out to reform his life and find the truth. In the seventeenth century the journalist might have wandered from sect to sect seeking one that was truly the church. The Friend saw his condition as analogous to Saint Paul's description of inward torment: "For I delight in the law of God after the inward man: But I see another law in my members, warring against the law of my mind, and bringing me into captivity, to the law of sin." Job Scott of Rhode Island (1751–93) described his misery: "My days I spent in vanity and rebellion, my nights frequently in sorrow and distress. . . . I knew myself a prisoner but I hugged my chains." The experience of God under these conditions was not pleasant. Thomas Story knew Jehovah

> only as a Manifester of Evil and Sin, a Word of Reproof, and a Law condemning and judging those Thoughts, Desires, Words, Passions, Affections, Acts and Omissions, which are seated in the first Nature and rooted in the carnal Mind.[10]

Even the stage of convincement, or realisation of the truth of Friends' principles, and the knowledge of what had to be done did not bring peace. Alice Hayes (1657–1720) described the contrast between her expectations and the results

> Instead of Peace, Trouble and Sorrow, Wars and Commotions, with frightul Sights and deeply distressed, fearing that my Condition was such, that never was the like, not knowing that the Messenger of the Covenant was come. . . . He whom my Soul had been seeking after, and that he must sit there *as a Refiner's Fire, and as a Fuller with Soap, to clear his own Place.*

John Griffith, in attempting to conquer temptations, first triumphed over the sins of the flesh and then found that Satan became an "angel of light" to make him mortify his body. After going around half-starved, with too little sleep, and attempting to work continually, he fell into a religious depression until a ministering Friend visited and told him that his torturing of the body was a design of Satan.[11] Although the complete acceptance of God ended the struggle, the Quaker would in some sense be engaged in a continuous attempt to feel God's presence for the rest of his life.

The desideratum of religious life was conversion or justification. The primary goal for the Quaker was experiencing conversion daily, and the only difference between the initial and the later encounters with God came from the mature Christian's greater familiarity with the beauty and demands of divine love. In meeting God a paradoxical situation was created in which the person had to undergo the abnegation of his own will and be filled with the will of Christ. Thomas Story experienced a most dramatic conversion in 1689, before he became a professing Friend. At the time, Story had been made conscious of his own sin, had been pursued by the Lord until he was aware of His presence, and had experienced disunity with all churches. While he was worshipping alone one first-day evening, the Lord "brake in upon me unexpectedly" as a "righteous, all powerful, all-knowing, and Sin-condemning Judge." Before God, Story's soul was filled with "awful Dread" and his mind seemed to separate from the body and plunge into eternal perdition. In his experience of death "a Voice was formed and uttered in me, as from the Center of boundless Darkness, 'Thy Will, O GOD, be done; if this be thy Act alone, and not my own, I yield my Soul to thee.' " These words brought instant "all-healing Virtue" and the vanishing of fear. "My Mind became calm and still, and simple as a little Child; the Day of the LORD dawn'd, and the Son of Righteousness arose in me, with divine Healing, and restoring Virtue in his Countenance; and he became the Center of my Mind." By this experience he lost his "old self," and saw all his sins condemned and forgiven. All his searchings and carnal reasonings and questionings ended. The next day his mind was "calm and free from Anxiety" and toward evening "my whole Nature and Being, both Mind and Body, was filled with the divine Presence, in a Manner I had never known before, nor had ever thought that such a Thing could be." Divine truth was now self-evident. Story experienced insight into the agony of Christ's passion; he was enlightened to see many mysteries of creation and divine redemption, and he could read the Bible with understanding.[12]

The moment of grace was rarely so dramatic and often came as a young man's realization of peace rather than as a sudden encounter. John Woolman had several experiences of seeking and finding God but then turning away. Finally he decided, "I must not go into company as heretofore in my own will, but all the cravings of Sense must be governed by a Divine principle." He then "felt the power of Christ prevail over all selfish desires." James Gough (1712–80) had moved to a new residence where "I was given plainly to see that my safety here and happiness hereafter, depended upon my yielding faithful obedience to his requirings by his light in my heart." This was his "espousal to Christ Jesus," and he was ready to sacrifice anything for Him. His poetry, which earlier he had delighted in composing, now appeared unworthy, and he burnt it. His satisfaction "was in the company of Christ my dear Lord," and he bade farewell to all the world's pleasures. John Griffith, caught between good and evil, realized that he had the power of decision. Afterward the Lord "broke in upon my soul, by his judgments mixed with mercy, in such a powerful manner, as that I was made willing to yield up thereunto, come life or death." John Kelsall (1681–1743), after experiencing the normal turmoil, gradually grew into Quaker customs.

> I made many Rules to myself that when I came among company I would not be light airy nor talkative but have a watch over my words . . . And thus I passed on for Some Seasons and by the Help of the Lord . . . I came by degrees to see that Nature that would have been up, in some measure to be subdued, and then there was a Zeal and Fervency begot in me against all such vanity.[13]

Many times during his life the Quaker would feel God's wiping out of his past sins and the creation within him of a new person. After his conversion the Friend witnessed a growth in what he was to do in order to measure up to the increasing demands of God. If the person were not already a plain Quaker, these trials would entail the adoption of a more simple style of dress, the use of the plain style of speech, the refusal to take oaths, the curtailment of business, the embarkation upon the ministry, and even traveling in the service of truth.[14] Friends also found that many times God seemed absent; this resulted either from their own straying from true virtue or from the Lord's unaccountably withdrawing Himself for a season. If the period of barrenness happened to a traveling minister, he might go to a village and appoint a meeting and then find he had absolutely nothing to say. In 1757 Anthony Benezet excused his delay in answering a letter because of a spiritual deadness.

> O my leanness, my leanness—it is beyond expression, and so sensibly felt by me, that I dare not as it were extend any further, lest I should defile God's jewels. Though a beggar may have a prospect of the order and beauty of God's house, and can even at a distance see, and apprehend he can distinguish the furniture of it, yet shall he presume, while clothed in rags, to enter therein?

John Griffith in the midst of his "high career" in the ministry lost his gift to speak for nearly five months. Finally the Lord saw his suffering and restored the ability.[15] These periods might last for weeks or months, but ultimately the Almighty was again pleased to make His presence known.

III

While these experiences of the spiritual elite show the goals of life, the average Quaker's normal religious activities can be seen by focusing on the less dramatic occurrences in the particular meeting for worship. The Friend had a great many opportunities to attend meetings. In Philadelphia there were two weekly meetings—from ten until twelve on Tuesday and Thursday—three meetings on Sunday, plus special meetings for youth. There were monthly and quarterly meetings for business and several days of sessions at yearly meeting. John Smith, who lived in Philadelphia and traveled often to Burlington where his parents resided, recorded that during 1745 he attended 162 meetings.[16] If one lived in backwoods Virginia or North Carolina, he might have only weekly and first-day meetings in his immediate vicinity except when a traveling minister visited. Any special activity such as serving on a committee as an overseer, helping in a business arbitration, or visiting families took more time. Since the Friends had no professionally trained full-time clergy, the responsibility for all tasks fell upon the laity.

Organized religious devotion took place at the meeting for worship. The meeting house was perfectly plain; no stained glass, ornamentation, or organ music were to distract the person from silently waiting upon God. The benches were hard and might or might not have backs; normally there was a raised platform or gallery at the front with a bench where the ministers and elders could sit facing the congregation. In keeping with what may have been an earlier practice of the English parish churches, men and women sat apart. Unlike the Puritans, the Friends did not buy pews. Except that ministers and elders sat in the gallery, no distinction was made in seating arrangements. Quakers were expected to enter quietly and sit down, filling the seats at the front first.[17]

Friends were supposed to approach the meeting house seriously. Frivolous matters were not to be discussed either just before or after worship. New England's discipline warned against levity in riding a horse away after meeting. The congregation entered, sat down, and waited in silence. Men kept their hats on, except when someone prayed. When a minister felt moved by the Lord, he stood up, removed his hat, and spoke. The meeting ended when a Friend (normally a clerk or an elder) shook hands with the person seated next to him. Behavior within the meeting was strictly regimented. Too frequent excursions to the necessary house, spitting, and chewing tobacco were condemned. The most frequent complaint was that someone was sleeping in meeting. In 1760 Ann Cooper Whitall recorded in her diary, "I thought it my business to tell Kate Andras of Sleeping in meetings so much as She does and her dear husband dead so little awhile." John Kelsall, an English Friend, for a time found it necessary to carry a pin to stick himself when feeling drowsy in order to stay awake. Friends were warned that too large a noon meal on Sundays led to drowsiness in afternoon meetings. A few disturbances of the meeting were allowed. For instance, when the cry of fire was heard, all went. But when a shower of rain came up and Friends left to keep their saddles from getting wet, "a hint was given at the close, touching on the inconsistency with spiritual pure worship, that appears, where small matters are allow'd to interrupt. This was found to touch some members, who shew'd a dislike to their Conduct being faulted."[18]

The best description of a Quaker meeting was written by Peter Kalm, the Swedish traveler, who attended Bank Meeting House in Philadelphia, December 7, 1750.

> Here we sat and waited very quietly from ten o'clock to a quarter after eleven. . . . Finally, one of the two . . . old men in the front pew rose, removed his hat, turned hither and yon, and began to speak, but so softly that even in the middle of the church, which was not large, it was impossible to hear anything except the confused murmur of the words. Later he began to talk a little louder, but so slowly that four or five minutes elapsed between the sentences; finally the words came both louder and faster. In their preaching the Quakers have a peculiar mode of expression, which is half singing, with a strange cadence and accent, and ending each cadence, as it were, with a half or . . . a full sob. Each cadence consists of two, three, or four syllables, but sometimes more, according to the demand of the words and means; *e.g.* my friends/ /put in your mind/ / we/ / do nothing/ /good of our selves/ / without God's/ / help and assistance/ /etc. In the beginning the sobbing

> is not heard so plainly, but the deeper and further the speaker gets into his sermon the stronger becomes the sobbing between the cadences. The speaker today made no gestures, but turned in various directions; occasionally he placed one hand on his cheek; and during most of the sermon kept buttoning and unbuttoning his vest with right hand. . . . When he stood for a while using his sing-song method he changed his manner of delivery and spoke in a more natural way, or as our ministers do when they say a prayer. Shortly afterwards, however, be began again his half-singing mode of expression, and at the end, just as he was speaking at his best, he stopped abruptly, sat down, and put on his hat.[19]

This sermon took half an hour. Thomas Clarkson in the first decade of the nineteenth century provided a description of several of the preachers he heard. The ministers spoke in an odd tone of voice which Clarkson called "unpleasant" and likened to the noise made by street vendors. The speakers began very softly and slowly, but their speech became louder and faster as the discourse progressed. As fuller involvement came, the minister spoke "beyond the quickness of ordinary delivery," and some were "much affected, and even agitated by their subject." The changes of speed in delivery resulted, Clarkson thought, from the minister's caution in outrunning his gift. When he began to talk, he knew neither where his opening would lead him nor what he was to say. As insight grew, the speed of delivery increased. This singing style of preaching became more prevalent as the eighteenth century progressed, and by the middle of the nineteenth century many Quakers did not esteen a minister who did not sing his sermons.[20]

The content and quality of preaching are difficult to judge, since the few surviving sermons of even the most famous ministers were written down by outsiders and often printed without the consent of the Friends. These sermons show amazing ability in organizing extemporaneous discourse and some variety in type: theological disquisitions of Protestant dogmas, defenses of distinctive Quaker tenets, ethical exhortation, scriptural exegesis, personal narratives, and even evangelistic emphasis. Occasionally an ecstatic element entered as a Friend would prophesy or relate a vision. Samuel Bownas maintained that a Quaker could legitimately preach about almost anything, so long as he was careful to speak under God's immediate direction. Speakers rarely used classical allusions or literary flourishes but assumed a minute knowledge of scriptural lore; prooftexting was common. Sermons invariably had a strong moralistic bent and concluded with some demand upon the listener. Ann Whitall, who attended Haddonfield meeting, recorded that ministers spoke on the final judgment, on the importance of not only listening to sermons but of reforming sins, on spiritual pride, on bringing children to meeting, on education of youth, and on the decline of Friends. Advice to children and youth and preparation for death ranked as the most frequent subjects.[21]

Some opinions that outsiders delivered of Quaker worship tell more about the observers than they do about the Friends. Such is the case with Dr. Johnson's apothegm on a lady preacher: "Sir, a woman preaching is like a dog's walking on its hinder legs! It is not done well; but you are amazed to find it done at all." A more insightful evaluation of Quaker principles was made by Thomas Clarkson. Clarkson found little intellectual merit or variety in preaching in England, for many Friends had "little erudition," and principles forbade premeditation upon the subject. Even Quakers noted the varying abilities of different men, reasoning that one type of sermon might reach the learned and another the illiterate. The sermons were always delivered with "great seriousness" and were "singularly bold and honest" in rebuking anyone who needed it, no matter how rich or powerful. Because the ministers claimed to be able to discern states, a preacher in the middle of his discourse might feel called to change subjects in order to speak to someone's needs. Since any cultivation of eloquence or preparation was forbidden and inasmuch as all inspiration was to come while the person was actually speaking, a polished discourse was nearly impossible. Yet the best of Quaker ministers, like Rachel Wilson who was compared with George Whitefield, were able to attract large crowds.[22] Friends ministered by fostering a sense of the presence of God rather than by arguing about the truths of Quaker theology.

Brevity was not a necessary quality. In 1710, John Banks stood and preached in Somerton, England, for one hour and a half. George Whitehead spoke in London Yearly Meeting in 1716 for nearly two hours. Sophia Hume, writing from Charlestown in 1767, reported that, although she had been ill, "divine goodness" had so strengthened her that she was able to "exhort the People for at least an Hour at a Time."[23] Friends did not take satisfaction, as did certain Puritan ministers, in how often the hourglass was turned over. One spoke as long as the spirit led him; when inspiration stopped, even if in the middle of a sentence, he sat down.

Some historians have questioned whether the Friend normally heard a sermon in meeting. Rufus Jones, in a two-volume study of the *Later Periods of Quakerism,* found such a decline in the eighteenth century in the amount of preaching in meetings that the worship was often held in complete silence. Two of the better recent histories of Friends, by A. Neave Brayshaw and Elfrida Vipont, echoed Jones's judgment "that for years together many meetings were held wholly in silence."[24]

Direct evidence about speaking in meetings is not easy to find. Journals are a more reliable source for deciphering an individual's feelings about his ministry than for determining the amount of speaking. A diarist discussed his own preaching during a journey but almost never commented upon that of his fellow travelers. One bit of contrary proof comes from the diary of John Smith, who recorded every meeting he attended in the Philadelphia area between January 1745 and January 1746. Of the 162 meetings he went to: 150 had prayers or preaching, 5 were silent, of 7 no information was given. Smith calculated that during the year he heard 657 prayers or sermons, an average of 4 per meeting. Women gave 275. He heard 50 different men and 40 women speak plus a few strangers whose names were not recorded. The most frequently heard men, Michael Lightfoot and Daniel Stanton, spoke 69 times. Next was Benjamin Trotter who preached or prayed 59 times. Sarah Morris, the most frequent woman speaker, appeared 38 times; next was Hannah Hulford who spoke 18 times. Among the men, those who can be identified as ministers constituted 75 percent of the speakers and made 91 percent of the appearances. For the women the comparable figures are 83 percent making 81 percent of appearances. Four men made slightly over one-third of all discourses.[25] Clearly, at most meetings only recognized ministers spoke. Since Smith was in the habit of attending meetings all over Philadelphia, his statistics provide an accurate index to the strength of the ministry in this area, but they should not be taken as applicable to the rest of America. Smith's figures fall in a period of time ten years before the revival of Friends during the French and Indian War.

Comparable figures for other areas are not available, but there is evidence that the frequent laments about the declining state of the ministry were an exaggeration. If there were ministers, then one can legitimately deduce that the probability of speaking increased. There are no statistics on the number of live ministers, but starting in the 1680s London Yearly Meeting recorded the number of ministering Friends who died. From this one can deduce, with a slight time lag, the number of preachers at any one time. The two tables in appendix C give the total number of Quaker ministers who died and the average deaths per year calculated on a five-year average. The figures indicate that there were more ministers during the eighteenth century in almost all decades than in the period from 1690 to 1700. From 1700 till around 1770 the numbers remain relatively stable; the end of the century shows a decline that continues into the nineteenth century. London Meeting for Sufferings calculated in 1756 that there were 487 particular meetings in England, not counting London and Middlesex. Since there were approximately 19 meetings there, this makes a total of 506 meetings. According to my figures, from 1740 to 1759, 486 ministers died; according to Charles Hoyland, 475. If one assumes an average ministerial career of twenty years, then most meetings had one minister.[26] Of course many undoubtedly had several and others none, but English Friends did not appear to be destitute of ministers during this period. Philadelphia Yearly Meeting did not begin making accurate lists of ministerial deaths until 1764. Fortunately for the historian, John Smith compiled memorials of all Quaker ministers before 1762. He searched monthly meeting records, wrote letters to Friends in Virginia, New England, and England, and visited elderly ministers.[27] While his information on ministers before 1720 is often sketchy, it is possible, by coupling Smith's figures from 1720 to 1762 with Philadelphia Yearly Meeting records from 1764 to 1779 to determine numbers of ministers. The ministry in Philadelphia Yearly Meeting did not decline in the eighteenth century; rather, the figures, even including the missing year of 1763, show a marked increase as the Revolution approached. (One cannot discount the possibility that the increase may be in part due to the two sources used for numbers.) Figures for the twenty-year period beginning in 1760 show 106 deaths from 103 meetings. The meeting-minister ratio is slightly better than in England. From the available evidence it is clear that there is no proof that there was a lack of preaching in eighteenth-century Quakerism. When a Friend attended a meeting for worship, he expected to hear a spoken ministry consisting of prayers or preaching.

In theory anyone could speak in meetings, but people were not allowed to infringe upon the captive audience very often. Friends who were not officially recognized as ministers were permitted to talk occasionally, but frequent preaching without the approbation of the monthly meeting was frowned upon. In 1726 Philadelphia Monthly Meeting informed Noble Butter that he was not to speak because "he is not esteemed a minister." In 1747 at the Bank Meeting House, "Sam Pennock made a long story, and would have done much longer, but Anthony Morris told him he had said Enough." Elders removed mentally disturbed people from meeting houses. When an outsider visited and began speaking, Friends had to listen although they could keep their hats on or stand as signs of disunity. During the Keithan controversy, his advocates invaded yearly meeting sessions and harangued assemblies. The Quakers sat in silence until the intruders left.[28]

While overseers and elders were often the older and more wealthy members of the congregation (who had the leisure to carry out the duties), neither age nor riches was of much consideration in the ministry. Howard H. Brinton, in his analysis of 100 Quaker journalists, found that the average age at which they began to speak in meeting was 26. James Jenkins noted that in the Yorkshire village of Highflatts one of the ministers, "Henry Dickinson, was an excellent man, and (his illiteracy and condition in life considered) ministered with great propriety of language, and connection of argument." John Smith recorded that apprentices occasionally spoke in Philadelphia meetings and, in 1741 he met a 10-year-old girl preacher. "Several have told me that She speaks very notably and very much to their Satisfaction."[29]

In the eighteenth century the elders supervised both the speaking and the conduct of the ministry. They were responsible for warning the preacher if he misquoted Scripture or outran his gift and for encouraging young people who were just entering the ministry. The elders were to be as "nursing Fathers and Mothers" to both young and old. Historians have tended to find in the growth of the institution of eldership a repressive influence upon the creativity of the ministers.[30] However, no journalist mentioned struggling against elders who suppressed the truth and, occasionally, a preacher who was rebuked by the elders commented on the help he had thereby received. The most scathing comments on preachers came from ordinary laymen and from diaries written by other ministers. Elders should not be held responsible for the theological conservatism that Quakers espoused throughout the eighteenth century. The whole Society stood against doctrinal innovation and the most devout—minister, elder, or ordinary Friend—assumed responsibility for continuing the old ways. Criticism and analysis of what was said in meeting were popular pastimes. Ann Whitall, after hearing people belittle a minister, commented, "I wonder if good men in that day [Bible times] did talk against one another as they do now." Nathaniel Greene, more noted for his Revolutionary War role than his earlier Quakerism, compared one sermon to a meal called "Whistle Belly Vengeance," the more you ate the worse it became.[31] Since some writers were often critical and rarely commendatory and others reversed these tendencies, a person's subjective state undoubtedly had much to do with his opinion of the sermons. Because the light within was involved in judging meetings and sermons, in theory no other criterion except internal feelings could be used. John Griffith seldom had much good to say about a meeting or another's sermon. George Churchman infrequently had praise for any minister except his father, John Churchman, while John Smith rarely blamed or censured a sermon.[32] If learning and polished discourses had been criteria, John Smith, an intelligent and well-educated Friend, was far better qualified to judge than George Churchman. Friends believed that God favored some ministers more than others and esteemed highly those individuals who were eloquent speakers and could bring variety to their sermons without distorting the Scripture.

IV

Quaker religious life was a preparation for the next world. The title of William Penn's very popular *No Cross, No Crown* shows the linkage between mortification in this life and glorification after death. Friends were to "be as strangers and pilgrims to the world, and all things therein, possess as though you did not possess them," for this earth was only a place of travail on the road to a final destination.[33] A devout Quaker lived every day as if it were his last. The small town flavor of colonial life and the degree of involvement of Friends with the meeting meant that an individual would be frequently exposed to people dying. Undoubtedly the ambivalent feelings of Friends toward death—desiring heaven yet dreading the unknown—occasioned the constant preoccupation with health that one finds in letters.

The fear of death and the hope of eternal life motivated not only the initial conviction of sin but the perseverance in the Christian path. Ann Whitall mused in her diary on January 11, 1762:

> I find it an excellent Thing to be as much as we can, always ready, and by being frequently thinking upon Death, it is not so surprizing when it does come: This is a great Point of true wisdom, to number our Days so, as to remember our latter end.[34]

Death was the climax to life, and the period just before the end was supposed to reveal either the righteous prevailing and triumphant or the wicked filled with fear and hesitancy. The journals and the testimonials or memorials to ministers and elders drawn up by the monthly meetings showed how pleasant death could be to a saintly Friend. In 1701 John Tomkins compiled a collection of the dying sayings and deathbed scenes of young and old Friends under the title *Piety Promoted* (which, with additions, was republished 29 times before 1800. The last American edition appeared in 1854.) In England, at the end of the eighteenth century, Friends assembled special editions made up of the death scenes of young persons from age 6 or 7 to the early twenties which were designed for the edification of children and youth.[35] Friends were not unique in their interest in death. In the seventeenth century, Catholics and Protestants issued collections of the dying sayings of children. In 1700 Cotton Mather added several stories to the anthology of James Janeway, an Englishman. Mather published the book under the title *A Token for Children Being an Exact Account of the Conversion, Holy and Exemplary Lives and Joyful Deaths of Several Young Children.*

Typical of this form of Quaker literature were the unpublished accounts of the death of Charles Pemberton, aged 19, drawn up by his mother, Rachel, and his brother, Israel Pemberton, Jr. The mother's account was an extraordinarily impersonal history of the events; the brother's was a very emotional story designed to be placed at his bedside for frequent reading. After Charles had been ill for some time and seemed near death, Israel Pemberton, Sr., warned him that "there Seemed little hopes of his recovery and that he hoped in this long time of Illness he had not been unmindful to prepare for his change." The father informed the youth that both his parents had been praying for him and had petitioned the Lord "to be near to him and grant him resignation of mind to his holy will" and to bring "Some assurance of his mercy and favour." After being informed by Charles of his submission to whatever God demanded, Israel, Sr., told the boy of his own religious experiences and of the Lord's mercy when undergoing "great affliction of body and mind." He offered to have any Friends that Charles wanted visit him. Some were paying him a religious visit five days later when he died.[36]

Unlike the mother, Israel Pemberton, Jr., stressed "The Great Love and Affection which Subsisted between me and my Dear Brother" and also the character of Charles as a "Youth favored of the Lord with a Good Capacity, great memory, good delivery, and a tender spirit." Israel thought that he could not survive the "Loss of him but the Lord was mercifully pleased to assist and help. Wherefore Let my Soul bless his name."[37]

Friends who survived the death of others stressed in Job-like fashion the necessity of submitting to the will of God. When John Reynell's only surviving child was about to die, the girl, age 15, "desired her Mother to give her up, and said She should be better provided for than any thing I could do for her." The father mourned but believed that it was better to "part with them while young, than to have them live to take bad Courses . . . the Lord sees not as Man seeth, He gives and takes away. Blessed be his Name forever and may [we] be Resigned to his Will, for he knows what is best."[38]

Complete resignation was expected not only from the survivors but also from the dying person who was not to desire life or death but was to welcome whatever the Lord brought. If death came, he welcomed it as a deliverance from this world of tribulation. If health returned, the person's submissiveness was seen as being rewarded by God.

The Friends' assurance of knowing the will of God carried over into the experience of death. When Charles Pemberton was dying, Sarah Morris, a ministering Quaker, was told by the Lord "not to be Concerned for him, for that he had a mind to take him unto himself and that his End should be peace, and that was enough." Israel Pemberton, Jr., recorded, quite naturally, how "greatly Comfortable" this testimony was to him. At times the knowledge came directly to the person. When Elizabeth Allinson lay dying, she told her sister that "since she had been on that Bed the Almighty had kindly favoured her and given her to see that all her former transgressions were forgiven and that if it should be his will to take her at that time, she had reason to believe she should be accepted."[39]

An entire household gathered in the death chamber to hear the final words of exhortation. If the Friend were very prominent many visitors, including young children, would come. There was nothing private about the final expiration. The individual was in his closest relationship with God, and the advice and pious expressions he gave were often taken down and kept as family memorials. At Samuel Allinson's death, his wife regretted that he had no opportunity to give final counsel to his children. Her father, Peter Cooper, did not trust to chance but left directions in writing that his coffin was to be perfectly plain pine and that the expense saved thereby should be given to the poor. He wrote out the reasons for his plainness and concluded with an address to his neighbors to suppress their desire for pomp. The paper was read at his funeral.[40]

The religious exercises of children were not often recorded except when they were dying. One 10-year-old boy bore a testimony to simplicity by asking his mother to remove from the house a pair of gilt teapots, a chimney piece shaped like a lion, and an ornamental china dish. After he had given to the assembled company a short speech on salvation, the grandmother returned thanks by saying, "*Oh Lord! That* this young Branch, should be a Teacher unto *us old Ones.*" The lad agreed that this was his role. Quaker children customarily gave advice to those around them, whether adults, playmates, or brothers and sisters. When Hannah Hill, aged 11, was on her deathbed, she rebuked those who wished for her recovery. Before dying she exhorted her sister and cousin to obey their parents and trust in the Lord.[41] Hannah Hill's religious exercises went through three editions between 1715 and 1717 and were later incorporated into *Piety Promoted.*

In order not to distract from the religious significance of the occasion and to guard against superfluities, the meeting approved only those burial customs that were free from embellishment. The Society opposed all outward signs of mourning. Normal clothing was correct funeral attire, and the wearing of black was an unseemly formality. The homage paid to the deceased was of no more significance than the opportunity it provided for the living to reflect upon their own deeds. Since there were few undertakers in colonial days, the care of the dead was strictly a family affair. After death the corpse was left at home until the time of burial. Although George Fox had testified against wakes as a heathen custom, by the time of the Revolution the practice had been revived, at least among Philadelphia Friends.[42]

Funerals were generally held within two or three days of death but, if the weather were hot, the burial might take place the next afternoon. Friends were given notification either by an announcement at the close of a meeting, or by personal invitation, or by both. The invitation meant that the person was privileged to partake of refreshments and dinner. The corpse, wrapped in wool in England but in a linen sheet in America, was buried in a wooden coffin. The wealth or strictness of the Friend or his family would determine the degree of ornamentation. John Woolman insisted that his coffin be made perfectly plain and from ash rather than oak because the latter "is a wood more useful than ash for some other purposes." More worldly Friends' coffins were made of mahogany with silver handles and lined with flannel.[43]

Friends disapproved of elaborate funeral processions. In early Pennsylvania the coffin was placed in the ground and then a meeting held. The format was the same as at a regular meeting for worship. Sometimes the meeting was held and then the coffin carried to the graveside. Friends believed that seeing the corpse in the meeting and then carrying the coffin to the cemetery and watching the burial was useful "for the propagation of truth."[44] Philadelphia Monthly Meeting adopted regulations on how the procession was to go from the meeting house to the cemetery. Friends were to follow "orderly . . . not exceeding four in breadth." At the graveside after a short pause during which members had an opportunity to speak, the coffin was placed in the ground. Friends permitted no marker of any kind on the grave, but, since having a tombstone was not a disownable offense, some appeared. If the meeting was large, families would not be buried together; rather, there would be a systematic filling up of the burial ground. An occasional grave site might be lined in bricks, but most Friends preferred to have the wood coffin placed next to earth.[45] Since the person was dust in the beginning and would return to dust shortly, elaborate care of the physical remains was sacrilegious.

Frequent references in yearly meeting disciplines to violations of the simplicity of funerals indicate that moderation was more easily advised than enforced. The most prevalent abuses were found in the serving of refreshments. Friends saw the necessity of providing some repast for people who came from far away, but they objected to the size and lavishness of entertainments that debased a solemn occasion into a "festival." The 1719 Philadelphia discipline listed the ofienses:

> Friends are desired . . . to break from and avoid that offensive and, unsuitable Custom of large provision of strong Drink, Cakes etc. and the formal and repeated servings and offers thereof. This indecent, and indiscreet custom, and practice has run to such excess, That invitations being made to greater number, than their own or Neighbours houses can contain the very Street and open places, are made use of for the handing about burnt wine, and other strong Liquors etc.

It was customary to provide cake and wine before a burial and a meal afterwards. An unverified Quaker practice was to pass the bottle around only twice at a funeral.[46] This was supposedly to prevent early guests from eating and drinking more than was compatible with the solemnity of the occasion. But even in the eighteenth century there were no records of elaborate formalities in the meeting or of the giving of gloves or rings to pallbearers.

V

The shared experience of the inward light in meeting for worship, private prayer, and Scripture or devotional reading shaped Quaker religious life. People converted and remained Friends because they believed that in silence God was found. The encounter with God first brought turmoil and anguish as the person measured his life by the divine standard, but eventually, as the Holy Spirit came to dominate the person's will, the godly enjoyed peace, consolation, and assurance. By reading the journals of weighty members and listening to ministers preach, Friends gained confidence that only the meeting provided pure and true religion.

Quaker ministers did not prepare a message but waited expectantly in meetings for the Holy Spirit to inspire them and the resulting "openings" could be a few words or a long discourse. The belief in divine afflatus did not preclude laymen from grumbling about the content of sermons or from occasional drowsiness. Publishing the journals of prominent Friends provided a method of proselytizing as well as reassuring the faithful, for a holy life stood as an affirmation of the power of God in Quaker religion. The narratives of dying Quakers, which occupy so prominent a position in *Piety Promoted,* testify to the belief that in the moments before his decease the person was in his closest relationship to God and could receive insight into realms beyond the grave. Emphasizing the closeness of eternity also served as a reminder that unrepentant evildoers went to hell and goaded lukewarm Friends to more diligence in religious observances.

The outward forms of worship did not change in the colonial period, but after 1690 the Friends' conception of themselves did evolve. Before the Act of Toleration, Quakers struggled to survive in a hostile environment. The Society saw its religion as a new spiritual phenomenon that would sweep all forms of apostasy from the earth. In the eighteenth century the emotional quality of Quakerism changed. Friends believed just as fervently as before in the truth of their doctrines, but they lost the hope of conquering the world for Christ. The novelty was ended and the excitement completed. The Friends' task became to preserve what was already established rather than to build anew. Any enthusiastic tendencies were disciplined and disappeared, for grace flowed in stable, well-defined channels. In short, the children of light became a respectable Protestant denomination. Frederick Tolles has argued that Quakers were unable to respond favorably to the fervor kindled in the Great Awakening because conservatism, wealth, and stability had sobered the meeting. An early sign of this change can be seen in Benjamin Coole's *Discourse on Inspiration,* printed in 1712, in which the author maintained that the Friend's experience of the grace of God was both "*safe* respecting the Sobriety it leads to, and *sound* respecting its Orthodoxy."[47] The hardening of a universal truth as preached by Fox, Barclay, and Penn into a creed professed by a small denomination made the Society of Friends into a conservative body. The eighteenth century was for them an age of orthodoxy in which tradition governed.

Notes

1 Thomas Story, *A Journal of the Life of Thomas Story* (New Castle, England, 1747), pp. 32–33.

2 Robert Barclay, *An Apology for the True Christian Divinity,* 13th ed. (Manchester, England, 1860), prop. 11, pg. vii, 223.

3 Howard Brinton, "Stages in Spiritual Developments as Recorded in Quaker Journals," in *Children of Light* (New York, 1938), p. 384; see also Luella Wright, *The Literary Life of the Early Friends* (New York, 1932), pp. 165–97.

4 John Woolman, *Journal and Essays of John Woolman,* ed. Amelia M. Gummere (New York, 1922), p. 173; Janet Whitney, *John Woolman* (Boston, 1942), pp. 150–51.

5 See the Preface to Story, *Journal,* pp. ii-iii.

6 James Jenkins, "The Records and Recollections of James Jenkins Respecting Himself, and Others from 1761, to 1821," ed. Mildred Campbell, Typed transcript, p. 8, FHL.

7 William Evans and Thomas Evans, eds., *Memoirs of Thomas Scattergood,* in *Friends' Library* (Philadelphia, 1844), 3: 3; Joshua Evans, *A Journal of Joshua Evans,* ed. George Churchman (Byberry, Penn., 1837), p. 5; Thomas Chalkley, *The Works of Thomas Chalkley* (London, 1791), pp. 3–4; Brinton, "Stages in Spiritual Development," p. 387.

8 Story, *Journal,* p. 11; Evans, *Journal,* p. 7; Woolman, *Journal,* p. 155; David Cooper, "Diary of David Cooper," p. 3, QC; John Griffith, *A Journal of the Life, Travels, and Labours in the Work of the Ministry, of John Griffith* (Philadelphia, 1780), pp. 8–9.

9 Brinton, "Stages of Spiritual Development," pp. 390–95; London YM, Christian and Brotherly Advices, pp. 271–72, FHL; William Penn, *Works of William Penn* (London, 1726), 2: 867; John Griffith, *Some Brief Remarks* (London, 1764), p. 36. In 1692 John Banks equated convincement with the first awakening and conversion with sanctification. See *A Journal of the Life . . . of John Banks* (London, 1712), pp. 247–62.

10 Jane Hoskins, *The Life of that Faithful Servant of Christ, Jane Hoskins,* in Friends' Library, 1: 460; Story, *Journal,* p. 12; Job Scott, *Journal of the Life, Travels and Gospel Labour of . . . Job Scott* (New York, 1797), pp. 26–27; Brinton, "Stages of Spiritual Development," p. 390; Romans 7 : 15–23; George Churchman, *Journal of George Churchman,* in *Friends' Library,* 6: 180.

11 Alice Hayes, *A Legacy, or Widow's Mite* (London, 1723), pp. 27–28; Griffith, *Journal,* pp. 17–19.

12 Story, *Journal,* pp. 13–15.

13 Woolman, *Journal,* p. 156; James Gough, *Memoirs or The Life, Religious Experiences and Labours in the Gospel, of*

James Gough, ed. John Gough (Dublin, 1802), pp. 21–22; Griffith, *Brief Remarks,* pp. 27–29; John Kelsall, "Diary," 1: 34–35, FHL.

14 Brinton, "Stages of Spiritual Developments," pp. 400–06.

15 Anthony Benezet to Samuel Fothergill, 10/1/1757, in George S. Brookes, *Friend Anthony Benezet* (Philadelphia, 1937), p. 222; Griffith, *Journal,* p. 31; John Pemberton to Israel Pemberton, Jr., 5/23/1751, PP, 7: 89, HSP.

16 John Smith, "Diary," vol. 2, Jan. 1745-Jan. 1746, Smith Mss, LC.

17 Eleanor Trotter, *Seventeenth Century Life in the Country Parish* (Cambridge, 1919), p. 50; *BFHA* 31 (1941): 29; Mary Leadbeater, *Annals of Ballitore, The Leadbeater Papers* (London, 1862), 1: 175–76.

18 New England YM, Discipline, 1708–38, 10, QC; *The Book of Discipline Agreed on by the Yearly Meeting of Friends for New-England* (Providence, 1785), p. 19; Ann Cooper Whitall, "Diary," 7/27/1760, 30, QC; Kelsall, "Diary," 1: 21–22; Churchman, *Journal* 1: 88, QC.

19 *BFHA* 31 (1942): 28–29.

20 Thomas Clarkson, *Portraiture of Quakerism* (London, 1807), 2: 281–83; Jenkins, "Records and Recollections," 1: 197, 214–15, FH.

21 *Concurrence and Unanimity of the People Called Quakers* (London, 1694), pp. 17, 55, 73–77, 111; Samuel Fothergill, *Two Discourses and a Prayer* (New York, 1768), pp. 1–14, 26; *A Sermon Publickly Delivered At a Meeting of People Called Quakers* (Newport, 1773); Thomas Story, *Sermons on Following Subjects: 1. Salvation by Christ . . . II. Nature and Necessity of . . . Silence* (Leeds, 1739); Samuel Bownas, *A Description of the Qualifications Necessary to a Gospel Minister* (London, 1750), pp. 47–48; [Thomas Letchwork?], *Discourse as Delivered at a Meeting (Supposed at Canterbury) of the People called Quakers, In the Year 1768* (Cork, 1776); Lucia Beamish, "The Quaker Understanding of the Ministerial Vocation" (B. Lit. thesis, Oxford University, 1965): Ann Whitall, "Diary," pp. 36, 39, 57–59, 71, 74, 81, 86–88, 108.

22 Martha Petel to Israel Pemberton 2/21/1770, PP, 21: 116. There is no evidence that Johnson ever heard a lady Quaker preach. G. B. Hill and L. F. Powell, eds., *Boswell's Life of Johnson* (Oxford, 1934), 1: 463; Clarkson, *Portraiture of Quakerism,* 2: 284–87.

23 Banks, *Journal,* p. 145; "Peter Briggins' Diary," in *Eliot Papers,* ed. Eliot Howard (London, 1895), 2: 68; Sophia Hume to Israel Pemberton, 6mo./1767, Letters of Sophia Hume, Charleston Mss, DR.

24 A. Neave Brayshaw, *The Quakers: Their Story and Message,* 5th (New York, 1938), pp. 249–55; Elfrida Vipont, *Story of Quakerism* (London, 1954), p. 150; Rufus Jones, *Later Periods of Quakerism,* (London, 1921) p. 63. Jones relied upon journalists and John Rutty's description of twenty-two silent meetings in Dublin in 1770. While one does find references to occasional silent meetings in various sources, the evidence from most localities indicates that total silence was exceptional and journalists who conducted silent meetings reported the disappointment of attenders.

25 Smith, "Diary," vol. 2, Jan. 1745-Jan. 1746. In 1762 Haddonfield had six ministers and a great deal of preaching. Whitall, "Diary," p. 120.

26 For laments of declining strength in the ministry, at a time when the figures show no such phenomenon, see London YM of Ministers and Elders, Minutes, vol. 1 (1757): 8–23 and the epistle sent by Philadelphia Yearly Meeting in 1754, in Epistles Received by London YM, 3: 361. It is not known what records Charles Hoyland based his calculations on. I used the deaths of ministers as reported to London Yearly Meeting, totaled the amounts in five-year periods, and averaged the figures for a per annum death rate. In the memorials collected by John Smith, the average time of service was twenty-seven years, but for many individuals no estimate of time spent as a minister was given.

27 John Smith, "Lives of Ministers Among Friends," 3 vols., QC; Smith Mss, 5: 178, 210, 225, 241, and 6: 91–98, LC.

28 Min. Philadelphia MM, 3 (11/26/1726): 141; Smith, "Diary," vol. 2, 4/22/1746, 11/27/1726; A. C. Myers, ed., *Courtship of Hannah Logan,* (Philadelphia, 1904), p. 120. Min. Philadelphia YM, 1 (7/23/1696): 59. Morris was an elder. Pennock made six appearances in 1746 but was not recognized as a minister.

29 Meetings were often exhorted not to pick their elders by wealth or age, a sign that this was probably done sometimes. Min. London YM, 12 (5/15/1761): 213; Brinton, "Stages of Religious Developments," p. 400; Jenkins, "Records and Recollections," 1: 31; Smith, "Diary," 1 (6mo./1741), and 2 (2/27/1746), and 3 (5/16/1747).

30 Arnold Lloyd, *Quaker Social History* (New York, 1950), p. 123; Lucia Beamish, "Quaker Understanding of the Ministerial Vocation," (Bachelor of Letters thesis, Oxford, 1965), pp. 107–109; Philadelphia YM, Christian and Brotherly Advices (1723), p. 120. Jones, *Later Periods of Quakerism,* pp. 120–28. Jones has an excellent discussion of the imprecision in functions of elders, overseers, and ministers.

31 Elizabeth Morris to John Smith, 1/20/1756, Smith Mss, 4: 251; Gough, *Memoirs,* pp. 42–43; Whitall, "Diary," pp. 36–37; C. P. Monahon and C. A. Collins, eds., "Nathaniel Greene's Letter to 'Friend Sammy Ward,'" in *Rhode Island History* vol. 15 (1956), p. 52.
32 Griffith, *Journal,* pp. 267–68; George Churchman, *Journal,* 1: 10mo./1760, 12, 6/1/1760, 9, 10/3–3/1762, 44; Smith, "Diary," 4: 2/26/1748.
33 George Fox, *Works of George Fox* (Philadelphia, 1831), 8: 18.
34 Whitall, "Diary," 1/11/1762. Evidently, a sermon on this subject had been preached in the meeting.
35 William Rawes, Jr., ed. *Examples for Youth in Remarkable Instances of Early Piety* (London, 1797); *Brief Memorials of the People called Quakers* (London, 1781).
36 Rachel Pemberton's undated account of her son Charles' death, ca. 3mo./1748, PP, 4: 112.
37 Israel Pemberton, 3/24/1748, PP, 4: 118.
38 John Reynell to Mary Groth, 1756, Letter Book 1756–59, Coates-Reynell Mss, HSP.
39 Israel Pemberton, 3/24/1748, PP, 4: 118; Katherine Smith, "Account of the Death of Elizabeth Allinson," 8/20/1768, Allinson Family Mss, QC.
40 *PMHB* 22 (1898): 257; Martha Allinson to William Allinson, 11/13/1795, Allinson Family Mss.
41 *A Seasonable Account of the Christian and Dying-Words, of Some Young Men Fit for the Considerations of All: But Especially of the Youth of This Generation* (Philadelphia, 1700), pp. 13–14; Hannah Hill, *A Legacy for Children* (Philadelphia, 1717), pp. 8–9, 19.
42 Fox, *Journal,* p. 107; Elizabeth Drinker, *Extracts from the Journal of Elizabeth Drinker,* ed. Henry Biddle (Philadelphia, 1889), p. 147; Penn, *Works,* 1: 870–71; Clarkson, *Portraiture of Quakerism,* 2: 39–41.
43 Smith, "Diary," 2 (5/2/1746); Drinker, *Extracts from the Journal,* p. 219; Alton Men and Women Friends, "A Testimony Concerning our deceased Friend, Elizabeth Merryweather," 3/15/1790, Allinson Mss; Woolman, *Journal,* pp. 324–25; *PMHB* 27 (1903): 53–54.
44 Myers, *Hannah Logan's Courtship,* p. 291; *PMHB* 22 (1898): 257, and 17 (1893): 456–58; Min. Philadelphia MM, 2 (12/22/1705).
45 London YM, Christian and Brotherly Advices (1717), p. 199; Min. Philadelphia MM, 1 (8/26/1694): 132; Min. Philadelphia YM, 1 (6/16–20/1732): 360; Clarkson, *Portraiture of Quakerism,* 2: 33–34.
46 Philadelphia YM, Christian and Brotherly Advices (1719, 1729, 1735, 1746, 1750), p. 12; Min. Philadelphia YM, (1719), 1: 223; Watson W. Dewees, "The Meeting at Work," in *225th Anniversary of Concord Monthly Meeting of Friends 1686–1911* (Philadelphia, 1911), p. 62.
47 Frederick Tolles, *Quakers and the Atlantic Culture* (New York, 1960), pp. 91–113; Benjamin Coole, *Miscellanies* (London, 1712), p. 61.

3 The Nature of Christian Discipline

Whilst we are in Unity with the Body of Friends, we must be very careful that we Act, nor Do, any thing contrary to the Principle or Discipline of Truth, because there is no Person that is a member that is Exempted from the Censure of the Church.

Min. Philadelphia YM, 7/19/1710

The process of salvation has thus far been traced, in both theological treatises and personal narratives, from the individual's awakening from sin through his justification and sanctification. While most of the preceding has been discussed in terms of the individual, one should remember that the Quakers belonged to a church, the Society of Friends. If the inward grace of God came to men singly, the group still met together communally to help the members prepare to receive and walk within the light. The defining of this strait-and-narrow way involved church authority. In their rationale for Christian discipline, Quakers created an effective method to control individual behavior.

During the Restoration in England, Friends were beset by two alternatives to their beliefs on discipline. On one side were the Ranters, a group that demanded inward revelation but refused to subject it to church scrutiny and consequently adopted moral practices that scandalized their contemporaries. On the other side were the Anglicans, Presbyterians, and many Puritans, who demanded a uniformity in belief for all Englishmen, used the authority of both state and church to insure Christian conduct, and denied the possibility of individual revelations equal to those known by the apostolic writers.

The Quakers experienced schisms and continued to be tormented by internal factions until after the Keithan controversy in America in the 1690s. In 1661–62 a group led by John Perrot asserted that when there was true spiritual worship, there was no need to remove a hat for prayer or shake hands to end a meeting. While not seeking to force their principles on others, followers of Perrot demanded the right to decide such matters for themselves. Another schism, known as the Wilkinson-Story controversy, began about 1675 as a protest against the growing hierarchy of monthly, quarterly, and yearly meetings. These dissident Quakers denounced the imposition of a uniform discipline and split away over the establishment of separate women's meetings. Their protest was not a denial of the ability of women to participate, but they opposed establishing separate institutions for them.[1] In 1674, against a backdrop of developing turmoil, Robert Barclay wrote a treatise on Christian discipline entitled the *Anarchy of the Ranters,* which was published in 1676 in the middle of the Wilkinson-Story dispute. Throughout the eighteenth century this book was used by Friends to justify the authority of the meeting over theological and moral issues.[2] An analysis of the *Anarchy of the Ranters* demonstrates clearly how Quakers in both the seventeenth and the eighteenth centuries supported church authority. One of the reasons why only Friends, of all the sects that sprang up during the Commonwealth period, were able to survive was that they managed to combine the liberty of personal authoritative revelation with a strong system of discipline and church control.

Quakers saw their religion as the restoration of primitive Christianity. Fox proclaimed that all Friends' beliefs and practices went back to Christ, and that the Quakers derived their authority directly from Him.[3] Any action taken by the early church under the direction of the Spirit could be taken by those who restored true Christianity. The problem, then, was to search the New Testament for precedents in church government.

> The ancient apostles and primitive Christians practiced order and government in the church; that some did appoint and ordain certain things; condemn, and approve certain practices, as well as doctrines by the Spirit of God: that there lay an obligation in point of duty upon others to obey and submit.[4]

The Holy Spirit showed the primitive church the necessity for the "same principles, doctrines, and points of faith." Even in apostolic days it was necessary to discipline apostates, sinners, and opposers, and any true church could do the same. The Society of Friends was also gathered by the Spirit and had found a unity in faith, doctrine, and behavior. The Quakers had formed themselves into a body to propagate and maintain Christianity and had an obligation to oppose any actions or principles that might hinder the propagation of the truth or bring "infamy, contempt, or contumely upon it."[5]

Order within the church was not tyranny; rather, it was the basis for holding the society together. Physical means, such as setting a time and place for meetings, were necessary because men were corporal beings. The exercise of control was limited to those within the meeting, and all those who professed to be or were deemed Friends by the Society were subject to the discipline. Quakers did not intend to compel outsiders to join them, but they did have a divinely imposed obligation to exhort strangers to enter the church and to condemn any outgoings from the light.[6] But the primary emphasis in discipline was to keep those who professed the truth in the truth. Toleration was defended because faith could not be forced, but toleration did not mean that others had any claim to grace. A hundred years after they had become reconciled to the fact that Friends were only one small denomination among others, their religious attitudes and disciplinary practices rested upon an assumption of Quaker truth and the world's error.

Although Quaker organizational structure resembled the English parish and the Presbyterian synod system, the rationale was always the New Testament precedents. In primitive times the chief marks of Christians had been their "Love and compassion" for each other. These attitudes fostered a desire to care for poor widows and orphans and to contribute to the poor. Temporal matters such as marriage and law suits were also within the scope of the church. Since Christians were to love one another and to exist in unity and harmony, any reference of a dispute to outside authority meant that one did not love, and could not trust, his brethren.[7]

The church also had control over matters of doctrine. All religious beliefs were matters of conscience, and no one could be coerced into the church. Christian freedom was the privilege to follow the lead of the Spirit as manifested in the unity of the fellowship. True liberty of conscience within the Society lay not in each individual's ability to define truth but in his right to exercise his gifts by preaching, or overseeing, or administering charity. Friends believed that all schisms within the meeting, whether in apostolic times or seventeenth-century England, occurred when persons left their proper places and demanded or attempted to exercise gifts that were not rightfully theirs. If the principles upon which the Society was formed were true, then to oppose the meeting would be to obstruct God, and to cherish persons who were in error was a false charity. Inward revelation was the ground of the church, but unchecked subjective experiences were not permissible. The practices of the Society of Friends were "received as true, and confirmed by God's Spirit in the hearts of the saints," and to introduce anything contrary to them would bring "reproach upon the truth" and "so stumble the weak." Therefore, "those who have a true and right discerning, may in and by the power of God authorizing them (and no otherwise) condemn and judge such things," and obeying their judgment would be "obligatory upon all the members."[8] The church would judge not only matters of great weight but also those of minor importance that might have a tendency to bring any practice of the body into disrepute.

The effects of the doctrines of church authority and unity, besides justifying the expulsion of members over so minor a matter as failure to remove hats during a prayer in meeting, were extremely inhibitive to any change. The martyrs of Quakerism put their stamp of approval upon the canon and any attempt to alter what the meeting regarded as authoritative would be seen as proceeding from a wrong spirit. Since every doctrine and practice was viewed as being under the guidance of the Holy Spirit, to change even minor matters for administrative convenience could be a major undertaking. (Quakers did distinguish between acts of the moment, such as repairing the meeting house, and matters on which spiritual insight was required.[9]) When confronted with the possibility of changing doctrines, Fox had declared:

> For when they that are ministers change and alter from that which they went forth first in, and brought the people into, it doth show that they are either gone out of the truth, or else were never in the truth.

When declaring against vain fashions, London Yearly Meeting, as early as 1675, enforced "Friends Ancient Testimony." After the trial of George Keith at London Yearly Meeting in 1694, one of the reasons frequently cited for declaring him out of unity was his "delivering the Doctrines of Truth in Unusual Words." In the eighteenth century, when certain quarterly and monthly meetings in both England and America petitioned their respective yearly meetings for changes in certain decrees prohibitive to marrying kin, the dispute was ended by referring to former advices of yearly meetings.[10] Since these had been delivered in a spirit of truth, to change the advice would be to alter God's eternal decrees. When changes in customs did occur, as in the case of slavery, the alteration was brought about by men like John Woolman and Anthony Benezet, who were so dedicated that no one could really doubt that they were in unity with the spirit of Friends. And this particular change evolved relatively easily because meetings did not reverse previously held tenets; rather, they gradually extended older advices (upon the evil in trading slaves who had been procured in war) first to forbid Friends' buying or selling slaves and finally to require those who owned slaves to free them. In this case, Friends asserted that following the light had brought a growth in understanding the requirements of God.

Since Friends maintained that revelation did not cease, the crucial factor in judging any sort of modification in doctrine or practice was the determination of whether or not it came from the Lord. Barclay affirmed that there were those in the meeting who had the power of discerning the grounds of actions or doctrines. If persons within false churches, by pretending to conscience, could judge, "then it must also be acknowledged, that such, to whom God hath given a true discerning by his Spirit, may and ought to judge such practices, and the spirit they came from." In any case of controversy "the spirit of God" would not desert the church as long as the people remained faithful to Him. God normally communicated His will through those persons who had gathered and nourished the true church.[11] When Barclay was writing, those persons were George Fox, the "first publishers of truth," and more recent converts such as William Penn, Thomas Ellwood and Isaac Penington. Later, the authorities to whom God entrusted His counsel would be "weighty Friends," in other words, those sitting in the gallery for ministers and elders. This practice opened up the possibility of the devout exercising oligarchical control, the beginnings of which had helped to precipitate the Wilkinson-Story schism in the 1670s and which came to prevail in the eighteenth century.

Friends throughout the seventeenth and eighteenth centuries, their only source of knowledge being the inward light, claimed the power to discern the states of men. In 1653 George Fox announced that "the Lord had given me a spirit of discerning, by which I many times saw the states and conditions of people, and could try their spirits." In 1748 John Griffith discouraged any from bringing information about the spiritual condition of a meeting that he planned to visit, for no minister needed faulty man-made knowledge when he had a "sure infallible guide within." In defending a rigorous interpretation of discipline in June 1768, David Ferris wrote to his brother Benjamin:

> If I believed, that Friends could not see, feel, smell, nor hear spiritually, so as to Discover the Situation of their fellow members, to know whether they were sincere or not, that is whether they were living members or dead, I would as live be of any other Society.[12]

Obviously some people who thought they were led by God to certain actions were mistaken. If the person were in error, the fault lay within himself. God was pure truth; His reception by mankind was also pure truth because man received God through pure supernatural senses. If a mistake occurred, the error came not from the communication of God to man, but, after the reception of truth or even before, from the fact that man's natural faculties had effaced God. Just as reason could operate infallibly under the right circumstances but could be destroyed by passions, so "some evil disposition of mind" could obliterate God. In the *Apology* Barclay maintained:

> For it is one thing to affirm, *that the true and undoubted revelation of God's Spirit is certain and infallible;* and another thing to affirm, that this or that particular person or people is led infallibly by this revelation in which they speak or write, because they affirm themselves to be so led.[13]

Barclay asserted that only the first proposition was maintained, but if the second were denied, then the whole foundation of certainty in having assurance, in speaking truth as a minister, in judging states, in fact, the whole epistemological basis for Quaker doctrine was founded upon sand. Quaker theology postulated an ultimate dualism, with God's virtue and man's corruption being totally divorced. The Puritans demanded to know why the interaction of good and bad resulted in pure good rather than a mixture of truth and falsity. Barclay was unable to explain this and, in effect, had agreed with the Puritans on the uncertainty of inward revelation.

The seeds of doubt may have been in Barclay himself, buried between propositions asserting the certainty of God-given knowledge. In spite of the fact that revelation was self-authenticating, the believer could check the light against Scripture, right reason, and the meeting's definition of truth.[14] With church, reason, and Scripture in theory subordinated to, but able to confirm, inward revelations, the Friends had weakened or at least disciplined the free grace of God. The collective total of the testimonies of the Quaker martyrs and the living church was sufficient to quell the intellectual doubt that any man could know for certain that God was speaking through him. While eighteenth-century ministers insisted to outsiders upon the infallibility of inward revelation, they acted more circumspectly within the meeting and showed some timidity in asserting their own purity. A major theme of the journalists was their fear of overstepping God's gift. Their defensiveness marks a major change in Quakerism; early Friends knew that they had the truth; later followers also had the truth but they worried about it.

While Quakers wanted only visible saints within the meeting, they recognized that most men—even those within the true church—were still liable to sin and periodically needed to be disciplined. Like the Puritans, the Friends saw their members as obligated to watch over their neighbors. In 1652 Fox had exhorted, "To that of God in you I speak, that ye watch over the weak, and see how the plants of the Lord grow." While Quakers were to "Let mercy overshadow the judgment seat," they were also to "Take heed of foolish pity," for all sin was to be cast out. John Smith, writing to an apprenticed Friend, Elias Bland, when both were young men, had summarized religious duty as "To do Justly, To Love Mercy, [and] T[o] Walk humbly with God," and he observed that justice was placed before mercy to emphasize that "our Mercy Should not Exceed the bounds of Justice."[15] Discipline was exercised to preserve truth from taint and to keep the City upon a Hill (a metaphor used by Quakers as well as Puritans) unblemished in order to show the world what Christianity should be. Dishonor within the church was an affront to God and to the visible saints. The goal of discipline was to cast out sins, not people. However, if the people were too wedded to their sins to forego them, the Society was to leave them to their deserved damnation.

The Puritans maintained civil and church discipline because the whole society was in covenant with the Lord. In normal times Quakers did not stress the religious origin of society, but in periods of urgency, such as during the French and Indian Wars, they relied upon a jeremiad formula to remind Friends that God had previously brought protection to his chosen people. In spite of the fact that they were a minority of the population, Friends saw God's judgment upon themselves. If repentance were delayed, God would cut off his once-privileged people. (At the same time, the Pennsylvania Quakers did not hesitate to blame the wars upon the perfidy of the proprietors in mistreating the Indians.)[16] Like the New Englanders, Quakers talked about the imminence of the eschaton, believing judgment could be avoided in England or America because a people of God existed there—a similitude to Abraham's quest of a few just men to preserve Sodom and Gomorrah.[17] Usually such theorizing about the entire society was avoided, though even after the Revolution some Friends continued to prophesy the dawning of the apocalypse.

II

The agency that handled all disciplinary problems was the monthly meeting, a unit that could be composed of one or several particular meetings in a township. While both men and women's monthly meetings were responsible for overseeing, only the men's had the power of disownment or actual public testimony that the sinner was no longer a Friend. All persons were to help maintain the discipline, but in practice the ministers, elders, and overseers did most of the ferreting out of sin. The elders (who were responsible for watching over the ministers) were not officially recognized until the eighteenth century, but their supervisory functions had been exercised long before that. In 1686 Philadelphia Monthly Meeting appointed a committee of three men to speak to any persons "professing truth that walk not according to it." Newport had a similar group functioning by 1700.[18]

Much of the inspection could be performed by the visiting of families. In the first quarter of the eighteenth century Friends discovered that family visits by weighty members gave an opportunity for worship, exhortation, and censure. Both London and New England's discipline advocated the procedure as early as 1708, although Newport meeting had to warn in 1715 that any who slighted or "undervalued" the service of visitors "shall not be Deemed fit and proper members." The Philadelphia Yearly Meeting recommended in 1710 the practice of calling on families ("going backward in their Worldly Estate") and in 1723 required meetings to make visits to all members.[19] The advice was sometimes ignored. As late as 1760 Bucks Quarterly Meeting did not bother to answer Philadelphia Yearly Meeting queries on family visits. Perquimans Monthly Meeting in North Carolina had never engaged in visits before 1756 when the Quarterly Meeting recommended them. After having postponed action on the matter for nearly two years, the clerk of Perquimans wrote that "friends of this meeting not finding any to be free to Undertake" such service referred to the quarterly meeting for advice.[20] The matter was not mentioned again. In both England and America, answers to queries show that meetings often had difficulty finding persons willing to carry out the time-consuming process of calling on all families in the Society.

When a visit took place, a group of weighty Friends would come to the house. The family, including servants and apprentices, would sit with the visitors in silence. After a time a visitor would say a few words of counsel or exhortation. These might concern someone's gay clothing, the frivolity of children, or frequent absences from meeting. At times the person called on might experience a concern to speak to his guests, but some ministers and elders disapproved of this practice.[21] At the conclusion the family might serve refreshments, and a more informal atmosphere would then prevail. Even a normal social occasion could become a religious visit at any time if someone felt moved by the Spirit.

The visitors could speak upon any subject, but meetings exhorted them to stay away from strictly personal affairs. This advice was not always heeded. Two elderly unmarried female ministers visited Robert Dudley, also a minister, soon after he had married his third wife

> Whether they had observed any particular fondness between Robert, and his wife, I know not, but it seems, he was warned by one of them against too fondly indulging in conjugal delights, lest, (like Samson formerly) he should loose the means of his strength, whilst reposing on the lap of his Delilah. The other minister felt (or thought that she felt) a like concern for *both,* and my friend assured me, alluded to some things about which, they (as old maids) could not have been supposed to know any thing. ———And all this too in the presence of a youth, the son and step-son of the parties![22]

This old maids' visit illustrates not only that a minister could lack social graces, but it also shows the existence in late eighteenth-century England of prudishness about sexual matters. Although in the seventeenth century Friends had cautioned against reading immoral classics such as Ovid's *Art of Love,* they were not concerned that youth and unmarried women should remain innocent of all sexual knowledge. However, the exhortation to beware of uncontrolled passions was a staple of many Quaker tracts.

Most disciplinary matters never reached the stage of formal meeting involvement. Every Friend who saw another professor misbehaving was supposed to upbraid him. If the person improved, the matter was to be dropped. If he did not, the Quaker went to several other members and together they advised the man to reform. If their help was still ignored, the matter was presented to the monthly meeting and an official committee was appointed to labor with the wrongdoer. If there was any chance of getting a recantation, the committee met repeatedly with the offender over a period of several months. The degree of tolerance depended upon the nature of the offense, the likelihood of a retraction, and the state of the meeting. If the sin took place during a period of reform (such as occurred in Pennsylvania in the 1750s and in New England during the 1770s), less leniency would be allowed. At no time did meetings desire to expel people, though sometimes elders showed more zeal for the purity of truth than they did patience with offenders.[23] Since Friends everywhere disavowed the use of the state to enforce religious discipline, their only weapon was disownment. (When Friends abdicated their majority in the Pennsylvania assembly, the meeting used a half-way punishment whereby Quakers who remained in the legislature were barred from attending business meeting or performing any tasks for Friends. Anyone under discipline was unable to perform such activities.) However, no one was ever stopped from attending meeting for worship, and the excommunicated could still regard himself as a Quaker.[24]

If the evildoer repented, he had to make formal acknowledgment, either orally or, more often, in writing, before the monthly meeting. If the offense were very serious, perhaps involving premarital sex or marriage out of unity, the sinner stood while the clerk read the paper of self-condemnation at the close of meeting for worship.[25] In his paper of acknowledgment the miscreant admitted that the deed was wrong, that he had knowingly committed a sin, and that he was truly sorry for bringing dishonor on truth. Often the statements blamed the lapse upon sickness, weakness, or the crafty spirit of Satan. The meeting scrutinized these depositions carefully and often refused to accept one if a true spirit of repentance was not manifest.[26] The difficulty in recognizing true contrition can be seen in this statement written by a woman of Bradford Monthly Meeting in 1769:

> Notwithstanding I am represented to the aforesworn common liars, by the Supporter of a Delinquent, and that by an old Delinquent, whose doings are well known to many had they a mind to expose him—I mean T. B. in the Screening and Supporting his Son all his Wickedness. Was the said T. in his Duty he would long Since have admonished his Son, instead of Supporting him in his folly at the Expence of my character. It is true I made one Mistake and am sorry for it and from that Down I defy the world for anymore. But I am not alone in the crowd. T. has Daughters himself. I wish he may do Well but to undertake in the house of the Lord to say he could prove me a liar and foresworn. I think he greatly polluted the same that ought to be called the Lord's Sanctuary. Now I request of thee that in Justice to me you should Read this in publick, and that I not only can prove that J. B. Did Swear, but that the said T. did play Cards with W. T. . . . And if you Doubt the truth as set forth pray let there be Enquiry made of Justice C.

Evidently the woman had some grounds for her charges because eight months later T. B. was disowned for profanity and "unbecoming Actions."[27] Most self-condemnations were far more humble than E. M.'s, and even then the meetings cautiously warned that the paper was "accepted for Satisfaction as their future Conversation shall make Manifest." If the person lived a godly life, his sin was to be forgotten. Fox specifically warned, and later meetings repeated his counsel, that:

> And when any thing is once condemned and judged, let it not be raised upon again, but keep it in the grave. . . . they living in the life and light which doth condemn and judge it.[28]

There were examples of ministers and elders who experienced discipline and later resumed positions of authority in the meeting.

If the person would not agree that he was in the wrong, the meeting expelled him while maintaining that the person had ostracized himself by sin. The official action merely confirmed that he was living out of the spirit of truth. When an offender was disowned, the monthly meeting directed that three papers be drawn up. The first copy went into the meeting records; the second was posted or publicly read; the third was delivered to the person concerned, who was advised of a right of appeal. A few persons did appeal to quarterly or yearly meetings where a committee investigated the claims of the appellant and the monthly meeting. Though there were instances of higher meetings overruling the local or quarterly meeting, normally the sentence was confirmed.[29]

While the theory of discipline, as set forth by Robert Barclay and reiterated by Friends in the eighteenth century, claimed divine authority for every act, in practice meetings acted with great restraint. The divine sanction tended to be used as a rationale for all acts rather than as a defense of individual actions. The appeals system operated in a thoroughly secular manner. Well-attested evidence rather than a spiritual discerning of states enabled matters to be brought before meeting.[30] In theory, a meeting had the right to discipline in spirituals (matters of faith) and temporals. Actually, after the Keithan controversy, there was little direct supervision of what people thought. One of the few American Quakers to be disowned for heresy was botanist John Bartram, whom Darby Monthly Meeting expelled in 1758 for denying the divinity of Jesus. Generally, only the publication of a book denying Quaker principles brought discipline, but even then the content might be ignored and the offense would simply be publishing without approval of meeting.[31]

The following list gives an idea of the variety of offenses for which people could be disciplined: marriages without Friends' approval or by an Anglican or Presbyterian clergyman, sexual offenses, drunkenness, gossip or slander, military service or privateering, quarreling or fighting, bankruptcy, going to law against a fellow Quaker, dishonesty, profanity, swearing, playing cards, abusive behavior to wife or children, and attendance at plays or horse races.[32] Offenses of dress or speech were usually mentioned only in connection with more basic sins.[33] Minor infractions of this sort could be ferreted out by overseers without requiring official meeting involvement.

Queries that were to be answered by monthly and quarterly meetings and reported to the yearly meeting provided one means of ensuring uniformity in discipline. Although English Quakers had used this procedure since the 1680s, Americans did not make use of the policy until later. New England Yearly Meeting instituted queries in 1701, and by 1737 Perquimans Monthly Meeting in North Carolina was answering questions. In 1743 Philadelphia Yearly Meeting adopted a set of questions and, in 1755, specified that they were to be answered in writing. Because the queries demonstrate the primary concern of business meetings, a summary of the 1743 Philadelphia questions is presented here:

1. Are Friends careful to attend meetings at the time appointed and to refrain from sleeping or chewing tobacco in meetings?
2. Do Friends stay clear of excess in "drinking Drams"?
3. Do young Friends keep company for marriage with non-Friends or marry without parental consent?
4. Are Friends clear from tattling, talebearing, and meddling?
5. Do Friends stay free from music houses, dancing, and gambling?
6. Are Friends careful to "train up their Children in the Nurture and fear of the Lord, and to restrain them from vice and Evil Company, and keep them to plainness of Speech and Apparel"?
7. Are the poor taken care of, their children put to school, and then apprenticed out to Friends, and do Friends apprentice their children only to Friends?

8. Are Friends cautious not to launch into business beyond what they can do?
9. Are Friends careful not to remove without a certificate?
10. Are Friends on guard not to deprive the King of his duties?
11. Do Friends stay clear of the importing or buying of Negroes?
12. Are Friends prudent in settling their affairs and in leaving wills?[34]

These seemingly negative advices were the essence of the business of meetings, and, although the nature of these concerns was limited, the impression one receives from monthly meeting minute books is that rarely was anything else discussed. A violation of any of the Quaker testimonies was a matter for discipline (but a hypocrite could perform these outward signs with no difficulty). The positive tenets of Quaker doctrine were not mentioned.

The stringency with which discipline was enforced varied with locality and date. From the founding of Philadelphia Monthly Meeting in 1683 until 1691, there is only one clear act of disownment. Except for approving marriages (always the most time-consuming function of business meetings), about all the meeting did was arbitrate business disputes, give charity, and supervise the placement of orphans. There were no marriages out of unity and only one sexual offense.[35] Jack D. Marietta's study of monthly meeting minutes in Pennsylvania showed that, except during the Keithan controversy, there were few offenses and even fewer disownments prior to 1720. With the influx of non-Quaker immigrants in the eighteenth century, the establishment of other types of churches, and perhaps some secularization of the entire culture, disorders rose, however, and by the 1730s eight of the existing eleven monthly meetings had twice the 1715 rate of delinquency; by 1755 the number of offenses had again doubled. With the reform movement of 1755 the number of prosecutions increased 75 percent, and between 1755 and 1774 there were 1,800 disownments.[36]

The fluctuations in discipline give rise to some reservations about prevalent ideas concerning Quakers and the American environment. Before 1720 Pennsylvania was close to being a frontier, and, supposedly, a wilderness environment leads to a breakdown in morality. During the time that religious fervor among Quakers was strongest in Pennsylvania, Friends were either extraordinarily lax in discipline or very moral or both. The infrequency of marriages out of unity can be partially explained by the small percentage of outsiders in the area. But this does not help us understand why there were so few sexual cases or other offenses. Clearly, the variation in enforcement makes it very difficult to use minutes as a method of determining changing social mores in America. The Society's insistence, after 1755, on tightening the discipline should be viewed in light of a trend to enforce the beliefs of the meeting. Friends did not suddenly end the Holy Experiment in 1755. The agreement, which was worked out by English Friends to keep some Quaker political power in Pennsylvania, specified only that Friends would not have a majority in the assembly in wartime.[37] Religious renewal came not as a sudden reaction to a discovery of institutional decay and growing worldliness but as a result of a gradually increasing concern for the purity of truth. The impact of the beginnings of the Great War for Empire, including Braddock's defeat in 1755 and Indian raids on the frontier, caused Friends to reexamine their moral shortcomings and tighten their discipline.

Philadelphia Friends attempted to influence other yearly meetings to embark upon a program of reform. In 1760 American Friends persuaded London Yearly Meeting to begin an inspection of all quarterly and monthly meetings.[38] At the urging of visitors from Philadelphia Yearly Meeting, New England and North Carolina Yearly Meetings revised their disciplines.[39] Even so, other American meetings did not follow Pennsylvania's pattern of a steadily increasing concern with discipline. For example, Symons Creek in North Carolina disowned 12 of 23 disciplinary actions taken between 1710 and 1719; such numbers were not reached again until 1760–69. Core Sound Meeting showed only a slight increase in disciplinary cases between 1740 and 1789, and the number of disownments remained low. Between 1770 and 1789 this meeting disciplined 21, disowned 6, and admitted to membership 37 adults and 32 children. The most prominent meeting in New England was Rhode Island Monthly Meeting. Before 1700 this meeting was quite active in enforcing discipline; then in the eighteenth century the number of offenses and disownments tapered off, although an upsurge in prosecutions and disownments occurred in the 1770s.[40] Although the numbers involved by 1770 were larger, approximately the same percentage of members was involved as in the pre-1700 period. Arthur Worrall, who has calculated the number of offenses per meeting in New England, has proved that the revival of discipline spread throughout New England Yearly Meeting after 1770. He argues that the revival did not come earlier in New England because of the small impact of the Great War for Empire.[41]

In Pennsylvania after 1755, in England in the 1760s, and in New England in the 1770s, Friends became increasingly rigid and more inclined to disown than to reclaim erring brethren. Meetings enforced parts of the discipline, such as the testimony on plain speech, that had rarely been used previously.[42] There were no theological innovations, only increased unwillingness to allow deviation in behavior. While Friends were bypassed by the Great Awakening, they found in the movement for discipline the same release that the revival brought to the Puritans. Both phenomena were attempts to recapture the past, to duplicate the faith of the fathers. The Great Awakening brought emotional religion and the theology of Jonathan Edwards. The Quaker awakening brought the movement against slavery and heightened concern over the implications of pacifism. The reformers, who gave Quakers their finest hour, attempted at the same time to turn the clock back to the 1650s. Their ancestors had found the truth; as descendants they would enforce its testimonies. What had once been vital issues in Puritan England now became shibboleths to strain away the unregenerate. Friends required no test of religious experience before membership but insisted that if one wished to remain a Friend he must be obedient to Quaker law.

Since theoretically discipline was supposed to be exercised over every sin, the elders and ministers had the right to delve into any affair, but yearly meetings advised discretion. In 1725, in reversing a conviction by both a monthly and a quarterly meeting, London Yearly Meeting warned others to "take care how they Interfere in the properties of persons." In 1732, elders and traveling ministers were asked to be prudent in advising and "not as Busy Bodies nor Meddlers with family or Personal Affairs."[43] The most complete statement about when to desist was made by William Penn in 1692, in defending the establishment of women's meetings as convenient but unessential to faith or liberty.

> I do not mean, by the Liberty, that we are to resign to the Benefit of *Society* That which is Private or Personal; No, this does not enter into Private or Personal Liberty, concerning which, the Apostle taught us to bear, and not offend one another; as about Meats and Drinks: I may add Clothes, Houses, Trades, &c. so as there is no Excess, for that is every where Wrong: These Things regard not Society, but a man's Self, and his private Liberty alone.[44]

Penn's very liberal view did not always prevail, and even he had allowed a loophole in condemning "excess." If the meeting could define superfluity, it could also define what was normal. John Griffith, a strong disciplinarian, defined as "flesh faith" the restricting of control over the outward testimonies. "The flesh faith, there is little in dress; religion doth not consist in apparel; there is little in language; there is little in paying tithes &c."[45] Some topics were often the subject of exhortation but rarely of discipline. Parental control of children, conjugal relations, and politics did not reach the meeting unless there was a gross abuse. In almost all instances those activities with which the meeting was concerned were straightforward matters of conduct. Friends could supervise that over which they had previously exercised authority, and even in the greater strictness in discipline after 1755 the rules of conduct were already clearly defined; all the renewal meant was more rigid enforcement.

Most of the restraints upon what meeting could do came from the difficulties of putting theories into practice. The main limitation in discipline was that it was self-imposed. A wealthy Quaker living according to his rank had difficulty censuring a practice in others that he engaged in himself. Visiting ministers could demand strictness, but elders and overseers were working with relatives and acquaintances.

> Oh! what mean cringing, stooping, and temporizing, is to be found in some! It is my son, daughter, near relation, or friend, that I am loth to offend.

If a son or a wife were disowned, the parents or the husband might withdraw from meeting. David Hall, writing in 1747, pled with those who had been chastised "that you don't entertain any Hardness or Resentment against" any Friend for engaging in church discipline.[46] A lover of peace might be inclined to forego checking minor offenses merely because he did not wish to become involved. Yet if some Quakers were too easy, others were overly censorious. In spite of the oft-repeated admonition that all discipline was to be done in a spirit of love, charity, and meekness (perhaps best exemplified by John Woolman's exercises on slavery),[47] certain Friends were unduly harsh. Job Scott, after visiting in New England in the 1790s, warned against "a want of charity in some few, very strict in outward plainness, who, from a misguided zeal, held others too much at distance on account of their not appearing equally plain." He grieved at the deviation from simplicity but suffered more at the "contracted, illiberal, and harsh spirit." No matter what the outward appearance, when charity was lost, religion became formality.[48]

In spite of the hierarchy of meetings, the yearly meeting's only power of enforcement was exhortation. The disciplines were filled with Christian and Brotherly Advices, not laws. Queries generally cannot be used as a source to describe what happened in meeting because the answers in both England and America rapidly became a stereotype of what had been said before.[49] Since any expulsion required the consent of the entire business meeting, a few individuals could stop the procedure. Both contemporaries and historians have commented on the oligarchy that could control the Quaker organization;[50] if certain leading Friends opposed an action, nothing could be done. High position in the community or the meeting may have enabled some to escape unscathed. James Jenkins noted that elders were always the most difficult to discipline, and Ann Whitall bemoaned the death of Jonah Tomson because no one else then alive dared to speak to a certain young man and woman of their misdoings.[51] But prominence did not always confer immunity. James Logan, David Lloyd, and William Shippen—three of the most famous early Philadelphia Quakers—were all forced to make acknowledgments of misdemeanors before meeting. Wealth or position might enable a few lapses to escape notice, but a glaring sin was disciplined regardless of the position of the offender. Friends had to cultivate an indifference toward the world and a deference before the meeting.

In almost every attack against the Society, in both the seventeenth and the eighteenth centuries, opponents mentioned the tyranny of meeting. Certainly Quakers exercised great power in the lives of members, but both Puritan and Anglican procedures were just as authoritative. Quakers defended their discipline by saying that no one was forced to become a member or remain one. Thomas Clarkson thought that the reason for obeying stemmed from the belief that the whole meeting had agreed upon the discipline and thought that their measures were "influenced by the dictates of . . . the Spirit of Truth."[52] The principle that required that all actions be taken by the sense of the meeting added extra power, for there could be no aggrieved minority. More mundane reasons might also have applied. The Society had a system of poor relief, schools, care for orphans, and assistance for the aged. Disownment would cut a member off from all privileges within the Society. Since Friends tended to trade with one another, the economic facts of life added another incentive to conform—particularly since Quaker masters might dismiss a wayward employee. A practicing politician in Pennsylvania would have many advantages in his search for power if he remained a Quaker. The pressure from family and social acquaintances would bear weight. When divine revelation, business and political interest, social contacts, and past custom coalesced, a person's acquiescence under the control of meeting was understandable.

The Quakers' rationale for discipline managed to remain both libertarian and authoritarian. Led by the Spirit of God, the believer arrived at truth, and yet his final position had been discovered previously by the members of the church. An individual's conscience would agree with the testimony of the group or the person sinned against what God had told him. Eighteenth-century Quakerism solved this ambiguity by ignoring it. In practice the meetings continued to exercise power over those parts of life which had come under the purview of early Friends. While, in theory, all thoughts and actions were subjected to scrutiny, the meetings' main efforts went into maintaining the Quaker testimonies about marriage, business, the plain style of speech and dress, and peace.

By the middle of the eighteenth century, as the percentage of Friends in the American population diminished, and as both religious and secular challenges to the faith increased, Quakers became more conservative and rigid. They tightened discipline at a time when disownment resulted in less social cost. Who, in 1760, would discriminate against a man disowned only because he had married a Baptist? By refusing to compromise and by trying to maintain all previous religious testimonies unchanged, the denomination turned its back upon the Enlightenment and the emerging American pattern of evangelical religion. The price of sectarian purity would be a smaller membership and decreasing influence in the contemporary world.

Notes

1 William Braithwaite, *The Second Period of Quakerism,* 2d ed. prepared by Henry J. Cadbury (Cambridge, 1961), pp. 228–36, 290–323.
2 *The Anarchy of the Ranters* was issued in England in 1676, 1692, 1717–18, 1733, and 1771 and in America in 1757, 1770, 1783, and 1831; Sydney V. James, *A People Among Peoples* (Cambridge, Mass., 1963), p. 174.
3 George Fox, *Journal* (New York, 1963), p. 385.
4 Robert Barclay, *The Anarchy of the Ranters and other Libertines, the Hierarchy of the Libertines, the Hierarchy of the Romanists and other Pretended Churches, equalled Refused and Refuted,* . . . in *Works* (Philadelphia, 1831), 1:487.
5 Ibid., pp. 475, 493–94.
6 Ibid., p. 494.
7 Ibid., pp. 501–04.
8 Ibid., pp. 515, 520, 524, 527, 530.
9 Ibid., p. 473; William Penn, *Works* (London, 1726), 2:775–76. If Barclay risked making all proceedings of the meeting holy, Penn seems at times to have made everything a matter of "order."
10 George Fox, *Works* (Philadelphia, 1831) 7:167; Min. London YM, 1:19 and 2:33; Min. Philadelphia YM, 1:241, 355, 366 and 2:12, 37, 39–44, 48, 54, 64, 75–76, 141–42.
11 Barclay, *Works,* 1:521, 535–36.
12 Fox, *Journal,* p. 185; Griffith, *Journal,* pp. 189–90; David Ferris to Benjamin Ferris, June 1768, Ferris Mss, FHL.
13 Barclay, *Works,* 3:574–79; Robert Barclay *Apology,* prop. 2, pp. xiii, 25.
14 Barclay, *Apology,* prop. 2, pg. 3–4, 26.
15 Fox, *Works,* 7:29, 328; John Smith to E. B., ca. 1739, "A Collection of Sundry Writings on Divers Occasions," Smith Mss, LC.
16 Min. Philadelphia YM, 9/22–28/1759, 2:149–51; Min. Philadelphia MM, 6 (8/28/1761): 390–92; David Cooper, *Diary,* p. 49. When relative peace came in 1761, Friends used a reverse jeremiad. God had shown his favor to Pennsylvania by ending the war, and so the governor was petitioned to reform the sins of Philadelphia as a thanksgiving.
17 Penn. *Works,* 1:224.
18 Min. Philadelphia MM, 1: (12/3/1682): 2 and (7/24/1686): 39, and (7/19/1694): 47. As early as 1682 Philadelphia appointed overseers who performed activities associated with supervision of membership as well as business concerns.
19 New England YM, Discipline 1708–38, pp. 12–13; Min. Rhode Island MM, 1: (11/27/1707): 214 and 2 (11/31/1715): 125; London YM, Christian and Brotherly Advices (1708), 117; Min. Philadelphia YM, 1 (7/20/1710): 283, and (7/14–18/1717): 184.
20 Min. Philadelphia YM, 2 (9/2–10/1760): 138; Min. Perquimans MM, 2 (8/4/1756-5/3/1758).
21 Barnaby Nixon, *Extracts from Manuscript Writings* (Richmond, Va., 1814), pp. 30, 35–36; Thomas Clarkson, *Portraiture of Quakerism,* (London, 1807) 2: 266; James Jenkins, "Records and Recollections," (Typed transcript, F H) 1:258–59.
22 New England YM, The Book of Discipline (1731), 87; Jenkins, "Records and Recollections," 1:260–61. This incident occurred in 1787.
23 Min. Philadelphia MM, 2 (10/26/1712): 150–51; Philadelphia YM, Discipline, 1704–1717; Min. Cedar Creek MM, 4/12/1755, 86. When T. S. was disowned for marriage out of unity, the period was only "until it may Please God out of his infinite goodness to bring him a Sense of his out goings."
24 Philadelphia YM, Discipline 1719, pp. 29–30; John Reynell to Joshua William 9/17/1767, Letter Book 1767–69, p. 23, HSP; Mary Leadbeater, *Annals of Ballitore* (London, 1862), 1: 175–76.
25 Min. Philadelphia MM, 3 (9/26/1742): 348; Min. Rhode Island MM, 1: (11/1/1705): 174; 2 (5/25/1732): 298–99.
26 Min. Philadelphia MM, 2 (10-12

mo./1706): 20, 24, 25–27; Min. Rhode Island MM, 2 (10/31/1728): 264; 3 (7/30/1771): 353; Philadelphia YM, Discipline 1719, pp. 26–27; London YM, *Epistles from the Yearly Meeting of the People Called Quakers* (London, 1760), p. 109.

27 Bradford MM, Certificates of Removals, Reports, Acknowledgments, 1760–69, 5/8/1769, p. 252, and 2/15/1769, p. 264, DR. The policy of the Quaker libraries at Swarthmore, Haverford, and at the Department of Records, Arch Street, Philadelphia, is to require the historian not to divulge the names of individual Friends who were disciplined by the meetings. In England, New England, and North Carolina, Friends who seem less concerned about hiding blemishes of their ancestors do not impose such restrictions.

28 Min. Rhode Island MM, 2 (10/31/1728): 264; Fox, *Works,* 7: 221–22.

29 Penn, *Works,* 1: 54; Min. Philadelphia YM, 2 (9/20-26/1755): 67–70, 76; Robert Sutcliff, *Travels in Some Parts of North America in the Years 1804, 1805, 1806* (York, England, 1815), p. 251.

30 John Griffith, *Some Brief Remarks,* pp. 86–87. L. C. was accused by R. H. of being the father of her child. He denied it; she persisted in the charge, even at a face-to-face confrontation. The committee reported that "there is some grounds to fear he is guilty of the charge." When L. C. continued to assert his innocence, the case was dropped. Min. Rhode Island MM, 3: 34. Philadelphia Monthly Meeting disowned a woman, whose husband had been long absent, for committing adultery. While admitting they had no "positive Proofs, . . . the strong probability is so persuasive in the Minds of all Observers, that such cannot by their Craft or thin Covers pervert the general Scandal and Odium which falls on them, and which is by many People thrown at the Community." Min. Philadelphia MM, 9/28/1729.

31 *BFHA* 31 (1942): 42; John Moon, *A Second Address to the People Called Quakers* (Stokesley, England, 1815),: pp. 9–10 Jenkins, "Records and Recollections," 1: 225-26.

32 Min. Philadelphia MM, 1 (10/29/1699): 171; 2 (5/29/1709-1/31/1710): 73, 76, 85, 87, and 2 (2/27/1711–12/29/1711/12): 110, 113, 116, 131; 3 (10/25/1747): 45–46; 6 (12/26/1760-3/12/1761): 305, 323; Min. Cedar Creek MM, 10/31/1759, pp. 130–131; 7/11/1767, p. 247; Min. Rhode Island MM, 2 (11/25/1714): 111, and 3 (7/30/1765): 264, 266, 270; Extracts of Min., Buckingham MM, 12/13/1758–10/2/1759; Min. Falls MM, 10/4/1689, p. 40; Bradford MM, Certificates of Removal, 5/8/1769, p. 252; Min. Goshen MM, 8/4/1723, in I. Sharpless, *Two Hundred Fifty Years of Quakerism at Birmingham, 1690–1940,* (West Chester, Pa., 1940) p. 56.

33 Philadelphia disowned W. P. for bankruptcy, leaving his family, neglect in attending meetings, and deportment showing "A Slight and Contempt to the Simplicity and plainness of the Truth." Newport expelled a man for horse-racing, gaming and "Running into superfluity of apparel." Min. Philadelphia MM, 3 (2/30/1742): 339; Min. Rhode Island MM, 2 (1/29/1720): 174.

34 Min. New England YM, 4/13/1701, p. 37; Min. Perquimans MM, 3/4/1737; Min. Philadelphia YM, 1 (7/17–21/1743): 434; 2 (9/20-26/1755): 73. Philadelphia YM, Christian and Brotherly Advices, 121–122, 160. The meeting did investigate the beliefs of ministers and elders. Their query number two read, "Are Ministers sound in Word and Doctrine, careful to minister in the Ability God only gives, and thereby kept from burdening the living?"

35 Min. Philadelphia MM, vols. 1–8, 1682–1777.

36 Jack D. Marietta, "Ecclesiastical Discipline in the Society of Friends 1682–1776" (Ph. D. diss. Stanford University, 1968), pp. 136–143, 148, 156. Marietta is continuing work on a computerized study of the changing patterns of Quaker disciplinary practices. Final conclusions as to the age, economic position, sex, and marital status of those who were disowned as well as statistics on the numbers of members must await publication of this research.

37 James Pemberton to John Fothergill, 11/27/1756, PP, 11: 20–22, 10: 137, and 11: 55, 61. In spite of a great deal of attention given to the reform movement of 1755, historians have not been able to agree on the causes or consequences of the movement. Three recent interpretations are Jack Marietta, "Ecclesiastical Discipline in the Society of Friends," pp. 150, 164; David Kobrin, "Saving Remnant: Intellectual Sources of Change and Decline in Colonial Quakerism, 1690–1810" (Ph. D diss., University of Pennsylvania, 1968), pp. 253–70; Richard Bauman, *For the Reputation of Truth* (Baltimore, 1971), pp. 1–64.

38 Min. London YM, 12 (5/28/1760): 91 and (5/16/1761): 220. Griffith, *Journal,* p. 294. The tightening of discipline in England, as in America, did not suddenly spring up. For example, in 1755 London added eight new queries that were to be answered by monthly meetings. *JFHS* 49 (1961): 214-15.

39 Min. North Carolina YM, 10/10-

12/1755, pp. 136–37; Min. Rhode Island MM, 7/29/1755, pp. 136–37; Min. New England YM of Ministers and Elders, 6mo./1755. Monthly meetings at Swanzey, South Kingstown, and Sandwich owned disciplines copied from London's discipline dated between 1756 and 1763.

40 Min. Core Sound MM, 1733–91; Min. Symons Creek MM, 1699–1785, Guilford College; Min. Rhode Island MM, 1676–1773.

41 Arthur Worrall, "New England Quakerism, 1656–1830" (Ph.D. diss., Indiana University, 1969), pp. 58–59, 212–13, 140–41.

42 Jack Marietta, "Ecclesiastical Discipline in the Society of Friends," pp. 71, 148–51.

43 Min. London YM, 6 (3/20/1725): 303, and (4/11/1732): 272.

44 Penn, *Works,* 2: 776.

45 Griffith, *Journal,* pp. 125, 172.

46 Ibid., p. 96; David Hall, *A Compassionate Call, and Hand reached forth in tender Gospel Love* (London, 1758), pp. 52–53; Min. Core Sound MM, 8/17/1763, pp. 60–61.

47 John Woolman, *Journal and Essays* (New York, 1922), 161–62; David Hall, *Memoirs* (London, 1758), p. 217; Philadelphia YM, Christian and Brotherly Advices, 160–61.

48 Scott, *Journal,* p. 91.

49 Min. London YM, 1 (3/27/1675): 18, and 9 (3/26/1743): 160–61; Min. Cedar Creek MM, pp. 207, 214, 232, 272. Cedar Creek in 1764 answered the queries as follows. "Meetings are kept up but not so well attended as could be desired; the plain language, drinking to Excess, Payment of Priests' wages, making wills, and the Education of Negroes are Complained of in Some . . . and Care hath been taken to Endeavour to Remove the above Complaints." Almost identical words were used long before and after 1764.

50 Jenkins, Recollections and Records, 1: 52, 157–58, 176½; Myers, *Hannah Logan's Courtship* (Philadelphia, 1904), 4/9/1748, pp. 197–98; Griffith, *Journal,* pp. 111–12; Theodore Thayer, *Israel Pemberton,* p. 33; Sydney James, *A People Among Peoples,* (Cambridge, Mass. 1963), p. 16.

51 Jenkins, "Records and Recollections," 1: 52, 160–65; Ann Whitall, "Diary," 10/24/1760, p. 52, QC.

52 Penn, *Works,* 1: 877–78; Griffith, *Some Brief Remarks,* p. 77; Clarkson, *Portraiture of Quakerism,* 1: 249.

4 Childhood: As the Twig Is Bent

Vere Lord was here. She did believe it never was harder to bring up Children to be good in any age of the world than it is now.

Ann Whitall, "Diary," 5/7/1760

When John Woolman was born on October 19, 1720, he became the responsibility of two groups, his parents and Burlington Monthly Meeting. His parents had the primary obligations of feeding, clothing, educating, and disciplining John. The authority of the parents was God given: "Honour your father and your mother, that your days may be long." The members of Burlington Monthly Meeting to which the Woolmans belonged thought of themselves as a second family, the people of God exercising a sacred responsibility to assist in the rearing of the child.

The Christian church had often referred to itself as one body in Christ bound by love, and since apostolic times it had encouraged the use of such family terminology as "brethren" and "sisters" to show the essential unity among members. In the religious Reformation of the sixteenth and seventeenth centuries, many sects claimed to restore the primitive church in all its purity, and their ideal of the early congregation included close fellowship among the elect. The use of family or kin terms for the church can be seen in the "Church of the Brethren," "The Family of Love," the "Moravian Brethren," and in the early Quaker name, "Children of Light." The metaphor was not unique among Friends, but its importance in Quaker life should not be slighted, for the family symbolized not only the bonds of unity and love among members but also the subordination of the individual to the group.

Fox called the meetings the "household of faith" and the "Family of God." Philadelphia Yearly Meeting addressed an epistle to London Yearly Meeting "to all God's flock and family." When Maryland and Philadelphia Yearly Meetings decided to send representatives to each other's gatherings, the visitors were welcomed "as Brethren of one Family." A women's meeting in Rhode Island addressed Friends as "near Relations."[1]

The Quakers justified poor relief not only by the scriptural precedent of almsgiving but because the needy were seen "as children of one father." Fox, defending the foundation of women's meetings, exhorted the ladies to be "mothers" of the church and to see that "nothing be lacking . . . and so to do good unto all, but especially to the household of faith." All legal disputes were to be settled within the meeting because the family should show love between members and not open differences to the outside world. Barclay noted that Friends became, through the spirit of God, "as one family and household in certain respects, [so] do each of them watch over, teach, and instruct, and care for one another."[2] The ties between Friends in Barbados, England, and America were maintained partially because all thought of themselves as members of a spiritual brotherhood. The extent of bonds among Quakers led, of course, to a certain degree of exclusiveness toward outsiders.

Within a few days of his birth, John Woolman was enrolled as a member of the meeting. In England the ceremony was more legal than religious, since, in the absence of baptism, the state required some test of legitimacy. The laws of Pennsylvania demanded registers of the inhabitants; the meetings formulated lists of births, marriages, and deaths, and all religious bodies were eventually required to keep such records. Because unnecessary frivolity was forbidden, the Friends were supposed to make no special preparations and have no feast at the naming of the child. Witnesses of the birth, weighty Friends, and the immediate family gathered. After a time of silence the father pronounced the name, which might be chosen for its religious connotations or because it was a family name, the witnesses signed a certificate of birth, and "John Woolman. Son of the said Samuel Woolman & Elizabeth his Wife . . . was born the 19th. 8 mo. 1720" was entered on the register of births and deaths.[3]

In his early years the meeting would serve John chiefly as an insurance policy. If the immediate family became financially insolvent, the meeting might make loans, give money, seeds, tools, or perhaps a cow to the Woolmans so that the family might survive. If there were too many brothers and sisters for the parents to support, the meeting could take the responsibility of placing some of the children in other good Quaker homes. If Friend Woolman died and John's mother wished to remarry, the meeting would demand that the boy's inheritance be preserved and that he be well taken care of. If both parents died, the meeting would serve as an emergency set of parents. John would be put out to Friends and later be apprenticed, with his master guaranteeing clothing, education, and training in a profession. The meeting would pay the apprenticeship fee, if necessary, and supervise the indenture so that no undue obligation would be placed upon the orphan.

II

The religious status of the infant in Quakerism was far different from that of the child of Catholic, Lutheran, or Calvinist parents. Before the Reformation, a mother and father took their baby to the church for baptism as soon as possible; the sacrament would save him from perdition by covering the taint of original sin. Lutherans, Anglicans, and Roman Catholics continued this practice. The status of a little child was more of a problem in the Reformed churches, for the harshness of the doctrine of predestination was apparent in teachings about children. All children were believed to be flawed by original sin and, in their natural condition, damned. If the infant were predestined to election, Christ would save him; but if he were not, infancy was no guarantee of salvation. The best that one could hope for a damned child in Michael Wigglesworth's *Day of Doom* was that he would be placed in "the easiest room in Hell." With the exception of the General Baptists, in no part of Christendom before 1650 was a baby thought of as being innocent at birth, for Adam's sin was considered to have been transmitted to all mankind.[4] Since Augustine's time most western European Christians had believed that sin was given to a child through the lust in the act of conception.

Since the Quakers had no sacraments, they could have no doctrine of infant baptism to provide protection for the child. True baptism occurred when one was an adult and capable of seeing the movings of the inward light in one's heart. Quakers approved the end result of Catholic or Anglican baptism because babies were secured, but they believed that the means was invalid. The Roman Catholics invented sacramentalism in order to increase mystery and thereby heighten clerical power. The Calvinistic predestination of infants was "absurd," "cruel," and contrary to God's mercy and justice. The Puritan doctrine of the imputation of grace through the loins of the parents was also belittled by Friends, who pointed to many biblical precedents where holy parents begot unholy sons. Neither sin nor grace was conveyed by heredity. George Keith questioned whether even the Puritans knew what sort of holiness was established in children by a covenant or federal relationship.[5]

Early Quakers were far more interested in denying the consequences of others' doctrines than in formulating the status of their own infants. George Fox argued that the sinlessness of a Quaker child stemmed from the innocence of the parents. If at marriage the parents either had attained or were working toward perfection, sex for them contained no taint and their children would be innocent. The corollary, not clearly expressed in Fox's pamphlet on the subject, was that non-Quaker children would not be innocent. William Smith in 1663 mentioned a "Root of sin" within children which was present because they were "conceived in Sin."[6] But the tendency or seed or root of sin did not germinate until the child actually sinned. Robert Barclay put the doctrine into a syllogism:

> Sin is imputed to none, where is no Law.
> But, to Infants there is no Law:
> Therefore sin is not imputed to them.

Infants (like idiots) suffered the disadvantage of being unable to learn about or know the law. Until a person could distinguish right from wrong, his acts were not classified as sin. Barclay did not deny that Adam had imputed a "seed of sin" to all men, but he insisted that a tendency toward something did not establish guilt. Although the act of conception might be sinful, the fault was the parents'. Just how children were saved or whether Christ's atonement was responsible were not discussed in the *Apology*. George Keith at least saw the problem, although he confessed his inability to solve it.

> And as for the general state of infants, and how they are particularly disposed of immediately after Death, who dye in Infancy, seemeth a great mystery, and is best known unto the Lord.

Neither Barclay nor Keith asserted absolutely that children were innocent; yet both seemed to back into that position. They preferred to have all children declared faultless and saved rather than to assert that any were damned solely for Adam's sin.[7]

In 1714 the American John Hepburn stated the doctrine in far more positive terms. "There is no fear . . . that Christ will cast away such holy, harmless, righteous, and innocent Creatures, as little Children are." Infants have so little time and so small a part of this world that "we need not doubt of their salvation." Children were directly under God's "Tuition and Government." He set the bounds to their acts and made certain they could never sin.[8] Eighteenth-century Friends did not hesitate to affirm that children were created innocent and remained so throughout infancy.

If the child were born saintly and by adulthood became depraved, then the logical question was at what age did the child fall. The writings of Friends provided no uniform answer. The infant had to have reached the age of reason to have learned the difference between right and wrong—and to have chosen deliberately to do wrong. Hannah Pemberton saw the "first dawnings of Reason" when her baby began to notice his surroundings and what people said to him. Isaac Norris II described 7-year-old Mary's writings as the "forerunners of Reason." John Woolman saw schoolchildren as "Innocent," but Anthony Benezet began his *First Book for Children* with, "Man was at first made in a state of bliss; but by sin he fell from that good state into a state of woe and misery."[9] The primer made clear that the schoolchildren who used the book were encompassed in Adam's fall. Since Quaker children usually began school at anywhere from age 4 to age 8, a child became aware that he was a sinner sometime within this period. George Keith and William Smith paraphrased the Book of Jonah, 4:11, and declared that when a child learned his right hand from his left he had reached the age of responsibility.[10]

One index to growing up might be the time at which little boys stopped wearing petticoats and started wearing coats and breeches. The pictures of children in Alice Morse Earle's *Child Life in Colonial Days* show that boys and girls dressed identically until age 5 or 6. John Penn, son of William Penn, was wearing breeches at age 4; Elizabeth Drinker's two boys put them on at age 5; William Dillwyn's son Lewis at age 6.[11]

When a child died, the parents sometimes extended sinlessness to a much more advanced age. The 7-year-old daughter of James Pemberton died in 1765, and the father wrote that she was "taken away at an age of undoubted innocence." Isaac Norris I declared at the death of his 12-year-old daughter: "But she was taken off sweetly and in a state of innocence." Hannah Hill was called innocent at age 11.[12] The earliest narratives in the *Piety Promoted* type of literature began with ages 7 or 8; the child supposedly could sin by that time and experience God inwardly. One corollary to the doctrine of childhood innocence was that the growth of reason and the development of the first seeds of grace were liabilities. The child could not sin before he was capable of distinguishing what he was doing. Growing into reason or experiencing the inward light might extinguish whatever means God had used to preserve the infant.

The relationship of the child to the church constituted a problem for Puritans and Quakers; both groups believed in a congregation composed only of saints. From the time of his baptism the Puritan child was under the care of the church, but he was not considered a full member until he was old enough to make a declaration of faith and receive communion. The New Englanders believed that children of the elect would be more likely than others to become visible saints. The seriousness with which the Puritans approached church membership and the failure to convert the children of members resulted, in

1662, in the adoption of a half-way covenant which gave to adult children of full members many of the privileges of belonging to the church, including that of having their children baptized. The decision for a half-way membership was taken only after a vigorous debate among the Congregationalists. By 1700, Puritan ministers concentrated almost exclusively on preaching to members and children of members. Edmund S. Morgan has argued that Puritanism turned into tribalism when the church forgot about converting the society and concentrated its efforts upon the offspring of the saints.[13]

Early Friends belittled the Presbyterians and the Anglicans for failing to restrict church membership to the holy. Robert Barclay declared in the *Apology,* "When men became Christians by BIRTH and not by conversion, Christianity came to be lost." Education and attendance at worship did not equal the experience of the inward light. Early Quakers insisted that the church was a gathering of saints, and only those who experienced grace were members. A few years after the publication of the *Apology,* and with no debate upon the subject, Friends in both England and America operated upon the assumption that the test for membership was simply to be a child of a member.[14] Friends became even more tribalistic than Puritans, for the Quaker child who grew into an adult member was not required to make a declaration as to what he believed or whether he had experienced the light. Membership became a privilege of birth.

Since the Quakers had no theological precept to justify such a practice, how had "birthright membership" come about? From earliest years, meetings issued certificates when a family moved. These were given to the new monthly meeting, thus providing Friends with a conception of belonging to a church. The meetings' registers of births and deaths served as legal tests of birth. One could recognize a Friend by his behavior, and no further criterion was necessary. Since there was frequent persecution in Restoration England, a man who adopted the Quaker customs of speech and dress and attended meetings with regularity needed courage.

In early Pennsylvania, the situation was much different. William Penn was proprietor; Quakers controlled the government, owned much land, and constituted a large majority of the population. Since most people used Quaker forms of speech and dress, the peculiar customs did not distinguish a man from his neighbors. A child of a Quaker might keep the religious testimonies from habit and not have experienced conversion. The Society of Friends never faced up to this danger. George Keith was the first to recognize what could happen. When Keith and a group of his followers founded their separate meeting around 1691, they drew up a discipline for use in regulating the church. Keith declared that "outward practices" did not constitute a Christian and that such signs should not be "esteemed by Friends as any full test or Touchstone of Trial or mark of distinction." The schismatic Quakers required the children of members to declare in their own words "their real convincement of the Truth and most common and generally received principles of Christian doctrine by Friends."[15] What Keith condemned in 1691 was a form of birthright membership.

One can find in the writings of orthodox English Quakers sufficient references to establish that birthright membership was practiced in England before 1700. John Banks, in 1692, exhorted Friends to go beyond acceptance of the intellectual truth of Quaker principles and to become truly converted. John Hands, in 1705, addressed a warning to the "Children of Believing Parents, and those that are Friends by Education, but not by Conversion." In certificates of removal or disownment in the early eighteenth century, people regarded as members were often defined as having their "birth and education" among Friends.[15]

London Yearly Meeting in 1737, Philadelphia Yearly Meeting in 1762, North Carolina in 1782, and New England in 1790 gave indirect formal recognition to birthright membership. These decisions, which defined membership, were designed to regulate which monthly meeting was responsible for giving charity. A Friend was declared a member of the meeting in which he was born or within whose boundaries he resided.[17] The theological implications of birthright membership were discussed by no Quaker until John Moon published two pamphlets in England in 1809 and 1815 opposing the practice. Moon claimed that Friends refused even to discuss the problem. The meeting disowned Moon because his pamphlets had not been submitted for approval before publication. The comments on birthright membership by individual Quakers and the offhand references to it in epistles and disciplines in England and America prove that Quakers were well aware of the practice.[18] The fact that they refused to discuss the relationship of the child to the meeting throughout the colonial period shows a fear of facing the issue. Friends became more concerned with their children than with theological consistency. The need to insure that their children became Quakers took precedence over the desire to make sure that all Quakers were Christians.

III

Historians have often commented on the rigors of infancy in colonial days. When the Quaker child was spanked at birth, he really had something to cry about because his early years would be harsh. If sickness did not kill him, the remedies of the doctors might. The frequency of disease and the fears of the parents were described vividly by Thomas Chalkley

> And consider the first month after thou wert born, oh the care and tender concern, the watching, labour, and charge, cannot easily be expressed! what running to the physician upon every symptom or suspicion of being ill, or out of order.[19]

Chalkley knew from personal experience what he was talking about, for he buried 11 children before they had lived ten years.

Using the birth, death, and marriage records of nine monthly meetings compiled by Robert Wade Hinshaw in *Encyclopedia of Quaker Genealogy,* Robert V. Wells has studied the demographic data on 276 families from the middle colonies who lived in the eighteenth and early nineteenth centuries.[20] The only families examined were those having full information as to dates of birth for husband and wife, date of marriage, number of children, and time when the first spouse died. One meeting's records were checked for accuracy against other available sources. Since the data are based upon meeting records, the figures are a reliable index only to those Friends who were not disowned and who had some interest in keeping their family records up-to-date. The conclusions should not be applied to the general population or to all Quakers. For example, of the 1,542 births documented in Wells' study, only 15 resulted from conception prior to marriage. Such data are unrepresentative, however, because those Friends whose children appeared before the parents had been married nine months were almost always disowned and thus disappeared from the records.

Based upon a sample of 271 couples, the average family size was 5.69 children. Forty percent of the families had 0 to 4, 45 percent from 5 to 9, and 15 percent from 10 to 14. The average number of children for completed families was 6.04 and for uncompleted 4.93. The average interval between marriage and first birth was 13.61 months, and between first and second birth 21.38 months; and the period lengthened for each succeeding birth. In the normal Quaker household a child would grow up surrounded by brothers or sisters who would share in the family chores and later divide any inheritance. Wells discovered significant changes in family size by dividing his sample into three groups: "prerevolutionary" women born prior to 1730 whose fertility was ended by 1775, "revolutionary" women born during 1731–55 whose fertility was over by 1800, and "postrevolutionary" women born during 1756–85 whose fertility was ended by 1830. For the prevolutionary group the average number of children was 6.68, for the revolutionary 5.67, for the postrevolutionary 5.02. A comparison of families completed by 1775 with those completed by 1830 shows a decline of 1.66 children per family. In the postrevolutionary period, the fertility rate declined for women of all ages. It seems clear that Quakers had begun to practice some kind of family limitation involving birth control. Such planning did not occur in the generation before 1730, and the evidence for the 1755 generation is mixed. The average number of children per family for Americans in 1800 was 7 and the national average did not fall to the Quaker rate of 5.3 until after 1850.

The questions of how and why Quakers began to practice birth control cannot be answered with any certainty. Birth control devices such as *coitus interruptus,* various types of contraceptives, and breastfeeding had long been known in Europe. There is no evidence that any of these techniques suddenly gained in popularity, or that women suddenly began to nurse their babies longer. The social or cultural factors which led to the change are also difficult to assess and could involve the high price of land or the social turmoil during the Revolution, in which Friends lost their influence in government and were regarded suspiciously by both belligerents. This chapter's thesis is that a cult of childhood developed about the time of the Revolution in which, for the first time, infants were recognized as having distinct personalities. Perhaps mothers limited their families so that they might have more time to spend with each child. There are also definite signs of Quaker prudery by the Revolution. Prudery may have extended within the marriage and resulted in a decline in the amount of intercourse between husbands and wives. Such questions will not be answered until we learn when other groups in America—defined by social status, religion, or nationality—began to practice birth control.

Records of the time of death were the most likely to be neglected by the meeting, because, unlike birth and marriage entries, the death dates served no legal function. English Friends had a ceremony called "Nomination" in which a baby's name was entered on a register. The stillborn infants and those who died shortly after birth might not be listed. On the basis of such incomplete evidence, Robert Wells' educated estimate was that 210 of each 1,000 children died before age 1 and 350 of each 1,000 died before age 5. Jacob Taylor, a Friend who published many works for Philadelphia Yearly Meeting, included in his 1745 almanac Sir William Petty's estimate that in England, Scotland, France, and Ireland only 40 of 100 children would be alive at age 16 and only 25 of 100 would be alive at 26.[21] While a demographer might blanch at Petty's impressionistic statistics, the Quaker's awareness of the frequency of death makes understandable parental anxieties before the child's birth and during his infancy.

Most births were attended by midwives, whose limited knowledge of medicine may have been an asset. While doctors could use forceps, their feeble understanding of the process of childbirth is illustrated by William Shippen, Jr.'s bleeding mothers just before labor in the belief that women who had not menstruated for nine months had a surplus of bad blood. Elizabeth Drinker believed that women who lived past childbearing age "experience more comfort and satisfaction than at any other period of their lives." She comforted her 39-year-old daughter Sally, who was in labor, by assuring her that if she could nurse for two years she might not be able to have more children.[22] Phineas Pemberton, Isaac Norris II, John Smith, and William Dillwyn's wives died in childbirth. One wonders how many such women, who died while still young, were debilitated from bearing and caring for children.

With the child mortality rate so high, parents tried to prepare themselves for these deaths. When James Logan's 13-month-old son died in 1727, he mourned to his brother, "The Loss of a Child so young . . . is very little thought of by others," but he added that he and his wife felt great distress. A Friend wrote Israel Pemberton, Jr., that Polly Waring's 3-week-old daughter died, "but such things will be, and there may be more [children born] some time."[23]

When trying to convince grown children not to neglect their parents, Thomas Chalkley pictured infancy as a time of turmoil.

> Now after our first month, what a deal of fatigue and trouble we give our mothers, who still, if they give us suck (as many mothers do, even queens and princesses, and many noble women, not disdaining to give their children suck from their own breasts, which certainly is the most natural way of bringing up and nourishing them; though on some considerations, a nurse may be dispensed with) how do we partake of their own blood, to the wasting of their spirits, and oftentimes the flesh also?
>
> Surely, nothing but love and duty would engage a mother to the great care and fatigue which she is obliged to in nursing and suckling her children, especially if beforehand in the world; who can express the toil and care to keep the poor unthinking little ones quiet, and the many weary steps and contrivances to keep them from crying?[24]

The defense of breastfeeding by Chalkley showed that the debate over whether the mother should personally feed her child was a controversial subject even in the eighteenth century. Religious writers since the Reformation had questioned whether the putting out of infants to be breastfed was proper, and Quakers joined the discussion. In 1701, William Edmundson cited numerous biblical women who had nursed their offspring, the most famous of whom were Elizabeth, the mother of John the Baptist, and the Virgin Mary. (There is no biblical evidence that Elizabeth or Mary nursed.) Sophia Hume, a prominent female minister who resided at times in South Carolina, severely censured the putting of "the poor Innocent" out to nurse to strangers. She maintained that the death of many children could be blamed upon the neglect by such hired help, "for how can we reasonably expect that a Stranger should take the due and tender Care, and faithfully discharge so troublesome an Office, which a Parent suppos'd to have a natural Engagement for her Infant, declines." Although women generally claimed a want of milk, Sophia Hume found the cause of "this Cruelty" centered in the sinful pride of mothers who feared bother, discomfort, or a change in "Shape." Priscilla Wakefield, in a tract written in England in 1798, emphasized as harmful "the destruction, or at least the diminution of that sympathy between the mother and child" that nature provided.[25] This discussion of the unique relationship or bond between mother and child, while certainly present in earlier writings, stands as an indication of the new importance of mother in childhood.

Most mothers undoubtedly fed their own children, and those who were not able used relatives or hired wet nurses. Advertisements sometimes appeared in colonial newspapers telling the readers to inquire of the editor for the name of a wet nurse. (Evidently this information was considered too personal to be advertised openly.) In wealthy families the nurse would come to live at the child's home; in poorer families the infant might live at the nurse's home. Mary Pemberton, wife of Israel Pemberton, Jr., first hired women to live in, but later "after much fatigue with nurses" placed the child out "with an honest Reputable woman, In an Airey Part of town." Finding a nurse of suitable character who was willing to live in was an onerous task. Sarah Buckley searched "Town and Country" for one in 1774, and Elizabeth Drinker, after employing three different women in ten weeks in 1781, mused that "it is a favour to be able to do that office oneself—as there is much trouble with nurses." When Margaret Morris gave birth to twins in 1760, their grandfather was happy that she did not attempt to nurse them, but he strongly opposed putting either of them out.[26]

Whether the child was nursed by a parent or outsider, there was no set age at which children were weaned. Because of poverty, Deborah Hill discharged a wet nurse at 6 months (which she thought far too early). William Dillwyn's daughters were weaned at 12 and 15 months; this was the age they began to have teeth. John Kelsall's daughter Elizabeth was weaned at 22 months and Susanna Cox at 16 months. Elizabeth Drinker weaned one child after 9 months (she was 3 months pregnant), one at 12, one at 17, and one at 26 months. The rich, who could afford to hire a boarding nurse or place the child out, had a definite advantage over the poor, who could afford to do neither. When scolding a husband for driving his wife out of the house, John Reynell lamented that she would now have to wean her own baby because her only means of support would be to nurse another's child.[27] The placing out of a child for a year or more must have meant that the importance of the mother in the very early years was diminished. By no means were all children breastfed. Sarah Meade wrote to Margaret (Fell) Fox in 1686 that if the mother was not able, and a good nurse not available, a child would be brought up "by the spoon." Dr. Richard Hill advised providing his granddaughter with a wet nurse or letting her be "brought up by hand, tho' this last method may be attended with some hazard to the child if she should not take kindly to feedings."[28]

IV

Any physical description of how the Quaker infant was brought up in early colonial times has to be founded largely upon surmise. There are descriptions of nursing, baby talk, weaning, first steps, and the great amount of affection lavished on children, but these do not originate before the middle of the eighteenth century, and most date from the revolutionary era. James Logan carried on an extensive correspondence; yet in a gossipy letter written in 1725 he confined his comments on his four children, aged from 10 years to 4 months, to, "I Can say nothing at all but that they are like their Neighbours." John Smith's diaries, which contained a wealth of materials about his habits and courtship, provided no description of how his daughter was raised except for an occasional reference to his taking her riding.[29] The large Quaker manuscript collections of the Historical Society of Pennsylvania and Haverford and Swarthmore Colleges are similarly lacking. This does not mean that young children were totally ignored; most business letters state the health of the sender's family and wish well to the members of the recipient's household. Friends wrote many books giving counsel on how to raise children, but parents rarely talked about the first 6 or 7 years of life. One would enjoy having some observer comment on how William Penn applied the many advices he wrote about how to rear children (particularly since his own sons did not meet his expectations). The lack of information is not a uniquely Quaker phenomenon; the massive works of Alice Earle and Edmund Morgan's studies of family life in New England and Virginia have much more to say about advice given than about how very young children were actually handled. Even Samuel Sewall's diary, a magnificent source of information about Puritan Massachusetts, only rarely mentions his children before they reached 9 or 10 years of age.[30]

To what is this neglect due? Undoubtedly to the nature of the documents that were preserved. Since business, politics, and religious affairs were of more lasting significance, such correspondence was saved. That most of the letters were written by men to men might also be a factor. Few purely social and personal letters were sent because postage was expensive. With the gradual improvement of both transportation and postal systems, more personal letters were written. Also, perhaps after 1760 a changing view of children was responsible for the increase in available documentation.

The absence of family papers discussing infancy and difficulties in interpreting the terminology used in religious tracts make impossible an adequate treatment of the psychological development of children. For example, in the seventeenth century "infancy" might refer to any age from birth until 7 years or later, and infrequently used adjectives like "early" or "late" infancy only complicate the issue; a "babe" can be 6 weeks old, in school, or older; "little" is just as vague; "child" was used interchangeably with "infant" and "youth," and there was no clear division between "youth" and "young men." Even when meetings gave advice on rearing children, their records make it difficult to distinguish what age group was being discussed.

Theological language further obfuscated the issues. Quakers could compartmentalize life, and terms useful for religious purposes may not have been applied in raising children. Reason and will were attributes of depraved man, but men in this world had to use such faculties to survive. There is no information as to what behavior was thought desirable or normal for a 2- or 3-year-old child and what seemed excessive or destructive. Did parents see sibling rivalry as a sign of sin or childish behavior, or did they just ignore it? Parents rocked cradles, but we remain ignorant about how often and in what circumstances. Quaker mothers were prohibited from singing lullabies (and all songs), but was cooing or humming to a baby considered singing? Most children were breastfed, but no data exist as to whether the infant was fed by demand or on a schedule. Parents feared the physical and emotional stresses from weaning, and some employed preventive measures (such as giving the infant honey) to ease the transition. Since the birth interval varied among different children in the same family, the limits for the age of weaning could change considerably. Perhaps wealthy children placed out to wet nurses were spared early weaning.

Was the Quaker father as head of the household reserved and stern or "tender hearted." Was the mother expected to be more affectionate, and, if so, what form did her affection take and did it change at a certain age? On the first four years of life (which include the crucial first three stages in Erik Erikson's analysis of *Childhood and Society*), there is almost no available information precise enough to be useful to a psychologist studying personality development.[31] What modern observers consider important about infancy did not interest seventeenth-century Friends, but what colonial Quakers did find important is made clear in dozens of books.

For the period from the 1660s to the 1760s, one can discuss Quaker ideas of children and not give much consideration to chronology, because the contents of yearly meeting advices, tracts, and journals rarely varied. A pamphlet written by Thomas Chalkley in 1730 described the process of growing up as occurring in three stages. Stage one went from infancy until age 7; at 7 came a key turning point, for the child went to school. By 14 formal education was completed and the youth was apprenticed to a trade. By 21, he finished his indenture and became a man who could enter business and marry. What happened to the child until he reached 7 was described thus:

> From the breast, and the arms, to the seventh year of our age, who can relate the world of trouble our parents have with us, to keep us out of harm's way, to keep us from bad company, to keep us in health as much as lays in their power; to clothe us and keep us whole and clean, and take care that we learn no ill words or manners; for about this time little youths are very apt to learn good or evil; and the careful, virtuous parents, would do well to endeavour to cultivate their tender minds, and to plant things good and profitable in them betimes.[32]

In rearing children in the eighteenth century, Friends emphasized seclusion from the world's evil. If the "infant and feeble" mind were exposed to good and evil, the child would not sift and winnow to arrive at good.[33] Rather, his natural inclinations to evil would predominate, and he would soon become so hardened in his vices that the grace of God could not reach him. In one sense this seclusion from the world involved a contradiction of early Quaker experience. George Fox and the first publishers of truth had been raised in what Friends thought were very evil surroundings and had managed to overcome them. Why could not the children of the second and third generations do the same? No Friend ever faced this issue. In 1689, John Crook skirted the subject by noting that often young people blamed their own sins upon the elders' bad examples. Parental faults were no excuse for the children's weaknesses since the first generation, who were pressed on every side by the "strong holds of *Satan,*" had conquered evil in the name of truth. The following generations had the example of these early Friends, who by a living testimonial to their faith made "the Passage . . . much more easy to those that followed." Rather than challenge young people to move out into the world to test their faith, Crook wanted them to stay in the "more easy" path and follow the pattern of their forefathers.[34]

The seclusion of children from the world could result in tribalism. If by tribalism it was meant that godly people should live and work as much as possible among other Friends, the Quaker approved. The true pilgrim ought to live as if the earth were transitory and, erecting a barrier against the enticements of evil, help the community of believers foster an attitude of living today for tomorrow. Quaker isolationism created a person who stood against the world as an individual but who, as a member of the church family, became submissive to the dictates of the meeting. One way to create Christians was to strictly control the environment of the young.

It would be hard to overestimate the importance that Friends placed upon the correct rearing of children. Their offspring were "next to our own souls" the "most immediate objects of our care and concern."[35] A great deal of the motivation behind the care of youth was due to fear. Perry Miller has argued that, underneath their calm assurance of certainty, the Puritans had a deep-seated suspicion that the "errand into the wilderness" might be a fool's journey.[36] Quakers in both England and America had the same kind of confidence in their mission and yet feared that their singularity as a "peculiar" people might be the result of oddity rather than of God's call. Their whole faith was a journey into the wilderness, an experiment in true spiritual Christianity, and they were haunted by the thought that the world had passed them by and that few really cared if they succeeded. In the eighteenth century, Friends were a small sect; by the time of the Revolution they comprised no more than one-seventh of the population, even in Pennsylvania. The founders had staked their lives on the fundamental importance of their religious principles, and the only way for the tenets to be maintained—the method by which Quakerism could be preserved—was for the children to adopt, preserve, and pass the faith on to their descendants.[37] The children had to hold to the truth with the same degree of fervor as the parents. The innumerable warnings about the decline of piety in youth and the necessity to educate the rising generation in the faith can be understood best as manifestations of a fear mechanism based on the suspicion that the Society of Friends might die.

Bernard Bailyn has reasoned that the mounting shrillness of the seventeenth-century Puritan exhortations to their children came from a changing family structure resulting from the colonial environment.[38] Quaker family literature in both England and America in the seventeenth and eighteenth centuries was strident, but its intensity was not the result of the effect of the frontier or of America on family structure. One could postulate and prove an

Americanization of the Quaker family only if the writings in England and America diverged. They did not. When changing perspectives about children grew up after 1760, the literature on both sides of the Atlantic showed the same evolution at just about the same time.

Fear may have been an underlying motive for the stress on correct child rearing but the ostensible reason was a religious one. The inward light of Christ was used by the Friends much as the Wesleyans used free grace. The light came to or was in everyone; therefore, responsibility for behavior and for being saved fell directly upon each person. The Methodist parent was to prepare his child for the acceptance of justification; the Quaker was to help the child cut the weeds of sin so that grace would enable the inward seed to sprout.

The primary responsibility for maintaining a godly atmosphere lay with the family. Quakers knew that the religion of the parents was not inherited by the children; yet they believed that pious parents had religious children. The attempt to merge these contrary beliefs was shown clearly in the 1747 epistle from London Yearly Meeting:

> For although virtue passes not by lineal succession, nor piety by inheritance; yet we trust that the Almighty will have an especial and gracious regard to the sincere endeavours of those parents, who have an early and constant care and concern for the welfare of their offspring.[39]

If the parents took special care of their offspring, they enjoyed a "reasonable" chance of success. The best way of evangelizing children within the home was by good example. In 1704 London's epistle advised members "to be careful to act in the Wisdom of God; that they may be exemplary therein to those that are young." Most children went astray by following the example of their mothers and fathers, "and so covetous Parents teach their Children covetousness; for their own minds being in that thing, they press their Children to the practice of it" under a "show of carefulness and prudence."[40] John Freame's catechism of 1713 noted that the first duty of parents was to be good examples because advice without action would not compel emulation. Parents should be careful of actions in the presence of children, for they "have very quick Eyes and Ears," and when once they spy the faults and form a "Mean Opinion" of parents, the counsel "seldom produceth any good Effect."[41]

If the father had experienced and lived according to truth, he was then fit to govern his family. In order to keep children pious, parents had first to "take heed to themselves, that their own spirits be rightly seasoned and directed." The family was a hierarchical structure with parents in control and children kept in due subordination. "Between a Man and his Wife, nothing ought to rule but *Love.* Authority is for *Children* and *Servants;* yet not without sweetness." Parents were told "you are set in your families as judges for God, and it is you that must give an account of the power committed to you." So long as the father and mother furnished food and clothing, their power was not just to "advise and persuade, but also to command," and they should be "absolute" in matters involving religion. Philadelphia Yearly Meeting referred all masters of families to the example of the Lord, who praised Abraham "for I know him that he will Command (Mark Command) his Children."[42] The authority of parents was founded upon natural right and scriptural precedent, and Friends cited the dire punishments suffered by disobedient children.

If the child rebelled, the parent was literally expected to crack the whip.

The mother and father were to begin to "govern, counsel, and correct" their children as soon as they could understand what they were being corrected for and knew "in measure" what they should say or do. This knowledge of right and wrong entailed some comprehension of the light. The children at a very early age must be made to realize that:

> *Their Wills* ought to be entirely subject to *Ours;* and that whatsoever we Command or Require, must be punctually comply'd with: But then *Care* must be taken, to require nothing of them that is Unreasonable, or not becoming a Religious and Tender Parent.[43]

If everything the child cried for were given, he, rather than the parent, would become the master. Friends were very certain that if a person were ever to be governed, the process had to begin while he was still "Little," because if one were subjected to authority early enough, he would grow up in "Duty and obedience." If the infant's will were conquered, then as he matured an admonition or even a nod rather than the rod would suffice to control him. The child was to be loved but not pampered. Benjamin Coole wrote that he always loved his offspring but was careful not to manifest too much fondness.[44] The parental station required tenderness but not softness.

The father was not to be a tyrant over the household. He was head of the family, yet he was to rule gently, for unnecessary harshness or severity would turn the children against him and his religion. Friends desired that all punishments be fitted to the nature of the offense and the disposition of the child. "Some will be more gained by Words fitfully spoken . . . than others will be by Correction." A schoolmaster counseled using first a rebuke, next a "timely restraint," and finally the rod. John Banks advocated a good thrashing if necessary but cautioned that he had found waiting a while and then talking to the child to convince him of his mistake to be more successful.[45] At age 12, John Woolman was reproved by his mother and made an "Undutiful reply." The father was away at the time, but when he returned he said nothing until John was riding home after meeting.

> He told me he understood I had behaved amiss to my Mother, and Advised me to be more careful in the future. I knew myself blameable, and in shame and confusion remained silent. . . . I do not remember that I ever after that spoke unhandsomely to either of my Parents.[46]

All Friends counseled against punishing when not in control of oneself. If a parent beat a child when the parent was angry, the like sentiment would be kindled in the child. "Wrath, Anger, and Passion, beget their own Likeness in Children, and rather make them more stubborn." William Penn, the most eloquent of all early Friends, summarized the Quaker attitude toward rearing children:

> If God give you children, Love them with Wisdom, Correct them with Affection: Never strike in Passion, and suit the Correction to their Age as well as Fault. Convince them of their Error before you chastise them, and try them, if they show Remorse before Severity, never use that but in Case of Obstinacy or Impenitency. Punish them more by their Understandings than the Rod.[47]

If a son became wicked on his own and his parents, in spite of their best efforts, could not keep him in the way of sobriety, reason, and religion, then the child was responsible. But if, through undue harshness, neglect, or softness by the father and mother, the child were lost, the parents would be judged and found wanting. Friends rarely mentioned a parent who was too severe, but sermons, journals, and tracts cited many examples of indulged children who dominated the household.

The Quaker child was to be subjected to the plain style of life from an early age. The infant was not dressed in frilly laced petticoats with ribbons attached so that he might not later succumb to the temptations of finery and pride in appearance. Children were not allowed to "babble many vain words with their tongues" for "thereby the tongue becomes an unruly member." A few toys might be proper to give the infant "an Idea of natural Things," but too many playthings were trifles which, when given as objects of value, led afterwards to a false esteem for such "Vanities and Toys." It was wrong to let children learn idle absurd sonnets and ballads or to teach "Fairy Tales, Histories of Giants, Tom Thumbs, and such like Stuff," which prepared them only to receive more "Ingenious Lies and Romances."[48] Thomas Clarkson, a sympathetic observer of Quakerism at the beginning of the nineteenth century, noted that one of the first objectives in education was the "subjugation of the will" so that "every perverse passion [could] be checked." So Quaker parents rebuked children for any expression of anger or raising of voices beyond "due bounds."[49] Above all else, children had to learn how to keep their places in due humility. One of the many reasons for condemning slavery and requiring Quakers to free their slaves was the ill effect that slavery had upon the family. A child accustomed to living in luxury and giving orders to slaves did not learn proper submissiveness. Friends perceived that there was something incompatible about teaching that Christianity required one to be a servant of all and then giving a child the power to rule adult Negro men and women.[50] Having servants could also expose children to the danger of superciliousness, but a Christian master would allow a godly servant to discipline and rule the child. Thomas Clarkson listed the curbing of children's spirits as an objective in the Quaker system of moral education. He had a conjectural Friend answer by agreeing and asserting that "spirit, or high-mindedness, or high feeling, is not a trait in the Christian character." From early years the child was accustomed to subjection, moderation, and religion; otherwise as he grew older the parents would have difficulty weaning him from the "ill-habits he has imbibed with his Mother's Milk."[51]

The Quaker child was to be under continual surveillance. London Yearly Meeting advised parents in 1731 to have "a constant watchful Eye in Love over them for their Good, and keep them as much as possible within their notice and observation." Parents were warned repeatedly that "no Opportunity be omitted, nor any Endeavours wanting to Instruct them in the Principle of Truth which we Profess," so that as the child learned about God his spirits might be "soft'ned and tendered" and he would be made fit to "Receive the Impressions of the divine Image." As in the Puritan household, Quaker parents were to be on the alert for a visitation of grace. Every sign of evil was to be banished and any seed of light was to be encouraged to grow. The sprouting of the seed was fostered by keeping the child enmeshed in the plain style of life in all things, in family devotions and meetings, in the reading of Scriptures, and by pious admonitions and holy example. John Banks recorded that, even in bed at night, his great concern was how to bring up his children. John Woolman's parents would gather the whole family every Sunday afternoon for prayer and Scripture readings. Samuel Fothergill remembered the power and eloquence of his father's tears during daily devotions. Robert Barclay's widow sat down with her seven children before breakfast each morning and "in a religious Manner waited upon the Lord." Abraham Shackleton's father died in 1704 when the boy was eight. The son's recollection was of the "tender concern of his pious father, who, following him to his bed-side, was wont, awfully, to recommend him to seek the Divine blessing."[52] The kind of religious instruction and encouragement that Cotton Mather and Samuel Sewall gave their children undoubtedly was duplicated in many Quaker homes, but there was a difference. Unlike Samuel Sewall, Friends did not begin with predestination and damnation and scare their children into conversion.

V

Concurrent to his life at home and in school, much of the Quaker child's time was spent in meetings. There is no definite record listing the age at which children began to attend, though parents were warned against delaying too long. Thomas Harrison testified that parents brought children to meeting beginning about age 4. The Drinker children attended by age 5, and Lydia Dillwyn behaved well in meeting at age 8. John Kelsall at age 6 played at going to meetings with a friend since his parents did not take him.[53] The worship was in silence with the only possible diversion being a sermon by one of the ministering Friends. Even the elders sometimes slept during meeting, and the children were probably very bored. One can imagine the difficulties that 8-year-old boys encountered in attempting to sit quietly for two hours twice every Sunday. From 1699 on, the minutes of Philadelphia Monthly Meeting contain many records of futile attempts to keep the scholars' gallery quiet. The meeting, which separated boys and girls and padlocked the door between them, also paid men to watch over disorderly children kept out of service, and, encouraging all youth to attend, asked for volunteers to sit in the gallery. Parents and schoolmasters were admonished to restrain their charges. The final solution was to have Friends serve for a term of one month in the boys' gallery; from the many names in the minutes, it would appear that everyone took his turn. John Cresson, enduring this "unpleasant" office in 1795, complained about the elderly Friends who sat near "ill-behaved Boys" yet took no notice of them. Little had changed since 1738 when George Harris was scandalized to see parents do nothing when children laughed during silent worship.[54]

Quaker rhetoric tended to combine the religious functions of meeting and family, but ambiguity in terminology never meant that family devotions could replace attendance at first day's service. The number and variety of occasions on which the epistles advised parents to bring children to meeting leaves no doubt as to the importance Friends attached to constant worship. When someone reported in 1700 that the youth in Philadelphia had too much "Liberty to wander on first days in the evening," a special meeting was appointed for that time of day. Many communities scheduled special meetings for youth at least four times annually. Everyone was invited to attend these gatherings, but the remarks were directed toward the youth present. The scholars at Penn Charter School always attended the weekday meetings in Philadelphia. Rebecca Jones, a ministering Friend and schoolteacher, warned her pupils to

> make no disagreeable scraping or rubbing of your feet against the floor or seat, nor use any unbecoming gestures or motions with any part of your bodies to disturb or offend any person, by biting your nails, pinching your fingers, lolling, stretching, yawning, spitting, staring about, or by any other means.[55]

There was no Sunday school or formalized religious training (outside of the classroom) in the eighteenth century. Children attended and sat through the same service as their parents. An English Quaker in 1802, while defending the practice of children attending for worship, suggested that sitting in the meeting often did not result in any positive instruction in the Bible or Quaker beliefs, with the result that "the children of our Society . . . are generally in a state of greater ignorance and darkness" than persons of similar ages in other denominations. Job Scott of Rhode Island saw in the meetings not only a place for children to wait upon the Lord but also a means of discipline. Sitting quietly for two hours taught "silence and subjection; it curbs their wills and habituates them to restraint, and a patient waiting."[56] There can be little doubt that repeated attendance at meetings led to a more quiet and relaxed tempo of life.

The impact of the constant religious emphasis in home, school, and meeting resulted in children being deeply committed to Quaker practice long before they experienced conversion. Although the journalists in general did not stress their early lives, they showed how deeply imbedded Quaker practices could become. Once when Thomas Chalkley was playing in the street, he came under strong convictions of sin and began to weep. As a 10-year-old boy he reprimanded grown men for swearing. After secretly buying a deck of cards and going to play at the home of his relatives, he stopped at a meeting and heard a declaration against gambling. He not only refused to play cards thereafter but brought the deck home and burned it.[57]

The narratives about dying children provide an excellent source for determining what the Quakers thought an ideal child should be. The infant paragons acted not as gay and vivacious little children but as serious small adults. They never complained, were very pious, and were dutiful to their parents. At an age when others played with toys, they remained home studying, praying, or meditating. They were described as even talking like adults. When Sarah Camm, age 9, was on her deathbed, she informed her father:

> Oh! my dear father, thou art tender and careful over me, and hast taken great pains with me in my sickness, but it availeth not, there is no help nor succor for me in the earth; it is the Lord that is my health and physician, and he will give me ease and rest everlasting.

Mary Post, who died in 1712, philosophized about her impending demise at age 8:

One must once die, and if I recover I must (or may) be sick again; and I had rather die when I am young. If I should live till I am older, the devil may tempt me to be naught[y], and I might offend the Lord. I am not afraid to die; through mercy I shall go to my rest.

In 1680 a 12-year-old was quoted as saying, "If this distemper doth not abate, I must die; but my soul shall go to eternal joy, eternal and everlasting life and peace with my God for ever."[58]

One boy at age 10 read Scriptures, wrote down pious sayings, and memorized them. He always acted dutifully toward his parents, and he cheerfully carried out every service asked. His mother was frail and, besides helping her, he wished for strength in order to do all her difficult tasks. The *Dying Legacy of Hannah Hill* included this description of an 11-year-old girl:

I Observed that she was always very Dutiful to her Parents, Loving to her Friends and Neighbours, and Kind to the Servants, both White and Black. . . . I also observed, That many times when other Children would be at Play in the Streets, (that which our *Youth* are too much addicted to in this City, and too much Winked at by their Parents) she would be either at her Book or her Needle, at both which she was very Dexterous, and it rather seemed a Delight to her, than a Burden.[59]

A discipline intended to create saintly children also created some devilish brats. John Kelsall, a schoolmaster in both England and Ireland in the early eighteenth century, wondered why Quaker children were always so much harder to discipline than others. John Banks told of hearing a parent tell her child to do a task and getting the retort "I will not" several times. The parent did nothing. Others complained of children who fretted about food and demanded to be served first.[60]

The official Quaker attitude toward childhood games and fun approaches the popular stereotype of Puritanism. Yearly Meeting advised in 1729, "Let Care be taken to preserve them from Idleness (That Nurse of many Evils)." The infant paragons felt guilty if they "loved play too well" and were commended for preferring prayer and work over fun and games.[61] No Quaker religious tract or advice in either the seventeenth or the eighteenth century directly advocated play for children. The only Friend who came close to saying that recreation was good was Anthony Benezet who included in his primer that maxim that "All work and no play, makes Jack a dull boy. . . . All play and no works makes Jack a meer toy." When sports were mentioned, it was usually in a derogatory manner. William Caton in his Latin textbook abridgment of Eusebius's history warned students not to participate in "*Folly, Plays, Sports,* and *Pastimes,* but rather betake your selves to your Books; or in some retired place, to wait upon the Lord." While those who played gained exercise for the body, those who waited upon the Lord received "Refreshment" for their souls. Friends condemned dancing, horse races, cock fights, plays, ball, and all games. Thomas Chalkley had a fearful vision of students stopping their reading of Scriptures in order to peruse "filthy and irreligious corrupt romances, and prophane play-books, often poison, and are the bane or ruin of youth."[62]

The lack of official statements giving a place in life to youthful fun and games throughout most of the colonial period forces one to question whether Quakers actually had a conception of childhood. Theologically, there were only two periods in life. The child was innocent until he grew old enough to sin; then he was completely depraved. There was no intermediate stage of partial innocence. When non-Quaker Thomas Clarkson wrote his *Portraiture of Quakerism* early in the nineteenth century, he provided a conception of childhood: Children live in a "kind of perpetual spring. Their blood runs briskly throughout; their spirits are kept almost constantly alive; and, as the cares of the world occasion no drawback, they have perpetual disposition to cheerfulness and to mirth. This disposition seems to be universal in them."[63] Clarkson's attitude, which expressed what Quakers believed in 1800, differed greatly from that of Friends fifty years earlier. The absence of this conception of the uniqueness and gaiety of youth in the early eighteenth century is striking.

At the beginning of the eighteenth century, Benjamin Coole advised his children to "Begin to be Old betime," and the correspondence of youths show how effective such counsel could be.[64] Quaker instruction and seclusion were expected to result in a disciplined life in which control over the self was always present. There was, in theory, no indulgence of weakness or high-spiritedness in children.

However, even if a conception of childhood was not present among Friends, parents looked on approvingly while boys and girls found time to play. John Reynell, an elder of Philadelphia meeting and a strict Friend, sent his nephew a whip and a top. When Elias Bland, an English Friend who had once served as his apprentice sent Reynell's 6-year-old daughter a doll, Reynell thanked him and said that his daughter would like the doll "the better for not being so Friendly" (i.e., plain). When John Smith's children received a gift of a "whirly-gig" from London, the toy was so complicated that no one could put it together and Smith was forced to request instructions. James Pemberton, when he journeyed to England, wanted to buy books for Israel's children but found them so given over to "romances and idle tales" that he purchased a new edition of *Aesop's Fables.* Mary Shackleton, who was a small child at the time of the American Revolution, reminisced that her grandfather made little pitchforks so that she and her sister could play at tossing hay. "He was kind to us, but was never pleased when he saw us playing with our dolls."[65] Babies received rattles and candy. Little girls had swings, drew on slates, cut out paper dolls with scissors, recited poetry, and played with doll houses and cradles. Boys flew kites, sailed boats, constructed wigwams and played at being Indians, rode hobby horses and later real ponies, collected rocks and bird eggs, attempted scientific experiments, gardened, and made pets of squirrels, guinea hens, dogs, and cats. Their activities did not always meet with parental approval—as when Jonas Dickinson dived into deep water in the Delaware River with a 40-pound weight in his pocket to prove his strength, or Billy Drinker came home with his face bruised after boxing, or Algernon Logan burned himself while playing with gunpowder. John Woolman repented of having thrown a stone and killed a bird, but others engaged in marksmanship contests of many kinds. John Watson's *Annals of Philadelphia* listed a large variety of games participated in by schoolboys, some of which were played in front of Friends' school. Among them were skying a copper, pitch-penny, chuckers—all games involving pitching a coin at a mark or into the air.[66] Friends disapproved of fox hunting and other forms of killing for "fun," but boys could justify hunting as providing food for the table, and no one had qualms about fishing. Quaker merchants and travelers sent home books, toys, and chocolates. One 10-year-old boy's vision of heaven was being offered a "rare Applepie" and then being told that "there were better Dainties for me." Yearly meetings meant school vacations; thus whole families attended for social as well as religious purposes. Fairs took place in many localities, and, although masters were instructed to hold school as usual in order to keep children away, there must have been opportunities to attend them. When there were not fairs, the stimulation of market day was excitement enough. Philadelphia parents were advised to restrain their sons from congregating with the rabble whenever the drum was beaten.[67]

Officially condoned games were allowed under the guise of exercise. Whether from reading John Locke or from common knowledge, Friends often advocated a rigorous regimen to harden the constitution. Penn advised, "Children can't well be too hardy bred: For besides that it fits them to bear the roughest Providences, it is more Masculine, Active, and Healthy." Parents took such counsel seriously; in 1788 George Dillwyn, not quite two, was plunged into a cold bath every other morning. William Massey, an English schoolmaster who kept a boarding school, listed as health-producing exercises for young boys "Tops, Suckers, Marbles, Hoops and Ball" and for older pupils "more strong and manly Sport." At his school for girls, Anthony Benezet provided for periodic breaks in order that the pupils could go into the next room for some exercises. Many Quakers found that the needed physical exertion could be accomplished through work rather than play. James Gough noted that his mother "made it her maxim in her plan of education to accustom her children to useful employment, frugal fare, and to have our wills crossed."[68]

In colonial days recreation usually took second place to the sheer amount of work needed to survive. Alice Morse Earle has described the staggering amount of labor necessary to process flax into linen or raw wool into mittens. Little girls played at being mother by learning to sew, spin, and cook, and they were soon taught to make clothing and to help with the innumerable tasks in the kitchen. Boys could help around the house or in the shop or garden or even hoe in the fields. Children were undoubtedly introduced to the required hard work even before they went to school. No matter where one lived in America, he was not far from farmlands and chores. Town families commonly kept pigs and chickens, and even in Philadelphia, until after the Revolution, the herdsman would stand on Dock Street near Second and blow his horn and all the cattle in town would come to him. After taking them to the meadow for the day, the herdsman returned with the cattle, blew his horn, and each cow found its way home.[69]

VI

Quaker catechisms show how the attitude toward children changed. In the eighteenth century the most popular catechism was Robert Barclay's (first edition, 1673), a 99-page book filled with abstruse questions. The answers were scriptural citations. The first problem will demonstrate the tone of the book:

Q. Seeing it is a thing unquestioned by all sorts of Christians, that the height of Happiness consisteth in coming to know and enjoy Eternal Life, what is it in the Sense and Judgment of Christ?

A. That is Life Eternal, that they might know the only true God, and Jesus Christ whom thou has sent. John 17:3.[70]

This was one of the easiest topics. Some subjects required questions and answers that filled almost half a page. The primer of George Fox, used by Quaker schools in the seventeenth and eighteenth centuries, had a catechism in the form of a dialogue between a "Scholar" and the "Master." Many of these questions and answers went on for several pages. An impersonal tone was also found in John Freame's *Scripture Instructions,* printed in London in 1713 and Philadelphia in 1754. Although Freame maintained that his book was designed especially for children and that he eschewed all "Controversial Points of Religion," the contents were similar to the material in the catechisms of Barclay and Fox.[71]

Friends cited the same scriptural precedents that appeared in the catechisms of other denominations, and there was no disagreement about the meaning of such verses. For example, children were informed why they were disciplined.

Prov. 23:13–14. Withhold not Correction from the Child: for if thou beatest him with the Rod, he shall not die. Thou shalt beat him with the Rod, and shalt deliver his Soul from Hell.

The emphasis upon parental authority was very strong.

Deut. 27:16. Cursed be he that Setteth Light by his Father, or his Mother.

Col. 3:20. Children, obey your parents in all things; for this is well-pleasing unto the Lord.[72]

Quaker parents found biblical precedents to support their ideas on authority, discipline, and restraint—the last to be exercised by both children and elders. Eph. 6:1, 4, for example, says: "Children, obey your parents in the Lord: for this is right. . . . Fathers, provoke not your children to wrath." The most frequently cited verse was Exod. 20:12: "Honour thy Father and thy Mother: That thy days may be long upon the Land." Quaker and Puritan children frequently began letters to their parents with "Honoured Father." There is no biblical passage that commands children to love parents or vice versa.

The Quaker father or mother did not worry about the harshness of the biblical injunctions in the catechisms. In a sermon published in New York in 1769, Rachel Wilson warned children that disobeying parents brought the judgment and wrath of God. Even those children who defied their elders by playing out-of-doors after being told to come into the house were in danger. She did not hesitate to quote the chilling scriptural prophecy: "The eye that mocketh at his Father, and despiseth to obey his Mother, the Ravens of the valley shall pick it out, and the young Eagles shall eat it." This is not to assert that Friends refused to stress the more humane and gentle side of their faith; but they saw no contradiction in addressing children on page one as "Dear

Little Friends, not tainted yet with ill, / By sense not biass'd nor misled by will," and warning on page two that the youngsters must "Fear, fear the Lord, his awful presence fear, / And dare not to sin, for he is ever near."[73]

The impersonal tone, the dangers of sin, and the frightening presence of God remained long into the nineteenth century in reprints of older catechisms, but newer books directed at little children and published in England and America showed an almost total change. In 1807, London Yearly Meeting for Sufferings published *Early Christian Instruction in the form of a Dialogue between a Mother and Child.* In earlier works, the questioner had been impersonal or the master. Now the mother was the central figure. Previously, the exhortations had been purely theological with long scriptural citations. Now the few verses of Scripture were not to be memorized. Here is the beginning of this official catechism:

> "Dear mother, I am sometimes uncomfortable. I want to be always comfortable and happy."
> "Then, my dear, thou must take the way to be happy."
> "What way, mother? What is the way to be happy?"
> "To let alone naughty and wicked things, and to be a very good child."
> "What things are wicked, mother?"
> "Telling lies is very wicked. So is using bad words; being disobedient; being cruel to dumb creatures; stealing; giving way to passion, and other things of that kind."[74]

After a long introduction of dialogue, Christian and Quaker contents were introduced. There was no mention of hell fire and damnation.

The author of *Parental Instruction in Familiar Dialogues* (1811) worried about exposing children to the fundamental truths of the "fall and redemption" of man since they could so little understand them. The term *sin* never appeared in this catechism; the child was "bad" or, more frequently, "naughty." The children were not pictured as treacherous small adults who had to be rigidly disciplined; rather, they were depicted as saccharine sweet and sentimental beings. The subject of religion was approached indirectly. Two children, William and Fanny, talked to their mother. They began by walking into a field and picking wild flowers; the beauty of creation served as an introduction to the nature of God.

> *Mother:* "Now, dear Children, I am ready to walk with you."
> *Fanny:* "May we go into the fields? It is so pleasant there."
> *Mother:* "I have no objection; but has William learned his lesson?"
> *Fanny:* "O! yes—he repeated it very well."
> *Mother:* "That is the way to enjoy your pleasures: I like to please you, but if you were idle and disobedient, I could not make you happy."
> *Fanny:* "I wish we were always good, then we should be *so* comfortable."[75]

Even when the cathechism was more conservative in tone, the same emphasis upon domestic happiness appeared. John Wigham's *Christian Instruction in a Discourse as Between a Mother and her Daughter* (three editions in Philadelphia, 1817–20) had Mother communicate religious truths to Mary.

The authors of these three catechisms departed from the traditional Quaker insistence upon imparting the substance of the faith in scriptural terms. Stress, strife, evil, and a judging Jehovah were obliterated by domesticity in these nineteenth-century instruction books. Friends had not forgotten the toughness of the world, but they deemed a harsh reality incompatible with the sweetness and innocence of children.

VII

When personal letters describing childhood began to appear in the late eighteenth century, parents left no doubt that they espoused a sentimental view of children and were fascinated with their offspring. Here, Sarah Buckley describes her children to her absent husband in 1774:

> our dear Billy is as hearty a[s] a Child can be she Eats drinks sleeps and sucks as much as is good for her begins to Notice all about her, as to knowing her Name she does not but call her Billy and she will Coee & talk her fashion half an hour.[76]

The uncle would stop by to play with the baby; he would put her on his lap on a pillow and she would fall asleep. Ann Wood noted in 1782 that although her son David would not walk, "he's took to Creeping and beats all at it I ever saw, he has scar'd one several times by getting all the way upstairs and peeping down. I expect to see him break his neck some day; there is no such thing as keeping him in the house." Both father and mother were intimately engaged in rearing their children. When Samuel Allinson was forced to be away from home on business, he told his wife, "Kiss little Davy for me and let him kiss thee for me." Parents raised children, but grandparents enjoyed them. John Smith of Burlington wrote his son-in-law acknowledging his kindness in letting the granddaughter visit and assuring him that she would be a "welcome guest" at any time and that "we shall be sort of blank without her." When Peter Cooper visited his grandson, the father described the meeting: "Little Davy was very well, and solicitous with his GrandDaddy to tell me he was a *Good Boy* not a Naughty Boy, answering his G D when he told him was a N Boy sometimes, 'but I is a good Boy now!' "[77] Deborah Logan enjoyed playing with her "lovely" and "excessively engaging" 1-year-old son who was "just now playing on the table and wanting much to have the Inkstand in his possession." The Pemberton family shows graphically the new emphasis upon infancy. There are almost no comments about Israel, Jr., James, or John Pemberton (born 1715, 1723, 1727), and none about their children. But their grandchildren, born just prior to the Revolution, call forth comments about giving kisses, "diverting companions," "domestic endearment," and sweetness.[78]

William Dillwyn, an influential Quaker minister who lived for a considerable period in America and then moved to England, wrote a series of letters to his daughter in Burlington describing the raising of five children born between 1778 and 1787. Dillwyn described one daughter as a "dear little Creature" and another as "a sweet little Darling." His son was a "precious Fellow." Susanna, the daughter in America, responded in kind, terming her nieces and nephew "our dear little Hannah," a "lovely little baby," and a "sweet little boy."[79] Discipline did not appear to have been severe. On one occasion Dillwyn noted that he was always in danger of spoiling his youngest. Two-year-old Nancy was "very engaging and makes thy Father do just as she pleases. He generally pets them at her age." When Nancy began to talk, her nurse once attempted to "check an unseasonable Midnight fit of Prattle." The child responded, "*Surely Nanny . . . Nancy may Talk.*" When greetings were sent from the children to their American sister, 2-year-old Lydia did not bother because she was so busy drawing flowers on a slate. Five-year-old Judy was a "listless Scholar, and a little Sewing *fatigues her exceedingly,* tho I believe there is not a greater Romp in the parish."[80] The children played with kites, cut paper dolls, rode horseback, celebrated birthdays, squabbled among themselves, and went on boat trips and outings to London. The general atmosphere of the household as described in these letters seems best conveyed by the father's comment when, to keep a promise, he allowed the children to stay up much later than usual: "I do not begrudge trifling a little when by it, I can please *any* of my Children, big or little."[81]

One can interpret in several ways the significance of the idyllic view of childhood contained in these letters. One might argue that Friends adopted a sentimental view of children early in the eighteenth century when the doctrine of children's sinlessness became normative. In this view, the absence of all documentary evidence referring to young children was due to factors relating to the view of the family, such as expense of paper, etc. The major weakness in this position is that it ignores the continuing theological strictures demanding rigid control of small adultlike beings.

A more plausible explanation is that there was a major shift in ideas after 1760. Friends readily used new concepts because they seemed to derive from the traditional doctrine of childhood innocence. There is evidence that such ideas were not confined to Friends. The stress on the bond between mother and child, the sweetness of infancy, and the importance of the early years appears in the late eighteenth-century pictures of family groups and children by Gainsborough, Reynolds, and Morland, in Blake's *Songs of Innocence,* and in Rousseau's *Émile.*[82]

Since the sentimentalization of childhood appears to have been a widespread phenomenon in England and America, to search for the causes of this change only among Friends would be futile. A possible explanation for the new importance of children lies in that complex shift of attitudes from neoclassicism to romanticism. William Wordsworth, a prime exemplar of the flowering of romantic poetry in Great Britain, pictured the child as "trailing clouds of glory do we come / From God, who is our home; / Heaven lies about us in our infancy."[83] An innocent baby fitted easily into romantic emphases upon the development of personality unfettered by institutional restraints, the desire for a simple and uncluttered life, and affection for the delights of home. Friends' contribution to the cult of childhood consisted not in originality of ideas but in the speed with which they assimilated new themes. A godlike child who would not need baptism to cover a taint of original sin fitted more easily into Quaker than Calvinistic theology.

Christopher Hill and Michael Walzer argued that the Puritans caused a transformation of the family by emphasizing its spiritual importance.[84] Quaker documents dating from the end of the seventeenth century confirm this view but suggest that family nurture became important after the new religion was solidly established, when the number of converts diminished, and as the children of early Friends matured. Even then the child remained a small adult and the parental role increased only for the purpose of religious instruction. Parents still did not assume that relatives or friends were interested in how their offspring behaved. The Quaker experience suggests that after 1760 fundamental changes occurred that resulted in the sentimentalization and glorification of the child. For the first time the child was recognized as having a personality from infancy. The parents secluded the child not only from evil but even from knowledge of his existence. Conversion could be postponed; happiness came first.

Notes

1 George Fox, *Works* (Philadelphia, 1831), 5: 5, and 7: 142, 145, 149; London YM, Epistles Received, 1: 137, and 2: 77, 197; Epistles Sent, 1: 105; Min. Philadelphia YM, 2, (9/24–27/1765): 212; New England YM, Ancient Epistles, Minutes and Advices, or Discipline, 4/6/1673, p. 14.

2 Min. Philadelphia MM, 10 mo./1685; George Fox, Works, 7: 15; Robert Barclay, *Apology for the True Christian Divinity,* 13th ed. (Manchester, England, 1869), prop. 10, pg. iii, 170. Philadelphia YM, Discipline of 1719, p. 3; Sydney James, *A People Among Peoples* (Cambridge, Mass., 1963), p. 34.

3 John Willsford, *A Brief Exhortation* (Philadelphia, 1691), p. 5; Burlington MM, Births and Deaths 1682–1800. William Penn, *Works* (London, 1726), 1: 870.

4 Michael Wigglesworth, *Day of Doom,* verses 166–81; William Lumpkin, ed. *Baptist Confessions of Faith* (Chicago, 1959), pp. 228, 330–31; *A Confession of Faith, Set Forth by Many of those Baptists, who own the Doctrine of Universal Redemption* (Newport[?], 1730[?]), pp. 3–4.

5 Barclay, *Apology,* prop. 4, pg. iv, 59; George Keith, *The Presbyterian and Independent Churches in New England* (Philadelphia, 1689), p. 86.

6 George Fox and Thomas Lawrence, *Concerning Marriage,* pp. 4–5; William Smith, "Universal Love" (1663), in his *Balm for Gilead* (London, 1675), pp. 76, 94–95. Smith came close to asserting that all children were born "innocent and harmless."

7 Barclay, *Apology,* prop. 4, pg. iv, 59–61; Keith, *Presbyterian and Independent Churches,* pp. 84–85. After he left Friends, Keith clarified the ambiguity in his position. The nature of children was corrupted even in the womb, he said, and "brutish Lusts" dominated before the age of discretion. God saved innocents not because they were innocent but because he was merciful. Keith, *Truth Advanced in the Correction of Many Gross and Hurtful Errors* (New York, 1694), pp. 33, 36.

8 John Hepburn, *The American Defence of the Christian Golden Rule* (Philadelphia, 1714), pp. 66–70; William Evans and Thomas Evans, eds., *An Account of the Gospel Labours and Christian Experiences, of. . . John Churchman* in *Friends Library* (Philadelphia, 1842), 4: 177–78.

9 Hannah Pemberton to James Pemberton 1/3/1778, "Exile Letters," DR; Isaac Norris to Prudence Moore, 9/21/1747, Norris Letter Book 1735–55, p. 48, HSP.

10 Anthony Benezet, A First Book for Children (Philadelphia, 1779), p. 22; idem, *Some Serious and Awful Considerations* (Philadelphia, 1769), pp. 14–20; Smith, "Universal Love," p. 95; Keith, *Presbyterian and Independent Churches,* p. 89.

11 Alice Morse Earle, *Child Life in Colonial Days* (New York, 1929), pp. 37, 51, 222; *PMHB* 22: 72; William Dillwyn to Susanna Dillwyn, 9/22/1784, 1: 22, Dillwyn Mss., HSP; Elizabeth Drinker, "Diary," HSP. At the Lateran Council in 1215 the Roman Catholic church decided that after a person arrived at the "years of discretion," he must take confession and communion once a year. Until 1910 the church did not define the age of discretion as seven, but as early as the Renaissance most authorities specified seven, although in some countries first communion was postponed until later. Henry Denzinger, *Sources of Catholic Dogma,* trans. Roy J. Deferrari (New York, 1957), p. 173; Henry Charles Lea, *A History of Auricular Confession* (Philadelphia, 1896), pp. 400–04.

12 James Pemberton to John Smith, 10/19/1765, Smith Mss, vol. 6; Hannah Hill, *A Legacy for Children* (Philadelphia, 1717), pp. 6, 16, 23; Isaac Norris to Mordecai Moore, 10/12/1711, *Correspondence between William Penn and James Logan* (Philadelphia, 1872), 2: 440. There are two difficulties with the term *innocent.* First a Friend who was

converted and sanctified died innocent; second, many Englishmen used *innocent* as a synonym for *children* in a context quite divorced from theology.

13 Edmund S. Morgan, *Puritan Family* (New York, 1966), pp. 177–82.

14 Min. London YM, 8 (4/1/1737): 316–18; Barclay, *Apology*, prop. 10, pg. v, 171; *JFHS* 51 (1967): 143–53; Richard Vann, *Social Development of English Quakerism* (Cambridge, Mass., 1969), pp. 45, 131–40. Charles Carter and Richard Vann have shown that the 1737 poor-relief policy of London Yearly Meeting marked no new departure in membership. What is still unclear is the origin of Quaker membership practices. Vann argues that early Friends did not define membership because, in the spiritual church, membership was invisible and Friends did not believe that they could judge inward states. Disownment was not excommunication but showing the world that the person had never been a member. This interpretation is incorrect. Friends always claimed that God gave them the power to discern inward states; conduct might be used as a test of spiritual estates because true belief and right action could not be divorced. A member could fall from grace at any time; when he became sinful he disowned himself, and the meeting's actions only confirmed this. Since in the meeting the visible and invisible churches were united, there was no theological principle against knowing membership.

15 *JFHS* 10 (1913): 73.

16 John Banks, *A Journal... With a Collection of his Epistles* (London, 1712), pp. 247–51; John Hands, *A Seasonable Epistle to Believing Parents, and their Children* (1705), p. 5: Philadelphia MM, Original Certificates, 1689–1713, no. 85, 6/6/1709; Min. Rhode Island MM, 2/26/1720, p. 175.

17 London Yearly Meeting began debating the problem of charity in 1710; in 1730 New England Yearly Meeting rejected following London's pattern because charity was not a problem. By 1755 South Kingston and Nantucket meetings defined membership; Core Sound in North Carolina defined membership in 1782 and the Yearly Meeting followed suit in 1790. Min. Core Sound MM, 2/13/1782; Min. North Carolina YM, 10/25/1790, p. 260; Min. New England YM, 4/11/1730, p. 4; Arthur Worrall, "New England Quakerism 1656–1830," (Ph.D. diss., Indiana University, 1969), p. 61; Min. London YM, 4: 137, 142–44, 298; 7: 64–65; 8: 317–18, 527; 9: 48; 13: 523–24: Min. Philadelphia YM, 2: 156, 166, 169, 171, 198, 213, 232.

18 John Moon, *Observations and Quotations on obtaining Church-Membership by Natural Birth and Education* (Stockton, England, 1809); idem, *A Second Address to the People called Quakers* (Stokesley, England, 1815); Joseph Phipps, *To the Youth of Norwich Meeting* (1775), p. 8; New England Yearly Meeting, *The Books of Discipline Agreed on by the Yearly Meeting of Friends for New England* (Providence, 1785), pp. 14, 21; New York Yearly Meeting, *Rules of Discipline and Christian Advices* (New York, 1800), pp. 65–66; Maryland Yearly Meeting, *Discipline of the Yearly Meeting of Friends* (Baltimore, 1806), pp. 21–23; Anthony Benezet to Samuel Allinson, 10/23/1774, Allinson Papers.

19 Thomas Chalkley, *Works* (London, 1791), p. 571.

20 The next two pages are based upon Robert V. Wells, "A Demographic Analysis of Some Middle Colonies Quaker Families of the Eighteenth Century" (Ph.D. diss., Princeton University, 1969), 46, 48–49, 57–58, 101–106, 114–121, 129, 131, 137–140, 141–142. Wells published his findings in "Family Size and Fertility Control in Eighteenth Century America: A Study of Quaker History," *Population Studies*, 26 (1971), 73–82; idem, "Demographic Change and the Life Cycle of American Families," *Journal of Interdisciplinary History*, 11 (1971): 273–282; *idem.*, "Quaker Marriage Patterns in a Colonial Perspective," *William and Mary Quarterly*, 39 (1972), 415–442. A few of the many recent books and articles on demography are John Demos, *A Little Commonwealth: Family Life in Plymouth Colony* (New York, 1970), and "Families in Colonial Bristol, Rhode Island: An Exercise in Historical Demography," *William and Mary Quarterly* 25 (1968): 40–57; Kenneth Lockridge, "The Population of Dedham, Massachusetts, 1636–1736," *Economic History Review* 19 (1966): 318–44, and *A New England Town: The First Hundred Years* (New York, 1970); Philip Greven, Jr., *Four Generations: Population, Land, and Family in Colonial Andover, Massachusetts* (Ithaca, New York, 1970), and "Historical Demography and Colonial America: A Review Article," *William and Mary Quarterly* 24 (1967): 438–54; Robert Higgs and H. Louis Stettler III, "Colonial New England Demography: A Sampling Approach," *William and Mary Quarterly* 27 (1970): 282–94; D. V. Glass and D. E. C. Eversley, eds., *Population in History: Essays in Historical Demography* (London, 1965).

21 Jacob Taylor, *An Almanack and Ephemeris . . . for 1745* (Philadelphia, 1744). Wells' conclusions about variations in birth rate can be compared with Greven's findings on Andover. In Andover the birth rate, the age of marriage, and

the death rate among different generations showed marked changes. While the death rate in the seventeenth century was extraordinarily low, the eighteenth century witnessed a rise in infant mortality to a rate comparable to that of the Quakers. *Four Generations,* pp. 24–27, 105–11, 185–93.

22 Cecil Drinker, *Not So Long Ago* (New York, 1937), pp. 48–50, 55, 144.

23 James Logan to William Logan 10/26/1726, Logan Letter Book, 3: 69,HSP; M. Bell to Israel Pemberton, 6/3/1768, PP, 20: 45, HSP.

24 Chalkley, *Works,* p. 571.

25 William Edmondson, *An Epistle Containing Wholesome Advice and Councel to all Friends* (1701), pp. 12–13; Sophia Hume, *An Exhortation to the Inhabitants of the Province of South Carolina* (Bristol, 1751), pp. 89–90; Priscilla Wakefield, *Reflections on the Present Condition of the Female Sex* (London, 1798), pp. 16–17.

26 Mary Pemberton to James Pemberton, 10/12/1748, PP, 4: 178; Sarah Buckley to William Buckley, 8/7/1774, Morris-Sansom Mss, QC; Drinker, *Not So Long Ago,* pp. 63–64; *Letters of Doctor Richard Hill and his Children* (Philadelphia, 1854), pp. 174–75.

27 William Dillwyn to Susanna Dillwyn 9/22/1784, 11/27/1790; Susanna Dillwyn to William Dillwyn 10/31/1789, Dillwyn Mss, vol. 1, HSP. John Kelsall, "Diary Extracts," 2: 108; John Reynell to Edward Day, 11/16/1757, Letter Book 1756–59, HSP; Elizabeth Drinker, "Diary," HSP.

28 *JFHS* 11 (1919): 169; Richard Hill to his daughters, 2/20/1760, Howland Mss, QC.

29 James Logan to James Greenshields, 11/2/1725, Logan Letter Book, 3: 51; James Logan to William Logan 5/26/1731, Letter Book, 4: 295–96, HSP. Albert Cook Myers, ed. *Hannah Logan's Courtship* (Philadelphia, 1904), 2/7/1750, p. 283.

30 Mark Van Doren, ed., *Samuel Sewall's Diary* (New York, 1927), pp. 30, 61–62, 110, 129–31. Sewall mentioned his children on christening days, or if they were very ill, or if some part of their behavior gave rise to religious reflections. Peter Laslett noted the same lack of sources about young children in Stuart England. See Laslett, *The World We Have Lost* (London, 1965), p. 104.

31 Erik Erikson, *Childhood and Society,* 2d ed. (New York, 1963), pp. 247-74. The first three stages are Oral-Sensory (Basic Trust vs. Mistrust), Muscular-Anal (Autonomy vs. Shame Doubt), Locomotor-Genital (Initiative vs. Guilt). Erikson related psychoanalytic thinking to historical biography in *Young Man Luther* (New York, 1958). David Hunt, *Parents and Children in History* (New York, 1970) attempted to relate the categories to child rearing in late sixteenth-century France. John Demos, *A Little Commonwealth,* pp. 134–39, quite tentatively applied the Erikson stages to Plymouth children and in "Developmental Perspectives on the History of Childhood" *Journal of Interdisciplinary History,* 11 (1971), 315–27, suggested that conflict and aggression in Puritan New England resulted from patterns of child rearing.

32 Chalkley, *Works,* pp. 571–80.

33 London YM, *Epistles From the Yearly Meeting,* (1723), p. 149.

34 John Crook, *The Design of Christianity* (London, 1701), pp. 336–39.

35 London YM *Epistles from the Yearly Meeting* (1706), pp. 103–04.

36 Perry Miller, *Errand into the Wilderness* (Cambridge, Mass., 1956), p. 3.

37 "The welfare and Interest of our Society in the next Generation in a Great Measure depends on the godly Care of Parents over their Children now in Being." Philadelphia YM, Christian and Brotherly Advices (1746), p. 149.

38 Bernard Bailyn, *Education in the Forming of American Society* (Chapel Hill, N.C., 1960), pp. 21–29.

39 London YM, *Epistles from the Yearly Meeting,* (1747), p. 228.

40 Ibid., pp. 228, 98; Smith, "Universal Love." p. 75.

41 John Freame, *Scripture Instruction* (London, 1713), p. xii.

42 London YM, Christian and Brotherly Advices (1731), p. 48; idem, *Epistles from the Yearly Meeting* (1688), p. 38, and (1731), p. 171; Penn, *Works,* 1: 826; Min. Philadelphia YM, 1 (7/16-19/1694): 41; John Griffith, *Some Brief Remarks* (London, 1764) p. 9.

43 Banks, *Journal* (1712), p. 348; Freame, *Scripture Instruction,* pp. xv-xvi.

44 Benjamin Cooke, *Miscellanies* (London, 1712), p. 2.

45 Banks, *Journal,* pp. 350–51; William Thompson, *The Care of Parents, is a Happiness to Children* (London, 1710), p. 7.

46 John Woolman, *Journal and Essays,* (New York, 1922) p. 153.

47 Banks, *Journal,* p. 343; Penn, *Works,* 1: 901.

48 Hume, *An Exhortation,* p. 93; Humphrey Smith, *To all Parents of Children upon the Earth* (London, 1660), p. 11.

49 Thomas Clarkson, *Portraiture of Quakerism,* (London, 1806) 1: 34.

50 London YM, *Epistles from the Yearly Meeting* (1758), p. 269; Woolman, *Journal and Essays,* pp. 341–43.

51 Clarkson, *Portraiture of Quakerism,* 1: 166; Thompson, *The Care of Parents,* p. 10.

52 London YM, Christian and Brotherly Advices (1731), p. 48; (1717), pp. 45–46; Elizabeth Jacobs, *An Epistle in True Love* (London, 1789), pp. 8–9; Freame, *Scripture Instruction,* p. xviii; Banks, *Journal,* pp. 130–31; Mary Leadbeater, *Memoirs and Letters of Richard and Elizabeth Shackleton* (London, 1822), vol. 1; John Gratton, *A Journal of the Life of . . . John Gratton* (London, 1720), p. 125; Morgan, *Puritan Family,* pp. 102–05, 137–38; Samuel Fothergill, *The Prayer of Agur* (Newport, 1773), p. 27.

53 George Harrison, *Some Remarks Relative to the Present State of Education* (London, 1802), p. 17; Elizabeth Drinker, "Diary," 6/30/1772; William Dillwyn to Susanna Dillwyn, 4/27/1793, Dillwyn Mss, vol. 1; John Kelsall, "Diary," vol. 1; David Hall, *Memoirs* (London, 1758), pp. 69–70.

54 Min. Philadelphia MM, 1: 198, 230; 2: 37, 69, 71; 3: 118–19, 360; 4: 73, 114; John Cresson, "Diary." 1 (4/5/1795); "Last Words of George Harris," Smith Mss, 1: 168, LC.

55 Min. Philadelphia MM, 11/31/1700, p. 187; 7/22/1697, p. 64; Min. Rhode Island MM, 11/31/1709, p. 38; 12/29/1710, p. 58; Overseers of Penn Charter School, Minutes, 1 (11/25/1755): 136, 296; London YM, Christian and Brotherly Advices (1696), p. 186; W. J. Allinson, comp., *Memorials of Rebecca Jones* (Philadelphia, 1849), p. 26.

56 Harrison, *Some Remarks,* pp. 17–18; Job Scott, *Journal* (New York, 1797), pp. 88–89.

57 Chalkley, *Works,* pp. 3–4.

58 William Rawes, Jr., *Examples for Youth in Remarkable Instances of Early Piety* (London, 1797), pp. 8, 15; *A Brief Account Of the Innocent Example and Pious Sayings of Rebeckah Toovey* (London, 1715), p. 11; *Brief Memorials of the Virtuous Lives and Dying Sayings of Several of the People called Quakers* (London, 1781), pp. 18–19.

59 Chalkley, *Works,* pp. 270–72; *A Legacy for Children, Being Some of the Last Expressions, and Dying sayings of Hannah Hill, Junr.* (Philadelphia, 1717), pp. 31–32.

60 Kelsall, "Diary," 1 (ca. 1710): 63; Banks, *Journal* p. 342; Freame, *Scripture Instruction,* Preface; Wilson, *Discourse,* p. 5.

61 Philadelphia YM, Christian and Brotherly Advices (1729), p. 27; London YM, *Epistles from the Yearly Meeting* (1733), p. 196; *JFHS* 26 (1929): 4.

62 Anthony Benezet, *Pennsylvania Speller,* p. 16; William Caton, *An Abridgment of Eusebius Pamphilius's Ecclesiastical History* (London, 1698), p. 14: Chalkley, *Works,* p. 574.

63 Clarkson, *Portraiture of Quakerism,* 1: 14.

64 Coole, *Miscellanies,* p. 16; Phineas Pemberton to James Pemberton 12/29/1777, and Sally Pemberton to James Pemberton, 1/7/1778, Exile Mss, DR.

65 John Reynell to Mary Groth, Letter Book 1756–59; John Reynell to Elias Bland, 10/4/1743, and 10/26/1746, Letter Books 1741–44, 1745–47; Smith Mss, 6: 151, 166; James Pemberton to Israel Pemberton, 11/10/1748; pp. 5; 43; Theodore Thayer, *Israel Pemberton, King of the Quakers* (Philadelphia, 1943), p. 27: Mary Leadbeater, *Annals of Ballitore,* (London, 1862) 1: 75.

66 Esther Robinson to Mary Robinson, 9/12/1792, Richardson Mss., NHS; Dillwyn Mss, 1: 33, 48, 52, 74, 82, 87, 110, 136, 195; Smith Mss, 5: 59; 6: 130, 136, 260; 7: 134; PP, 7: 77; 20: 88; Elizabeth Drinker, *Diary Extracts,* p. 144; Deborah Logan to Isaac Norris, 8/28/1785, Maria Dickinson Logan Family Papers, HSP; Mary Norris to Debby Logan, 12/16/1795, Norris of Fairhill Mss, 2: 81, HSP; Rachel Preston to Mary Dickinson, 3/14/1704, Norris of Fairhill Mss, 2: 9: John Watson, *Annals of Philadelphia* (Philadelphia, 1830), p. 240: Woolman, *Journal and Essays,* p. 152.

67 *A Seasonable Account of the Christian and Dying-Words, of Some Young Men* (Philadelphia, 1700), p. 13: Min. Philadelphia MM, 1 (9/27/1702, 2/30/1703); Philadelphia YM, Christian and Brotherly Advices (1714), p. 24; Overseers of Penn Charter School, Minutes, 2 (9/21/1775): 47.

68 Penn, *Works,* 1: 851; William Dover, *Reasons for Erecting an Additional Number of Schools* (London, 1752), pp. 3–4; William Dillwyn to Susanna Dillwyn, 11/27/1788, Dillwyn Mss, 1: 78; William Massey, *Instructions for a Boarding School,* (n.d.); Gough, *Memoirs,* p. 5.

69 Alice Morse Earle, *Home Life in Colonial Days,* chapters 8 and 9; John Watson, *Annals of Philadelphia* (Philadelphia, 1857), 2:421.

70 Robert Barclay, *A Catechism and Confession of Faith* (Philadelphia, 1726), p. 1. This edition was ninety-nine pages long.

71 George Fox, *Instructions for Right Spelling* (Philadelphia, 1702), pp. 38–57; Freame, *Scripture Instruction,* pp. iv-v.

72 Freame, *Scripture Instruction,* pp. 38–45.

73 Rachel Wilson, *A Discourse, Delivered on Saturday the 10th Day of August 1769* (New York, 1769), pp. 5-7; Anthony Purvery, *Counsel to Friends Children,* 1st ed., 1737 (London, 1801), p. 2.

74 *Early Christian Instruction in the Form of a Dialogue between a Mother and Child* (London, 1807), pp. 5–6.

75 Charlotte Rees, *Parental Instruction in Familiar Dialogues* (Bristol, 1811), pp. 1–20, 36, 41; John Wigham, *Christian Instruction in a Discourse as between a Mother and her Daughter* (London, 1815). The latter treatise was reprinted in Philadelphia many times.

76 Sarah Buckley to William Buckley, 3/18/1774, Morris-Sansom Mss, QC.

77 Ann Wood to Martha Allinson, 7/21/1782; Samuel Allinson to Martha Allinson, n.d., Allinson Mss, QC; John Smith to William Dillwyn, 2/11/1770, Howland Mss, QC. David Allinson was born in 1774.

78 Deborah Logan to Isaac Norris, 8 mo./1784, Maria Dickinson Logan Family Letters, HSP; Israel Pemberton to Mary Pemberton, 12/26/1777; Mary Pemberton to Israel Pemberton, 1/15/1778, 1/29/1778; Rachel Pemberton to James Pemberton, 1/28/1778; Sally Pemberton to James Pemberton, 11/7/1778, Exile Mss, DR; PP 22: 1.

79 William Dillwyn to Susanna Dillwyn, 6/23/1783, 2/8/1785, 8/23/1783, 8/23/1788, and Susanna Dillwyn to William Dillwyn, 2/12/1783, 11/4/1785, 4/29/1787, 11/27/1788, Dillwyn Mss, vol. 1, HSP.

80 William Dillwyn to Susanna Dillwyn 7/17/1785, 10/28/1786, 1/3/1786, 2/3/1787, Dillwyn Mss, vol. 1.

81 William Dillwyn to Susanna Dillwyn 10/28/1787, 8/10/1791, 3/29/ 1790, 8/2/1783, 1/25/1786, 2/18/1790, and Susanna Dillwyn to William Dillwyn 9/4/1786, Dillwyn Mss, vol. 1.

82 E. K. Waterhouse, *Reynolds* (London, 1941); idem, *Gainsborough* (London, 1958); idem, *Painting in Britain, 1530–1790* (Baltimore, 1962); C. H. Collins Baker, *English Painting of the Sixteenth and Seventeenth Centuries* (New York, 1930); Walter Gibby, *George Morland, His Life and Works* (London, 1907).

83 William Wordsworth, "Ode: Intimation of Immortality from Recollections of Early Childhood," in *Major British Writers,* ed. G. B. Harrison *et al* (New York, 1954), II, 243.

84 Michael Walzer, *The Revolution of the Saints* (Cambridge, Mass., 1965), pp. 183–98; Christopher Hill, *Society and Puritanism in Pre-Revolutionary England* (London, 1966), pp. 433–81.

5 "A Guarded, Religious, and Useful Education"*

Quaker concern with primary education dated from the early years of the Society. In 1667 Fox recommended starting a school for boys at Waltham and a school at Shacklewell "for instructing girls and young maidens in whatsoever things were civil and useful in the creation." Fox wrote a primer in conjunction with Elias Hookes, and a number of other Friends wrote Latin and Greek textbooks. L. John Stroud has determined that from 1669 to 1691 Friends established at least 46 schools in England.[1] Since refusal to take an oath constituted a crime in Restoration England, and since Quaker schoolmasters refused or were unable to obtain licenses to teach from the bishops, the early schools were more or less fly-by-night affairs, and the authorities often closed them.

With the establishment of toleration by James II in 1687 and by Parliament in 1689, Friends enjoyed a relatively peaceful period and could devote more energy to founding and maintaining schools. Around 1687 the tone of epistles sent out by London Yearly Meeting changed drastically. Friends had earlier been exhorted to hold fast to the faith under the storm of persecution; the whole emphasis was upon endurance. Now, in a period of liberty, the advices stressed the maintenance of fervor and the difficulties of raising a younger generation in the faith. London Yearly Meeting began issuing epistles in 1675, but until 1688 it made no mention of either children or schools. After this 13-year delay, a discussion of education was included in fifty-one of the next 71 epistles.[2] When toleration forced Friends to consider how small a minority they were, their response was to emphasize the roles of the family and the school in the Christianizing of their children.

The advice contained in London's epistles of 1688 and 1690 was duplicated in various forms throughout the eighteenth century. In 1688 the meeting asked parents to be good examples "in the educating [of] your children and servants in modesty, sobriety, and in the fear of God." Education was not the province of schools alone; Friends used the word to refer to the proper rearing of children. In its 1690 advice London Yearly Meeting specifically mentioned attendance at school and told members to provide "faithful Friends" as teachers rather than to send pupils to the schools of outsiders where they would learn "the corrupt ways, manners, Fashions and Language of the World and of the Heathen in their authors and names of heathenish gods & goddesses." Meeting again admonished parents to train their children in the "nurture and admonition and fear of the Lord," to require the plain style of clothing and language, and to be good examples.[3]

*Moses Brown, Clerk. *From the Meeting for Sufferings in New England, 1782*

The effort to establish and maintain educational institutions was a local responsibility, but yearly meeting took an active interest. Meetings first reported their progress to London in 1695; in 1697 monthly and quarterly meetings began to inspect all schools in their bounds, and by 1700 queries on education were read and answered at every yearly meeting. These questions did not specifically mention schools, so local meetings could interpret "education" as involving only religious upbringing or as implying the need to provide schools.[4]

The Quakers did not found schools because they blindly followed the traditional idea that learning was the province of the church. Since they wanted their children to be able to read, write, and cypher, Friends had the choice of founding their own schools or of sending their children to Anglican or Puritan schools. They thought that their distinctive religious beliefs involving dress, speech, and silence could not survive in institutions controlled by others, and their stress on education at the end of the seventeenth century coincided with their growing emphasis upon their own peculiar customs. Throughout the eighteenth century the epistles of London Yearly Meeting advocated educating children in the faith in order to preserve the heritage of the founders and enable youth to gain the skills necessary to survive in the world. It was felt that young people could only be preserved in the faith through control of the environment. Isolation from vice was part of Puritan and Anglican theories of child nurture, too, but Quakers, because of their minority position, placed far more stress upon it. A boy was supposed to associate and play with other Quakers, attend only Quaker meetings, go to a Quaker school, be taught by a Quaker teacher—all in order to protect him against the profane and secular world. Anthony Benezet believed that it was "while the inclinations are yet flexible, that the mostly lasting impressions are likely to be made," and that a spirit of true devotion once instilled would eventually prevail in spite of the passions of youth and the allurements of the world.[5] Friends fervently believed in Proverbs 22:6: "Train up a Child in the way he should go, and when he is Old he will not depart from it." The child was malleable and should be shaped into a Christian pattern. Since all children had within them a principle of goodness, the duty of the school was to establish a disciplined life so that saintliness would become a habit. Friends wanted the school to serve all of life, in this case a life of work and religion. Their attitude was summarized by Penn, who wrote to his children that "Education is the Stamp Parents give their Children."[6]

Since Quaker education was not directed toward preparing boys for college and thus the study of Latin and Greek was not seen as the end-all of learning, the Friends were very free in their criticisms of traditional schools. While there is no definite proof that early Friends were influenced by Johann Comenius, John Locke, or dissenters in England, the criticisms that Quakers made of older teaching methods were very similar to those made by other educational reformers.[7] William Penn in *Reflections and Maxims,* a tract read in many schools in America during the colonial period, defined the trouble with English practices: "We are in Pain to make them Scholars, but not *Men*! to Talk, rather than to know." When the child went to school, he was burdened with "Words and Rules: to know *Grammar* and *Rhetorick,* and a strange Tongue or two," while his "natural Genius to *Mechanical* and *Physical* or natural Knowledge" was ignored. Penn did not condemn the study of Latin, but he wanted classical learning combined with the study of useful knowledge. "Children had rather be making Tools and Instruments of Play; *Shaping, Drawing, Framing* and *Building,* &c. than getting some Rules of Propriety of Speech by Heart: And those also would follow with more Judgment, and less Trouble and Time."

Penn did not draw the present-day distinction between secular and religious education; rather, he stressed that a knowledge of creation should lead to a fuller appreciation of the Creator. An ideal textbook would introduce "Mechanicks" in Latin, instruct gardeners and farmers in the "Reason of their Calling," and show the learned man "Rules that govern" the artisan's "Workmanship." For the Quaker, as well as for the Puritan, natural learning could not contradict revelation. One studied the world not only because the knowledge was practical but also because the earth wore the "mark of its Maker."[8]

In 1685 Thomas Budd wrote a clear expression of Quaker ideas about educational reform entitled *Good Order Established in Pennsylvania and New Jersey in America.* The pamphlet recommended the following: that the legislature found schools that would be supported by a grant of 1,000 acres of land each and that the produce within them be grown by the pupils; that the poor (and the Indians) receive free training in a curriculum consisting of an amalgam of practical and traditional subjects. All were to learn to "Read and Write true English, Latin, and other useful Speeches and Languages, and fair Writing, Arithmetic." While the boys received instruction in bookkeeping and a trade such "as the making of *Mathematical Instruments, Joynery, Turnery,* and making of *Clocks* and *Watches, Weaving, Shoemaking,*" the girls would learn "*Spinning of Flax* and *Wool,* and *Knitting* of *Gloves* and *Stockings, Sewing* and making all sorts of useful *Needle-work,* and the making of *Straw-Work* as *Hats, Baskets,* etc."

Budd recommended that the school run for eight hours each day; that there be two hours of formal instruction in both the morning and afternoon and two more hours in each session for practice or work in the trade or art that the person "most delighteth in." Lunch, a leisurely occasion of two hours, might provide time for recreation as well as for eating. The pamphlet suggested that the scholars study for six days per week; on Sunday a special meeting of masters and students would take place, at which time teachers would examine the conduct of pupils.[9]

Although Budd's proposals were never implemented, his concern for useful training was recognized, and Quakers studied far more practical subjects than did schoolboys in non-Quaker grammar schools in New England or England. But Quaker boys learned a trade from their fathers or through a system of apprenticeships rather than in school.

When Friends founded their "Holy Experiment" in Pennsylvania, both the charter and the laws made provisions for schools. In the 1682 frame of government, the provincial council and the governor had the power to "erect and order all public schools." One committee of the council was to supervise "manners, education, and arts" in order to suppress vice and ensure that youths were trained in "virtue and useful knowledge and arts." The 1683 charter reenacted these provisions. In the laws agreed upon in Pennsylvania in 1683, the colonists ordered that all parents, guardians, or trustees of children "shall cause such to be instructed in Reading and writing; So that they may be able to read the Scriptures; and to write by the time they attain to twelve years of age;" at 12 they were to be taught some "useful trade or skill." The law provided for a penalty of £5 for neglecting to comply with these directions; this was an extraordinarily severe penalty, since for profane swearing the fine was only 5s.[10] The early court records of Bucks and Chester counties showed that no men were prosecuted for violating this statute. In 1683 the provincial council hired Enoch Flower to teach an elementary curriculum of reading, writing, and cyphering, and it set the fees for his school. The council also discussed the need for a more advanced educational institution but took no action.[11] In 1689 Philadelphia Monthly Meeting founded a Latin school, now known as the William Penn Charter School, under a charter granted by the proprietor in 1687. William Penn later yielded to pressure from influential Philadelphia Quakers and donated land for the school and granted two new charters.

The state's positive role in education in Pennsylvania ended before 1700, and the charter that Penn issued in 1701 contained no mention of any state responsibility for education. Penn was in debt, and the proprietary government had no money to spend for schools. The growing religious diversity in Pennsylvania made the Quakers realize that state supervision of schools should be kept to a bare minimum. If the government controlled the schools, what would happen to Quaker schools if the crown revoked Penn's charter or if Penn surrendered the government? Safety lay in establishing schools under the supervision of the meeting, as was the case in all other American colonies. Unlike the New England Puritans, Quakers in America were not compelled by law to start or support institutions of learning.

Since London Yearly Meeting sent epistles throughout the colonies until long after the American Revolution, Quakers in the New World kept abreast of English ideals of education. Similar goals were evident in the disciplines and minutes of American yearly and monthly meetings. Pennsylvania and New Jersey Yearly Meeting wrote, in the 1704 discipline, that anyone who did not educate children in the way of truth or endeavor to bring them up to read and write was to be admonished by overseers. New England Yearly Meeting's first formal discipline (1708) told Friends to be sure that Quaker masters taught their children. If none were available, the parents should teach the children at home. The meetings demanded rather low minimum standards of knowledge throughout the colonial period. Philadelphia Yearly Meeting, which encompassed the best and the largest number of schools, required only training in reading and writing. If the parents could afford more, the child should receive some practice in arithmetic and the keeping of accounts.[12]

II

Before the impact of Quaker theories about the necessity and functions of schools can be assessed, it is necessary to show what percentage of Quaker children attended school. Between 1920 and 1936 Professor Thomas Woody and several of his students wrote a series of monographs about Quaker educational practices in North Carolina, Virginia, Maryland, New England, Pennsylvania, and New Jersey. This material clearly demonstrates that the density of the Quaker population and the area in which they lived determined to a large extent the opportunities for schooling. William Dunlap's conclusion about schools in southern Virginia summarized most of the findings about the South. "The author has found but little evidence that these meetings were able to establish schools under the direction of the meeting." Zora Klain discovered that in North Carolina the records revealed "no mention of educational activities of any kind" until the first decade of the eighteenth century. After 1715, meetings became interested in schools, but not until after 1750 was there much emphasis upon learning—and the main concern did not come until the nineteenth century.[13] In New England the Puritan regard for formal education did not influence Quaker neighbors in Massachusetts or Rhode Island. Rhode Island Monthly Meeting, which included Newport and Portsmouth, founded an elementary school, but whether it operated steadily throughout the century is uncertain. In 1780, when New England Yearly Meeting took a comprehensive survey, it found no schools directly under the care of monthly meetings and only one standing committee on education. Friends in New England studied at dame schools, which were not under the meetings' control, or in private homes.[14]

Only in the area encompassed by Pennsylvania and New Jersey Yearly Meeting was there a widespread effort to provide instruction for children. The only attendance records for Quaker schools came from the system established under Penn's charter in Philadelphia, and even here, since the accountings were not systematic, the historian has a difficult time. In petitioning for an enlargement of the charter in 1759, the overseers claimed that "there have been constantly upwards of two hundred Children instructed therein and in some other Houses in different Parts of this City." The pupils were not all Friends, and charity was administered to children of any religious denomination. In 1765 the overseers recorded 127 poor scholars: 72 Friends, 33 Anglicans, 5 Baptists, 1 Moravian, 8 Presbyterians, 8 Roman Catholics (probably Acadians). Instruction in all schools was heavily influenced by Quaker teachings, and a non-Friend had to take the chance that his child would be converted. In 1767 the overseers decided that, owing to a shortage of funds, the policy would henceforth be to take poor Friends first and then others if places remained. In 1779 a survey of Quaker education in Philadelphia disclosed that there were 184 pupils in four schools. Friends supervised five other schools for which no figures were provided.[15]

Children in Philadelphia probably mastered at least the contents of a primer and many were exposed to much more material. Since the overseers visited the schools once a month to scrutinize the teachers and quiz the students to find out how much they were learning, the standards were fairly high. Any Friend who wanted an education could receive one, and for poor children the overseers provided complete support (books, ink, tuition, etc.). Statistics on education outside the city are little more than guesses. Thomas Woody in his study of Quaker education in Pennsylvania estimated that by 1741 there were at least 6,000–7,000 school-age children of Quaker parentage. At that date there were no more than 40 schools under Quaker control. If all the children attended school, there would have been an average of nearly 180 pupils in each school. With the exception of the Penn Charter school system, Quaker schools rarely had a student body of 60. Woody concluded, therefore, that "it is apparent that the schools *regularly* established were in no way adequate to [service] the school population."[16]

An absence of facilities for education did not mean that Quakers in these areas were illiterate, however. Bernard Bailyn has called attention to the amount of learning that took place in the home in colonial America. Sometimes this was by choice and sometimes by necessity. If there was a choice between sending the child to a Presbyterian school or keeping him at home, meetings said to keep him at home. Expense may have been a factor in certain cases, but there are instances where prosperous Friends tutored children at home rather than send them to school. William Penn told his wife to employ tutors because schools exposed children to too many evils.[17] James Logan wanted to teach his son William (as he did his daughters), but his wife persuaded him that the boy's slowness and his own impatience would not mix. Since Philadelphia schools were ruled out because of the licentiousness of the town, William went to England. When John Smith removed his son from the Latin school, Robert Proud, the master, acquiesced, noting that the care of a father was worth far more than that of a teacher. Susanna Dillwyn started to attend school but her health was delicate, and so her uncle taught her at home.[18] The father's abilities, the health of the child, the location of the school, and the character of the master were all factors to consider. Since teachers at dame schools had no formal training, and since most primary education was rote memorization, children could be taught just as well, and more cheaply, at home.

There were more schools in England than in America during the seventeenth and eighteenth centuries but not nearly enough for all Quaker children; yet historians have commented upon the absence of illiteracy among Friends. Dorothy Hubbard found that, even in the first period of Quakerism, there were almost no marks (in lieu of signatures) and that even the letters written by servants "show considerable ease in writings and expression." The record was good in the Midlands and East Anglia and even better in the Northwest. John Stroud believed that "almost without exception, every Quaker of the second and succeeding generations could read and write." Thomas Clarkson noted that poor Friends had more school learning than other English children of comparable situations.[19]

If these estimates are accurate, Friends had a far better educational record than the English population as a whole. In Gloucestershire in the 1660s all men had to sign their names when applying for marriage licenses; about one-quarter could. In Surrey in 1642 two-thirds of the males over 18 found it necessary to make marks on a protestation of loyalty to Parliament. The Hardwicke Marriage Act of 1753 required bride and groom to sign a register. In East Yorkshire only two-thirds of the men and one-half of the ladies could sign. Lawrence Stone estimated that the average male literacy rate in 1640 was 30 percent; by the middle of the eighteenth century it had risen to 53 percent. Signatures imply little more than bare literacy. The inventories attached to the wills of propertied people before 1700 suggest "that something like one in ten propertied persons possessed books."[20]

One can attempt to determine the amount of Quaker literacy in America by examining signatures on marriage documents. Since a person learned to read before he began to write in schools of that time, signatures should result in a lower percentage than a test for reading ability alone.[21] Of 89 original marriage certificates dated between 1680 and 1801 at Friends' Historical Library, only 6 contained marks. The law required at least 12 witnesses and oftentimes more than 50 would sign a document. However, only bride and groom had to sign the certificates; illiterate attenders might not. Thus, in order to determine the rate of literacy I counted only the newlyweds.

The lowest percentage of illiteracy occurred in New England. Of 720 signatures from Salem, Pembroke, Greenwich, and Rhode Island meetings between 1676 and 1780, there were 27 X's (only one male) leading to a rate of not quite 4 percent. Cecil Monthly Meeting in Maryland had 27 percent illiteracy between 1689 and 1710 but from 1710 to 1780 only 2 percent. In North Carolina, Rich Square, and Cane Creek meetings, whose marriage certificates begin in 1760 and 1746, the illiteracy rates were 3 and 10 percent, respectively. Symons Creek Monthly Meeting, whose records began in 1680, had 35 percent female and 11 percent male X's; of the males who could not sign their names 82 percent married before 1740, while 50 percent of the illiterate women did so.[22]

The greatest variability in time occurred in the middle colonies. Three of the oldest meetings—Burlington, Haddonfield, and Philadelphia—exhibited an initial good record, then a drop, and finally a recovery to virtually universal literacy. Burlington, for example, in 33 certificates between 1680 and 1689, had no marks; yet between 1700 and 1709 it had 19 percent illiteracy and 16 percent in the following decades. Philadelphia went from zero before 1690 to 21 percent before 1700; by 1710 the percentage dropped to 3 and there were only four female X's out of a total of 595 marriages between 1710 and 1779. Before 1700 Haddonfield had 12 percent, from 1700 to 1709 22 percent, from 1710 to 1719 40 percent. Falls Monthly Meeting's certificates begin in 1700, and the highest percentage (25) occurred during the first decade.[23] By 1730 illiteracy had waned everywhere in Pennsylvania and New Jersey, and by the Revolution, X's were as rare in the middle colonies as in New England. These results suggest that part of the price of migration to America was a large drop in literacy for the first generation raised in this country. New England Friends showed little variation in rate of illiteracy because their settlements were established long before Quaker records began. As settlements matured, illiteracy decreased either because schools were established or because someone in the family or neighborhood had time to teach.

Since these figures for literacy rest upon the unproven assumption that signatures can be correlated with reading ability, the favorable results need to be evaluated in the light of other observations about learning. Stephen Grellet, a traveling minister who visited the South in 1800, recorded that in both Carolinas and Tennessee the education of the young was generally neglected, with the result that few children or parents could read. Moses Brown complained that Friends in New England were an "Illiterate and I may Justly Say an Ignorant Set of People Compared with others." Only about five or six in the entire yearly meeting were acquainted with any language except English and "many Cannot Write Even their Names."[24]

Frederick Tolles has described the large libraries of such Philadelphia

Quakers as Isaac Norris II, John Smith, James Logan, and Dr. Lloyd Zackery. Some merchants received and read English newspapers like the *Spectator*. James Logan, who read widely in the classics and compiled one of the best libraries in early America, was very interested in the controversies over deism and carried on a wide correspondence on scientific matters. Tolles described John Smith of Burlingon as a "literary Quaker" because he had read widely and could quote from books as varied as *Paradise Lost* and *Tom Jones*.[25] Philadelphia also had Quaker merchants like John Reynell who, after reading a treatise by the English deist Thomas Chubb, commented that the author appeared to be "one of the Worst sort of free thinkers" whose book was intended "for no good but mischief." In order to prevent such ideas from contaminating Pennsylvania, Reynell threw the book into the flames and suggested that if Chubb did not repent, he also would eventually end in the fire. The estate of Israel Pemberton, Sr. was appraised at over £9,000 but his library was worth £5.[26] The necessity for Philadelphia Monthly Meeting to send to London for schoolmasters for the Latin school throughout the colonial period shows how thin the veneer of learning was. In 1760, when no Englishman was available, the Latin school was suspended briefly. Except for the Presbyterian Charles Thomson who taught from 1757 to 1760, all masters of the Latin school were imports. And Pastorius' primer, issued in 1698, was the only textbook written by an American Friend before 1774. John Churchman, a country Friend and later an esteemed minister, went to school for three months and was instructed by a weaver who sat at his loom as John recited his lessons. General John Lacey characterized his Quaker father as having an average education for a country farmer, since he "wrote a tolerable plain hand, understood Common arithmetic and kept his own accounts."[27] Outside Philadelphia, this was undoubtedly the extent of intellectual attainment for most Friends.

III

After the first decade of the eighteenth century, Quakers seemed gradually to lose interest in schools. There were few pamphlets about education, records of monthly meetings rarely mentioned schools, and overseers seem not to have visited classrooms. Quarterly meetings in England answered the queries of London Yearly Meeting with stock phrases showing little thought. Around the middle of the century however, Friends on both sides of the Atlantic became more concerned about their schools. Historians have listed several causes for this. First, the meetings discovered that parents were not setting good examples or providing Quaker schoolmasters. Second, Quakers became involved in the educational competition among denominations that resulted from the schools founded after the Great Awakening. Third, Friends realized the implications of birthright membership; that is, since membership was hereditary, Quakers needed a system of schools to train their children in religion.[28] All of these reasons are partially true but none of them really offers a wholly satisfactory explanation. For example, the lack of Quaker schoolmasters was seen as early as 1700. Why did London Yearly Meeting not take steps until 1760, and Philadelphia until 1778, to solve this problem? The Great Awakening caused an interest in denominational schools, but not for reasons that Friends approved. The traditional hostility to a trained clergy and theological institutions would not compel any emulation of New Light efforts. Birthright membership, practiced long before 1700, was rarely commented on before the nineteenth century.

A more reasonable explanation for the revival of interest in education is that the general tightening of discipline in both England and America after 1755, which led to more scrutiny on other matters of conduct, also prompted Friends to inquire whether their advices on education had been implemented. Late eighteenth-century society generally was more concerned about education. In England the great response to the schools of Joseph Lancaster, a Friend, and the beginnings of the Sunday school movement show this trend. For America the evidence is less conclusive, partially because of uneven documentation, vast area, and a variety of educational institutions. Robert Middlekauff has determined that in New England in the period following the Revolution, a great number of private academies were founded. Yet these schools rose as older tax-supported grammar schools declined. Daniel Boorstin and Bernard Bailyn found in the colonial mentality a thirst for education as a means of attainment. Lawrence Cremin claimed that "there is every indication that the number of schools and the extent of schooling increased more rapidly than the increase in population."[29]

After the late seventeenth century the first real sign of interest in formal education came in a 1752 pamphlet by the English Quaker William Dover. Dover thought that Friends generally neglected education, and he proposed that several Quaker boarding schools be established.[30] The meetings ignored Dover's proposals. In 1760 London Meeting for Sufferings called for an accounting of the number of schools under Friends' influence. They found, to their dismay, that in many counties in England there were no Quaker-controlled schools and that, in spite of a few excellent boarding schools run by Friends, pupils generally could not obtain advanced training in any Quaker educational institution. The difficulty in founding and maintaining schools resulted from the small number of Friends in many areas and the slender pay provided for masters. London recommended that several counties cooperate to found and support schools, and that a new institution be started in London to provide specialized training of a more advanced caliber. Answers to the queries in 1761 announced either that no progress had been made or that the whole project was impractical.[31] If the advanced school in London was ever established, it did not last long.

The minor revival that took place in America antedated the English concern by a few years. In January 1749 the overseers of Penn Charter School decided to visit all Quaker schools in Philadelphia at least four times a year in order to see whether the scholars were progressing, the rates were adequate, and more rules were necessary.[32] With adequate supervision, able teachers, and good financing both from subscriptions and investments, the Philadelphia schools provided the best system of Quaker education anywhere. After its own house was in order, Philadelphia Quarterly Meeting took the initiative in attempting to persuade the yearly meeting to end the neglect of educational institutions. In 1750, Philadelphia Yearly Meeting proposed that every monthly meeting should have a school and pay a teacher. In those areas that did not already have schools, the almost universal reaction was that "by reason of the distance they live from one another" such an undertaking would be impossible.[33]

During the middle of the Revolution, at the time when British troops occupied Philadelphia, the Yearly Meeting appointed a committee to study the problems of education. A committee report, signed by Anthony Benezet and Isaac Zane, was submitted in 1778 and approved. It noted that, in spite of frequent recommendations on schools, "very little has been effectually done therein." The key problem was to obtain and support teachers, and the committee recommended that meetings provide subscriptions to finance schools and also to furnish houses and some land for the masters. During the next year a delegation from the Yearly Meeting visited all quarterly gatherings and had conferences on the subject of education.[34] The committee's report was also circulated to other yearly meetings in America. The implementation of schooling was still seen as a local responsibility; the central body merely admonished the local groups.

In England in 1779 a much more revolutionary program was taking place under the leadership of Dr. John Fothergill. A group of wealthy London Friends bought, without official sanction, a recently abandoned foundling hospital to convert it into a school for the children of poor Quakers. (There was no shortage of Quaker grammar schools for the children of the wealthy.) London Yearly Meeting later approved the purchase and assumed the financing and supervision of the school. Ackworth School, as it was named, opened in 1779 and survives to this day. Although designed specifically for the poor, many middle- and a few upper-class Friends sent their children. Past experience—notably the 1760 proposals—had shown that monthly and quarterly meetings could not support enough schools. Thus, Ackworth was financed and attended by Friends from all over England. Within two years it had a total enrollment of 309 boys and girls and a staff of 41. The school was so popular that by 1783 the age for admission was raised, and there was a waiting list of 40.[35]

Propaganda for Ackworth circulated freely in America, and attempts at imitation occurred from New England to Virginia. Since Ackworth was the culmination of eighteenth-century Friends' thinking about education, the rationale behind the system is of some significance. The school was established to provide a "pious, guarded, useful education of the children of Friends not in affluence."[36] The discussion of other Friends' schools show that this "guarded" education was crucial. Friends' workhouse and school at Clerkenwell in London had failed to inculcate godliness, because the boys and girls had occasionally been allowed to roam the streets or to go home and witness bad examples on the part of parents; the elderly poor who also lived at Clerkenwell were not monuments of rectitude for the children to pattern themselves after either. Ackworth School offered complete control of the environment. All masters, housekeepers, domestic staff, and students were Friends. No vacations were allowed, and parents who visited were not permitted to take students off the premises.[37] The school itself was to be a "family." Although scholars had often boarded with masters and been treated as members of their households, the idea of creating an institution that attempted to duplicate a family was new. All students were to be treated equally, regardless of rank. The original plans called for all to dress identically in order to discourage social distinctions and encourage students to think of themselves as members of the family. Later, requirements changed and students dressed in garments provided by their parents. Each pupil received an equal allowance and was allowed to write home four times a year. Family terminology permeated the school's entire set of rules. The treasurer (later named superintendent) and the "Mistress of the Family" were to ensure that the "Family rise" early, assemble in an orderly fashion at meals, and go to bed at proper times. The children kept silence before and after meals; while eating they could whisper only when necessary "for transferring their victuals." Supervision was rigorous; the student was never out of sight of his masters or monitors.[38]

The curriculum was very circumscribed, perhaps because the school was established for children of the poor. All students learned English grammar, writing, and arithmetic. In order to prepare the girls to be housewives, they were instructed in needlework and helped with ironing, mending, and occasionally cooking. There was little purely vocational training for boys, although they did help with the farms and were encouraged to have their own gardens. After completing schooling, boys became apprentices. The students were allowed time to exercise, because mixing "Learning and labour" resulted in a "sound mind and a healthy body." The school was coeducational, but any intermingling between boys and girls was frowned upon. In short, sound discipline, religious instruction, and academic training combined

> to promote a tender, teachable disposition, inuring them to bear that yoke in their youth, which will moderate their desires, and make way for the softening influences of divine good-will in their hearts, fitting them for the faithful discharge of every duty in life.[39]

The literature about Ackworth and the report by Anthony Benezet and Isaac Zane reached America's yearly meetings at about the same time. Moses Brown noted that the external impetus coincided in New England Yearly Meeting with a proposal for a school sent up from a quarterly meeting. Under Brown's tutelage, New England Yearly Meeting investigated its educational institutions, and in 1783 it founded a boarding school at Portsmouth. Although this failed, a later institution now named Moses Brown school has survived.[40] In 1792 Wilmington, Delaware, which already had a school, adopted Philadelphia's recommendation to establish a subscription to educate the children of poor Friends. In 1796 New York Yearly Meeting founded a boarding school named Nine Partners near Poughkeepsie. In 1778 Warrington and Fairfax Quarterly Meetings in Virginia set up a committee on education and founded a school in 1799. In 1801 came the establishment of the Southern Boarding School within the bounds of Duck Creek Meeting in Virginia. Baltimore Yearly Meeting founded a boarding school at Fair Hill in 1815.[41]

The strength of the English influence can be shown by examining the early history of Westtown School in Pennsylvania. Individual members of Philadelphia Yearly Meeting had founded boarding schools in 1761 and 1780, and although both had failed, a small group of reformers continued to agitate for a new academy. Ackworth's success showed that sponsorship by a yearly meeting could ensure adequate attendance and financial support. In 1790 Owen Biddle published a plan for a boarding school modeled on Ackworth that would provide vocational and academic training in a family-like atmosphere.[42] Philadelphia Monthly Meeting took up the project in 1791, and eventually the yearly meeting appointed a committee. A series of bequests plus the donations of Quakers living in Philadelphia, some of which were given as an impetus for the yearly meeting to act, provided the means to purchase 600 acres of land, erect buildings, and open the school in 1797. It was an immediate success.[43]

Like Ackworth, Westtown offered an opportunity for total control of the environment. Because of their belief that pupils in city schools could not be insulated from evil influences, Friends deliberately picked a secluded site in the country. The committee of men and women that drew up the regulations possessed a copy of the Ackworth rules, and several Friends involved in the planning and supervision of Westtown had visited Ackworth. Westtown was to be a "family" living in "harmony and love" whose teachers would instruct in both religious and literary endeavors. Tutors ate and slept in the same rooms with the students, and writing masters examined every letter sent home. There were no vacations, and visits home, which at first were allowed every six months, were soon forbidden. Westtown was not far from Philadelphia and parents and religious visitors were welcomed, but children were not allowed to leave the premises. While there was no uniform dress, any garment deemed insufficiently plain was altered at the parents' expense. Letters of parents, descriptions by visitors, and a journal kept by Rebecca Budd, a teacher, show how the child was enveloped in a religious atmosphere.[44]

Westtown attracted rich and poor, and the early curriculum offered a wide range of subjects including Latin, French, English grammar, bookkeeping, mathematics, geography, astronomy, reading, and writing. Girls who so desired could learn to sew and knit, and many samplers still decorate walls of the school. Students followed a strict schedule and kept silent at meals but were allowed "sufficient time to unbend our minds from Study: and exercise enough to keep us in health."[45] Girls had no organized games and could not wander through the woods at will, but boys, who enjoyed both these privileges, gardened, built wigwams in the woods, and constructed an outdoor schoolroom. The masters' "Black Book," which listed offenses such as talking in meeting or putting pepper on a neighbor's food, showed that punishments, such as copying a page in the dictionary or confinement to the yard, were rather mild. When James Harper lost the right to play ball, he muttered "that he will forget how. Asked if he came to Weston to learn to play ball: Ans. Yes."[46] The school was coeducational, but conversation between sexes was confined to that between brother and sister—and then only in the presence of the tutors.

IV

From the 1670s until after the American Revolution, Friends wanted schools to provide two types of instruction: practical learning and religious indoctrination. Children needed to learn to read, write, and cypher in order to study the Bible, manage a farm, or become shopkeepers and merchants. If his learning came in an institution dominated by Anglicans or Puritans, the child might become contaminated by heathen beliefs and practices. Whether in the home or classroom, Quakers expected education to be religiously oriented. The child went to school to become a better Quaker.

In America the quantity and density of Quaker settlements in any area determined the amount of meeting schools. The large numbers of Friends in Pennsylvania and New Jersey meant that schools were established in most towns, but in the South and in New England, Quakers were widely dispersed and there were few institutions of learning. No colony had enough schools to educate all the Quaker children. However, the statistics compiled from marriage certificates show that most Friends in all regions were literate enough to sign their names. With the shortage of schools, many children probably learned to read and write in the home.

In an effort to improve the quality and quantity of Quaker education after 1750, London and Philadelphia Yearly Meetings tried a variety of schemes. Those that depended upon the activities of local meetings were not satisfactory. Success came when London Yearly Meeting founded, supported, and supervised the Ackworth School for poor children. Ackworth provided the seclusion from sinful ways and the practical instruction so prized by Quakers. Since frequent visits from outsiders were discouraged, the school became a substitute for parents and was thought of as a "family." In a series of boarding schools established in the late eighteenth century, American Friends put into practice the family idea of education with corresponding control of the environment and supervision by the yearly meeting.

The boarding schools eased the problems of supporting schools in districts where there were few members. The ideology behind the school was a response to the declining power of the Quaker traditions of the plain style of dress and speech. After 1755, when the monthly meetings severely tightened discipline and expelled members for a huge variety of offenses, the number of disownments began to jeopardize the survival of the sect. Creating a new generation of the devout could not be done in an open society where the distinctive testimonies appeared as oddities rather than marks of divine favor. Children had to be removed from the profane world in order to grow into adult Friends who would hold fast to the faith. If a family living in an increasingly secularized society could not instill truth, then an artificial family at school could substitute.

Notes

1 George Fox, *Journal* (New York, 1763), p. 461; L. John Stroud, "The History of Quaker Education in England" (Master's thesis, University of Leeds, 1944), p. 169.

2 These calculations are based upon the collection of epistles of London Yearly Meeting printed under the title *Epistles from the Yearly Meeting* (London, 1760).

3 Min. London YM, 1 (3/4–6/1688): 182–83; London YM, *Epistles from the Yearly Meeting* (1690) pp. 47–48.

4 London YM, Christian and Brotherly Advices, pp. 269–74; Dorothy Hubbard "Early Quaker Education" (Master's thesis, University of London, 1940), pp. 72–73.

5 Anthony Benezet, *The Pennsylvania Speller* (Philadelphia, 1779), pp. 5–6.

6 William Penn, *Works,* (London, 1726), 1: 901.

7 Frederick Tolles, *Meeting House and Counting House,* (New York, 1963) p. 207; Janice L. Gorn, "John Locke's Educational Theory and Some Evidences thereof in Pennsylvania" (Ph.D. diss., New York University, 1963), pp. 380, 398–401.

8 William Penn, *Works,* 1: 820–21.

9 Thomas Budd, *Good Order Established*

in Pennsilvania and New Jersey in America (Philadelphia, 1685), p. 4.

10 Staughton George, Benjamin Nead, and Thomas McGamant, eds., *Charter to William Penn, And Laws of the Province of Pennsylvania, Passed between the Years 1682 and 1700 . . .* (Harrisburg, Penn., 1879), pp. 95–96, 142, 238.

11 James Wickersham, *A History of Education in Pennsylvania* (Lancaster, Pa., 1886), pp. 40–41. Wickersham thought that the statute on literacy was enforced because of the prosecution of a master by an apprentice for neglecting education. While this case could have come under the law, it might also have arisen from the contract of indenture. Provincial Council of Pennsylvania, Minutes, 1683–1700, in *Colonial Records of Pennsylvania* (Philadelphia, 1838), 10/26/1683, 11/17/1683; 1: 36, 38.

12 Philadelphia YM, Discipline of 1704; Christian and Brotherly Advices (1722), p. 251 and (1746), p. 180; New England YM, Discipline 1708–38, p. 8.

13 William Dunlap, *Quaker Education in Baltimore and Virginia Yearly Meeting* (Philadelphia, 1936), p. 168; Zora Klain, *Quaker Contributions to Education in North Carolina* (Philadelphia, 1926), pp. 327–28.

14 Min. Rhode Island MM, 2 (7/27/1727): 249; 3 (6/29/1749): 75; (5/28/1771); 350; (6/25/1771: 350; (4/7/1772): 367. In 1771 when Clarke Rodman desired to keep a school in the schoolhouse, the meeting had to empty the building of people who lived there. Moses Brown, Clerk, *From the Meetings for Suffering in New England* (Providence, 1782), p. 3. William Redwood to John Pemberton, 3/5/1770, PP 21:118

15 Overseers of Penn Charter School, Minutes, 1 (10/17/1754): 185, and (8/29/1765): 291–92; 2 (7/9/1779): 97–98. Included in the 1779 survey were dame schools, schools for girls only, coeducational schools, and two that permitted non-Quakers to attend.

16 Thomas Woody, *Early Quaker Education in Pennsylvania* (New York, 1920), p. 271.

17 Bernard Bailyn, *Education in the Forming of American Society* (Chapel Hill, North Carolina, 1960) pp. 14, 26; Min. New England YM, pp. 44, 97; William Penn, *A Letter from William Penn to his Wife and Children* (London, 1761), p. 7.

18 James Logan to Alexander Arscott, Letter Book, 4 (10/14/1730); James Logan to William Logan, 3/22/1731, pp. 252–53; James Logan to William Logan, 1/3/1732/3, pp. 315–318; Robert Proud to John Smith, Smith MSS, 6: 16; William Dillwyn to Susanna Dillwyn, Dillwyn MSS, 1 (7/9/1786): 42; (2/15/1786): 42.

19 Dorothy G. B. Hubbard, "Early Quaker Education," pp. 10–11; L. John Stroud, "History of Quaker Education in England," p. 34; Thomas Clarkson, *Portraiture of Quakerism,* (London, 1807), 3: 230.

20 Peter Laslett, *The World We Have Lost,* p. 196; Lawrence Stone, "Literacy and Education in England 1640–1900," (London, 1965), *Past and Present,* no. 42 (1969): 101, 108, 109, 110.

21 J. W. Adamson, "The Extent of Literacy in the Fifteenth and Sixteenth Centuries," *The Library,* 4th ser. 10 (1930): 163–64, 193. This distinction may hold more value for England than America. As soon as pupils learned to read in a dame school in America, they began to attempt to write. Undoubtedly, some who could write nothing else could sign their names. See also Lawrence Cromin, *American Education* (New York, 1970), pp. 544–51.

22 The books of marriage certificates for Pembroke, Greenwich, and Salem meetings belonging to New England YM are temporarily housed at the John Carter Brown Library; Rhode Island MM marriage records are at the Newport Historical Society; Core Sound and Symons Creek records are at Guilford College; microfilm copies of Cecil and Rich Square MM marriage certificates are at Friends' Historical Library.

23 Microfilm copies of the marriage records of Falls, Burlington, Philadelphia, and Haddonfield meetings are at Friends' Historical Library.

24 Stephen Grellet quoted in Klain, *Quaker Education in North Carolina,* p. 57; Moses Brown to Anthony Benezet, 10/2/1780, George S. Brookes, *Friend Anthony Benezet,* (Philadelphia, 1937), p. 434.

25 Tolles, *Meeting House and Counting House,* pp. 161–204; *PMHB* 65: (1941): 300–333.

26 John Reynell to Elias Bland, 12/28/1746/7, Letter Book 1745–47; Tolles, *Meeting House and Counting House,* p. 201.

27 John Churchman, "Journal," ed. William Evans and Thomas Evans, *Friends' Library* (Philadelphia, 1842), 4: 178; *PMHB* 25 (1901): 3.

28 Sydney James, *A People Among Peoples* (Cambridge, Mass., 1963) pp. 70–71.

29 Laslett, *The World We Have Lost,* pp. 197–98; Stone, "Literacy and Education in England, 1640–1900," pp. 92, 113–15; Robert Middlekauff, *Ancients and Axioms: Secondary Education in Eighteenth-Century New England* (New Haven, 1963), chapters 9–10; Daniel J. Boorstin, *The Americans: The Colonial Experience* (New York, 1964), pp. 277–90; Bailyn, *Education in the Forming of American*

Society, pp. 21–22, 26–27, 32–36; Cremin, *American Education*, p. 500. Cremin's evidence came from a variety of sources, including newspaper advertisements, circulation of newspapers, literacy statistics, and the number of colleges.

30 William Dover, *Reasons for Erecting an Additional Number of Schools* (London, 1752), pp. 11–18, 30–31.

31 Min. of London Meeting for Sufferings, 6/20/1760, pp. 440–451; Min. of London YM, 12 (5 mo./1761): 163–99, 224–25.

32 Overseers of Penn Charter School, Minutes, 1 (11/25/1749): 77–78. When Philadelphia Yearly Meeting adopted queries in 1743 and revised them in 1755, it included education for the poor. But the main emphasis in these questions was on rearing children in the "fear of the Lord" and in "Plainness of Speech and Apparel."

33 Min. Philadelphia YM, 2 (7/15–19/1750): 18, (7/14–18/1751):22, and (9/15–19/1753): 37.

34 Philadelphia YM, Christian and Brotherly Advices, 1778, pp. 182–83; Minutes, 2 (9/26–10/5/1778): 410, and (9/29/1779): 435.

35 General Reports of Ackworth School, vol. 1, folio J. 1780–1820. Friends' Reference Library, London. Elfrida Vipont, *Ackworth School* (London, 1959), is an undocumented but readable history of the school.

36 John Fothergill, *A Letter to a Friend in the Country, Relative to the Intended School, at Ackworth* (London, 1779), p. 35; the phrase was also used by Moses Brown.

37 *Rules for the Government of Ackworth School* (London, 1790), p. 17; Thomas Pumphrey, *History of Ackworth School* (Ackworth, 1853), p. 42; John Fothergill quoted in Owen Biddle, *A Plan for a School on an Establishment similar to that at Ackworth* (Philadelphia, 1790), pp. 22–23; "Instructions to Agents and Others," General Reports, 1782, vol. 1, folio J; Fothergill, *A Letter to a Friend in the Country*, p. 62.

38 *Rules for the Government of Ackworth School* (London, 1795), p. 14, 16–17; Sarah Grubb, "Appendix Containing an Account of Ackworth School," in *Some Account of the Life and Religious Labours of Sarah Grubb* (Dublin, 1792), pp. 257–58, 262–67; F. M. J. Pinn, "Parental Views on Education with Special Reference to Ackworth School," (thesis for Teachers' Certificate, University of London, 1953), pp. 34, 59.

39 Sarah Grubb, "Appendix," pp. 258–60, in Fothergill, *A Letter to a Friend*, pp. 13–14, 57, 63; Min. London YM, 6/13/1778, reprinted in a broadside. Criticisms of the limited curriculum and suggestions that more subjects be taught so that bright boys could be trained as teachers came very early. John Morton, *A Letter to a Friend, Concerning the School at Ackworth* (London, 1782), p. 27.

40 Brown, *From the Meeting for Sufferings in New England*, p. 7. Rayner W. Kelsey, *Centennial History of Moses Brown School 1819–1919* (Providence, 1919). The school founded by Friends in New Bedford in 1810 did not conform to the Ackworth ideology. James, *A People Among Peoples*, p. 277

41 Dunlap, *Quaker Education in Baltimore and Virginia Yearly Meeting*, pp. 100, 105, 265–59, 312–13, 536.

42 Helen Hole, *Westown Through the Years* (Westtown, Penn., 1943), pp. 12–14; Biddle, *A Plan for a School*. Biddle quoted lengthy excerpts from Fothergill's description of Ackworth. Biddle desired a school organized like a family with groups of students living in small cottages under the supervision of a couple who did not serve as schoolteachers.

43 Jonathan Evans, Clerk, "At a Meeting of the Boarding School Committee, held the 24th of the Ninth Month, 1796," p. 2

44 "Rules and Regulations For the Government of Friends School at West-Town," p. 5; John Cox, Jr., Letter, 9/23/1799; Jonathan Evans to William, Joseph, and Mary Evans, 1779–1800, copies in Box 2, Westtown Archives; Rebecca Budd, "Diary," Chester County Historical Society; Watson and Sarah Dewess, *History of Westtown Boarding School* (Philadelphia, 1899), pp. 28, 74, 78; Owen Biddle, Memorandum, 1790, Westtown Archives.

45 M. Yarnall to William Darlington 5/7/1800, Box 2, Westtown Archives; Dewess, *History of Westtown*, pp. 66–67.

46 "Westonian Kabbies' Report alias Black List." Dewess, *History of Westtown*, p. 68.

6 Quaker School Life

Any reconstruction of the pattern of eighteenth-century Quaker education must stress the role of teachers, since meetings were often exhorted to obtain morally and intellectually qualified men. In theory, Friends had a very high conception of the importance of teachers. Next to preaching the gospel, the opportunity to prevent evil and instill virtue in youth was seen as "the greatest and most acceptable sacrifice and service we can offer to the great Father." John Woolman emphasized the importance of entrusting children of tender age to those fit to set an example for them. David Hall believed that no "truly conscientious" master would teach pupils arithmetic or reading without also instructing them in the "first principles" of religion. Next to the home, school provided the best opportunity to mould lives. A master was told to make the school a "Place of *Delight* and *Recreation*" rather than a "House of Correction." To do so he must be "Discreet and Prudent" and guard against disciplining for trifles or when he was not in complete control of himself. Being a teacher was no easy task

> Schoolmasters should be grave and meek, but authoritative; patient in hearing and acute in instructing; prudent in reasoning and laborious in convincing of Errors; reluctant to correct, and then with Lenity . . . diligently inspecting the Tempers, Capacities and Memories of their Pupils, and adapting Conduct that may best improve the first, Instruction that may be easiest imbibed by the second, and longest retained by the third.[1]

Perhaps this idealistic conception of a teacher cherished by masters such as Benezet, Woolman, and Hall was not entirely shared by laymen.

The New England Puritan system of education maintained high standards because the instructors were, like John Adams, men who had studied at Harvard or Yale and were deciding on professions. Those few who did not choose a merchant's, minister's, or lawyer's career sometimes became teachers. The problem of financing education was solved by public taxation, and Massachusetts towns spent a large proportion of their budgets on school systems.[2] The Quaker situation was somewhat different, however. A shortage of teachers plagued Quaker education in England and America throughout the eighteenth century. Friends had no former college students to staff their schools. Quakers were barred from English universities, and one can easily imagine that Friends would not have felt very comfortable at eighteenth-century Yale. Since the salaries were not high enough to attract men anxious for material rewards, teachers tended to be either men of outstanding religious convictions, who saw teaching as a Christian service, or transients who taught for a while until something better came along.

The overseers of Penn Charter School sent boys to both English and Latin schools in order to qualify them as teachers; although the persons who became masters were usually intelligent, they were often poor, lame, or frail and not able to work at hard physical labor. Israel Pemberton, Jr., contributed the cost of a year's instruction to John Kirk, who had rheumatism. Although Kirk did become a teacher, he married out of unity with Friends and thus was lost to the community. London Yearly Meeting recommended that local meetings assist young men "of Low Circumstances whose Genius and Conduct may be suitable for that Office" to gain the intellectual qualifications for school teaching.[3]

A major deterrent to setting up a strong educational system was the parsimony of Friends. In 1719 James Logan wrote Thomas Makin, who had once taught mathematics in Penn Charter School, advising him not to return to Pennsylvania because there were no prospects for a schoolmaster there. In 1778 Anthony Benezet inquired into methods of recruiting teachers. Four years earlier, he had advised a young English Quaker against coming to America to be a master. If a teacher were lucky enough to find rural Quakers who would pay him an adequate salary, he still might find himself dismissed as soon as the neighborhood children attained a bare minimum of education. In 1774 Joseph Clark, a young and qualified English schoolmaster, could not find employment as a teacher around Philadelphia and lived in the Friends' alms house.[4]

Even if the country schoolmaster were successful in attracting pupils, other problems presented themselves. John Woolman complained that instructors had difficulties in supporting their families unless they accepted so many pupils that they could not "fully attend to the Spirit and disposition of each Individual as would be profitable to the children."[5] Moreover, the time required to manage the outward affairs of the institution forced the master to neglect his students.

In the rural areas the tutors were often young men who boarded from house to house. In 1745 London Yearly Meeting suggested that those Friends who had teachers living with them "accustom them to a solemn reading of Holy Scriptures" and "to the observation of the christian precepts therein contained." Benjamin Ferris complained that before the Revolution well-to-do Quakers in Delaware hired, as private tutors, itinerants who might be lacking in ethics or, who if sufficiently moral, knew very little. Both Ferris and Benezet charged that in country schools anybody could be hired if his remunerative demands were low enough—even if he could barely, read, write, and cypher. Some teachers, hired for a three-month term, spent most of their days sleeping off the effects of the previous night's drinking. The Philadelphia Yearly Meeting's report on education strongly condemned the boarding system and the hiring of transients, contending that the persons obtained were of no stability and little principle, knew nothing about education, and stopped teaching whenever a more profitable occupation appeared. The committee advised monthly meetings to purchase a plot of ground for the teacher. This plot should be "sufficient for a garden, orchard grass for a cow etc. and a house, stable, etc. [to] be erected thereon."[6] The meetings were told to guarantee the master an annual minimum salary. Only by giving a man financial security could Quakers hope to attract someone with a family who might become a permanent teacher.

Because of the shortage of school records (the only complete ones available are for Penn Charter School), it is difficult to determine the scholarly attainments of the teachers. The Latin schoolmasters, like Francis Pastorious, George Keith, and Robert Proud, were very well-educated. Prominent teachers of the English or elementary schools, like Anthony Benezet and John Woolman, were not highly trained, but reconstruction of their libraries has shown that they were extraordinarily well read.[7] Since the books available to Quaker schoolmasters would have been those distributed by London or Philadelphia Yearly Meeting, the teachers must have been well versed in the history and doctrines of Friends. Many monthly meetings collected tracts and these served as a school library. Thomas Woody compiled a list of the volumes most frequently mentioned in the records of seventeen monthly meetings and Philadelphia Yearly Meeting. He listed nine journals, eight treatises (such as *Anarchy of the Ranters* and *No Cross, No Crown*), three histories of the Society of Friends, three collections of epistles, one catechism, and one treatise on slavery. In 1769, when Joseph Pemberton retired from teaching English school in Philadelphia, the overseers made a list of volumes belonging to the school; this gives us an idea of the curriculum and the school equipment.

Buckhams Universal Penman
7 Bibles
3 History of England
3 Roman History
2 Barclay's Apology
6 Collection of Tracts
6 Miscellanies
Seneca's Morals
Wilson's Surveying
Potter's Mathematics
a Theodolite and Chain
an Instrument to prick Copy Books
4 Doz. copperplate copies and 6 copper plate pieces set in frames[8]

One can gain some appreciation of what was expected of rural teachers from letters written to or about them. When John Hunt sent over a potential master from England, he stressed that the man qualified in all respects, but that his handwriting might be improved. Benezet told a young teacher that his letters were "as well expressed as could be expected," but that he ought to avoid always beginning and ending letters with the same phrases. Benezet advised him to purchase a dictionary, study spelling, and endeavor to attain "some further insight into grammar; it is of more consequence to thee than thou art aware of."[9] Some country-school teachers probably knew little more than their students. General John Lacey, born in 1755 to Quaker parents, described his teacher as not able to "read or write correctly, as he knew nothing of Grammar, it was not to be expected he could teach it to others." Grammar was not taught in his school nor in any of the schools he was acquainted with. A Bible and a primer were the only books country Friends would permit. The Quaker parents of Jonathan Roberts (born 1773) hired a Roman Catholic teacher who was learned but too short-tempered to teach in a country school. Roberts's next master required the pupils to memorize the rules of English grammar, since he himself could not explain them. Nathanael

Greene complained that country Quakers in Rhode Island allowed only Fox, Barclay, and a few tracts to be read in school, and the resulting education was so narrow that it bred "Ignorance and Superstition instead of piety."[10]

II

The qualifications of the teacher varied and were tailored in part to the kind of education that Friends desired. Most schools outside Philadelphia provided instruction in the three R's and not much else. Friends' schools in Newport, Rhode Island, and Wilmington, Delaware, had no Latin in their curriculum until after the Revolutionary War. In Philadelphia there were at least four types of education. The dame schools taught the alphabet, spelling, and reading. Girls also learned to sew and make samplers. The more advanced girls' school, of the kind that Benezet established and at which Rebecca Jones later taught, included instruction in penmanship, French, and, if the mathematics copy book owned by Miss Jones is an adequate index, some advanced arithmetic.[11]

Any boy whose education went beyond reading and whose station in life ranked below the so-called upper class attended English school. Here he received not only a broad but also a practical education. First he mastered reading, penmanship, and spelling. He was then introduced to the complexities of English grammar to an extent (if the textbooks were mastered) far beyond that of most Americans in high school today. Besides elementary arithmetic, the student learned a smattering of algebra and geometry and had rigorous training in figuring interest rates and converting currencies. A sample problem might require the student to figure the price of a mixture of three types of grain when each was of a different cost and amount. The theodolite, an instrument to measure angles, was used to teach surveying. Geography (at least the use of globes) was included in the curriculum. When Anthony Benezet submitted an application to teach in an English school in 1742, he listed his qualifications:

> Reading and writing. I think I could teach every hand in writing except, the Italian. I apprehend that care and a good method in the writing master with a tolerable hand will answer the end.
>
> Arithmetic in all its chief branches, which besides the Small rules is Single and double rule of three, Fractions, Vulgar and decimals, practice, fellowships, Alligation, Position, exchange, and extraction of the Square, and cube roots, which rules comprehends what is commonly called Arithmetic, the next step is Algebra.
>
> Merchants Accounts
>
> The French language
>
> The German language I would undertake to teach, so far, as that, the learner might read, and perfectly understand the Bible, and talk it so as to be enabled to buy, sell and talk of common things, but I would not undertake to teach any one, the whole variations of the nouns and irregular verbs.
>
> I would also be careful to teach the Children to Spell, and indite.
>
> I have also some knowledge in measuration viz. in measuring timber, bridgework, Land, and gaging but I would not engage to teach any thing but what I seem assured I can bring to perfection.[12]

Although in theory Friends valued practical training above a classical education, the most esteemed masters were found in the Latin school. A succession of highly qualified teachers taught students a curriculum corresponding to those of the dissenting academies of England and the grammar schools of New England. Not everyone was expected to attend Latin school. The fees for the English school were £2, for the Latin school £5. In a catalogue of Latin school students compiled in 1754 the names Logan, Biddle, Pemberton, Paschall, Meredith, Morris, and Lloyd appeared. The families described by Frederick Tolles as "Quaker Grandees" sent their sons to this Latin school, and since the overseers tended to be wealthy Friends, the school received far more attention and money than its numbers warranted. A few free scholars also attended the Latin school; these boys had shown unusual genius in other schools or were slated to become teachers. Nicholas Waln, a free student in 1754, later became a lawyer and an esteemed Quaker minister. That Quakers valued the Latin over the English school is shown in the salaries paid the masters. Anthony Benezet earned £50 from the overseers for teaching 15 poor students in 1760; the Latin teacher received £150. In 1761 when the overseers hired Robert Proud, they paid him £200, and his usher received £80.[13] This high wage was partly the result of an attempt to obtain a British teacher. In 1770 the overseers described the kind of person they wanted as someone who would be prepared to teach Latin and Greek, arithmetic, the "most useful parts of mathematics," geography, and the use of globes and who would be able to prepare the students for business by instructing them in accounting and good writing. The master "should be a friend both in principle and practice, and if possible to be had of an easy agreeable disposition fit to have the care and education of youth."[14]

The Latin school was only one division of Penn Charter School, and it generally enrolled less than 40 pupils.[15] The child of a New England Puritan was far more likely to receive a classical education than the child of a Quaker.

III

A discussion of the textbooks used in Friends' schools indicates what was normally taught. The first primers employed in America were written by George Fox (first English edition in 1673 and first American printing in 1702) and Francis Daniel Pastorius (1698). Both books were notable in that they made little attempt to clarify the contents for the beginning child or to arouse interest in the materials. After listing the ABC's, Fox's first word list, organized in alphabetical order, started with such words as "abolished, abomination, absence." After seven pages of similar words (which a five- or six-year-old was expected to learn by rote), the student came to the first reading lesson. "CHRIST is the *Truth. Christ* is the *Light. Christ* is my *way. Christ* is my *life. Christ* is my *Saviour. Christ* is my hope of *Glory.*"[16] Having presented four pages of doctrine, Fox introduced the students to Bible stories—again with no attempt to simplify the vocabulary. Pastorius first presented the ABC's, then listed words in a more logical order of from one to seven syllables—compressed into three pages—and followed with seven pages of rules of pronunciation and capitalization. The student then learned the names of the books of the Bible (some of them in Hebrew). The first reading lesson set forth a doctrine, such as "Being by Nature Children of Wrath, even as others," and this was followed by a scriptural citation that the student was to find in the Bible and read. After a page of doctrine, Pastorius listed 80 sins, beginning with "Adultery" and ending with "Youthful Lusts."[17] If the masters explained the meaning of "Concupiscence," "Extortion," and "Fornication," it must have been a memorable lesson. The tables of contents of these two early primers followed no logical sequence and the emphasis was on memorization of lists of words, rules, and biblical subjects.

Stephen Crisp's *New Book for Children to Learn in* (1681) was also used in both England and America. The primer began, much like those of Fox and Pastorius, with the alphabet and lists of words to be memorized. The first reading lessons introduced both easy and complex words and the only simplification made for beginners was that difficult or multisyllabic words were divided. "A wise Child pre-ser-veth himself from Cor-re-cti-on by O-be-di-ence; but a Foo-lish Child pro-cur-reth Stripes by his re-bel-li-on." After 10 pages of similar exhortations, the pupils read a 38-page epistle from George Fox. The only way one would know that Fox meant this for the young was that "Little Children" appeared in the title and frequent addresses were made to "children." In all other respects, the document was an adult theological tract containing the doctrine of God, Christ and the Trinity, the Light, fall, sin, and so forth. Fox's tract was followed by two sermons by Crisp; these, too, made no allowance for children who at this point were just learning to read.[18] William Thompson's *The Child's Guide to the English Tongue* (1711) contained similar lists of words and rules to be learned. The reading lessons in the book were short and printed first with the complex words divided and then repeated in normal fashion.[19] Again, there was almost no gradation to help the child progress from simple to difficult words.

Inventories of American Quaker schools listed the primers of Crisp and Fox all during the eighteenth century. Fox's was the most popular. After its first London edition in 1674, Christopher Taylor two years later translated all except the very beginning into Latin under the title *Institutiones Pietatis.* Barbadians used the primer in either the English or the Latin edition in 1686 and required students to memorize and recite portions of the catechism and proverbs. Friends reprinted the English edition in Philadelphia in 1702 and 1737 (of this edition of 2,000, 1,000 were sent to New England), Newport in 1769, and Boston in 1743. North Carolina schools used the Boston edition. Philadelphia Yearly Meeting authorized the publication of Pastorius' textbook in 1698 in an edition of at least 200 copies, which were distributed to the individual monthly meetings. Although the records of meeting libraries rarely mentioned this primer, one suspects that Pastorius used his own book until he stopped teaching about 1718.[20] None of these early school books was issued in the quantity required for mass consumption. Perhaps only the teachers had copies and the pupils had to be content with hornbooks. A primary purpose of the primers was to introduce students to the reading of Scriptures, and the volumes mainly emphasized memorization of long tables and rules. Teachers taught reading by familiarizing the students with sounds, such as "ba, be, bi, bo, bu," then introducing tables of words, and finally reading passages worthy of adult minds.

The increasing concern that Quakers felt for children after 1760, seen in personal letters, catechisms, and the revival of schooling, can also be found in the textbooks. The change here was not as much in the conception of childhood as in an increasing mastery of the technique of teaching. This change was not pioneered by nor peculiar to Friends; rather, Quakers adopted practices used in other primers. Thomas Dilworth's *New Guide to the English Tongue,* written by a non-Friend, was used in Quaker schools in the late eighteenth century, although perhaps the book's set prayers were omitted in editions used by Friends. After listing the alphabet in correct order, Dilworth scrambled the letters to make sure that the students could identify each.[21] He simplified the manner of learning to read also; the pupils still recited the total possibilities of sound and then learned long lists, but the gradualism in word length made the vocabulary easier to master. For example, the first section contained one syllable words of two letters; the next list was of one syllable words with three letters, many of which rhymed: "bib fib nib rib." Later, the student was introduced to pages of difficult words, and to the sections on grammar, which contained many rules, were presented in catechistical fashion, and had to be memorized.

> Q. *What is a Noun* Substantive? A. It is the Name of any Being or Thing, perceivable either by the Senses, or the Understanding; as a *Horse,* a *Book.*

The primer concluded with prose selections, verses, and fables, which were introduced more for pious thoughts than to cultivate a taste for fiction. One story told how a mother goat, before going out, told her kids to lock the door and be certain to look out the window to see who was there before they opened the door. The wolf, who overheard her charge, came to the door and counterfeited the mother's voice. The kids forgot to look out the window, opened the door and were eaten by the wolf. The moral:

> Children should obey their Parents, who are always better able to advise them than the Children can themselves. It is convenient also for young Men to lend an Ear to the Aged, who being more experienced in the Affair of the World, can give them better Counsel. . . . Witness *Eli's* Sons and *Rehoboam's* Fall.[22]

Anthony Benezet's primer, *Pennsylvania Speller,* a product of 30 years' teaching experience, proved that Benezet knew how children learned. The book was written for Quakers and other religious people and could be used in schools or by parents teaching their children at home. The lessons were short to ease memorizing, constructed to include both review and progress, and moved gradually from the simple to the slightly difficult to the complex. After the alphabet was introduced, Benezet listed the vowels and had exercises to depict the different sounds. The pupil was next taught two-letter words which were then made into such phrases as "I am" and "we go." Following the drill on three-letter words, the first simple sentences came, often in poetic form.

> The sun is up my boys,
> get out of bed.
> Go see for the cow;
> let her eat her hay.

When the student had progressed through four- and five-letter words, easy two-syllable and difficult one-syllable words, Benezet listed a few maxims and some short scriptural passages, usually from Psalms. The Bible stories were fast moving and poetry, fables, and some moralistic history provided variety. Benezet showed that a dedicated teacher could provide the moral instruction so important to Friends and do it subtly enough to arouse student interest. Learning to read did not need to be a dull task.

Benezet was conscious of the improvements in his book. He believed he had simplified Dilworth's speller by introducing easy two-syllable before difficult one-syllable words since children could learn the easy ones faster. In the first edition he had attempted to divide syllables by ear rather than by formal rules, but this brought so many complaints from masters and students accustomed to the Dilworth method that the second edition omitted this. Benezet simplified grammar by leaving out distinctions used by Latin teachers that needlessly complicated the study of English. Rules of grammar and spelling were introduced only at the end of the book because they were difficult to learn and apply. The *Pennsylvania Speller* had a wide circulation. Benezet sent copies to England, where it was used in drawing up a primer for use at Ackworth School, and at least one edition appeared in Ireland. The overseers of Penn Charter School distributed 300 copies of the primer to schools in Philadelphia and in the country, and schools as far south as Nottingham, Maryland, made use of the book. Moses Brown, after sending to Philadelphia for several hundred copies, had the book reprinted at Newport in 1781 in an edition of 6,000 copies.[24]

A scholar who mastered one of the Quaker primers would have acquired a good vocabulary, for he would be able to define and spell words such as affinity, detrimental, acerbity, perpendicular, abnegation, and anathema. His grasp of mathematics would be more problematical. Multiplication tables were provided in Fox and Pastorius; Benezet ignored such information probably because, by the 1770s, separate mathematics texts were used—or students made their own by solving problems and then copying the rules and problems into a cyphering book. In Philadelphia basic arithmetic was taught in all the schools as were writing and spelling. Benezet believed that dictations by the master to the students, which could then be corrected and recopied, would make up for the lack of a classical style. Pupils began to write with ovals and gradually learned to shape the letters; both good posture and a correct grip were necessary in order to write with a "strong, free hand." The Bible was used in every school both for practice in oral reading and for religious instruction. Since the Scriptures were difficult, pupils read history or religious books to learn proper emphasis and a consideration of punctuation marks. In the early schools, pupils studied all sorts of rules and tables; Benezet remarked that the "abstruse" and not "generally necessary rules" of grammar and mathematics should be left to pupils of "brightest genius."[25]

The chief aim of education was "the amendment of the heart." Thomas Chalkley wrote to his daughter's schoolmaster, "Although my care is great for my children's learning their books, yet it is much more so as their learning true piety and virtue." James Logan expressed similar sentiments to his son when the boy left to attend school in England.[26] Fox's grammar included a catechism, and the Philadelphia schools used Barclay's catechism. The pupil learned that he was depraved and would be damned if he did not experience the inward light.

> And if I be a *Child of God,* I must not grieve him, but must be meek, and sober, and gentle, and loving and quiet. . . .
>
> So if I be wild, forward, wicked, heady, highminded . . . and do not the *Truth,* and forget *God,* such *God* turneth into *Hell,* that grieveth him.[27]

Pastorius advised his pupils that their duty was to be subject to their elders, kind to each other, and sober minded. Benezet included poems on the danger of delaying repentance and on "Praises for Mercies Spiritual and Temporal." Pupils were reminded that "the eye of God is on us, all the day." Friends never separated theology and ethics, and pupils were told not to kill a fly needlessly or prolong the agony of a worm when baiting a hook. Maxims inculcated other virtues: "Go to the *Ant,* you that love sloth, Think on her ways and be wise," and "Soon to bed and soon to rise, / Will tend to keep thee well; / and tend to make thee wise." Primers warned students not to fight with classmates or brothers and sisters. Friends believed, above all else, that a Christian life involved discipline, and the ideal child was to be so intoxicated with God that the external world meant nothing.

> Thro' each event of this inconstant state,
> Preserve my temper equal and sedate;
> Give me a mind that wholly can despise,
> The low designs and little art of vice;
> Be my Religion such as taught by thee,
> Alike from pride or superstition free;
> Inform my judgment, regulate my will,
> My reason strengthen, and my passion still.[28]

While the newer primers contained definite improvements in presentation of materials designed to facilitate learning, the more advanced books changed much less—with the exception of the inclusion of a discussion of methodology. Since the seventeenth century pedagogical writers had stressed the need to do away with complex rules. When Christopher Taylor wrote a *Compendium Trium Linguarum* in 1676, the preface to the second edition (not written by Taylor) cited the contents as designed to reduce rules to a minimum. If English, French, or Polish could be learned without rules, why could not Greek, Latin, or Hebrew? Language came before grammar, not grammar before language. Rules and exceptions "wholly nauseat[ed]" pupils, who became so discouraged that they left school.[29] John Gough's English grammar, used in Philadelphia and New England's Quaker schools just before the Revolution, claimed to teach students English without burdening them with Latin grammar. However, after the pupil conquered 48 pages of orthographic tables and 34 pages of selected vocabulary, he encountered 68 pages of rules. In 1786 Thomas Coar wrote a grammar for the use of Ackworth School. The first 240 pages contained nothing but rules and no relief from monotony. Coar also wrote a simplified version for Ackworth. On the title page he quoted a motto from Edgeworth's *Practical Education:* "Perhaps nothing can be more practically useful, than to simplify Grammar, and to lighten as much as possible the load that is laid upon Memory."[30] The easy version contained 25 pages of rules which the author wanted to be learned by memory but not verbatim.

No improvements in the teaching of grammar occurred until Maria Hack published *First Lessons in English Grammar* early in the nineteenth century. She, like Thomas Coar, quoted the motto of Edgeworth and went further to introduce parts of speech by showing how baby brothers talk. The first words a child learned were interjections like "Ah! Oh!" and so forth. The rules were kept to a minimum and the lessons shortened. After each subject, exercises were provided so that the child could apply what he had learned. As a way of review, she relied upon a common seventeenth-century device of teaching by the use of poetry.

First comes the little particle
Grammarians call *an article,*
And then the mighty *noun:*
Great store of fancies that may bring,
A Noun, it may be any *thing,*
A Person or *a town.*[31]

Perhaps this grammar was made easier because it was to be used by very small children. The more advanced grammars still placed full emphasis upon pure memorization.[32]

By the end of the eighteenth century Friends in both England and America began to use English-language readers. These were designed to supplement Bible reading and included a variety of stories, usually containing moral exhortation. The Ackworth reader included stories such as "Androcles and the Lion," "Snow" (a scientific article), "On Filial Duty," and "On Large Cities, and their Evil Tendencies."[33] Lindley Murray, an American Friend who emigrated to England, wrote textbooks that were extremely popular until after the Civil War. Murray was careful not to include any reading that might "gratify a corrupt mind, or, in the least degree, offend the eye or ear of innocence." He allowed only passages that brought "due reverence for virtue" and inculcated "sentiments of piety and goodness." While a few amusing pieces were admitted, Murray feared to include many, for, if one excited the imagination of youth, he then had to strive harder to make them heed right reason. Murray also wrote a catechism designed to introduce Friends' children to religion; this book was most notable for its omission of nearly all distinctively Quaker beliefs. Only by the sections on pacifism and oaths could one know that this was a book not written by a Methodist.[34]

The mathematics texts that Friends are known to have used in American schools are John Gough's *Practical Arithmetick* and Thomas Dilworth's *The Schoolmaster's Assistant.* Gough's book, written in 1773, encompassed many stages from counting to square roots and logarithms. The text followed the mathematical progression from addition and subtraction to multiplication, division, and fractions. When the student began addition, he learned rules at the outset and the first problem was not to find the solution of two plus two, but to add three figures, each of which was over a thousand. Simplification or gradation was not attempted. Dilworth, at least, presented some slightly easier studies. For instance, in Gough, the first number that the student learned to write was three thousand six hundred and forty-four; in Dilworth he was expected to write "Twenty-nine, Three hundred and forty-eight, Seven thousand two hundred and twenty-six." The emphasis in both textbooks, and in Rebecca Jones' copybook, was on learning shortcuts or working problems mentally. Dilworth suggested that when multiplying by a number between 12 and 20 one should "Multiply by the Figure in the Units Place, and as you multiply, add to the Product of each single Figure that of the Multiplicant, which stands next on the right hand."[35]

IV

John Gough, who taught in a Friends' school in Ireland, included in his grammar a curriculum for an Engish school. First the pupils learned to read, spell, and write. Writing was so important that two hours a day were spent practicing it through most of the rest of the curriculum. Next came English grammar, in which the scholars studied the rules and applied them. The reading of a book such as *Aesop's Fables* provided examples of a variety of constructions. After mastering reading, spelling, and grammar, the child progressed to geography, which he learned through maps and travel books. Then came the study of the history of England and of the ancient world from Cyrus through Rome, and students also began reading newspapers along with their other work. Arithmetic was not introduced until the boys were "tolerable Masters of Grammar and Geography," and then they devoted half of each day to it. After arithmetic came bookkeeping, geometry, surveying, navigation. How many of these were studied depended upon a boy's future vocation. Scholars of real genius could be instructed in some parts of physics or natural science. They could read, for style and content, articles on religion and morality in the *Spectator* or *Tatler,* write a biography of a remarkable person, or practice penning letters of all kinds.[36]

Anthony Benezet never wrote a detailed plan for a curriculum, but his correspondence with future teachers and influential Quakers provides an outline of what he believed should be taught. The *Pennsylvania Speller* contained basic reading and grammar. Benezet combined instruction in spelling, punctuation, and writing by dictating passages which the students copied and brought to him for correction before recopying them in a commonplace book. Because arithmetic books with difficult problems might discourage the pupil, Benezet recommended that very easy ones be used at first. Advanced mathematics was taught in a special evening class attended by boys only. Here students learned double-entry accounting, square and cube roots, decimals, and many tables involving lands, liquids, dry measures, and longitude. In advanced school, pupils gained a "general knowledge of the Mechanical powers, Geography and the plain elements of Astronomy." By charting the paths of the stars (also useful for navigation) and looking at insects through a microscope, scholars saw the vastness and complexity of creation. Teachers included those parts of history that showed the dreadful effects of war, the corruption and depravity of humanity, and the advantages of moral living. Anatomy was taught so that scholars could see the healthful effects of a "plain simple way of life." Benezet cited Penn's maxim that education should be useful and enable students to be of service to others.[37]

The model education proposed by John Gough or Anthony Benezet included no mention of Latin or a classical curriculum. This omission was intentional. John Gough stressed the need for an English grammar while maintaining that many of the supposed advantages of studying Latin were illusive. Latin did not increase one's vocabulary or make English grammar any easier. The study of English demanded full attention unhampered by the transfer of knowledge from other languages. Benezet hoped that instruction in English grammar would make "unnecessary" the use of learned languages. Long experience had taught him that the difficulty in attaining knowledge of the classics and the status achieved from being proficient in Latin and Greek had "a natural tendency to wed to the world" even when pious authors rather than Ovid, Horace, or Virgil were used.[38] Perhaps Benezet had noted the tendencies to worldliness in sons of Quaker grandees who attended the Latin school in Philadelphia.

Since the educated clergy of other denominations saw Latin and Greek as qualifications for the ministry, a distrust of classical learning became a characteristic of Quakerism from the very beginning. Friends came closest to an outright condemnation of all classical learning in a 1669 tract included in *A Battle-Door for Teachers and Professors to Learn Singular and Plural.* The bulk of the book was an exposition written by Benjamin Furly justifying the Quaker use of "thee" and "thou" as good grammar by showing how the distinction between singular and plural in the second person or "you" form was maintained in 34 languages. Following this impressive display of erudition was a diatribe against heathen learning written by John Stubbs (an educated man), who cited the biblical precedent of God telling the Israelites to study the law and shun and destroy all heathen inventions. The early Christians had learned of the dangers and had cast into the flames works of Virgil, Ovid, Horace, Terence, Plautus, and Cicero. If the students were to be taught Latin, they should read the Scriptures in that tongue. Stubbs analyzed several popular texts used for teaching children Latin and found them full of vulgar expressions. What he denounced shows conversely what he thought permissible for youth. He condemned any expression involving an oath or violence or any vain usage of the name of the Deity such as "Yea, so God help me" or "As God love me a comely fellow." Stubbs's censure of all words that belittled men, such as knave, villain, varlet, graceless rascal, or hangmanly thief, shows the strain of Christian egalitarianism in early Quakerism. Sexually immoral or erotic passages, such as those found in Ovid's *Art of Love,* were severely castigated. Any saying advocating playing ball, drinking, idleness, or the use of "you" for the singular was criticized.[39] The *Battle-Door,* the only pamphlet that actually listed offensive passages, advocated a tame religious literature designed to protect innocent children from evil thoughts. That the Bible, the proper subject of education, contained as many corrupting passages as Terence or Virgil was not acknowledged.

Many early Quakers condemned the contents of school books. In answering a question about the Quakers' opposition to Latin, the English Quaker Thomas Lawrence distinguished between the usefulness of the language in learning English, traveling, doing scholarly work, and comparing translations of Scripture and the evilness of the "filthy, lascivious, unclean expressions" in the books used to teach it. Christopher Taylor translated Fox's primer into Latin and also published a book to be used in the teaching of Latin, Hebrew, and Greek. He planned to expurgate part of the classics for the use of children, but there is no record that he did so. Thomas Lawson, an early schoolmaster, thought that the "Pagan Ethics, Physicks, and Metaphysick" taught in "Devils books" in schools enslaved the minds of men. Lawson proposed teaching Latin and natural science together so that the student's learning would be relevant and more interesting. Lawson's aims were similar to those of William Penn, who wanted instruction in Latin to be practical.[40]

Although New England Puritans did not seriously debate the relevance of a classical curriculum until after the Revolution, Friends on both sides of the Atlantic had been discussing the subject for over a century.[41] Richard Hutton, who taught at Clerkenwell school in London early in the eighteenth century, charged that most students could find better subjects to learn "than to Murder three or four Years time in Learning Latin to little or no purpose." Only those with a definite need, lots of time, and an "able Purse" should study classics. Shopkeepers and merchants should consider what possible use their sons could make of the traditional subjects. London Yearly Meeting in 1737 recommended that youth be instructed in modern languages for use in trade and in the traveling ministry. In 1760 Meeting for Sufferings said that parents' esteem for a little exposure to Latin was a discouragement to both teachers and pupils.[42]

In spite of the current of criticism, Friends' schools continued to teach the classics and use heathen editions. The boarding schools in England provided a traditional grammar-school curriculum. In 1714 Robert Scantlebury wrote from Sidcot school that, during five years of attendance, he had studied "Grammar, Latin Testament, Corderius, Castalion, Textor, and Tully." James Logan, who had no illusions about his son's lack of aptitude for learning, sent him to school in Bristol, England, to study, hopefully to become a master of spoken as well as written Latin and to become conversant enough in Greek to read the New Testament. William kept a commonplace book, wrote verses, themes, and letters in Latin, and read a variety of authors including Virgil, whose first *Georgics* James recommended in case William became a husbandman. Charles Mifflin, who attended Union School in Germantown, compiled a record of his education between June 26 and September 24, 1764.

> I said 64 morning Lessons; Read English History, 59 times, Read Poetry 26 times, Read Roman History 24 times, Attended Lecture on Latin Grammar 62, Attended Lecture on English Grammar 48 times, Said 82 lessons on Corn. Nepos; Made 48 Latin Exercises had Trials for Places at the Table 12 times, Place in 1st Class Head 3 times, Foot none, Absent none, Read 113 Chapters in the Holy Bible, Attended Divine worship at Friends meeting 12 times, Had 8 Lectures on Geography Maps. Wrote 8 Copies.[43]

In Philadelphia, the Latin school taught Greek and Latin from sources not known to have been censured. When John Wilson resigned from the grammar school in 1769, he asked the overseers whether instruction in Ovid, Horace, Juvenal, and Lucretius made for godly living.

> Is it not monstrous? That Christian Children intended to believe and relish the Truths of Gospel should have their early and most retentive years imbued with the shocking Legends and abominable Romances of the worst of Heathens should be

> obliged to be Pimps to the detestable Lusts of Jupiter and Mars attend the thefts and Villany of Mercury or follow Aeneas on his Murdering Progress.[44]

In 1787 Robert Proud, Tory master of the Latin school, bewailed the fact that people "who cannot see the Utility of what they do not understand" were hostile to the classical education and those who taught it. James Logan insisted that studying the classics taught discipline, provided moral instruction, and could be useful in commerce with foreign countries. Richard Shackleton, a strict Friend and Irish schoolmaster, recommended that his grandson learn Latin, not for financial gain but because it was the foundation of a "liberal education," would be helpful in learning English, and gave the opportunity to read the best historians and poets in the original language. Moses Brown, whose son studied Latin, answered Benezet's critique by maintaining that Latin was useful for studying medicine and for maintaining contact with the learning of Europe.[45] The tradition of teaching Latin, the esteem of classical civilization, and the fact that Latin and Greek were still the languages of learned men kept the classics in the classroom. A grammar school education was considered important as a sign of gentility. An artisan- or merchant-turned-gentleman, as many a Quaker in Philadelphia and Newport was, saw a grammar school education as distinguishing his son from the mechanics and ruder sorts.

V

From a variety of sources one can piece together a picture of daily experiences in school. Thomas Chalkley described formal education as beginning at age 7 and ending at 14. In Philadelphia schools there was no set age to enter or leave, and pupils began as early as age 3 or 4 and as late as age 14 or 15. Westtown accepted students from ages 8 to 15. In 1700 Philadelphia Monthly Meeting, finding that the women's school was crowded with too many very young children, recommended that "the School be not hereafter troubled with such children till they learn their Letters and are of age to be under Government." Benezet believed that pupils too young to write should be placed in a special school, since taking care of them took up too much time and they were "with difficulty kept quiet." This sort of counsel was not always heeded. When her 8-year-old sister Hannah went to school, Susan Cox, not quite 3, went along because she did not like to be left behind. Seven months later Susan could spell words of three syllables. Samuel Allinson sent his son William, barely 3 years old, to Thomas Powell's school. The father requested the master to let the boy gradually become accustomed to school, to question him about his letters, and occasionally to help him over those he miscalled "in such a manner as to make him pleas'd with his own performances in that way." An older boy went along to help take care of his little brother. "In a Week or fortnights trial if he is too troublesome let me know and I must Remove him—I do not Accompany him lest he shou'd want to Return with me."[46] The normal age to begin education was between 6 and 8, and pupils stayed until ready to leave. In some instances boys attended English school first and then went on to grammar school. The few notations in the Penn Charter School records stating why pupils left mentioned that they had gone to sea or were apprenticed. There was no record of any class structure, graduation, or diplomas. Admissions could take place at any time of year. At the same school some might attend half and others full days. Starting from what they knew, the students probably went through the primers at their own pace. There could be little uniformity of class teaching in a school encompassing boys of all abilities at all different levels of preparation.

During the summer months school began at 7:00 A.M.; the winter at 8:00 A.M.. Students were called to the building by a bell; at least there was one at the Latin school. Although a few of the dame schools contained both boys and girls, normally the sexes were taught separately. (However, John Woolman instructed older children of both sexes at the same time.) School lasted eight hours a day, six days a week, although some of the elementary and the girls' schools ran for half days. On the fifth day, scholars came prepared to go to meeting and at quarterly intervals all attended special youth meetings.

The behavior desired in school is shown by a list of rules drawn up in 1748:

> That no Boy shall presume to absent himself from the School without producing a note from one of his Parents. . . .
>
> That strict obedience shall be paid to the Monitor[s] in discharge of their Office, and that none shall take the Liberty of entering into any disputes with them, but if any Boy Conceives himself aggriev'd, he shall make his Complaint to the Master.
>
> That in coming to School and returning home every one shall behave with Decency and Sobriety. . . .
>
> That in all their Conversation they shall use the plain Language . . . and shall be careful never to utter any rude or uncivil Expression, nor to call their Schoolmates or others by any Nickname or Term of Reproach.
>
> That in their hours of Leisure, they shall avoid ranting Games and Diversions, and every occasion of Quarreling with each other.
>
> That none shall at any time play or keep Company with the rude Boys of the Town, but shall Converse, as much as they can, with their own Schoolfellows. . . .
>
> That no Boy of this School shall be allowed to go into the Backyard, during School time, unless he be sent on an Errand by the Master.[47]

Masters and ushers were always to be within hearing distance of the boys. To promote justice, the teachers were to pay careful attention to any complaint; but the pupils were not to be encouraged in needless "tatling and talebearing." In 1790 Robert Proud drew up regulations for the Latin school that were similar to the 1748 code. The regulations required the boys to enter the school quietly, go to their seats, and remain there. If a student wished to speak, he should do so in Latin. If a fellow were punished, the boys were not to divulge the fact to outsiders "lest it may sometime happen to be thy own case." The masters expected the scholars to be helpful and industrious so that the school might avoid punishment or "servile fear" and be a "place of pleasure and delight."[48]

The methods of enforcing discipline varied. The Pemberton family thought Francis Pastorius too strict. Phineas Pemberton wrote to him apologizing for the lateness of his little girls in coming to school and noting that his sickness had kept them at home doing errands. Pastorius replied that the maidens had not been threatened or disciplined but saw others corrected and so feared for themselves, "which argueth their good disposition, and that the very shadow of a rod will do more with them, than the Spur with others." The result of disciplining Israel Pemberton, Sr., was not as successful. According to Israel, not an impartial observer, he was on good terms with Master Thomas Makin who always received questions with good nature. When Makin was absent, however, Pastorius, who did not show "any respect to me as a scholar," took that "opportunity to Thrash me." Once after a "small difference" between Israel and another student, Pastorius severely whipped Israel. Israel's sister told the father. Phineas Pemberton inspected the boy and saw "the tokens of his Correction still remaining upon me about five weeks since" and removed Israel from school. Makin wrote to Phineas the next year asking for Israel's return to learn mathematics in a school where he would have no contact with Pastorius, and soon after the boy returned to school.[49]

Some parents were not as censorious as Phineas Pemberton concerning discipline. Thomas Chalkley once wrote to a master, "As to the school-learning of my children, I leave to thy management, not questioning thy ability therein; and if they want correction, spare not the rod." Ackworth, which at first showed some tolerance in disciplining, by 1785 reverted to whipping, hitting fingers with rods, public confession, solitary confinement, and deprivations in diet.[50] Anthony Benezet supposedly never spanked pupils; instead, he appealed to their sense of honor and right. Perhaps this was one reason that he found teaching English school so strenuous and, after 1754, began teaching only girls. John Todd, who taught in the English school after 1763, had a quick temper and a veritable passion for beating his students. The quiet of the schoolroom would be broken by a slap on the ear, and then Todd would drag the boy to the center of the room where he would be strapped with a bridle rein which left a "fiery red streak at every slash." The more ideal teacher preserved a mean between unnecessary harshness and lack of discipline.

> Some indulgent parents mightily hurt their youth by tying up the hands of their teachers from discreet correction. No discreet teacher will use broom or mop-stick, or door and window-bar, to correct their youths; that would be unmanly, as well as unwise; but the rod never did hurt, in a skillful hand.[51]

Quakers wanted their children to be good students—but not from hope of gain or fame. The overseers of Penn Charter School fined themselves two shillings for missing an inspection trip in order to finance rewards for the best scholars, who were selected by a competition. When overseers visited a school, pupils recited memorized Latin orations or scriptural passages, a practice one Quaker thought more inclined to build vanity than promote piety in students. John Woolman refused to countenance the practice of rewards, arguing that a little slower learning was preferable to working hard for the wrong reasons.[52] No grades were given.

Schools were in session all year long, although in the summer country schools were usually maintained only for the very young; the older brothers worked on the farms. Yearly and quarterly meetings brought holidays and occasionally the masters would grant play days. A cunning child might procure more vacations. The day after he was kicked by a horse, Billy Allinson persuaded his mother that he should stay home from school, but he was able enough to be "busy running about." Since masters required a written excuse after an absence, truancy was not unknown. In 1704 James Logan wrote to Jonathan Dickinson:

> I shall acquaint thee that thy two rugged boys are very lusty, love the river much better this hot weather than their masters' countenance, and the fields and boats far before schools or books.[53]

Friends recognized that not all students were capable of higher learning. Jonathan Dickinson, who was rearing his brother-in-law Isaac Gale's sons while teaching them business, wrote that one boy was very steady and showed great ability in the counting house and the store. The other son, Jonathan, needed to be put to some other task, and "as to Latin all that I Can do with those matters Cannot get them though." Dickinson, perhaps trying to console the father, noted that Latin presented a stumbling block to youths who were "fit for any active Employment" and added that such might easier adjust to the world "than Some Scholastic all Blockheads who by Identity of Letters have Lost their Reason." Dickinson's own son, John, was no better than his cousin since, when he went to London at age 16, his father admitted that his former Latin teachers "gave hopes but they failed by one means or Other." Mary Allinson, a little girl with exquisite handwriting, evidently did not excel in other pursuits since the only encouragement the master gave her was "that he has had duller scholars." She found grammar such a "dry, laborious" subject that she feared she could not soon master it.[54]

During the Revolutionary period the boys in the Philadelphia Latin school started a variety of short-lived student newspapers that shed much light on Quaker youth. These handwritten papers, which sold for a sheet of paper, were produced by children of wealthy Philadelphia Friends. Their fathers' concerns were echoed in the papers, as the students debated whether everyone in the school should vote, issued bills of credit, required loyalty oaths, drew up constitutions, elected presidents, judges, senators, and army officers, and created their own miniature state. This "shadow" government insisted that, even during a time of constitutional revision, debts must be paid; when the master dismissed school early, the paper rejoiced in the restoring of the scholars' "just Right." The students formed a militia and enforced discipline to protect themselves against the tyrannical encroachments of the Toddites (members of the English school). The only allusions that might enable one to tell that these inhabitants of Latonia were Friends were the apology of one editor for using "we" to refer to himself and a mention that the overseers censured one master for wearing too gay apparel. When a student general, signing himself "Caesar," talked about the necessity for a good army, he aroused understandable scepticism in Benezet, who declared that studying heroic exploits in heathen classics was not conducive to the development of meek or pacifist Christians.[55]

The newspapers included comments on a wide variety of matters. Articles on natural history discussed how flies made noise. One feature was "Caddy Crabsticks Conundrums," which included a variety of riddles to which no answers were ever given. "What is that which God never saw kings seldom see but we often see?" "What is that which sometimes will bear an hundred pound weight and at other times not an ounce?" The writers wondered if John

Thompson would resign as master, if John Webster would succeed him, if the mathematics master left to avoid impressment or to teach school in the country, and if the British or Americans would close the school. When rumors spread that George Smith was leaving to keep a school west of Schuylkill, a correspondent observed:

> that Mr. Smiths keeping a boarding School depends upon his Marriage with a certain Lady and he cant help observing that unless he makes greater Progress in her Affections than he has done lately the Time will be more distant that what has been mentioned.[56]

One student who lost half his fortune in the lottery that the pupils conducted to treat the army to a party bemoaned both his fate and the decline of business that made it impossible to recoup his losses. One satire of a mooning lover paying a visit to his sweetheart would have done justice to Laurel and Hardy. School news also appeared. Mr. Moses Marks "slipped thro' the Hole of a necessary House and remained supported by the Excrements until Mr. Todd Governor of the English School" pulled him out with a rope, evincing a skill which "would do honor to the most experienced Gold Finder."[57]

The boys of the Latin school were generally too young to pay much attention to females. One time the boys were threatened by "Amazons." During a club meeting a boy suggested that they should say more in praise of the beauty of the fair sex. "Here followed a deep silence." A sister of one of the inhabitants of Latonia wrote noting that "you do not say enough of the female Sex and that dear enchanting Part of your Species which your morose Pendants out of pure Envy distinguish by the Name of Fobs." She offered to write a column telling which lady had the most admirers, the finest voice, the best shape, and the ability to tell which boy wore the most fashionable clothes. The offer was declined. On the cover of someone's volume of *The Student Gazette* was written in different handwritings, "Patty Jones Betsey Wister Becky Jones Sally Wister Junr." and below in another hand "four unmatched Ladies certainly, in their own opinions at least."[58] The Latin scholars were, to say the least, antifeminists.

Quaker girls did not write newspapers, and one can find only a few letters giving information about their behavior in or out of school. An undated letter of Sarah Hill (born 1739) is extraordinary, for it imparts some flavor of the mentality of a young maiden.

> Dear papa came and ask'd me, what News I had got, I told him the best I could have received, that you were all well, and put the letter in his hand; he smiled and told me, he didn't like to pry into Secrets. I thought he looked pleas'd and I said there was no secret but what he was welcome to see.
>
> I went out Just now, to look for strawberries, but I couldn't find any, but a few little ones. . . . I am sadly afraid I shall get poisoned, for there's a great many poison weeds in the strawberry patch, but if I should Die I shant be missed much, and then there will be less for Dear papa to maintain, for I know I'm a great Trouble to him and everybody else—I beg my Dear Sister Peggy my one apron one handkerchief. That's all.
>
> P.S. I am just killed with this ugly Tooth ache every night, and I'm forced to set up some times till most day. Pray send me word who them packets are for and

a few nuts for my squirrel. I can't get any, without buying; I haven't got a penny here.[59]

Phineas Pemberton, who had sent his children into Philadelphia for schooling after his first wife died, wrote to his daughter Phebe to learn her book well so that she could soon come home. Abigail Pemberton asked her brother Israel how Priscilla, age 10 years, liked being at school and whether he thought she would learn "anything worth her while to be kept at school." Pastorius carried on a correspondence with Elizabeth Hill in order to improve her command of French.[60] At age 4 James Logan's daughter Sarah was adept at needlework but just beginning to write. By 9 Sarah was studying French and kept busy in the "dairy of the plantation, in which she delights as well as in spinning." As an experiment to test the capacity of women, Logan taught Sarah the Hebrew alphabet. However, although she passed the test, he did not intend to instruct her in any learned language. Logan did give his two daughters a broad education, though. They read poetry by Milton, Pope, Dryden, and Thomson, devotional books by Thomas à Kempis, Jeremy Taylor and Sir Matthew Hale, and—in translation—works by Lucan, Homer, Juvenal, Horace, Seneca, Pythagoras, Epictitus, and Xenophon. In addition, the young ladies could use their father's magnificent library. Their brother William, who attended grammar school in England, learned from the same kinds of books, but he worked in the original languages, seems to have read more widely, and studied subjects useful to merchants, such as accounting.[61]

Deborah Hill wrote in 1750 approving her eldest daughter's decision not to send her little girls to school but to have them taught at home. She hoped that they would be able to "write a copy or two a Day" and sent needlework so that their minds could be kept "innocently Engaged."[62] The accounts kept for Sarah Powell (born 1755) who attended school in Philadelphia from 1759 to 1764 provide a glimpse of a young lady's education. Sarah attended a variety of Quaker dame schools where she studied reading, writing, arithmetic and paid special fees for instruction in French and "architect[ure]." She purchased pious books such as Watt's poems and Hervey's *Meditations and Letters* in four volumes, which she may have read in school. Sarah spent less for books than for materials used to make china, wax fruit and flowers, and shell arrangements. Four months at a dame school cost 13s., but a Dutchman charged £2 7s. for teaching the art of working with wax. Sewing was done at dame schools, but special fees were paid for embroidering. Purchases of scraps of velvet and six "wax babies" make one suspect that little girls learned to sew by making doll clothes.[63] Isaac Collins, Quaker schoolmaster and also a printer-bookseller, taught his daughter Latin and higher mathematics, subjects generally reserved for boys. Susanna Dillwyn informed her father that in spite of her "almost unconquerable . . . aversion" to arithmetic, she knew the first four rules (numeration, addition, subtraction, and multiplication), which "some persons think is enough for a woman." Susanna escaped mathematics because her father "had rather see thee *healthy* than *learned,* and good than *either,*" but he rejected her proposition on female education as degrading "the Dignity and Capacity of the Sex." Susanna studied French, a little geography and astronomy, and read through an English grammar. William Dillwyn taught his other children French but only the boys were sent away to grammar school.[64] The education of most Quaker girls rarely progressed beyond reading, writing, and cyphering. The fortunate few who attended an advanced girls school, such as the one Benezet founded in 1754, occupied much the same social position as the boys who went to the Latin school. While Friends recognized the spiritual equality of women, they did not esteem their intellectual capacities very highly.

VI

The emphasis upon higher education, so characteristic of Puritans in New England, was completely alien to Friends. While Harvard was founded in 1636 and Yale in 1701, the first Quaker college did not grant degrees until 1856. Since Congregationalists and Friends held so many similar attitudes, why did the Quakers neglect advanced learning? From the beginning, there was within Quakerism a distrust of scholarly endeavors stemming from the almost exclusive concern with the inward light of Christ. The only way for a man to be saved was to hearken to the grace within and live a holy life. Every man had a spark of the divine, and no amount of learning could strengthen the truth. Religion became, therefore, a completely subjective and spiritual phenomenon.

The Quaker opposition was directed not at learning per se but at training in religion at the universities. Since college education in the seventeenth century was predominantly theological, the Friends, who insisted that logic, philosophy, and foreign languages could not possibly lead to a correct understanding of Scripture, saw no need for it. Universities were disliked because they trained a hireling ministry, and this negative view of theological training continued throughout the colonial period. After the founding of Dartmouth College, David Ferris, a former Yale student turned Friend, wrote to Eleazor Wheelock that colleges were "an invention of the Devil" that had not existed until the church fell into apostasy. What was taught in such institutions was nothing but "the dead Letter," which could in no manner bring men closer to salvation. Well-educated ministers were apt to be "dead Carnal men" who could preach the letter but not the Gospel.[65]

Although theological concerns provided the main reasons for opposition to universities, Friends were also biased against other educated professions. George Fox denounced lawyers and doctors as being "out of the wisdom of God," and although Friends did later enter these professions, the normal method was by an apprenticeship. Penn echoed the general belief of Quakers that "Our Universities have made more Loose, than Learned" and that wickedness that began there was usually completed "abroad, or at our Inns of Court at Home."[66] By the middle of the eighteenth century the prejudice against higher education had abated somewhat, and certain Philadelphia Quakers sent their sons to Edinburgh for medical training. Haverford School, founded in 1833, offered a college curriculum, but because of Quaker prejudice against the name *college,* it did not become one until 1856.

Because early Friends opposed university-taught theology, one should not infer that they were ignorant. George Fox was the only one of the leaders who can be said to have been poorly educated, and he made clear his support of learning.

> I would not have any to think, that I deny, or am against schools for teaching children the natural tongues and arts whereby they may do natural things.[67]

William Penn, Robert Barclay, George Whitehead, Ambrose Rigge, Isaac Penington, George Keith, and Thomas Story were only a few of the well-educated leaders among the early Quakers.

Both members and outsiders commented upon the anti-intellectual tendencies within Quakerism. Thomas Clarkson, who thought Friends should place more emphasis upon education, noted that the controversy over learning and the clergy, although kept in balance by the educated, was misunderstood by others who assumed that, since intellectual training was not essential for the ministry, it thus was not required at all. In the seventeenth century, Jonathan Dickinson extended the belittling of reason into secular matters, and one of the synonyms Friends used for the devil was "the Old Reasoner." In the late eighteenth century, James Jenkins criticized those Quakers who feared using carnal wisdom.

> Almost every Friend was a *feeler;* no act of scarcely any importance without first *felt* to be right . . . and I am afraid that the hacknyed profession of *feelings* was often an unnecessary display of our common belief in divine revelation.

Not only in religion but in normal social conversation "was the soundest reason decried, and even reprobated."[68]

When attempting to start new schools in England, New England, or Pennsylvania, proponents had not only to contend with inertia, but they also had to refute the widespread view

> that much learning is unfriendly to virtue; that it puffs up the mind, and diverts it from true good, that it inspires vanity and pride; and more particularly, that, by leading into a great comixture with mankind, it operates . . . against the preservation of our testimonies.[69]

The dilemma faced by those wanting better education was that they dared not say that learning fostered spirituality, yet they did not wish to emphasize secular reasons. They circumvented their opponents by stressing that only in Quaker schools could one be secluded from the world's evil and asserting that the institutions would solve a chronic problem by providing a supply of godly teachers. Secondly, they retreated to the past to warn against a misapplication of the founders' doctrine. Fox, Penn, and Barclay had endorsed the value of an education, and the number of well-educated early Friends proved that any fault lay not in learning but in its application. Even the "best things" were liable to "great abuses," but this was no argument against education.[70] The impetus to found new boarding schools attracted both the wealthy and the devout Friends. The prevailing side included the Pembertons, the Fothergills, Issac Zane, Moses Brown, William Rotch, Anthony Benezet, George Churchman, and the Dillwyns. When one considers that a large number of eighteenth-century Quakers opposed advanced learning as unnecessary or even antithetical to piety, the meetings' successes in establishing and supporting schools in many localities become most remarkable.

VII

A shortage of teachers and a lack of funds plagued Quaker educational efforts all during the colonial period. Schools relied for support upon fees of students and grants from the meeting. Masters in rural schools were often transients who taught only until a more lucrative occupation appeared. In England and America a few teachers became noted for their ability to instruct as well as their piety, and these men played a significant role in meeting affairs.

The clientele and the locality of the school determined the curriculum. Those English and American institutions patronized by the children of prosperous Quaker merchants stressed a classical curriculum equivalent to that obtained in a dissenting academy or grammar school. The student newspapers of the Penn Charter Latin School provide a glimpse of daily life far removed from the somber picture presented in religious tracts and monthly meeting minutes. Most Quaker children attended some type of elementary school where they learned the contents of a primer, writing, and arithmetic. If a child lived in a city, he could go to an English school to learn surveying, navigation, geography, accounting, letter writing, English grammar, and natural philosophy. Friends wanted girls to have a basic education but not much more. Upper-class young ladies might study French, fancy sewing, and working with wax in an attempt to attain gentility. Supporters of more advanced learning for boys or girls had to struggle against an anti-intellectualism based on the Quaker principle that the inward light was sufficient without humane learning. During the entire colonial period, Friends made no effort to found or support any college.

The first primers used in Quaker schools showed little imagination in simplifying the learning process. Authors required beginning pupils to memorize long lists of rules and vocabulary words, and the reading lessons were difficult and dull. The essential task for the primer was to give the student enough instruction so that he could learn to read the Bible. By 1770 elementary school books had been revolutionized. Religious and moral exhortations still dominated the contents, but the materials were arranged with skill. Students began with easy lessons and gradually learned more difficult subjects, and the introduction of poetry, short stories or fables, and fast-paced Bible lessons made the books more stimulating. The advanced textbooks of the same period showed little improvement over previous efforts. Major improvements in the teaching techniques used in the school books for the very young, a greater emphasis upon education, and the sentimentalization of childhood occurred at the same time. These phenomena indicate the increased importance given children in the late eighteenth century.

Notes

1 George Brookes, *Friend Anthony Benezet* (Philadelphia, 1937), p. 230; John Woolman, *Journal and Essays* (New York, 1922), p. 391; David Hall, *Memoirs* (London, 1758), pp. 83–84; John Freame, *Scripture Instruction* (London, 1713), p. xxiii; William Dover, *Reasons for Erecting an Additional Number of Schools* (London, 1752), p. 14.

2 New England was unique in the rela-

tively good supply of teachers; elsewhere in the colonies teachers were in demand but salaries remained low. Robert Middlekauff, *Ancients and Axioms* (New Haven, Conn., 1963), pp. 23, 30–31, 45, 70; Lawrence Cremin, *American Education* (New York, 1970), p. 188.

3 John Kirk to Israel Pemberton, 3/2/1763, Letters of American Friends, QC; George Churchman to Israel Pemberton, 11/6/1764, PP, 17: 105; London Yearly Meeting, Epistle, 3/27–31/1761, QC.

4 James Logan to Thomas Makin, 6/9/1719, Logan Letter Book, 2: 72; Brookes, *Friend Anthony Benezet,* p. 317.

5 Woolman, *Journal and Essays,* pp. 429, 391–92.

6 London YM, *Epistles from the Yearly Meeting* (1754), p. 222; Brookes, *Friend Anthony Benezet,* p. 232; Benjamin Ferris, *History of the Original Settlements on the Delaware* (Wilmington, Del., 1846), pp. 285–86; Philadelphia YM, Christian and Brotherly Advices, 1778, p. 182; Anthony Benezet, *Pennsylvania Spelling Book* (Philadelphia, 1779), pp. 163–64.

7 *BFHA,* 31 (1942): 72–82; 23 (1934): 63–76; 25 (1936): 83–86.

8 Thomas Woody, *Early Quaker Education in Pennsylvania* (New York, 1920), pp. 200–01; Overseers of Penn Charter School, Minutes, 1 (11/23/1769): 332.

9 John Hunt to Israel Pemberton, Jr., 7/14/1750, PP, 6: 105; Brookes, *Friend Anthony Benezet,* pp. 209–10.

10 *PMHB* 25 (1901): 3; Jonathan Roberts, Memoirs, 1: 52–59, HSP; C. P. Monahon and C. A. Collins, "Nathanael Greene's Letters to 'Friend Sammy' Ward," *Rhode Island History* 16 (1957).

11 Ferris, *History of the Original Settlements,* p. 286; William Redwood to John Pemberton, 3/5/1770, PP, 21: 118; Rebecca Jones, "Arithmetick Book," 1766, Allinson Collection, QC.

12 Anthony Benezet to Israel Pemberton, 11/24/1742/3, Copy in the Edward Bettle Collection, QC.

13 Overseers of Penn Charter School, Minutes, 9/5/1761, p. 232; 7/25/1754, p. 120; 11/28/1754, p. 124; 9/3–5/1761; Frederick Tolles, *Meeting House and Counting House* (New York, 1963), chapter 6. Student fees fluctuated greatly during the colonial period. At times the charge for the English school was £2 when the Latin school charged £3. The fees went up when the salary of the master increased. The highest amount that Benezet received from the overseers was £80. Women teachers received much less. When Rebecca Jones taught in the girls school, she received £20. In some cases, student fees were deducted from the pay that the overseers gave; in others, what the pupils paid was in addition to the compensation that was for poor scholars.

14 Overseers of Penn Charter School, Minutes, 2/26–28/1770, p. 336. The master's salary was not to be over £200, and the student body was limited to twenty-four.

15 Ibid., 2/21/1757, pp. 152–53.

16 George Fox, *Instructions for Right Spelling* (Philadelphia, 1702), p. 10.

17 Francis Daniel Pastorius, *A New Primer or Methodical Directions to Attain the True Spelling, Reading & Writing of English* (New York, 1698), pp. 23–24.

18 Stephen Crisp, *A New Book for Children to Learn In* (London, 1706), pp. 7, 16, 55, 63. This book had to be used by small children since the size was approximately three inches by three inches. The primer was issued in 1681 and reprinted several times in the eighteenth century in England and America.

19 William Thompson, *The Child's Guide to the English Tongue* (London, 1711), p. 17.

20 *BFHA,* 29 (1940): 102–06; Zora Klain, *Quaker Education in North Carolina* (Philadelphia, 1928), pp. 51–52; Min. Rhode Island MM, 2 (6/31/1725): 231–32; Min. Philadelphia YM, 7/22/1697, p. 62; Min. Philadelphia MM, 10/7/1696.

21 Thomas Dilworth, *A New Guide to the English Tongue* (Philadelphia, 1770), p. 1. The 1770 Bradford edition of Dilworth's primer at the Library Company differs from the copy at the American Antiquarian Society. The Library Company's copy (which is not the final version) contained a pictorial alphabet to ease learning, the same device used in the *New England Primer.* Whether this variation was due to a printer's mistake or a change of mind is unknown, but different editions of the same primer often show changes. Dilworth's primer appeared in America about 1740, and by 1785 it had gone through twenty-five editions. By the middle of the century primers were issued in vast quantities. Benjamin Franklin issued 35,100 primers between 1749 and 1765. One can conclude either that more Americans were going to school or that of the Americans going to school, more had textbooks. *PMHB* 23 (1893): 122.

22 Dilworth, *A New Guide to the English Tongue,* pp. 4, 99, 143.

23 Brookes, *Friend Anthony Benezet,* p. 328; Benezet, *Pennsylvania Spelling Book,* pp. 9–11.

24 Brookes, *Friend Anthony Benezet,* pp. 369, 358, 388; Overseers of Penn Charter School, Minutes, 2, (2/26/1778): 77; William Dunlap, *Quaker Education in Baltimore and Virginia Yearly Meetings* (Philadelphia, 1936), p. 217; Moses Brown to J. Crukshank, Letters,

6/9/1782, p. 906; 8/25/1784, p. 927, Rhode Island Historical Society, Brown Papers.

25 Benezet, *Pennsylvania Spelling Book* pp. 165–66.

26 Ibid.; Thomas Chalkley, *Journal* (London, 1791), pp. 218–19; James Logan to William Logan, Logan Letter Book, 4, 5/4/1730; William Logan to John Fothergill, 5/11/1768, New York Public Library.

27 Fox, *Instructions for Right Spelling,* p. 12.

28 Pastorius, *A New Primer,* pp. 23–24; Benezet, *Pennsylvania Speller,* pp. 12, 16–17, 90, 127–29.

29 Christopher Taylor, *Compendium Trium Linguarum* (London, 1679), preface by J. M. Taylor also wrote a Latin translation of Fox's primer. These were the only school books in Latin written by Friends during the colonial period.

30 John Gough, *A Practical Grammar of the English Tongue* (Dublin, 1764); Thomas Coar, *A Grammar of the English Tongue* (London, 1796); idem, *An Essay Towards an English Grammar for Ackworth School* (York, England, 1800).

31 Maria Hack, *First Lessons in English Grammar* (London, 1813), pp. 1, 74.

32 The only improvements in grammar books involved the issuance of easy and advanced ones. Lindley Murray also designed an exercise book to be used along with his grammar. Lindley Murray, *English Exercises Adapted to Murray's English Grammar* (Philadelphia, 1809).

33 *Lessons for Youth Selected for the Use of Ackworth and Other Schools* (London, 1795).

34 Lindley Murray, *The English Reader: or Pieces in Prose and Poetry* (Philadelphia, 1803), p. 5; idem, *A Compendium of Religious Faith and Practice Designed for Young Persons of the Society of Friends* (York, England, 1815), pp. 54, 56.

35 John Gough, *Practical Arithmetick* (Dublin, 1773), pp. 22–23; Thomas Dilworth, *The Schoolmasters Assistant* (Philadelphia, 1781), pp. 18, 42; Overseers of Penn Charter School, Minutes, 10/12/1761, p. 235; Woody, *Early Quaker Education in Pennsylvania,* p. 195.

36 Gough, *Practical Grammar of the English Tongue,* pp. vi–xi.

37 Brookes, *Friend Anthony Benezet,* pp. 467, 332–33, 390.

38 Ibid., pp. 360–62, 389–90; Gough, *Practical Grammar of the English Tongue,* pp. ii–vi.

39 G. Fox, J. Stubbs, and B. Furly, *A Battle-Door for Teachers* (London, 1660), pp. 1–4, 6–13, 17, 20, The page numbers in this group of treatises start at one on several occasions.

40 Thomas Lawrence, *The Streight Gate and Narrow Way* (1673), pp. 18–19; Thomas Lawson, *Dagon's Fall Before the Ark* (1679), pp. 72, 86–88; Thomas Lawson, *A Mite into the Treasury* (London, 1680).

41 Middlekauff, *Ancients and Axioms,* p. 120.

42 Richard Hutton, *Commonplace Book,* ca. 1714, pp. 10–12, Ms at Saffron Walden School, England; Min. London YM, 8 (4/4/1737): 440; Min. London Meeting for Sufferings, 30 (6/20/1760): 441.

43 Robert Scantlebury, 6/21/1714, quoted in L. John Stroud, "History of Quaker Education in England, (Master's thesis University of Leeds, 1944), p. 56; James Logan to Alexander Arscott, Letter Book, 4 (5/25/1731): 273; *PMHB* 33 (1909): 365–66. The Germantown School was not under Friends' control, but special provisions were made so that Quakers attending could use the plain style of speech, etc.

44 John Wilson to Overseers, 12/28/1769 quoted in Jean Straub, "Quaker School Life in Philadelphia before 1800," *PMHB* 79 (1965): 138–39.

45 Robert Proud to Board of Overseers of the Public School, 6/2/1787, Robert Proud Mss, HSP; James Logan to William Logan, 12/12/1731, 6/30/1731, and James Logan to Alexander Arscott, 8/9/1731, Letter Book, 1731–32, pp. 36, 15, Letter Book, 4: 286, HSP: Mary Leadbeater, *Memoirs and Letters of Richard and Elizabeth Shackleton* (London, 1822), pp. 138–39; Brookes, *Friend Anthony Benezet,* pp. 433–34.

46 Thomas Chalkley, *Works,* pp. 573–74; Min. Philadelphia MM, 1 (5/26/1700): 180; Brookes, *Friend Anthony Benezet,* p. 371; Susan Dillwyn to William Dillwyn, Dillwyn Mss, 1 (5/6/1791): 140, and (2/14/1792): 155; Samuel Allinson to Thomas Powell, 5/8/1769, Allinson Mss, QC.

47 Overseers of Penn Charter School, Minutes, 4/26/1753, p. 102

48 Woody, *Early Quaker Education in Pennsylvania,* pp. 183–85.

49 Phineas Pemberton to Francis Daniel Pastorius, 2/12/1698; Francis Daniel Pastorius to Phineas Pemberton, 2/12/1698; Israel Pemberton to Thomas Makin, 5/22/1698; Thomas Makin to Phineas Pemberton 2/28/1698, Pemberton Papers, vol. 1, Etting Collection, pp. 76–78, 83, HSP. This correspondence has been reprinted in Marion Dexter Learned, *Life of Francis Daniel Pastorius* (Philadelphia, 1908), pp. 175–80.

50 Chalkley, *Journal,* pp. 212–13, *JFHS* 42 (1950): 51–66.

51 John Watson, *Annals of Philadelphia* (Philadelphia, 1830), pp. 249–50; Chalkley, *Works,* pp. 573–74.

52 Overseers of Penn Charter School, Minutes, 1 (12/15/1755): 137; Woolman, *Journal and Essays,* pp. 390–91; Thomas Redman's Observations to Trustees and Teachers on School, 4/4/1786, Allinson Mss.

53 Martha Allinson to Samuel Allinson, 3 mo./1775, Allinson Mss; James Logan to John Dickinson, 4/12/1704, *Penn-Logan Correspondence,* 1: 293

54 Jonathan Dickinson to Isaac Gale, 10/13/1717; Jonathan Dickinson to Thomas Mayleigh, 9/23/1717, Dickinson Letter Book, 1715–23, p. 164, HSP; Mary Allinson to William Allinson, 2/2/1796, Allinson Mss.

55 "Universal Magazine and Literary Museum," no. 1, 8 mo./1774; no. 6, 12/6/1774, p. 84; "Student Gazette," 1, issue 2, 6/18/1777; 2, issue 13, 9/3/1777; 3, issue 24; 6, issue 53, 6/17/1778. These newspapers are in the Norris of Fairhill Collection, HSP. Jean S. Straub has published three articles making extensive use of these student newspapers. *PMHB* 89 (1965): 447–58; *QH* 55 (1966): 38–45; *PMHB* 91 (1967): 436–56.

56 "Universal Magazine and Literary Museum," no. 6, pp. 82–83; no. 2, 3 mo./1774, pp. 23, 39, 64; "Student Gazette," 6 no. 56, 7/8/1778.

57 "Student Gazette," 6 no. 55, 7/1/1778; 2 no. 20, 10/29/1777.

58 "Universal Magazine and Literary Museum," no. 6, p. 84; "Student Gazette," 2 no. 15, 9/17/1777; 2, no. 16, 9/24/1777.

59 Sarah Hill to Peggy Hill, n.d., Howland Collection, QC.

60 Phineas Pemberton to Abigail Pemberton, 4/9/1697, PP, 2: 154; Abigail Pemberton to Israel Pemberton, 10/20/1702, PP, III, 2

61 James Logan to William Logan 2/8/1728, 12/12/1731, 8/12/1732, 5/18/1734, Logan Letter Book, 3: 198, and 4 (1731–32): 36, 82; James Logan to Captain Wright 9/30/1731, 8/28/1741, Letter Book, 1731–32, pp. 28, 139; James Logan to Alexander Arscott, 8/9/1731, Letter Book, 1731–32; James Logan to Thomas Story, 8/25/1724 in Myers, ed., *Hannah Logan's Courtship,* (Philadelphia, 1904), p. 8

62 Deborah Hill to Hannah Moore, 2/23/1750, Howland Collection.

63 Deborah Morris's Account Book, "Sarah Powell's Board, Clothing and Schooling 1759–1769," Morris Papers in Coates-Reynell Collection, HSP. The Vassar College reference librarians aided me in tentatively identifying Harvey's *Meditations* in four volumes as James Hervey's *Meditations and Contemplations* and *Letters.* Hervey (1714–58) was a very popular devotional writer whose works were published in many editions in England and America. Friends would have disapproved of his defense of predestination.

64 Susanna Dillwyn to William Dillwyn 11/12/1783, 12/27/1790; William Dillwyn to Susanna Dillwyn 2/15/1786, 7/9/1786, 1/28/1793, Dillwyn Mss, 1: 12, 42, 47, 177, LC.

65 George Fox, *Journal,* (New York, 1963) pp. 75–76; Davis Ferris to Eleanor Wheelock, 7/10/1773, Ferris Mss, Friends' Historical Library, Swarthmore.

66 Fox, *Journal,* p. 98; William Penn, *Works,* (London, 1726), 1: 738.

67 George Fox, *Works,* (Philadelphia, 1831), 5: 373–74.

68 Jonathan Dickinson to his brother, 3/14/1696, 5/29/1698, Dickinson Letter Book, 1698–1701; James Jenkins, "Records and Recollections," 1: 51–53; Hannah Harris to John Pemberton, 2/16/1767, PP, 19: 47.

69 John Griscom, *Considerations Relative to an Establishment for Perfecting the Education of Young Men* (New York, 1815), p. 5; Raynor Kelsey, *Centennial History of Moses Brown School, 1819–1919* (Providence, 1919), pp. 26, 40.

70 London Meeting for Sufferings, Minutes, 30 (6/20/1760): 448; Moses Brown, Clerk, *From the Meeting for Sufferings for New England* (Newport?, 1782), pp. 2–3; Owen Biddle to John and Mary Dickinson, 2/16/1793; John Dickinson to Samuel Pleasants, 1/22/1788; George Dillwyn to John______, 8/4/1786; Samuel Allinson to Owen Biddle, 7/31/1790; John Pemberton to Owen Biddle, n.d., Westtown School, Vault, Box 1; Owen Biddle, *A Plan for a School* (Philadelphia, 1780).

7 Youth: The Age of Temptation

He must in a few years like birds fully fledged be turned off to Fend and provide for himself, and then it will avail him nothing to consider in what nest he was bred. He must like them find his own food or perish therefore . . . nothing is or shall be wanting to him on my part for his education.

James Logan to William Logan, 5/25/1731

"The prime" and "the most Critical Time of Life" lasted from age 14 until marriage. Seclusion from the world had to end as the young Quaker confronted the evils from which parents and school had tried to protect him. Friends' children were exposed to their greatest "Temptations" at a stage in which they believed themselves "Qualified to Judge and Choose for themselves, when it is indeed, a time that stands the most in need of a Guide and Instructor" to help them steer between "Austere Restrictions" that might check their "dawning Faculties and a foolish (and often Sinful) Indulgence of their Youthful Appetites and Desires."[1] The monitors—parents, masters, and weighty Friends—had lived through and surmounted the dangerous period and now were obliged to walk the delicate path between the exercise of too much fondness and too great strictness with the realization that either extreme could provoke wickedness.

Both friend and foe commented on Quaker children. *News from Pennsylvania,* an attack upon Penn and his colony inspired by Anglicans and published in England by Francis Bugg, contained a severe indictment of Quaker youth.

> For tho' they pretend to raise up into the Lord, yet their Young Fry (for the most part) having no Restraint, nor Trained up in Virtuous Actions, are the most Lewd and Prophane, for Ranting, Singing, Gaming, Swearing, Cursing, Whoring and Drinking, upon the Face of the Earth.[2]

At the beginning of the nineteenth century, Thomas Clarkson found Quaker youths to be mature far beyond their ages, though he mentioned that, if a Quaker child threw off the restraints of the discipline, he usually ended in complete debauchery.[3] Quakers were well aware that some of their children did not turn out according to expectation. William Shewen described three types of youth. There were those who followed their parents' example and came to a realization of the light within; others kept the outward forms, but their religion, which was based solely upon "Education and Tradition," withered under the sun like "Corn upon the house tops." A third group were rebels who, contemptuous of any authority, cast off all modesty, temperance, chastity, and plainness. If these last returned to the church, it was a miracle.[4] The necessity of repeated exhortations to parents to inculcate in their children the value of plainness in speech and apparel and to restrain them from mixing with the world must mean that some mothers and fathers slighted these duties. A petition in 1696 to the provincial council of Pennsylvania, signed by male and female Quakers and outsiders, asked for the suppression of the "great rudeness and wildness" of the youth of Philadelphia who gambled daily in the streets.[5] Similar complaints directed to the government or to Friends were issued throughout the eighteenth century.

The frequency with which meetings took disciplinary action against marriages outside the faith gives evidence that some young adults did not conform to parental wishes. Although William Penn's *Advice to Children* was a popular tract, Penn's children did not mature as he had wished. John and Thomas became Anglicans, and William Penn, Jr., proved something of a rake in Pennsylvania, becoming involved in a fight with the watch at a tavern and paying indiscreet visits to Lady Cornbury when his lordship was absent.[6] Mordecai Yarnall, a Philadelphia minister, saw his son, age 18, confined to a cell in the hospital because he drank himself into a stupor every night. Friends who visited Charles Read, who had killed a man on the docks in 1789 and was subsequently condemned to die, said he showed no remorse. More penitent was Joseph Jordan, who during a drunken brawl in the house of his father-in-law, Israel Pemberton, fatally stabbed Thomas Kirkbride in the stomach. Isaac Zane, Jr., whose good Quaker father sank heavily into debt to help him buy an ironworks on Cedar Creek, near Winchester, Virginia, later was disowned and lived in splendor in a mansion with Miss Betsey McFarland, his confessed mistress, and their son.[7] Joseph Pemberton, son of Israel Pemberton, Jr., had to be put under strict regulation at night; if he were allowed out on his own, he would use the cover of darkness to hide his misdeeds. As an adult, Joseph lived extravagantly in the worldly planter society of Maryland, gambled heavily, and went bankrupt, greatly embarrassing his father, who had to collect nearly £10,000 to pay off the debts.[8]

Some Quakers sent their sons on voyages in hope of improving them. Joseph Gamble of Barbados hoped that a young man of good Quaker parents voyaging to Philadelphia would "exchange his wild Oats for some of your more Substantial Grain." Edmond Peckover wrote Israel Pemberton from London to ask him and his whole family to watch over and, if necessary, assist his son. The youth had a weakness for alcohol and bad company and, since he had not yet been disowned, the father sent him abroad in hopes of a reformation. If none occurred, Pemberton was to permit the boy to sail for the West Indies. Above all, Pemberton was asked to keep the letter secret and under no circumstances to give the boy money, since he was supposed to be earning his own way.[9] In an attempt to control the wild behavior of youthful Quakers sent abroad to learn trading practices, the yearly meetings required the young men to obtain certificates from their local meetings, which were to be presented to and endorsed by Friends residing in the various ports. If a trader misbehaved, the foreign Friends would refuse to sign his certificate.[10]

If parents found it impossible to control their children, they could always turn to the meetings for help. The process was similar to that used in disciplining. At first a few Friends would talk to the child privately. If he remained obstinate, the matter was presented to the monthly meeting and an official delegation counseled him. If the youth still did not reform, then the meeting took steps to disown him.[11] Friends were well aware of the economic powers of parents. Early Quakers such as Edward Burrough, Thomas Ellwood, and James Parnell had been disinherited by their Puritan fathers. Later Friends could use these occurrences as precedents, though they knew that such actions had rarely proved efficacious. Lancastershire Quarterly Meeting in England suggested that Friends deprive of their patrimony any children who strayed from the truth and were not repentant. The first Philadelphia discipline advised that a child's estate be lessened in order to encourage his reformation.[12] Benjamin Furly objected to the clause in Penn's charter giving equal inheritance to all but the eldest son as depriving parents of the power to reward "Virtue, obedience, and sweetness," and punish "Vice and refractoryness."[13] James Logan once threatened disinheritance if his son did not write home more often (Logan had received one letter in a year), but the threat was mostly bluff, and Logan soon sent assurances that the boy would be well treated on his return.[14] The German Lutheran minister Henry Muhlenberg noted in 1748 that children in Pennsylvania were legally "almost in bondage" to their parents who, if displeased, could punish, disinherit, or sell them (into apprenticeship or indenture). Even after minority, disinheritance "occurs frequently."[15] Pennsylvania was an agrarian society in which the father's power to bestow lands gave him potentially great economic power over his children, but Quakers seem to have had no inclination to exercise such power. The only known instance of disinheritance by a Friend occurred in England before 1700, and then Quakers condemned the action.[16] A far more usual attitude was expressed by James Logan when he advised William Penn that no matter how disappointed he was in William, Jr., he should be tender with him, "for he is and must be thy son, and thou either happy or unhappy in him. The tie is indissoluble."[17] Methods employed by Friends in dealing with their disobedient children were similar to those used by religious parents today. They wrote long letters of advice, warned the child of the ill consequences of his actions, and prayed (often in the child's presence, as William Penn's father tried to do) for improvement. Finally, if all were to no avail, they kept the hurt to themselves and treasured their offspring no matter how they behaved.

Like all orthodox Christians, the Quakers saw any disregard of filial duty as rebellion against God and as upsetting to the natural order. The father was placed in his family as a deputy for the Lord, and Friends did not hesitate to invoke the fifth commandment to secure obedience. But Quakers, unlike New Englanders, resisted any attempt to equate the authority of the state with that of parents. The magistrate, through the exercise of law, could take away human life, whereas parents could not; therefore, their respective authority was not based upon the same power.

> Paternal and Majestratical Authority are of two different Species, the one is Natural, the other is Political, and each has their particular Rules to walk by; the first is Love and Mercy, the last is Justice and Power; by the first, Families are propagated, by the last, Commonwealths are Maintained, and Supported.[18]

The state could intervene to support the father. The "Great Law" agreed upon at Chester in 1682 ordered that anyone who assaulted or threatened a parent be committed to the house of correction to toil at hard labor "during the pleasure of the said parent." After being abrogated, this law was reenacted in 1693. In 1700, the statute was modified and strengthened. Anyone who attacked or menaced "his or her parent" was to suffer six months imprisonment at difficult work and to be "publicly whipped with thirty-one lashes on his or her bare back, well laid on."[19] A servant who was guilty of a similar offense against his master received a six-month sentence but was not whipped. The authority of the state, while different in kind from that of the father, could be invoked in extreme instances to aid the family. These laws show the importance that Friends attached to the authority of parents; but the separation of church and state greatly limited the use of secular authority in any religious dispute between parent and child. These two laws were the only attempts by Pennsylvanians to enforce family authority during the period of Quaker hegemony.

II

Since eighteenth-century Quakers disapproved of university training, their sons and daughters who completed English or Latin school usually did not continue their formal education. A boy might finish school by age 14, but he could not begin a career as an independent merchant or artisan until he was 21, because the law forbade him from transacting business in his own name. The interval between school and legal accountability served as an age of transition in which the Quaker youth became adjusted to adult life by learning a trade.

Friends believed that all persons—rich or poor—should learn a skill, because a wealthy man never knew when he might become destitute, and, besides, idleness was morally dangerous. The youth's first task was to pick a vocation. The trade chosen was determined by the wishes of the boy and his parents. Children needed to be taught "such honest, lawful *Callings*, as the Lord inclines them to, or makes them *Capable* of."[20] The business was to be neither too high nor too debased for the ability and station of the child, and it had to be a useful occupation and one that would not expose the person to undue temptations. William Penn recommended choosing what he termed "God's trades" before man's. Plowing, gardening, shepherding were natural tasks and so were morally superior to work done in a city. Mechanics and handicrafts, while needed, were secondary and far inferior when compared to rural employments. (An agrarian bias can also be found in the writings of American Friends who, like many eighteenth-century people, preferred farming to mercantile pursuits and who viewed cities such as Philadelphia or London as places of dissipation.[21]) John Woolman, after traveling with the sailors in steerage in a Quaker-owned ship and witnessing the treatment and behavior of three Quaker apprentices, counseled against placing boys as apprentices at sea. He doubted the usefulness of most commerce and communication between lands and thought the "channels" used were frightfully impure.[22] Sarah Woolman was greatly disturbed to hear a Friend say that a particular child was to become a doctor or lawyer, for she feared the parents' motive was wealth rather than eternal happiness.[23] When Samuel Allinson (1739–91) was apprenticed to a lawyer, he defended his chosen field by asserting that an honest man need not be corrupted by law.

> I should be very sorry and Utterly Reject any Calling which I was Convinced would Corrupt or Hinder me from that Duty which I know most Behoves all to prize. . . . I have now arrived at the Age 16 and upwards and have liv'd part of the While in that Calling, I think Long Enough to form an Idea thereof: and I found Its not Impossible to be an Attorney at Law and an Honest M[an].[24]

As he grew older Allinson became less certain of the innocence of his occupation, and when, around 1771, he became a strict Friend, he gave up the practice of law and resigned his position in the New Jersey courts. Certain trades, like those involving drama, music, jewelry, or war, were closed to Friends. In 1713 Rhode Island Meeting decided to allow no one to sell strong drink without its approbation, and, while they disciplined a man for selling liquor without their allowance in 1723, they issued no permits.[25] Devout members experienced qualms over making unnecessary wigs or adding superfluous laces to garments, but others sold supplies to armies, catered to luxury tastes as cabinetmakers or silversmiths, armed their merchant ships, and stocked goods not in keeping with Quaker plainness.

Since most Quaker boys grew up on farms, they made a gradual transition from helping with the chores as youngsters to working the farms as adults. Rural schools did not meet during the summer, and Quaker youths spent their vacations working for the family. A boy could learn husbandry and provide needed labor simply by helping his father. The girls assisted in the kitchen and acquired the skills for managing a household that they would need in marriage. A wife and children could help the urban artisan or merchant with his shop, which often was located on the ground floor of their house. Even after they finished attending school, offspring provided too valuable a source of labor to be cast off without very good cause. Sons, though taxable at 16 if living alone, were not taxed in colonial Pennsylvania if they stayed at home, and could be required to work for their parents without pay until they married or reached 21 years of age. Youths who became artisans could be trained by parents or relatives—a procedure that provided labor and saved apprenticeship fees. A famous product of family training was the non-Quaker Benjamin Franklin, whose father first taught him candlemaking and later sent him to his elder brother, James. As Franklin's secret indenture to his brother showed, family arrangements for learning a craft could be formal or informal. Young John Woolman, while a shopkeeper, paid his master a fee to teach him tailoring. Daniel Stanton was apprenticed to a ship's carpenter, but when he discovered that he disliked the job, he returned home and later was bound to a joiner.[26] The legal codes for New York, Massachusetts, and Pennsylvania insisted that boys be taught a trade, but they did not require any specific method for learning it.

Unfortunately, little information is available about those children who worked for their parents. When Quakers mentioned persons gaining a skill, they usually confined their remarks to apprentices. The number of apprentices was not large; even in an artisan center such as Philadelphia, apprentices did not comprise 10 percent of the population. If an historian wishes to know anything about the life of adolescent Quaker boys, he may confine himself to the scanty information about religious turmoil found in the diaries or concentrate upon apprenticeship. Quakers thought of apprenticeship as a method of both education and social control, and they made the master's responsibilities include religious as well as vocational training. The ideal of the apprentice-master relationship was familial, and the advices of the meeting do provide insights into how fathers were expected to deal with their children.

III

The apprenticeship contract defined the legal relationship between master and boy. The master was to instruct the youth in the "art and mystery" of a trade. Often he was responsible for clothing, lodging, and feeding the apprentice, and he was expected to give some kind of freedom dues at the end of the term. Normally, in America, but not always in England, some degree of educational attainment was required.[27] The apprentice was to obey faithfully all his master's "Lawful Commands," (which usually meant obeying the master's wife as well), serve him dutifully, and preserve all his trade secrets. He could engage in no economic activities without his master's approbation, and he was forbidden to lend, steal, waste, or do damage to any of his master's goods. He was not allowed to "haunt" taverns or playhouses, to play at "Cards, Dice, Tables" or any "other unlawful games," and he could not "commit Fornication, nor Contract Matrimony" within the term of service. He was to be at every moment at the command of his master and was never to be absent without leave for any reason.[28] The contents of the contract were generally the same, whether the parents were Friends or Anglicans. Usually some kind of printed form was used, with blanks provided for term of service, type of work, and any special qualifications for the indenture.

William Mather in *The Young Man's Companion,* a guidebook for youth first written by a Friend (but which in many later editions became completely nonsectarian), noted that "Servants and Apprentices are accounted Slaves, during the time of their Service, and are put to the worst of Drudgery for the most part." He cautioned masters against undue severity and advised treating their servants fairly in the "Fear of God."[29] Eleanor Trotter has described apprenticeship in a seventeenth-century parish in the north of England as being less like a teacher-pupil than a lord-serf relationship. If the master abused the apprentice, the boy had recourse to the courts, but only with difficulty could he prove his case, and if he succeeded the only punishment meted out to the master was termination of the contract. (This was also true in America.)[30] If the apprentice ran away, the authorities sought him out, punished him, returned him to the master, and lengthened his obligation to serve. In certain cases the masters took apprentices only for fees and abused the boys in the hopes that they would desert so that the contracts would be forfeited.

Because of the harshness of the terms of indenture, Quaker parents attempted to ease their restrictions. The youth had some say in what skill he chose. At times there was a trial period during which the master and the would-be apprentice would learn about one another and the boy would decide whether he liked the trade. Usually this was done before the indentures were signed. Israel Pemberton, Sr., was not content to stay at home or serve his brothers, who could not teach him a trade. With his stepmother's permission, in 1702 he apprenticed himself to Samuel Carpenter for seven years. During the first year he was to learn "Baking and Bulting" and the next four "Traffic and Merchandise."[31] Jonathan Dickinson's son, John, was given permission to apprentice himself to Walter Newberry of Newport or Thomas Nyam of London, both of whom were relatives. Dickinson, a permissive parent, allowed his sons to go to England and gave them considerable leeway in what they did, in spite of the fact that John was badly educated and "too forward" and Joseph was a "Rough Impolished Youth having his head filled with Notions. Could he gain some better furniture will be highly prized by us his parents."[32]

Friends attempted to guard against the exploitation of children by assigning them only to members of the meeting who were, of course, under the discipline. There were instances, both in England and America, where monthly meetings censured masters for cruelty to servants, but the only punishment available was disownment.[33] In an attempt to guard against the negligence of parish officials or orphans' courts, some parents left instructions in their wills for the meeting to supervise the rearing of and putting out of their children. Most such instances occurred before 1725, however.

Like the Puritans, Friends wanted the masters to be religious men. The attempted seclusion at home and in school carried over into apprenticeship. The early advice of London and Philadelphia Yearly Meetings specifically enjoined the placing out of children to Quakers. The New York discipline of 1800 warned parents that disregard of this counsel could result in disownment. Friends were asked to keep their fees low and to grant special privileges to children of members so that a proper religious upbringing might be guaranteed.[34] When parents were unable to find a Quaker willing to take their child, they applied to the monthly meeting for help. In rare instances the meeting granted permission to bind the youth to a non-Quaker.[35] A good master reared the child "in the truth" by holding family devotions, giving advice, and requiring attendance at meetings. The crowning glory for a Quaker master came when he could boast, much like Cotton Mather, of converting his household. John Banks succeeded in rearing godly children and Christian servants.

> And as my Soul's Desire was chiefly for their eternal Good, so the Lord was pleased accordingly to answer it, in raising up three of my Servants with a Testimony for his Name, Truth and Glory, (together with one of my Daughters of late Years). . . .[36]

The quest for a religiously unified family conflicted with the desire for servants, since there were more families desirous of servants than there were Friends willing to be domestics or laborers. George Fox advised masters to choose their servants for their religious qualities and to require their attendance at family devotions and meeting. In letters of strict Friends, one occasionally finds requests for Quaker housekeepers or governesses, and some servants did adopt the master's faith. When he was converted to Quakerism, Moses Brown managed to persuade his wife's servant to leave the Anglican church. William Logan dismissed an overseer, originally recommended to him by a Quaker minister, who was later disowned when he married out of unity.[37] But other Friends were more lax. In 1681 Thomas Maule of Salem, Massachusetts, had a Roman Catholic maid. Quakers in Pennsylvania and Rhode Island owned slaves and bought German and Irish indentured servants who could work in the fields or the households. The Drinker family of Philadelphia contained female servants who attended chapel or Presbyterian services. Perhaps many Friends, like Abraham Redwood of Newport, esteemed themselves fortunate to find a "sober" coachman and trusted the power of master and mistress to create a godly environment in which servants at least outwardly conformed to the religious tenets of their employers.[38] At any rate, no Friend took credit for doing without servants because he could not find religious ones.

From 1650 until after the American Revolution masters were considered heads of family groups which included apprentices and servants. Fox wrote in 1656, "Dear friends, exhort all your families at times and seasons, whether they be servants or children, that they may be informed in the truth."[39] As late as 1814 Baltimore Yearly Meeting referred to the necessity of educating freed Negroes "who are in Friends' families," and in 1816 James Mott reminded members that "servants or hired people generally make part of the family."[40] The epistles of London and Philadelphia Yearly Meetings normally grouped advices to children, servants, and apprentices. Parents and masters were told in 1688 "to use your power in your own families, in the education [of] your children and servants." The 1757 query asked if parents, by precept and example, endeavored to "train up their Children, Servants, and those under their Care" in godly conversation.[41] When Robert Sutcliff traveled in America in 1804, he noted approvingly that on his deathbed Joshua Rowland called his domestics—two white servants, two Negro boys, and an orphan—to his bedside and after a short pause "addressed each of them in the language and accents of a father; for indeed as a parent he had always conducted himself towards them."[42] The only indication of a change in this attitude came in England. Southwark or Horslydown Monthly Meeting in London drew up membership lists in 1737, 1762, and 1782. In the two early lists children, apprentices, and servants were listed with mothers and fathers. In the 1782 list, servants and apprentices were omitted, even when the servants were Friends who worked for Friends.[43] Unfortunately, one cannot determine whether or not this was a general practice, since no other meetings in England or America drew up such detailed lists of members at periodic intervals.

The father, as head of the household, was responsible for the behavior of all members of his family. The apprentice could be treated as if he were his child, because he was generally an acquaintance's son or daughter. Since managing a servant was similar in nature to rearing children, familial language was appropriate; and most of the advice given about governing servants duplicated meetings' counsel regarding children.[44] The master had first, through self-control, to set a correct example. Discipline, though within his province, could never be meted out in anger, because passions and lack of moderation easily passed from master to servant. Owners were "generally gainers" from the service of their apprentices, said Thomas Chalkley, and so should use them well and not attempt to overwork or oppress them.[45]

The pitfalls for bound servants were the same as for children. Masters tried to keep apprentices in due submission at all times, "for youth, if they be let loose, are like wild asses and wild heifers" running into "airiness" and wickedness.[46] Some Friends esteemed apprenticeship primarily because it offered a legal instrument to control adolescents. Ireland Yearly Meeting's epistle in 1701 suggested that fathers who were teaching their offspring their own trade should bind them as apprentices so as to "keep them Close to their business as a good means to humble their mind and greatly help their Growth in Truth."[47] Jonathan Dickinson wanted to put "under Covenants" a "crassly Disorderly Young man" named Richard Wharton as a means of reforming him, but Wharton's parents through "their foolish pity (that hath brought him to what he is)" would not consent.[48] A servant's idleness could cause financial hardship for a master and could constitute a moral danger for himself. Thomas Chalkley advised that all youths, no matter what their social station, be apprenticed as a means of teaching them how to work. Since schooling was normally finished by age 14 and business could not legally begin until age 21, there was a seven-year interval of potential idleness, which might endanger the person's physical and spiritual well-being. The master was warned to enforce the contract's prohibition of gambling and drinking and to make sure that he supervised every moment of the boy's time.[49]

A person's wealth and position were important in attracting apprentices. When only 25, James Pemberton, the brother of Israel, Jr., had Samuel Powell Emlen, the son of a prominent Philadelphia Friend, as an apprentice. When James went to England, Samuel was left under the immediate supervision of John Pemberton, age 21. An apprentice could be a very valuable investment. John left instructions to Samuel Emlen to be in the store as much as possible, sell items at set prices, take accountings of all arriving cargoes, keep the books, check credit, foreclose, load ships for Barbados, and make an inventory of all goods. Above all, James advised Samuel, never to be idle. Samuel wrote back to James, whom he addressed as "Dear Master," "that I have hitherto been fully employ'd about one Thing or other ever since thou left us, and see no Likelihood of its being otherwise until thy Return."[50] Since Samuel was being instructed not only by James from London, but also by Israel Pemberton, Sr., Israel's wife, Israel, Jr., and John Pemberton, he must have wished for the return of a single master.

Friends did not hesitate to use Paul's admonition to masters to be "just and equal" and forbear threatening; so also they quoted his advice that servants "be obedient to . . . Masters . . . as unto Christ: Not with Eye-service, as Menpleasers, but as the Servants of Christ." Financial inducements were added to religious considerations. Many hard-working pious youths who began with little money and small natural abilities had risen to become "prosperous, rich and honourable Masters."[51] Quakers warned that good apprentices became successful tradesmen and bad ones ended in destitution. Masters were careful about the kinds of lads they accepted. John Reynell wrote that he would take Abraham Redwood's son, "but if he be high Spirited and Proud I should be glad to be excused from taking him for that Temper or a sour morose one would no ways suit me."[52] Since no one in Philadelphia knew the boy, Reynell insisted on a trial period before the indenture was signed. Even if Quakers did not approve art works such as Hogarth's *Idle and Industrious Apprentice,* they were well aware of the difference between industrious and idle workers.

James Logan's indecision about his son William's future shows a good deal about what Quakers expected from apprenticeship. When William was 13, James decided that the boy could not learn in American schools and so sent him to England where he spent the next three years in grammar school. In 1733 James concluded that Billy was not learning very much in England either and should be apprenticed. The schoolmaster discussed the matter with William to determine what profession the boy preferred. William had no definite choice, and the father debated whether trade was the best occupation considering that the British dominions were overrun with merchants and business conditions were so uncertain. William's occupation should be so useful that the world could not subsist without it, not that riches lead to happiness but because the best that man could hope for in this world was to "slide thro as easily as possible." An English apprenticeship would cost £200 (double what one would pay in America) and bring only questionable benefit. Apprenticeships were "7 years Servitude to slave for others" and the most that could be gained from them was an inclination toward business, "inur'd to diligence, and thereby prevented from falling in their most dangerous years into idle courses." James Logan had broken his hip, was lame, and believed that William could learn diligence and morality at home while being useful to his parents. Yet both parents feared that at home William could not be kept under "Streit rein" and would fall into idle and dissolute habits. In spite of the danger of being exposed to the "licentious" youth of Philadelphia, Logan decided to apprentice William for three or four years to his own former apprentice and new business partner, Edward Shippen, but the mother refused to agree because Shippen was not a Friend. Finally, James bound William to Israel Pemberton, Sr., a prosperous merchant and strict Friend, whose son, Israel, Jr., could serve William as a model of piety and industry.[53]

The relationship between a master and his apprentice depended partially upon the station of the youth and the fees he paid. A charity case would be treated as a servant; a relative or high-paying person as a member of the family. Abraham Redwood, Jr.'s, station in life was such that it was improper for him to serve as the younger apprentice who swept floors, fixed the fire, and did other menial tasks. Two years after being bound in 1759, Abraham left his lodgings with a Friend, who reprimanded him for taking undue "liberty with the Young Ladies in My Family."[54] Jesse Kersey, bound in 1784 to a Friend who appeared concerned for his welfare, found that the man treated his apprentices as inferiors who ate the leftovers after the family had dined. Kersey, who had hoped to be treated as a member of the family, had to associate with the other apprentices who swore, fought, caroused at night, and went to plays.[55] A nearly ideal father-son relationship was established by John Reynell and Elias Bland, a boy who came from London and paid a fee of 100 gn. sterling. The apprenticeship was arranged by one of Reynell's correspondents, a London Friend, who assured the father, a London goldsmith, that Reynell was "a Gentleman under whose Care his son would be perfectly safe" and would not be forced into activities beneath "one in his Station." The apprentice was to "dine at thy own Table with thyself and Family and in all things treat him as thou wouldst desire another to use a Son of thy own."[56] The father wrote requesting that the boy be allowed to attend weekday meetings and instructing that "he may be kept fully Employed And not have

Liberty to be absent at Evening or any other Time without Thy Leave."[57] The period of servitude was viewed by the elder Bland as an opportunity for his son to establish personal connections with American merchants, and Elias Bland later traded with Reynell, John Smith, and the Pembertons. After a stay of five years Bland returned home with a commendatory letter from Reynell noting that, though the youth was a little unsteady, with hard work and careful management he could become a good merchant.[58] Reynell wrote to his correspondents in London and elsewhere praising the new businessman and did business regularly with Bland, even though the young man's performance in later years did not always conform to Reynell's expectations. A constant stream of letters of advice on how to live and trade came from Reynell and, in return, Bland sent books and presents for the Reynell family. When Bland quarreled with his father, John Reynell managed to repair the relationship.[59] In spite of Bland's later personal shortcomings, Reynell continued to remain on the closest of terms with him. This business relationship, reinforced by personal friendship, showed the apprentice-master association at its best.

John Smith, James Logan, and John Pemberton maintained friendships with former apprentices, but the relationship between master and servant did not always end harmoniously.[60] In 1776 David Greene of Newport tried to obtain the release of his brother from a master who abused him. Joshua Barker beat with a horsewhip an apprentice who sneaked away from the house one night and the next morning refused to say where he had been.[61] Jonathan Roberts I (born 1731) suffered from want of food during his indenture; Jonathan Roberts II (born 1773) worked well with his master, whom he treated like a father and with "due deference." However, he had a few difficulties with the wife and was tormented by an older lazy boy who wished to camouflage his misdeeds. Roberts survived by "patient endurance" but warned his children that apprenticeship was hazardous to any but "inert or humble minds" and should be avoided by would-be farmers. Even the opportunity to marry into the master's family did not always work out well. Nathan Roberts' master was not only an "unfortunate" influence, but the master's sister, whom he married, was "unamiable in temper."[62] Joseph Fox was lucky, for his bachelor master, who died in 1737, left the bulk of his estate to Fox and another apprentice.[63]

Many Quaker merchants first acquainted their sons with business by sending them abroad, usually to England. The trip, serving as an introduction to England and an opportunity to test a boy's moral fiber, combined vocational with intellectual pursuits. Jonathan Dickinson entrusted one son with £200 and told him that was his stake. When he had used it all, he was to come home.[64] Israel Pemberton, Jr., on his trip to England, traded so extensively that he embarrassed his father. When the other sons went, Israel, Sr., advised them not to indulge in trading, and John traveled over England as a companion to John Churchman, a Quaker minister.[65] Francis Rawle, George and Thomas Mifflin, Isaac Norris, Jr., Samuel Powell, Isaac Zane, Jonas Redwood, and William Logan's sons George and Charles were also sent to England. John Smith made a trip to Barbados before settling down as a Philadelphia merchant. Friends realized that these journeys were the result of wanderlust rather than an interest in business, as when Thomas Pleasants and his cousin from Virginia journeyed to Philadelphia "to see fashions Learn Wit and Get Wives, if they can."[66] A voyage gave a young man who served as supercargo business experience, allowed him to see the world (something that established merchants had difficulty doing), and gave him an opportunity to form business and personal relationships with merchants in London or the West Indies. This American version of the European grand tour was engaged in only by the sons of the most wealthy Friends.

Edmund S. Morgan has found that in Puritan New England wardship or apprenticeship, besides serving an economic role and preserving the family from the strains of enduring an adolescent, was useful as a means of preventing parents from spoiling their children. Even wealthy Puritans might put out their offspring, and Morgan found instances where a father placed out his own children and took in others.[67] William Penn strongly condemned the placing out system.

> They do with their Children as with their Souls, put them out at Livery for so much a Year. They will trust their Estates or Shops with none but themselves, but for their Souls and Posterity they have less Solitude.[68]

Penn's children were raised at home, but after their father's death Richard and Thomas were bound out. In 1800 Elizabeth Drinker castigated those who were in a "Great hurry . . . to get rid of their children" and sent them to Westtown boarding school. The Drinker children stayed at home, yet the family accepted white boys and girls of less than ten and black boys as young as six or seven on trial as potential apprentices or servants.[69] John Reynell's sister invited him to send his daughter to England, a request he refused and instead asked her to send a son of hers to Philadelphia.[70] James Logan would have liked to have sent his daughters to England (because he saw no future for America), but the children and their mother refused. Israel Pemberton, Sr., who apprenticed himself after the death of his father, taught his own sons his business. Jonathan Dickinson reared the boys of his brother-in-law, Isaac Gale, but sent his own sons elsewhere to learn merchandising. Wealthy merchants such as Abraham Redwood, James and William Logan, and John Smith apprenticed their sons. The available evidence suggests that most Friends who bound out their children did so for economic reasons. A father might be retired, living in a remote place, disabled or dead, or know nothing about his son's chosen trade. Yet the apprenticeship of Joseph Pemberton, son of Israel Pemberton, Jr., to John Reynell cannot be explained by such factors.[71] Whatever the other reasons, such as a father-son conflict or fear of spoiling the child, the parents did not mention them.

Bernard Bailyn has argued that in America the function of apprenticeship changed. With the great labor shortage and the need for skilled artisans, the traditional methods of apprenticeship were inadequate. The functions that had originally belonged to the master, such as education, were transferred to the schools and a new institution, the evening school, grew up as a vehicle for instructing apprentices. In New England the master was exhorted by church and government to exercise parental control and the boy to accept a filial relationship; however, even in the seventeenth century, "both sets of obligations were increasingly neglected." Masters treated their apprentices as laborers, and apprentices used their masters as a means to gain a few skills. In short, during the colonial period, according to Bailyn, apprenticeship declined quantitatively and deteriorated qualitatively.[72]

There is little evidence that the nature of Quaker apprenticeships changed during the colonial period. The exhortations issued by George Fox to masters and servants in the seventeenth century did not differ markedly from the advices pronounced by American meetings just before the Revolution. A quantitative evaluation of the strength of apprenticeship for both Quakers and outsiders can be made by comparing two lists of indentures kept by the mayors of Philadelphia covering 1745–46 and 1771–73.[72] The earlier record has 922 entries, of which the overwhelming number were for indentured servants from Ireland or Germany. There were 72 cases of apprenticeship. In 28 cases the father signed the indenture; 4 of these were for such long periods that charity was probably the purpose. In 31 instances a mother or uncle or brother signed the contract; in 12 the overseers of the poor were the contracting parties. Since a father would normally sign the indenture, the 31 cases in which another relative was involved showed that the father was absent, disabled, or dead. In 47 instances the apprenticeship arose from the needs of poverty or from the fact that the father probably was not able to impart skills to his offspring.

During the year beginning October 3, 1771, a total of 579 boys and girls were apprenticed in Philadelphia (397 males and 116 females).[73] The length of service for these children varied from a few months to seventeen years and there was no standard term. For example, 92 contracts were for the periods of less than four years, while 155 ran over eight years and 94 of these over ten years. Almost all the males were to be trained in artisan trades, and most of the girls were apprenticed in "housewifry." Some schooling or a level of education to be attained was specified in the contracts of 55 percent of the males and 82 percent of the females. Normally the indenture mentioned instruction in reading, writing, and cyphering to the rule of three (a proportion where given three numbers, the fourth can be determined); rarely were the demands higher and sometimes, particularly for girls, lower. Usually the amount of schooling was circumscribed with attendance limited to one quarter per winter or to an evening school for several quarters, and often the parents or guardians were expected to pay for it. Those who received formal education might have gone to school for several years before being apprenticed. James Allinson, bound out to a tailor after the Revolutionary War, was given one quarter's schooling but the boy had already completed several years of formal instruction.[74] The instances where educational attainments were completely ignored suggest that the youths had already finished schooling. Several of the contracts in this category were for bookkeeping or navigation, skills demanding a knowledge of mathematics. Thomas Chalkley's description of the stages of life showed apprenticeship beginning only when education ended. These indentures illustrate that, at a time when there was no compulsory school system in Philadelphia, much of the artisan class gained or completed their education through the apprenticeship system.

The difference between the 71 cases in 1745 and the 579 indentures in 1771 is explained by the increase in population of the city and the growth of Philadelphia as an artisan and mercantile center. In 1743 Philadelphia contained approximately 13,000 inhabitants; those who were apprenticed that year comprised .54 percent of the population.[75] In 1772 Philadelphians numbered 40,000, and the number of children apprenticed equalled 1.1 percent of the population. In both periods the number of apprenticeships in a given year was less than 2 percent of the population. This scattered fragmentary evidence from one locality suggests there was no quantitative decline in apprenticeships. Such information does not prove Bailyn's hypothesis wrong, but it does suggest that historians need more definite evidence about the nature and extent of the practice of apprenticeship in the early colonial period before declaring that a change occurred in the institution.

During the colonial period Quakers (and other colonists) practiced four types of apprenticeship. They continued the traditional English practice of putting out small children who were either orphans or children of the destitute. Apprenticeship here was essentially a charitable institution whereby the child could have some semblance of a normal family relationship as well as training in a craft. George Fox believed that such charity indentures were an excellent way of building up decayed families, since in time the children could be expected to take over the care of their parents.[76] The apprenticeships in Philadelphia which in 1771 ran longer than eight years (about 25 percent of the total number) were probably charity indentures.

The middle and poorer classes used apprenticeship as a method of gaining the necessary occupational skills in a variety of artisan trades. Fees here were a secondary consideration. For example, of the 579 contracts in Philadelphia in 1771, 492 listed no fees for either party. The labor provided by the apprentice was considered equivalent to the value of vocational (and perhaps moral) training received. In those 81 cases where fees were paid, the highest amount was £20, and, rather significantly, in 83 percent of such cases no educational requirements were mentioned. Clearly, such fees meant that apprenticeship was a form of hired labor.

Finally, during the eighteenth century, letters of wealthy Friends disclose that apprenticeship became a prestigious form of class distinction. The fees for being trained by one of the leading merchants were far above the range of the commonality and thereby excluded them from the business community. John Reynell's standard charge was 100 gn. sterling and the father was to provide clothing. Even at this cost he was crowded with applicants. When wealthy Abraham Redwood of Newport wanted to apprentice his son, he suggested that either Reynell take him or inquire of other Quaker merchants if they had openings. Reynell, who at that time had several apprentices, found that the Pembertons and William Logan also had all they needed. However, since he had three young men leaving within a year, Reynell finally agreed to accept the boy at his customary fee. Richard Partridge, for a time Pennsylvania's colonial agent in London, sent instructions for his grandson to be apprenticed to William Logan, Reynell, or one of the Pembertons.[77] The attractiveness of these men was due not only to their financial ability but also to the fact that they were known as devout Friends.

Quaker children learned an occupation within a family group. Agricultural and artisan trades were organized on a household basis, and parents could teach skills while gaining labor from their children. If a child were indentured, he left his parents and joined another household. Friends thought of apprenticeship in terms of a family relationship, with the master's role as analogous to that of the father and the apprentice's to that of the son. The advices that meetings gave to masters and apprentices duplicated those given to fathers and sons. By insisting that the master be a Friend, Quakers continued their attempts to guarantee the youth's virtue by preserving him from contact with evil. A person mature enough to learn a trade could not be completely isolated from the ways of the world. Between fourteen and twenty-one seclusion gradually ended and a youth proved either that plainness had been grafted on to new stock or that unsteadiness and dissipation had taken root. The colonial period disclosed no apparent signs of decline in the number of youths who were indentured, and there is no evidence that Friends began to see apprenticeship as providing purely secular vocational training. Undoubtedly, some masters neglected their spiritual obligations, but the meetings often reminded them of their religious responsibilities, and wealthy and highly esteemed masters managed to combine business and religion. When a young man finished his term of servitude, he could enter into adult life and assume the responsibility for forming his own family.

Notes

1 William Smith, "Universal Love," in *Balm from Gilead* (1675), p. 90; Paul Johnson to Israel Pemberton, Jr., 2/17/1733, PP, 3: 15; David Cooper, *Diary*, 1747–95, p. 30.
2 *News from Pensilvania* (London, 1703), p. 32.
3 Thomas Clarkson, *Portraiture of Quakerism* (London, 1807), 3: 270–71.
4 William Shewen, *A Brief Testimony Against Tale-Bearers, Whispers, and Back-biters* (Philadelphia, 1701), pp. 19–20.
5 *BFHA*, 43 (1943): 31–32.
6 *Correspondence between William Penn and James Logan*, (Phildelphia, 1870) 1: 315, 320, 346.
7 John Smith to Uncle John Smith, 2/9/1763, Smith Mss, 6: 40; Susan Dillwyn to William Dillwyn 2/26/1789, Dillwyn Mss, 1: 84; PP, 14: 80, 84; Carl Bridenbaugh, *The Colonial Craftsman* (New York, 1950), pp. 25–26.
8 Benjamin Lightfoot to Israel Pemberton 1/29/1762, Letters of American Friends, QC; Theodore Thayer, *Israel Pemberton: King of the Quakers* (Philadelphia, 1943), p. 196.
9 Joseph Gamble to John Smith, 6/15/1748, Smith Mss. 3: 62; Edmund Peckover to Israel Pemberton, Jr., 5/10/1745, PP, 3: 169.
10 Min. Philadelphia YM, 7/28/1698, 1:74.
11 Philadelphia YM, Discipline 1704–19.
12 London YM, Epistles Received, 1: 272; Philadelphia YM, Discipline 1704–19; Rufus Jones, *Quakers in the American Colonies*, (New York, 1966), p. 313.
13 *PMHB* 19 (1895): 298.
14 James Logan to William Logan, 2/28/1733, p. 234, and 3/26/1734, pp. 395–96, Logan Letter Book, vol. 4.
15 *Journals of Henry Melchior Muhlenberg*, trans. T. G. Tappert and J. W. Doberstein (Philadelphia, 1958), 1: 197. For an excellent discussion of parental economic power in Andover, Massachusetts, and a critique based on Plymouth Colony, see Philip J. Greven, Jr., *Four Generations*, pp. 72–99, 272–73, and John Demos, *A Little Commonwealth* (New York, 1970), pp. 164–70.
16 John Tomkins to John Rodes, 1/18/1698, in Mrs. G. L. Lampson, ed., A *Quaker Post-Bag* (London, 1910), p. 160; Richard Vann, *Social Development of English Quakerism* (Cambridge, Mass., 1969), p. 184.
17 *Penn-Logan Correspondence*, 1: 346.
18 Benjamin Coole, *Miscellanies*, pp. 50–51; Min. London YM, 4/4–6/1688 pp. 182–83.
19 George *et al.*, eds., *Charter to William Penn, and Laws of the Province of Pennsylvania*, (Harrisburg, Penn., 1879), p. 113; Mitchell and Flanders, eds., *Statutes at Large of Pennsylvania* (Harrisburg, Penn. 1896) 2: 13.
20 William Salt, *The Light, the Way, That Children Ought to be Trained Up In* (London, 1660), pp. 2–3.
21 William Penn, *Works* (London, 1726), 1: 895; Joseph Scattergood to James Allinson, 8/18/1792, Allinson Papers, QC; *PMHB* 4 (188): 341–42.
22 John Woolman, *Journal and Essays* (New York, 1922), pp. 291–95, 302–03, 398–400; Janet Whitney, *John Woolman: American Quaker* (Boston, 1942), p. 86.
23 Sarah Woolman to———, 1 mo. /1776, Letters of American Friends, QC.

24 Samuel Allinson to Jacob Allinson, ca. 1755, Allinson Papers.
25 Min. Rhode Island MM, 2 (5/28/1713): 89, and (5/30/1723): 205, 266; Min. Philadelphia YM, 2 (9/20–10/4–1777): 376.
26 Woolman, *Journal and Essays,* p. 164; Daniel Stanton, *Journal* (Philadelphia, 1772), pp. 8, 18.
27 Richard B. Morris, *Government and Labor in Early America* (New York, 1960), p. 380. An examination of sixty-eight Quaker apprenticeship certificates belonging to Southwark Meeting in London confirmed Morris's conclusion that rarely was provision for education included in English indentures. Southwark Mss, vol. 5, Friends' House, London.
28 This paragraph is based upon the indentures found at Friends' House, London, and in the Historical Society of Pennsylvania. Indentures of Apprentices, 1677–1849, Miscellaneous Collections, HSP.
29 William Mather, *The Young Man's Companion,* 12th ed. (London, 1723), p. 129.
30 Eleanor Trotter, *Seventeenth Century Life in the Country Parish* (Cambridge, 1919), pp. 154–57; Morris, *Government and Labor,* p. 377. Apprentices may have been better protected in England than in America, because, in addition to the courts, the guilds actively enforced the contracts. Ivy Pinchbeck and Margaret Hewitt, *Children in English Society* (London, 1969), pp. 228–31.
31 Alice Pemberton to Samuel Carpenter, 8/18/1702, PP, 2: 185; Certificate of Indenture, 5/17/1702, PP, Miscellaneous Mss, no. 3.
32 Jonathan Dickinson to Thomas Mayleigh, 7/24/1717, p. 152; Jonathan Dickinson to John Asker, 3/3/1718, 190, Dickinson Letter Book, 1715–21, HSP.
33 Min. Rhode Island MM, 6/25/1719, p. 169; Philadelphia MM, Original Certificates, 1686–1713, 4/5/1709, p. 83. Men were more frequently disciplined for abusing a servant than for ill treating an apprentice. Here is the apology of C. L. on 4/15/1768: "After deliberately Considering my Case Respecting William McGuire I find it my duty to Condemn my Conduct in having any hand in Pouring Liquor on the said McGuire's hair which caused him to misbehave and taking in hand to Correct him I did it with too Large a stick and as I looked upon him to be my servant at the time this happened I hope friends will take this acknowledgement." Bradford MM, Certificates of Removals, Reports, 1760–69, p. 226, DR.
34 Philadelphia YM, Discipline, 1704–19; Christian and Brotherly Advices, p. 161; Min. London YM, 6/11–16/1753; New York YM, *Rules of Discipline and Christian Advice* (New York, 1800), p. 81.
35 Min. Perquimans MM, vol. 2A, 7/7/1773, 8/4/1773.
36 John Banks, *A Rebuke to Unfaithful Parents and a Rod for Stubborn Children* (London, 1710), p. 4.
37 George Fox, *Works,* (Philadelphia, 1831), 8: 22–23; Smith, "Universal Love," pp. 76, 97–98; Mack Thompson, *Moses Brown: Reluctant Reformer* (Chapel Hill, North Carolina, 1962), p. 85; William Logan to John Smith, 2/28/1758, Smith Mss, 5: 55; PP, 16: 52; Philadelphia MM, Original Certificates, 1714–19, pp. 296, 298.
38 M. B. Jones, "Thomas Maule, The Salem Quaker, and Free Speech in Massachusetts Bay," *Essex Institute Historical Collections* 72 (1936): 9–10: *Extracts from the Journal of Elizabeth Drinker* (Philadelphia, 1889) pp. 146, 186, 231, 289; Abraham Redwood to Stephen Greenleafe, March 6, 1750, Abraham Redwood Letter Book, vol. 3, Newport Historical Society.
39 Fox, *Works,* 7: 116.
40 Min. Baltimore YM, 10/10/1814, quoted in William C. Dunlap, *Quaker Education in Baltimore and Virginia Yearly Meeting,* p. 447; James Mott, *Observations on the Education of Children* (New York, 1816), p. 26.
41 London YM, *Epistles from the Yearly Meeting* (1688), p. 38; Christian and Brotherly Advices (1757), pp. 273–74.
42 Robert Sutcliff, *Travels in Some Parts of North America in the Years 1804, 1805, and 1806* (York, England, 1815), pp. 280–81.
43 The List of Friends at Horslydown Monthly Meeting, 1737, 1762, 1782, 1795, Mss at Friends' House, London.
44 Smith, "Universal Love," pp. 81–82. The official legal relationship between master and apprentice was *in loco parentis.*
45 Thomas Chalkley, *Works,* (London, 1791), p. 576; George Fox the Younger, *A Collection of the Several Books and Writings* (London, 1662), pp. 42–44.
46 Fox, *Works,* 8:24.
47 Min. London YM, 2 (5/10/1701): 338.
48 Jonathan Dickinson to his brother (Isaac Gale?), 3/2/1715, Letter Book, 1715–21.
49 Chalkley, *Works,* pp. 575–77; "The Ancient Testimony of the People called Quakers, Revived," Philadelphia YM, Christian and Brotherly Advices, p. 251. This treatise, originally written by Barclay, was reissued in 1722 by Philadelphia as a statement of Quaker practices.
50 John Pemberton's Directions for Samuel Emlen, 3/21/1749, PP, 5: 87; James Pemberton to John Pemberton, 10/19/1748, 5: 5; Samuel Emlen to James Pemberton, 11/23/1748, 4: 167, and 5/31/1749, 5: 98.
51 John Freame, *Scripture Instruction* (London, 1713), pp. 48–49; David

Hall, *Memoirs* (London, 1758), p. 120.

52 John Reynell to Abraham Redwood, 12/4/1746, Reynell Letter Book, 1745–47.

53 James Logan to William Logan (Uncle), 12/12/1731, p. 37, and 7/16/1732, p. 76; James Logan to Alexander Arscott, 8/10/1732, p. 80, Logan Letter Book 1732–33; James Logan to William Logan, 12/27–28/1732, pp 316–18; 3/30–31/1733, 5/25/1733, p. 341; 7/1/1733, p. 342; James Logan to William Logan (son) 2/28/1733, Logan Letter Book, Vol. 4.

54 George Cradock to Abraham Redwood, 5/29/1759, 1/20/1761, Abraham Redwood Letter Book, 4: 23.

55 Jesse Kersey, *A Narrative of the Early Life, and Travels and Gospel Labors of Jesse Kersey* (Philadelphia, 1851), pp. 24–33.

56 Lawrence Williams to John Reynell, 7/12/1737; Daniel Flexney to John Reynell, 6/26/1737, Reynell Papers, 1736–37.

57 John Bland to John Reynell, 6/18/1737, Reynell Papers, 1736–37.

58 John Reynell to John Bland, 4/21/1743, Reynell Letter Book, 1741–43.

59 John Reynell to John Bland, 6/1/1753; John Reynell to Elias Bland, 6/1/1753, Reynell Letter Book, 1752–54. When Bland overextended his business and fell into debt, Reynell wrote that Bland's good behavior in the future would please him "as if thou were my Own Child."

60 Richard Partridge to John Smith, 6/20/1755, Smith Mss, 4: 231: Isaac Foster, Jr., to John Pemberton, 10/22/1757, PP, 12: 76.

61 David Greene's Book Bought in Newport, p. 53, John Carter Brown Library; Richard Smith, Jr., to John Smith, n.d., Smith Mss, 3: 155.

62 Jonathan Roberts, "Memoirs," pp. 9, 19, 73, 80, 82–83, HSP.

63 *PMHB* 32 (1908): 178.

64 Jonathan Dickinson to Thomas Mayleigh, 7/24/1717, Dickinson Letter Book 1715–21, p. 152.

65 Thayer, *Israel Pemberton: King of the Quakers,* pp. 6–7; Israel Pemberton, Sr., to James Pemberton, 9/23/1748, PP, 4: 165; John Pemberton to James Pemberton, 10/31/1748, 5: 14.

66 Robert Pleasants to John Smith, 10/9/1752, Smith Mss, 4: 81; William Logan to John Pemberton, 7/7/1751, PP, 7: 109; John Smith, "Diary," vol. 1, 10 mo./1741.

67 Edmund Morgan, *The Puritan Family,* (New York, 1966), pp. 75–78; John Demos, *A Little Commonwealth: Family Life in Plymouth Colony,* (New York, 1970), p. 74.

68 Penn, *Works,* 1: 901.

69 Drinker, *Extracts from the Journal,* pp. 159, 161, 216, 231, 242, 248, 250, 255, 278; John Smith, "Diary," vol. 7, 3/7/1749, and vol. 10, 6/18/1750. Some of these children were sent by the parents to the Drinkers, while others came after a payment was made.

70 John Reynell to Mary Groth, 9/29/1754, Reynell Letter Book, 1754–56; Jonathan Dickinson to Isaac Gale, 7/7/1717, and Jonathan Dickinson to John Asker, 3/3/1718, Dickinson Letterbook. John Pemberton to John Smith, Smith Mss, 6: 209.

71 Bernard Bailyn, *Education in the Formation of American Society* (Chapel Hill, North Carolina, 1960) pp. 29–36.

72 "Record of Indentures of Individuals Bound out as Apprentices, Servants, etc. and of German and Other Redemptioners in the Office of the Mayor of the City of Philadelphia, October 3, 1771, to October 5, 1773," *Pennsylvania-German Society Proceedings* 16 (1907) 1–325; "Account of Servants Bound and Assigned before James Hamilton, Mayor of Philadelphia, 1745 and 1746," HSP.

73 In the mayor's records for 1771 apprenticeships and indentured servants were distinguished, except during the first month. There were sixty-six cases where the contract terms were those of an apprenticeship, but neither the term *apprentice* nor the term *servant* was used. These sixty-six are treated as apprentices.

74 Martha Allinson to William Allinson, 7/26/1794, Allinson Papers; Chalkley, *Works,* pp, 575–76.

75 Carl Bridenbaugh, *Cities in the Wilderness* (New York, 1938), p. 303; idem, *Cities in Revolt* (New York, 1955), p. 216. Bridenbaugh's conclusions about the size of Philadelphia at the time of the Revolution are questioned in Sam Bass Warner, *The Private City* (Philadelphia, 1968), p. 225.

76 George Fox, "A paper to be read in Women's Meetings," in Antient Epistles, Minutes and Advices, New England Yearly Meeting, ca. 1672.

77 John Reynell to Abraham Redwood, 10/4/1746, 12/12/1746, Reynell Letterbook 1745–47; Richard Partridge to Israel Pemberton, Sr., 7/10/1750, 6: 102.

8 Choosing a Wife

Neither Puritans nor Quakers accepted the traditional Christian view that marriage was a less blessed state than celibacy. The Book of Common Prayer duplicated the Roman Catholic lists of reasons for matrimony: the procreation of children, the remedying of sin, and mutual help. While Anglicans and Catholics emphasized the first two conditions, Puritans stressed the latter. Marriage was, to use Milton's phrase, not only "a prescribed satisfaction for irrational heat" whose main function was the propagation of the species; it was also a blessed state entered into so that husband and wife might fulfill each other intellectually, spiritually, and physically.[1] While children were the proper result of and a blessing to the union, they were not the prime reason for it. New Englanders saw the family as the foundation of church and state and insisted that single people, whom they viewed with some distrust, live in a family and submit to the authority of the father. While Friends believed marriage to be important, their advocacy of it was less inclusive. They did not assert that all needed to marry or that a celibate life was inferior to wedlock. In 1663 William Smith noted that "Singleness is a good state, and in that state Temptations may be resisted as in any state." The bachelor was endangered by "ease and security," for, after providing for a comfortable, settled life, he might be prone to pile up riches. The married man was apt to become so engrossed in the activities and duties within the family that he would forget God. The Pennsylvania council in 1683 discussed a proposal requiring all men to wed, but the assembly never passed it into law.[2] In none of the Quaker colonies were single men required to enter a household in order to be under family government, and a sizable percentage of men did not marry. When Jonathan Roberts, Sr., married at age 29 in 1760, he could count 30 older cousins still unmarried. Robert V. Wells's study of Quaker families indicated that, of the children alive at age 50, 12 percent of the sons and 16 percent of the daughters had never married.[3]

Puritans and Quakers agreed that wedlock was blessed because God had ordained the institution. George Fox argued that God had made a mate for Adam and had joined them together before the fall. Thus, since Adam and Eve remained sinless after their nuptial rites, matrimony was clearly innocent. In 1669 when Fox, at age 45, wedded Margaret Fell, the widow of Judge Fell and mother of several grown children, he defended his action by insisting that marriage was not just for the purpose of procreation and that matrimony was honorable for all.[4] While Roman Catholics and Anglicans defended its sacramental nature, the Puritans made marriage a secular ceremony and gave jurisdiction to the magistrates. The Quakers, who had no sacraments, agreed to register the event of a marriage ceremony with the government, but they insisted that since God alone could join people in holy wedlock the meeting should participate in all formalities.[5]

While marriage was permitted to everyone, only those Friends in a sanctified state could have a godly union. "The honourable marriage is when the bed is undefiled, transgression finished, freedom from sin witnessed, victory over the world known." In other words, persons who had not had carnal knowledge of each other and were "perfect" could have a Christian linkage, but those who had not attained full grace could join "if they do believe there is such a freedom from sin and do endeavour to attain it." In such cases God "winked" at a little taint. God joined only those who believed in or had attained a state equal to Adam and Eve's, and those who denied that such perfection was possible or were not working toward it had a defiled bed, even though they were morally upright. Such persons were marrying "in their own wills and affections" no matter where the ceremony occurred, and they would "have trouble in the flesh, cares, differing, children unclean, and many sad effects which are incident to all marriages in the fall."[6]

Seventeenth-century Friends argued in favor of marriage to counter both the Ranters' belief in free love between Christians who had attained perfection and the inclination to celibacy among those who thought the physical body evil.[7] Eighteenth-century Quakers felt no need to justify monogamous marriage in which husband and wife contributed to each other's happiness and comfort and served as spiritual helpmates. They assumed the value of a family, and their efforts aimed at making their marriage constantly serve religious function.

Since the marital union should contribute to the piety of the couple, Friends postponed the age to wed until the husband and wife were mature enough to participate fully in the life of the meeting. The popular stereotype of colonial women marrying in their teens, bearing a dozen children, and then dying young is not confirmed by the demographic statistics of Friends. At marriage the average age for Quaker women was 22.8 and for men 26.5; the median age for women was 20.5 and for men 24. One-third of the females married before 20 but less than 3 percent of the males did. Of the females 87 percent were 18 or older before marriage, and 85 percent of the males were at least 21. Fifty-one percent of the women married between 18 and 22 and 53 percent of the males between 21 and 25. During the eighteenth century the age at which males married showed little variation, but the age at which women married showed a slight but steady rise. Those women born after 1780 married a year and a half later in life than those born before 1730. This change could be due to different economic conditions such as higher prices for land in the thickly settled areas where Friends lived, or to an imbalance in the ratio between the sexes due to male migration to the frontier.[8] For the cultural historian the essential continuity in the age of marriage for males during 75 years of economic and politcal transformation in the middle colonies is more significant than the woman's slightly later age. Clearly, for a man changing business conditions were of less importance than past customs in determining the age to marry. In all periods marriages of the very young rarely occurred, and the ages of marriage were remarkably similar for New Englanders and Quakers.

The average duration of a marriage was 31 years, but 18 percent were dissolved by the death of one spouse before the fifteenth anniversary and 38 percent before the twenty-fifth. (A first child would have a much better chance of reaching adolescence or early adulthood before either of his parents died than a sibling born five or ten years later.) In all periods completed families (where the wife lived to at least forty-five and presumably finished child bearing) predominated. Despite the hazards of childbirth, wives tended to outlive their husbands. While widows and widowers were not uncommon (primarily because the remaining member lived longer than his mate on an average of slightly over 20 years), remarriage was not too common. Of all marriages in Wells' study, 97 percent of the women and 88 percent of the men entered wedlock for the first time. After the death of a mate, the average time for a widow to wait before remarrying was 6.2 years and for a widower 3.6 years.[9] Quakers did not conform to the image of the colonial husband surviving several wives. The demographic evidence makes clear that most Friends married only once, would have several children, and that the family would endure for several decades. Since the piety of the parents would inspire their children to devotion and, thereby, ensure the survival of the meeting, Friends insisted that God's approval of the marriage was a prime requisite.

II

Quakers believed that the inward light formed the bond of unity between a man and his wife who loved each other because they first loved God. Robert Barclay proposed marriage to Christian Molleson and suggested that while his reason strengthened and encouraged his affection for her, "that which is *before all and beyond all,* is, that I can say in the fear of the Lord that I have received a charge from him to love thee." The danger for both of them lay in being drawn into desire for the world, and Barclay hoped they could abide *"in the pure love of God; in the sense and drawings whereof, we can only discern and know how to love one another."*[10] Unlike the Puritans, Barclay did not worry about expressing his love for fear that he might love God less. Rather, he found in God his reasons for loving Christian and esteemed her for her godly virtues. William Penn wrote to Hannah Callowhill, soon to become his second wife, expressing the same feeling. "Is [*sic*] not virtue, religion, sweetness and Goodness the motives of loving her, and of her returns for the same?" Penn loved Hannah "above all other considerations" because *"the loveliness that the tendering and blessed Truth hath beautified thee with, hath made thee amiable in my eyes."*[11]

The essential task for a Friend who was courting was to make sure that his desire was based on God's will and not on the person's attractiveness or money. Just as Fox insisted that a man knew if he were in a state of grace, so he would know without doubt if God were commanding him to wed a certain woman.[12] The Swarthmore manuscripts show the intense desire of early Quakers to make certain that their motives were pure. Thomas Holme justified his marriage to Elizabeth Atherton in 1654 by writing:

> I was immediately commanded of the Lord to take her to wife that day having before seen it clear in the light eternal and had a vision of it long before as likewise she had. So in obedience to the Command of the Lord I took her to wife contrary to my will.[13]

Robert Weaver expressed his agonized uncertainty over whether he should marry the sister of John Abraham, a Friend. On several occasions when he had seen the maiden, "she being laid before me, something of her being my wife, which I could not entertain being afraid of that thing." He kept trying to decide whether the impulse was from God or from an "earthly end, being her mother kept a shop."[14] If he acted for carnal reasons and married, he might lose his experience of God, but he feared to delay since God might be commanding him to wed. Unfortunately, Friend Weaver's letter is a fragment, and since no answer exists one cannot be certain what he decided.

At times the insistence upon a clear notice from God led to difficulties. Martha Plats received directions to marry Edward Langford, but he was not similarly moved. When Martha asked William Smith whether her feeling might be wrong, he declined to judge while advising her to mind the power within. After an interval she continued to experience the same notice; but Langford was still unwilling. Miss Plats then became furious with Smith for misleading her. Smith wrote to George Fox informing him of the details of the case and advising him to deal carefully with the woman.[15] Other instances of women's initiative were more successful. There is a tradition that Elizabeth Haddon, the founder of Haddonfield, New Jersey, proposed marriage to John Estaugh, a traveling minister. He promised to consider it during his journey, and on his return he accepted.

The inward light not only told Friends whom to marry but when. Once a man decided to look for a wife, he might survey the available prospects. John Kelsall, after consulting with Friends, made a statement of intention to marry a certain young lady. After experiencing intense inward conflict, he had to drop the matter since he became convinced that proceeding further would not be pleasing to God, "but it appeared like a Thing below the Truth."[16] David Ferris, a Yale man who converted to Quakerism, noted that in 1733 he began to "think of settling myself, and to marry, when the way should appear without obstruction." He found a "comely young women, of a good, reputable family; educated in plainness; favored with good natural talents; and in good circumstances." After several hints from the family and Friends that his courtship would meet with success, he came to call. The maiden and her mother received him pleasantly,

> but I think I had chatted with them more than half an hour, before I heard something, like a still small voice, saying to me, "Seekest thou great things for thyself? Seek them not." This language pierced me like a sword to the heart. It so filled me with confusion, that I was unfit for any further conversation.

Ferris left immediately without mentioning to either mother or daughter the reason for his visit. His experience left him "confused and benumbed," and it was several months before he could submit to the Lord's dispensation. One day, after learning to bear his disappointment, Ferris sat down at a table with some Friends and "observed a young woman sitting opposite to me, whom I did not remember ever to have seen before." Though at first he took little notice of her, "a language very quietly, and very pleasantly, passed through my mind, on this wife, 'If thou wilt marry that young woman, thou shalt be happy with her.' " He now paid attention and found the girl very comely and pleasing. As the company moved from the table, Ferris noticed for the first time that she was lame and became unhappy "that I should have a cripple allotted to me." After wrestling with his pride and reason for some time, he came to see that if he chose his own wife, "she might be an affliction to me all the days of my life . . . or she might fall into vicious practices." The Lord, who knew best, had provided a wife who could make a happy household and bring a blessing upon his children. Ferris wed the crippled maiden and claimed that he never repented of it during 40 years of married life.[17]

Sometimes the Lord's wish could not be immediately determined. In 1740 James Moore was twenty-four and "had some thoughts (if it was the Lord's will)" to marry. Having heard of Ann Starr who was esteemed a "sober, religious young women," he went to see her. Moore needed to stay only a short time before his "affections seemed, in some degree, drawn towards her." Upon his return home, James experienced second thoughts, particularly as he considered the results of the many rash and inconsiderate marriages. So he waited on the Lord to learn His will. After remaining at home for three months, the Lord "was pleased to open my way," and James proposed to Ann Starr.[18] In 1753 Joshua Evans, at age 22, squandered much time "going from one young woman to another, in a thoughtless way, endeavouring to gain their affections, without considering the consequence." Quite unexpectedly he "gained the affections of a virtuous young woman, to whom I was nearly attached before I was aware of it." He became alarmed, experienced second thoughts, and concluded that marriage might be too weighty a procedure for his present condition, and told the young lady so. Her answer was "so discreet, that a solemn weight came over us, and the matter became more serious to us both." Evans consulted his father, who consented, and her parents also approved. This courtship and marriage resulted in Evans's giving up all "libertine company" and becoming "more settled in stability of mind."[19]

Except for Evans's religious qualms in the midst of the courtship, his conduct would have met with the opposition of most Quakers. First of all, he courted at random, seeking to engage the affections of many young ladies. In 1694 Philadelphia Monthly Meeting warned that young men should not

> go from one Woman to another and keep Company and sit together, especially in the Night-Season, spending their precious Time in Idle-Discourse, and drawing the Affections of one another, many times, when there is no reality in it: As one said in his day, These things make more like Sodom than Saints.[20]

Secondly, Evans became involved with a girl and discussed marriage before talking to either set of parents. A Quaker youth was supposed to inform the parents of his intentions before he came to court or in any way became emotionally involved with a girl.[21] In 1698 Thomas Pryor wrote an apology to Phineas Pemberton because he had twice come to the house to see Abigail without asking Phineas's consent.[22] At times the man spoke to the maiden before he endured the ordeal of approaching her father. But, if the meeting discovered this, the suitor was forced to apologize to Friends and make satisfaction to the parents.[23] The correct form of courtship was recorded by the English Quaker Peter Briggins, who noted in his diary on May 26, 1716, that "to the yearly meeting J. Barber's father acquainted us of his son's intentions." On May 28: "J. B. spake his mind to our daughter Mercy;" and in a marginal notation: "J. B. acquainted my daughter M. of his love &c."[24] Before he married, William Penn counseled against matchmaking by parents, preferring to let the man decide under the Lord's direction, but, in his instructions to his wife before leaving for Pennsylvania in 1682, he informed Gulielma to "see that they [his children] have worthy persons in their eyes, of good life and good fame for piety and understanding."[25] In 1683 the laws of Pennsylvania declared that a marriage could not be formalized until parents or guardians were consulted. In 1701 the law was strengthened so that a person under twenty-one or an indentured servant who married without the consent of parents, guardian, or master could be fined £5. When in 1762 Rev. Henry Muhlenberg performed a marriage for an underage girl who did not have her Quaker guardian's consent, he exposed himself to a £50 fine.[26]

Before he went to ask a father's permission a young man might confer with other members of the meeting. William Penn noted that this was often done.[27] John Smith, already a prominent member of Philadelphia meeting, was told by a Friend to court Hannah Logan, a procedure which Smith had already decided upon, and Sally Morris, a minister, wrote to James Logan on Smith's behalf.[28]

Parents had the right to consent to the marriage of a son or daughter no matter what their ages, but there were limits to their authority. For example, they were not supposed to force a girl to marry without her consent.[29] If they had once permitted a person to call and engage the affections of the daughter, they were not to withdraw permission for any worldly cause.[30] In 1699 in Concord Meeting in Pennsylvania, Jonathan Thatcher and Hannah Dix requested leave to marry; her father refused. The meeting investigated, found no sufficient reason, and so allowed the marriage.[31] In 1746 John Head refused to consent or not to consent to his daughter's request, saying, "There is a time to Speak and a time to be Silent, the Time of Speaking is past, the Time of Silence is now, and I have no more to say." The meeting disciplined him for "Obstinacy."[32] If, however, the parents allowed or did not actively oppose a marriage out of unity, Friends might discipline them and the newlyweds. Although it was not official policy to hold the father and mother responsible for their sons' and daughters' activities until 1752, parents had been exhorted to control their children's outgoings in marriage since the 1690s, and early in the eighteenth century parents were censured or disowned for permitting mixed marriages.[33]

Friends who migrated sometimes had difficulties in gaining parental consent. A father could require permission of Friends who lived in the area or allow his boy to marry whomever he chose.[34] When John Reynell, already an established merchant in Philadelphia, wrote in 1730 for freedom to wed, his father refused since he did not know the character of the girl. (Reynell's request may have been premature since he did not actually ask for and obtain permission to marry until five years later.[35]) The parental check could be used as a means of discouraging unwelcome suitors. When William Allinson, a widower with several children, asked Peter Cooper for the right to court his daughter Martha, the young lady asked her father to tell him that she was not interested. Peter Cooper refused to do this, forcing his daughter to act for herself.[36] She married William Allinson!

Although the first requisite in marriage was to hearken to the leadings of the Lord, Friends saw no incompatibility in listing the desirable qualities of a mate. The yearly epistles gave as much instruction to parents as to youth since, according to correct practice, parents had an opportunity to screen out all unsuitable prospective sons-in-law. The qualities a Friend desired in a husband were similar to those esteemed by Puritans or Anglicans. In 1722 London Yearly Meeting told parents to choose a person "of religious inclination, suitable disposition, temper, sobriety of manners, and diligence in business."[37] Only one Quaker writer, William Smith, in 1663 interpreted Paul's "Be not unequally linked" to apply only to religious factors and saw no hindrance to marriage in differences of age or wealth.[38] Thomas Chalkley advised that young and old not be matched; he believed that only financial considerations bred such marriages and that such factors should be secondary.[39] Richard Hill, a wine merchant who lived in Philadelphia and Madeira, advised his son

> that virtue, good sense, good temper and an agreeable person of a good family are so essential that scarce any one of them must be wanting. As to money it's only to be considered as a good contingent and by no means as a principal motive.[40]

Young Henry was warned not to be so entranced by a good family or a large dowry as to be "blinded" to some personal defect. Husbands and wives were expected to be helpmates in all matters. The wife needed to be modest, plain, frugal, and hard-working. A shrew could make a husband unhappy; a prodigal woman could bankrupt him; an irreligious one could corrupt him and lead him —and herself as well—to hell.

While marriage for money was universally condemned, Friends did not consider wealth unimportant. The piety of the daughters of Margaret Fell was evident, and so was the family's concern for the financial well-being of the future sons-in-law. The girls, who had received substantial portions from Judge Fell, married prosperous and devout Quakers.[41] Mary Penington feared that she could find "none of my rank" and disregarded the reproaches of some who said that there were no religious gentlemen, trusting that the "Lord would provide such a one for me." In 1654 she married Isaac Penington, son of a mayor of London.[42] Penn told his children to marry not wealth "but sufficiency." Richard Hill advised making certain before marriage that there was no one available of equal merit and agreeableness and a better family. Like many other Englishmen, Friends attempted to marry virtuous, wealthy girls of good background.[43]

A few English and American Quaker sources reveal the same sort of haggling over dowries that was characteristic of some of the New England Puritans. Quaker parents were no more generous than the Puritans in endowing sons and daughters with money. When Robert Barker courted the sister of John Rodes in England, her mother offered £1,500 but refused to accede to Barker's desire for 2,500 and would not even compromise at 2,000. The match floundered.[44] A most acrimonious dowry dispute occurred in Wales in 1722 between the Lloyd family of Dolobran, makers of iron, and the Extons, the aunt and uncle of the intended bride. The negotiations opened on February 20, and satisfactory solution seemed to have been reached by April 28, when the couple proposed their intentions before the meeting. The dispute flared up after the marriage when the Extons asserted that the husband should "take more Delight in their Business &c & to carry himself more respectful." Charles

Lloyd was willing to accommodate them provided that they remembered him in their wills and signed over their personal estate in return for an annuity. Finally, after prolonged bickering which involved the newlyweds in several quarrels, an agreement was reached on October 23, 1723.[45] William Penn engaged in a long and bitter dispute with William Aubrey, his son-in-law, and suffered a crippling stroke just after discussing Aubrey in a letter. James Logan continued the battle on the Penns' behalf until Aubrey's death. In other disputes Logan and Isaac Norris II disagreed on the terms of Sarah Logan's dowry, and John Griffith, an esteemed minister, used John Pemberton as an intermediary in his battle with his son-in-law. When John Smith courted his daughter, James Logan asked Smith what he was worth. Smith had £3,000. Logan offered to give £750 sterling and revealed that Hannah owned 500 acres of land and would receive £2,000 at his death and £1,000 at his wife's.[46] Smith's difficulty in preparing for this marriage lay not in the greater wealth of rival suitors Thomas Crosby or Charles Norris but in persuading Hannah to say yes.

It becomes obvious that while finances were in theory of secondary importance, they were in fact frequently a prime consideration. James Logan, former schoolmaster and secretary to Penn, did not have great wealth or standing early in life; nevertheless, he courted Anne Shippen, daughter of Edward Shippen, a prominent Philadelphia merchant. His rival was Thomas Story, a renowned minister and wealthy lawyer. Anne preferred Logan to Story, who was twice her age, and her brothers, Joseph and Edward, also favored Logan, but the parents wanted Story. Story proposed and Anne refused; so Story brought Logan before the monthly meeting in 1703 on a charge of breach of promise. After arbitrating the affair, the meeting burned the papers because of the prominence of the men involved, and Anne later married Thomas Story.[47] In 1711, on a visit to England, Logan and Judith Crowley, who had a dowry of £10,000, wished to marry, but the girl's family intervened because they did not wish her to leave her ailing father, and they hoped for a wealthier match. Logan suggested elopement, but Judith refused to leave against the wishes of her family. After obtaining money through the fur trade and land speculation, Logan had little difficulty in persuading Sarah Read of Philadelphia to marry him in 1714.[48]

When in 1750 Samuel Mifflin married Rebecca Edgell, worth about £10,000 sterling, Samuel Emlen wished him "much pleasure with his Light Wife and heavy purse." After John Hunt, a London merchant and minister, married, John Smith wrote to Elias Bland the news that Hunt had obtained "an agreeable Woman (a Widow) . . . with a fortune of Two Thousand Pounds." Gideon Wanton of Rhode Island, though informed by a young English maiden that she had no fortune, persisted in courting and asked her to marry until he learned that she really was not worth the £900 he had thought. He then switched his attentions to another girl so suddenly that the meeting demanded an explanation. After James Pemberton married Hannah Lloyd, he was complimented for choosing a partner with "great Merit beauty and fortune."[49] Even ministering Friends picked mates with an eye to their wealth. John Griffith mentioned the extent of his wife's estate to show the "Lord's kindness . . . in so fully answering what I had so often desired, viz. that in case I ever married and settled, I might be so placed and circumstanced, as to entertain the Lord's servants and messengers in an agreeable manner."[50]

Samuel Bownas, a prominent eighteenth-century English minister, made his fortune by marrying a rich widow. A Friend who thought the proposed match unsuitable wrote him an epigram that if to marry, he "inclined, / Choose the virtues of the mind." Samuel replied, "If to marry be the best,/I must have money with the rest."[51]

Nearly all the instances of the link between money and matrimony occurred among wealthy Friends in England and America and show that, like rich Puritans and Anglicans, prosperous Quakers saw marriage as involving a financial arrangement. The very few dowries mentioned in correspondence and the absence of Quaker marriage contracts preclude generalizations about the majority of members. Poorer Friends in city and country could have ignored wealth, or been just as mercenary as the merchants in selecting wives, even if the amounts of money involved were small.

In England in 1797 a few members of the Society of Friends set up a "Marriage-Portion Fund" to provide virtuous young servant women with dowries so that they would not need to postpone marriage. The need for some kind of financial settlement was considered far more important in England than in rural America where the high price of labor and the availability of land made the amount of work that a woman could do her most important asset. Jacques Pierre Brissot de Warville, who traveled in the United States in 1788, believed that most American women married without dowries.[52] In rural areas a father might contribute some livestock, however, and his daughter might accumulate feathers for a bed, linens, some pewter, or a chair.

III

The Old and New Testaments contained prohibitions against Jews or Christians marrying unbelievers. After commanding the children of Israel to destroy the nations around them, the Lord warned, "Neither Shalt thou make marriage with them; thy daughter thou shalt not give unto his son; nor his daughter shalt thou take unto thy son." Paul wrote to the church at Corinth, "Be ye not unequally yoked with unbelievers: for what fellowship hath righteousness with unrighteousness?"[53] The canon law interpreted these prohibitions as applying to Muslims, Jews, and pagans. When the Reformation came, Protestants and Catholics extended the ban to each other. Both Anglicans and Puritans continued to assert that one should not wed a nonbeliever, but since the number of Catholics or Jews was not large in relation to the total population, the law was of no great importance. For Friends and Baptists, who were a minority wherever they existed, the restriction that members must marry within the faith became of fundamental importance in preserving the meeting from the outside world.

Originally, the grouping of all others as heathens stemmed from the assurance that only Friends had the truth. Since a marriage involving a non-Friend entailed being wed by a cleric, the testimony against hireling priests was also violated. The practical difficulties of maintaining a household in which one member refused to say "you" to a single person, to pay tithes, to bow, to use any luxuries, and to attend communion must have been immense. George Fox asserted that all involved in mixed marriages were "bastard

Quakers" who esteemed their "affections and lusts" above God's truth.[54]

After Friends became reconciled to the fact that theirs was only one among many denominations, their exclusiveness became harder to defend. In 1707 Moses West, an English Quaker, wrote *A Treatise Concerning Marriage,* which was reprinted several times in both England and America because it provided the most complete exposition of Quaker beliefs about mixed marriages.[55] West, like Fox, maintained that the biblical commandments against marrying heathens still applied because mixed unions led to a decline in godliness. When a man and woman were bound in holy wedlock, they became helpmates in physical and spiritual matters. If the faiths of the couple were not the same, they could not help each other walk a Christian path and could not set a good example for their children. West did not assert that non-Quaker Christendom should be equated with paganism such as surrounded either the Jews or the early church; nevertheless, he insisted that the fact that two people believed in Christ was not sufficient religious similarity for marriage. West passed over the close relationship between dissenters and Quakers and chose to focus on the largely imaginary danger of intermarriage with Roman Catholics. When a Quaker wed a Protestant, either unity of worship would not prevail or one party must lose "Peace of Conscience." Truth's demands could not be met only half way, for compromise equalled surrender. If the matters at issue were only externals or outward judgments, then disagreements within a family would be of little importance, but when the safety of the soul was at stake, any weakening involved the danger of everlasting perdition. The Old Testament proved that lust and covetousness were the real motives behind marrying heathens; Quakers who married Presbyterians were directed by the same low desires.[56] While Friends may have been in essential agreement with nonconformists in many of their attitudes, they believed in strict adherence to their distinctive God-given theological and social tenets.

The records of monthly meetings in America illustrate the great amount of time devoted to the problem of improper marriage. Throughout the colonial period marriage out of unity was the most frequent offense for which Quakers were disowned. The revival of discipline after 1755 had its clearest expression in the far greater stringency used in dealing with offenders in this matter—primarily because Friends believed that meetings' laxity in such cases encouraged others in the same sins.[57] Jack D. Marietta argues that Friends saw marriage out of unity as particularly dangerous and treated it with more severity than any other offense because the result of such a union was the failure of the family to provide a religious upbringing for its children. He discovered that in Pennsylvania the number of disownments for marriage with outsiders, which did not amount to ten in the decades before 1700, reached 228 in the 1740s and 748 in the 1760s. The percentage of exogamous marriages to total marriages grew from a minority in 1725 to a majority of three-quarters or more by 1765. John S. Rowntree estimated that between 1800 and 1850 one-third of Quaker marriages in England were out of unity.[58] Parents and elders tried to discourage such marriages by visiting the Friend before he wed. If he still married after such a warning he could be disowned without further notice. Quakers were disciplined even for attending a marriage not done "according to the good order used amongst us, if the persons to be married have or do make any profession of Truth or be Friends' children."[59] If a Friend managed to wed an outsider before being spoken to, he was visited by elders and given an opportunity to repent. In practice, even after the tightening of control in the 1750s, anyone who appeared to be sorry and was willing to confess his sin could in time gain readmission. Meetings were exhorted to inspect confessions carefully to make certain the parties were sincere; but only good behavior and a show of contrition were demanded. The admission of guilt was not required for marrying a particular person but for violating a tenet of the Society. In practice, this distinction might have appeared technical to an outsider. Some of the disowned joined other denominations; others continued to attend meetings for worship, and eventually either they or their children became members. Friends may have gained some converts by their marriage policy, for some maidens would not marry until their beaux became Quakers.[60] Moreover, their habits of marriage undoubtedly made Quakers more exclusive and tribalistic. But, since large numbers left or were disowned when they married outsiders, Quaker beliefs about marriage hindered the growth of the Society.

While there were no direct challenges to the endogamous pattern of marriage in meetings, both the frequency of marriage out of unity and the occasional comments show that some Quakers questioned this tenet. After Richard Hill's daughter married out of unity, he defended her actions and insisted that he had consented for "the best of reasons"—the character of the man. When Molly Drinker and Sammy Rhoads eloped and married in Quaker fashion by a magistrate, James Pemberton and James Logan II tried to persuade the father not to be too stern. Ann Warder, who moved to Philadelphia after the Revolution, noted with dismay that Friends socialized with persons married by a priest as if nothing had happened.[61]

Unlike the Anglicans, Quakers did not recognize a precontract as a valid marriage. They did not agree with the Puritans that espousals or betrothal constituted a half-way marriage.[62] The only religiously valid ceremonies were those performed within the meeting. Couples who were wed either by priest or magistrate, even though legally joined, were subjected to discipline for marrying out of unity. The wedlock was a fact but it was not holy.

Anglicans and Puritans annulled all marriages in which people were of too near kinship. Leviticus 18:3–8 listed the degrees of relatives whose "nakedness" should not be uncovered. The forbidden degrees of kin first labeled in Roman Catholic canon law were retained by Anglicans, Puritans, and Quakers. Pennsylvania statutes of 1682 and 1700 outlawed incest without clearly defining just what was "uncleanness betwixt near relations in blood." After these laws were disallowed for vagueness, a new law was passed in January 1705. Relying upon English precedents, the Quakers forbade a man to marry his mother, his father's sister, his mother's sister, and the daughter of a son or daughter. All these were blood relations. The man was also forbidden to marry his father's wife (who was not his mother), his son's wife, his son's daughter (even if he were only the stepfather), his wife's daughter, the daughter of his wife's daughter or son. These unions were outlawed because of affinity.

The advices of Friends went beyond the legal prohibitions. The Bible stated that when a man and woman married, they became one, and so Quakers declared (along with many other Protestants) that a man was as closely related to his wife's sister or her children by a previous marriage as his mate was. A man could not marry his own kin to four degrees; so also he could not marry his wife's.[64] If a man married a widow, he was not allowed to wed her child, her child's child, her sister, or her sister's child. He was also forbidden to marry the close relatives of her first husband. No man could marry his own first or second cousin or the first or second cousin of his wife. Meetings forbade first cousins to wed and discouraged marriage between second cousins. New England's discipline asked that even third cousins not marry, and advised meetings to discourage although not forbid wedlock between second cousins. Rhode Island Monthly Meeting did permit children of first cousins to marry in 1728. Until the Revolution, Philadelphia meetings automatically expelled married first cousins, although the yearly meeting agreed to readmit one couple "since their marriage must remain sure and binding, their sincere repentance it is hoped, may stand accepted with God."[65] Anthony Benezet wrote to Charles Moor in 1782 informing him that since Eber Woolman, who had married a first cousin, had been reinstated in meeting, Moor also could be taken back into membership. In 1759 and 1760 a long controversy ensued when Shrewsbury Quarterly Meeting asked whether the acknowledgment of a man who married his former wife's half sister should be accepted. Shrewsbury was told to refuse membership.[66]

There was no dispute about forbidding marriage because of a blood relationship, but the biblical precedents justifying a prohibition within four degrees of affinity were not very clear and occasioned controversies in English and American yearly meetings throughout the eighteenth century. In 1725 Chester Quarterly Meeting wanted revision of the prohibited degrees of affinity; in 1760 Shrewsbury suggested the same thing. In 1755 Bucks and Burlington Quarterly meetings wished to change, but Chester, Gloucester and Salem, Woodbridge, and Shrewsbury were satisfied. Philadelphia Quarterly Meeting was so divided that it could come to no decision. In 1748 Merion and Abington Monthly meetings wanted revision, but the other meetings composing Philadelphia Quarterly Meeting postponed the matter. (It has generally been thought that the city Friends were more agreeable to change, but on this issue Philadelphia remained more conservative than several of the rural meetings.) In the end no change in the forbidden degrees of kin marriage occurred, because those who supported the old ways were always in the majority; they had the weight of tradition on their side.

Just as the meeting supervised the selection of eligible first husbands and wives, so it laid down instructions on choosing a second partner. The Puritans sometimes wed with great haste. The father and mother of Governor Winslow of Plymouth had been widower and widow 12 weeks and 7 weeks respectively when they joined in wedlock. Samuel Sewall's first wife died on October 19, 1717; by February he was wondering whether to remarry. He accompanied the Widow Dennison home in March soon after the funeral of her husband and told her his intentions.[67]

George Fox advised that before remarrying Friends should wait at least one year in order to show "both chastity, and virtue, and temperance."[68] Philadelphia Monthly Meeting forbade the second marriage of John English in 1688 because his first wife had not been dead a year. In 1700 Philadelphia Yearly Meeting laid down as official policy that no widow or widower was to "make or Accept any Offer Application or Procedure, in order to Marriage before Nine, or Ten Months be Expired, after the Death of the Wife or Husband of such Person."[69] Since the man had to court, propose, be accepted, and pass two monthly meetings before the ceremony, for all practical purposes the one year limitation defined by Fox was still in effect and was eventually reinstated in disciplines throughout America. There were few cases where permission to wed was refused because of haste, although a few speedy remarriages did occur.[70] In 1760 Ann Whitall recorded:

> more sorrowful news . . . Abe Chatting and Ruth Wood married together and his wife dead eight months and her husband four months. O what a shame, O how abominable is it in the sight of him that made us all. . . . O monstrous! What sort of woman is she?[71]

IV

Quaker epistles and tracts offering advice on selecting a wife or husband rarely mentioned love before marriage. Was love assumed to be present, or was it not deemed necessary until after the wedding? Edmund S. Morgan has argued that for the Puritans love did not become essential until after the marriage, and even then it was a rational love, although this did not in the least dampen its affectionate nature.[72] So long as spiritual concerns predominated, a Quaker could decide to marry and even select a partner on a rational basis, since his financial situation and her character should be considered. Friends did expect a religious love before marriage, however. Such love was described by Thomas Ellwood—perhaps in imitation of Adam's relationship with Eve before the fall—as "chaste desire" that came from God, had no connection with anything earthly such as sex or self-gratification, and was closely akin to sympathy.[73] This godly love bore no relationship to the emotions, and one can find nothing in official statements that would permit a blind romantic love to sweep aside all impediments to matrimony. In 1696 Joseph Sleigh advised his sons to make sure from "what ground your Love springs" and told his daughters not to accept the first "that may proffer Love to you, as in relation to marriage" but to wait for the Lord's counsel.[74] William Penn wrote: "Never marry but for Love; but see that thou Lov'st what is lovely." His sons were told to marry "your Inclination rather than your Interest: I mean what you Love, rather than what is Rich . . . and be sure you are belov'd again." The love that Penn wanted never sprang from lust; Christian affection was based upon a "*Union of Souls*" rather than a "*Union of Sense.*"[75] But Penn did demand genuine feeling between two people before marriage, and his letters to and about both his intended wives were permeated with affection. Samuel Morris, after warning his nephew Samuel Powell about beauty or fortune, asked rhetorically, "Must we marry without Love? No, but let consideration and judgment precede it."[76] A relationship religiously arrived at could become romantic, and the few surviving letters of Quaker courtship shift easily between pious phrases and terms of endearment. Meetings recognized that romantic love did exist, for parents were warned that contracts should be decided before the boy and girl became very attached. Symons Creek Meeting in North

Carolina allowed a couple after one appearance before the meeting to drop the affair "for want of Love" but demanded an acknowledgment of fault. In 1726 Rhode Island Monthly Meeting found a couple who were too near kin to marry but permitted the wedding because "their affections were Drawn toward Each other before they knew the order of Friends in that Respect."[77] Friends recognized that romantic love could not be turned off and on at will.

While Friends continued to discuss courtship and marriage officially in religious terms until the nineteenth century, the actual narratives of courting show considerable interest in romance. Other concerns, such as those for property and religion were present, but love seems to have been the primary requisite. Since the course of romance has rarely been cut and dried, Quaker courting had its share of hectic and traumatic moments. The story of Israel Pemberton, Jr.'s, first marriage in 1737 reads like fiction. Before going to England on business in 1735, Israel had shown interest in Sarah Kirkbride, but he made no formal overtures before leaving. During his absence Anthony Morris, Jr., frequently visited the Kirkbrides and proposed marriage to Sarah, who neither accepted nor refused. Upon Israel's return he did nothing for three weeks but then informed his father that he had intended to propose to Sarah, for he believed she had an affectionate regard for him. Israel, Sr., tried to discourage his son, but Israel, Jr., visited the young lady—in the presence of Anthony—and informed her of his intentions. The Morris affair continued and his family blamed the Pembertons for intervening. After parental coercion, Israel, Jr., paid no more calls for six weeks and agreed to do nothing until Sarah either accepted or rejected young Morris. Finally Anthony demanded a decision; Sarah said no. Morris retorted that Sarah had been so free with her favors that she would have to become his bride. Her father announced that his daughter would never marry him even if she were in dire disgrace. For all practical purposes, this outburst ended the Morris-Kirkbride courtship, and Anthony soon wed another. Israel then married Sarah.[78]

While neither piety nor wealth was absent from the courtship of John Smith and Hannah Logan, the romantic attitude predominated. Smith was a prosperous young merchant whose habit of listing in his diary only the names of females who went on outings with him around Philadelphia would incline one to believe that he had looked for a wife for a prolonged period. The first concrete sign of romance was Smith's recording in his diary that he had spent an evening at William Logan's in the company of "that dear Creature H. L., the Charm of whose Conversation Excells, if possible, those of her person. . . . Oh, could I be Blest with the favour of Retiring to it upon every occasion."[79] For several months his courtship was confined to seeking Hannah's company as often as possible and writhing in agony when he thought the girl displeased with him. He also informed his father that he wanted to marry Miss Logan. Eight months after confessing his love to his diary, John attempted to find an opportunity to see Hannah alone to ask permission to court. At the home of Anthony Benezet he broached the subject and stammered out his proposal "in a good deal of Confusion"; the maiden, who neither encouraged nor discouraged him, agreed to receive a letter. The epistle was most eloquent; Smith praised the girl's beauty, intelligence, and virtue and also mentioned that a Friends' minister had recommended her to him. She consented to receive him. Smith's state of mind during this time of good fortune was revealed in one of his entries in February 1747: "Drank tea at I. Pemberton's of Hannah Logan's making—Nectar and Ambrosia."[80]

The next stage was to visit the home and ask James Logan's permission. William Logan, the brother of Hannah, had delivered John's first love letter and now brought him to the Logan home. The way had been smoothed by Sally Morris, a minister and friend of the Logans, who wrote a letter to the father recommending the young man. Perhaps because he recognized a kindred intellect, and also because he wanted Hannah to marry so that he could settle his estate, James Logan heartily welcomed John Smith and rebuked William for not bringing him more often. The father took great pains to entertain his daughter's suitor in the library, but Hannah became ill and Smith was so unnerved that he failed to ask the father's consent. On the next visit Smith asked both parents for permission and they agreed that if Hannah preferred him, she could marry him. Logan, in later visits, informed Smith that he had said a few words to his daughter on his behalf and advised "how to Court, to have perseverance."[81] The sole problem was Hannah's consent, and Smith made frequent visits, went fishing with the family, and accompanied them to meetings and funerals. At one point Smith had to convince the maiden that her religious life would not be hindered by setting "affections upon any man."[82] John Smith's father helped the courtship by sending Hannah a four-wheeled chaise. In June 1748 Hannah determined to call the whole affair off, and though Smith obtained permission to visit again, "she told me she could not give me the least hope by putting it off to a future time." Smith did not call again for slightly over a month, but then in a meeting:

> I waited in it for a sense whether it would be suitable for me to renew my visits to dear Hannah Logan; and in my waiting my mind was filled with sweetness, and enlarged in pure Love and a particular openness and freedom, so that I determined in the affirmative.[83]

Absence softened this fair lady's heart for that evening Hannah confessed to John Smith that she loved him. On December 7, 1748, they were married.

When Richard Hill left Philadelphia in 1739 and moved to Madeira to enter into the wine trade, his young children stayed behind with a married daughter. While his daughter Rachel was courted by Richard Wells, grandson of Richard Partridge, the colonial agent, Friend Hill wrote a series of letters in which he gave his thoughts on love and marriage. His view of the parents' role and romantic love was far different from that contained in the meetings' advices.

> As I think the happiness of a married state depends principally on a mutual and well grounded affection between the parties, So I never intend to constrain nor overpersuade a Child of mine to marry any man for whom she has not such an affection. As Love is not always voluntary it may some times happen to be govern'd by fancy or other motives without reason and fixed on a worthless person of bad principles or bad temper; For either of which no set of features, no shape, no qualifications or fortune ever so great can make a woman amends. She must be a slave or miserable for her life or at least for his, except he should happen to have grace enough to be reclaimed by her which when this has been done in such Cases, has generally been the work of many years and commonly has been effected so late that the parties have received but short benefit by it.[84]

No prudent woman would ever run the risk of falling in love with a wastrel. If a daughter were about to "throw herself away upon such a man," Hill confessed that, while he would do everything in his power to dissuade her, he would not absolutely forbid it "because she might thereby become as unhappy as by marrying the man."[85] In this exposition love was not a rational learned duty, a necessity only after matrimony, which proceeded from an esteem of the partner's virtues. Rather, love was a blind, compelling, romantic force which might be checked but which might not accept governance of reason or religion.

Rachel Hill's hesitation to marry came after some extraordinary behavior by her suitor. He returned without a cargo all the way from England to court and promised to settle in Philadelphia; but he refused to marry until he had more money. The question was whether he was haggling for a large dowry from Doctor Hill, wanted a partnership, or was just a very cautious young man. The father was amazed that the man "should act so unlike most young lovers, who seldom let prudential considerations have too much weight with them." A person who placed business above love "must certainly be of a singular turn of mind and have very preposterous notions of Love, marriage, and Life." When Rachel could not make up her mind, her father wrote that the decision was hers alone.[86] Richard and Rachel married soon after.

Samuel Allinson, a lawyer who was not a member of the wealthy Quaker aristocracy of Philadelphia, showed the same concern for romance and true love. In a letter written to Elizabeth Smith in 1764, he pleaded that her statement that his proposal be "at present" dropped not be made a permanent refusal.

> Believe me Betsy, The Greatest frown of Fortune, I can bear, better, than thy displeasure. Pity the man that thinks himself unhappy without thee and caste him not to despair . . . I sue for thy Affections upon the Merit of my own and am Reduc'd to this single Argument to obtain my end "I Sincerely Love thee."[87]

Elizabeth could not resist such a declaration, and they were married on April 4, 1765.

The diaries of Elizabeth Drinker for the 1760s, Sally Wister during the Revolutionary War, and John Elliot Cresson during the 1790s show that the romantic, sentimental view of courtship predominated in the middle and upper classes. Elizabeth Sandwich's diary, which reveals a long romance, interrupted by Henry Drinker's visit to London, proved that a man and woman had ample opportunity to know each other intimately. Courtship in colonial days was not always carried on in parlors with young ladies being carefully chaperoned at all times; it often involved walks in the garden, short trips for recreation, parties, ice skating, and sleigh rides. John Cresson, when admonished by his father for sitting up with his "precious Molly" until 1:00 A.M., complained, "Alas, if Age is imprudent and unwise, ought there not to be some Allowance, and more than is commonly made, for the Ardour of Youthful Affection."[88]

Three worldly European travelers who visited America after the Revolution—Francisco de Miranda, Moreau de St. Méry, and Robert Hunter, Jr.—noticed the beauty as well as the coquetry of Quaker maidens.[89] In the Marquis de Chastellux's *Travels in North America,* the author commented on the "extreme liberty" of flirting between the sexes in the 1770s. George Grieve, who visited America in 1783 and who first translated the *Travels* into English, noted that he had once seen a "grave Quaker" and his family sitting on a bench outside their house in Philadelphia while alongside the apprentice boy and a servant girl or daughter were "not only kissing and embracing each other, but proceeding to such familiarities as would shock modesty"—all without reproof from the Friend.[90]

A diary kept by Sally Wister, a 16-year-old girl, during the British occupation when her family lived with Friends named Foulke, 15 miles outside Philadelphia, demonstrates that having a romance was a major preoccupation of young ladies. Parts of the Foulke house were taken over by the American army and used as the headquarters of General Smallwood of Maryland, and the single officers frequently visited, drank tea, made small talk, sang songs, played practical jokes, and carried on mild flirtations with the girls. Sally Wister and the other young ladies with whom she corresponded had completed schooling and spent much of their time helping around the house and dreaming of love. Occasionally their essentially juvenile nature crept out, as when Peggy Rawle wrote that she had locked herself in the library "to keep my Troublesome little Brother out."[91] The letters written by Debby Norris, Peggy Rawle, and Sally Wister show the normal adolescent wish to find a friend to whom all can be confided. Miss Wister's journal, a completely secular document, was devoted chiefly to a discussion of the officers. Major William Stoddard, from a wealthy Maryland family, at age nineteen was "vastly bashful; so much so he can hardly look at the ladies. (Excuse me, good sir: I really thought you were not clever; if 'tis bashfulness only, we will drive that away.)" When Sally played with her 19-month-old baby brother, the major lost his shyness and Sally found a method to become well acquainted. A small romance developed. When Robert Tilly of Virginia came in,

> his appearance was elegant; he had been riding; the wind had given the most beautiful glow to his cheeks, and blow'd his hair careless around his face. Oh, my heart, thought I, be secure! The caution was needless, I found it without a wish to stray.

The officers were frequently invited to tea, but when Sally, her 13-year-old sister Betsy, and 21-year-old Lydia Foulke wanted to send their "compliments to the Captain and Watts, Prissa [aged 33] insists it vastly indelicate, and that she has done with us. Hey day! What prudish notions are those, Priscila! I banish prudery."[92] Obviously the young ladies had no fear of romance with these non-Quaker soldiers. The flirtations continued until the British left Philadelphia and the family returned to the city. No marriages resulted. Two years later 18-year-old Deborah Norris wrote Sally:

> I sometime take a retrospective view of the happy days of our childhood, our school-day friendship, and always recall the idea with pleasure. The visionary Swains, my dear, are just as my romantic fancy has often painted. But when will they make their appearance.[93]

Deborah Norris married George Logan not long after, but Sally Wister died in 1804 still single.

V

The social historian faces formidable obstacles in determining the antecedents of Friends' practices and beliefs about marriage. Difficulties in the nature of the source materials and ambiguity in terminology make difficult any precision in locating the sources of Quaker ideas of love.[94] While seventeenth-century Puritans denied the Quaker claim that the Holy Spirit gave personal direction in matters of courtship, the Puritans did stress the spiritual unity between a man and wife and saw marriage as requiring physical and religious love. There were also precedents for Quaker beliefs about marriages to people outside the faith. Early English Baptists had adopted stringent regulations about marriages to nonbelievers—regulations similar to those used by Friends. Before 1660 those Puritans who believed in reforming the Church of England from within were not faced with the problem of mixed marriages, except those to Roman Catholics. After the Glorious Revolution, the Nonconformists desired to promote marriage within their faith. Daniel Defoe designed his *Religious Courtship* (ten editions between 1722 and 1762) as a guide to marriage for all pious Englishmen. Defoe described at length the inconveniences of a mixed marriage when one party was an Anglican and the other a dissenter.[95] The moralists of Georgian England saw in the ideal courtship and marriage a combination of *Sense and Sensibility.* Addison in the *Spectator* and Dr. Johnson in *The Rambler* savagely ridiculed marriages based only on love as well as those based solely on wealth. Such writers instructed their audience, composed of men and women, to select their mates on the basis of affection, virtue, equality of station, and compatibility of temper and intellect.

Throughout the colonial period the meeting continued to insist upon spiritual unity as a foundation for a God-inspired love between a man and a woman. Such a love was supposed to be completely divorced from physical attraction, wealth, or romance. Affection between the parties was a needed, but by no means sufficient, reason for marriage. While data on early Quaker marriages are sketchy, the theory and the practice were in harmony. Even in the nineteenth century, a few Friends described their courtship and marriage in terms that followed the meetings' standards. The information presented in this chapter suggests that in the eighteenth century middle- and upper-class Quakers, without repudiating the meetings' counsel, used the same trinity in courtship as other wealthy Englishmen did—religion, wealth, and love. The increasing number of disownments plus the narratives of those who married within the faith show that nonreligious factors gained the adherence of many young Friends. Since few admitted that they had married for money, most courtship stories revolved around love. The love was different from the union of souls wanted by Penn or the rational but affectionate love desired by the Puritans. Perhaps it can be most aptly described as courtly love linked to marriage.

The increase in Quaker marriages to outsiders may be one index to the rise of the dogma of romantic love in America. Similarly, the concept of romantic love might offer an explanation for the rapid increase in marriages to nonbelievers. The supplanting of spiritual love by romance also helps to account for a trend that historians have often asserted but have had difficulty pinpointing: why was there an increasing secularization of life in an age when people continued to profess religious values?[96] Choosing a wife after falling in love is far different from having God point out your helpmate. While we still know very little about colonial patterns of marriage, it seems reasonable to assume that Friends were not unique in succumbing to romantic love. What is still uncertain is whether or not what happened to the Friends was indicative of a general reorientation in English or American culture. Did Friends help to pioneer this change or did they lag behind? Did the religious caste of Pennsylvania Quakers (and New England Puritans) delay or foster a romantic view of marriage? Such questions, which are basic to the understanding of the family, cannot be answered until we have more understanding of the varieties of marriage customs in England and America. What is certain is that many eighteenth-century Quakers were forced to choose between religious purity and romantic love.

Notes

1 Chilton Powell, *English Domestic Relations 1485–1653* (New York, 1917), pp. 122, 94.

2 William Smith, "Universal Love" in *Balm from Gilead* (1675) p. 88. *Minutes of the Provincial Council of Pennsylvania, Colonial Records of Pennsylvania* (Philadelphia, 1838), 1:38.

3 Jonathan Roberts, "Memoirs," pp. 6–7, HSP; Robert Wells, "Quaker Marriage Patterns in a Colonial Perspective," *William and Mary Quarterly,* 39 (1972): 426–428. The numbers of Quakers who did not marry increased in the late eighteenth century and may be far higher than ten percent. Perhaps the stringency with which Quakers enforced their regulations requiring marriages within the faith but not to near kin resulted in many persons not being married.

4 Thomas Lawrence and George Fox, *Concerning Marriage* (1663), pp. 6–7; Moses West, *A Treatise Concerning Marriage* (London, 1726), p. 3; George Fox, *Journal,* ed. Norman Penney (Cambridge, 1911) 2:154. Fox insisted that God had commanded him to marry.

5 William Hull, *Benjamin Furly and Quakerism in Rotterdam* (Lancaster, Pennsylvania, 1941), pp. 61, 64–65. George Fox, *Works,* (Philadelphia, 1831), 8:281.

6 Lawrence and Fox, *Concerning Marriage,* pp. 1, 3–7, 10.

7 Wells, "Quaker Marriage Patterns in a Colonial Perspective," pp. 415–42; idem, "A Demographic Analysis of Some Middle Colonies Quaker Families of the Eighteenth Century" (Ph.D. diss., Princeton University, 1969), pp. 68–79. Wells argues that seventeenth-century Americans had larger families than Europeans because colonial women married earlier and thus had more time to bear children. By the end of the eighteenth century the American marriage pattern more closely resembled the European system.

8 Wells, "Quaker Marriage Patterns," pp. 421–26.

9 George Fox, "Sermon delivered at a Women's Meeting in Rhode Island," 4/18/1672, Antient Epistles, Minutes, and Advices, or Discipline, New England YM.

10 Robert Barclay to Christian Molleson, 12/28/1699, in John Barclay, *Diary of Alexander Jaffary* (London, 1834), pp. 295–96. See also Thomas Lower to Mary Fell, ca. 1666, and John Abraham to Rachel Fell, 12/26/1681, quoted in Isabel Ross, *Margaret Fell: Mother of Quakerism* (Plymouth, England, 1949), pp. 207–10, 315–16.

11 *PMHB* 27 (1903): 296, 299, 300

12 Lawrence and Fox, *Concerning Marriage,* pp. 6, 12.

13 Thomas Holme to Margaret Fell, 8 mo./1654. Swarthmore Mss, 1:195; "Letters and Documents of Early Friends," 2: 345–46. The Swarthmore manuscripts are letters and papers of early Quakerism which are housed at Friends' Reference Library, London.

14 Robert Weaver to Margaret Fell, 1654, Swarthmore Mss, 1: 91; "Letters and Documents of Early Friends," 3: 803–05.

15 William Smith to George Fox 4/21/1664, QC.

16 John Kelsall, "Diary Extracts," 1: 106–07. The volumes of Kelsall's diary are inaccurately labeled. Volume 1 is a summary of the events of his early life.

17 David Ferris, *Memoirs of the Life of Da-*

vid Ferris (Philadelphia, 1825), pp. 56–62.

18 "Account of James Moore," in *Friends' Miscellany,* ed. John and Isaac Comly (Philadelphia, 1835), pp. 158–59.

19 Joshua Evans, *Journal* (Byberry, Pa., 1837), pp. 10–11.

20 Philadelphia YM, Christian and Brotherly Advices, 1694, 23.

21 Min. Philadelphia YM, 1 (7/16–20/1721): 239; Min. London YM, 1 (4/9–11/1690): 239; 3 (4/2–7/1707); London YM, *Epistles from the Yearly Meeting,* (London, 1760), pp. 48, 106.

22 Thomas Pryor to Phineas Pemberton, 8/14/1698, Pemberton Papers in Etting Collection, 1: 78, HSP.

23 Min. Goshen MM, 1, (1722) 1; (1723): 23

24 "Peter Briggins' Diary," *Eliot Papers,* no. 2, p. 68.

25 William Penn, *A Letter From William Penn to his Wife and Children* (London, 1761), p. 7.

26 *Charter to William Penn, and Laws of the Province of Pennsylvania,* pp. 101, 151; *Statutes at Large of Pennsylvania,* 4: 153. *The Journals of Henry Melchior Muhlenberg,* trans. Theodore Tappert and John Doberstein (Philadelphia, 1942), 1: 502.

27 William Penn, *Works* (London, 1726), 1: 876.

28 Albert Myers, ed. *Hannah Logan's Courtship* (Philadelphia, 1904), 12/5/1747/8, pp. 146, 162.

29 Lawrence and Fox, *Concerning Marriage,* p. 6.

30 London YM, *Epistles from the Yearly Meeting,* 1707, p. 106.

31 Min. Concord MM, 11/8/1699, p. 79.

32 John Smith, "Diary," vol. 3, 11/30/1746/7.

33 Min. Rhode Island MM, 1/23/1708, pp. 3, 18; Min. Philadelphia MM, 11/31/1695/6, p. 140, and 3/29/1696, p. 142; Min. Cedar Creek MM, 5/10/1755, p. 80; Min. Philadelphia YM, 2 (7/23–27/1752): 31; Min. London YM, 10 (5/22/1752): 369.

34 John Hinton to William Hinton, Letter on back of certificate from Nailsworth MM in England, 11/6/1717, Original Certificates of Philadelphia MM, 1714–29, no. 179.

35 Samuel and Sarah Reynell to John Reynell, 1/10/1730, Reynell Papers, 1729–32. The parents granted permission 11/15/1731, but John Reynell did not marry until 1736.

36 Martha Allinson's Memorial to her husband Samuel Allinson, 1791, Allinson Papers, QC.

37 London YM, *Epistles from the Yearly Meeting,* 1722, pp. 146–47. See also "Peter Briggin's Parting Advice to his Children," 1717 *Eliot Papers,* 2: 75.

38 William Smith, "A Few Words of Counsel unto Friends Concerning Marriage" (1664), *Balm From Gilead,* pp. 154–55.

39 Thomas Chalkley, *Works,* p. 580.

40 Richard Hill to Hannah Hill, 9/25/1752, QC.

41 Ross, *Margaret Fell: Mother of Quakerism,* pp. 187, 208, 360.

42 Mary Penington, "A Brief Account of Some Exercises from my Children, written by Edward Penington," 1680; Thomas Scattergood, Notebook, no. 3, p. 5, DR. Mary Penington (1625–82), the widow of Sir William Springett, married Isaac Penington in 1654.

43 Penn, *A Letter to His Wife and Children,* pp. 7, 14–15; Richard Hill to Hannah Hill, 9/25/1752; Richard Hill to his Children, 9/2/1752, Howland Mss.

44 Martha Rodes to Sir John Rodes, April 2, n.d., Mrs. G. L. Lampson, ed., *A Quaker Post-Bag* (London, 1910), p. 29. For another example, see Philip Eliot to John Eliot, 7/8/1749, *Eliot Papers,* no. 1, pp. 12–13.

45 John Kelsall, "Diary Extracts," 3: 2, 19–20, 24, 94–98, 138.

46 PMHB 20 (1896): 386, 449; John Griffith to John Pemberton, 12/10/1767, PP, 19: 148; Myers, *Hannah Logan's Courtship,* 2/1/1748, p. 179.

47 Frederick Tolles, *James Logan and the Culture of Provincial America* (Boston, 1957), pp. 76–77.

48 Ibid., pp. 84–85; Edward Armstrong, ed., *Correspondence between William Penn and James Logan* (Philadelphia, 1872): 2:437; see also *JFHS* 47 (1955): 73.

49 John Smith, "Diary," 1: 2/14/1741; Samuel Emlen, Jr., to John Pemberton, 9/3/1750, PP, 6: 99; Smith Mss, 5: 5; James Briket to James Pemberton, 5/31/1751, PP, 7: 95.

50 John Griffith, *Journal* (Philadelphia, 1780), pp. 41–42.

51 James Jenkins, "Records and Recollections," pp. 68–69, 112, FH. Widows with large estates were greatly desired as wives. Pennsylvania's laws provided that a widow received at least one-third of her husband's property. The second husband usually did not receive a widow's property if there were children from the first marriage, but he did control the income from it during her life. *Charter to William Penn, and Laws of the Province of Pennsylvania,* pp. 141, 142, 174, 231, 265.

52 "Marriage-Portion Fund," London, 1797, Broadside. Jacques Pierre Brissot de Warville, *New Travels in the United States of America,* trans. M. S. Vamos and D. Echeverria, ed. D. Echeverria (Cambridge, Mass., 1964), p. 257. Stevenson Fletcher, *Pennsylvania Agriculture and Country Life, 1640–1840* (Harrisburg, Penn., 1950), p. 420.

53 2 Corinthians 6:14; Deuteronomy 7:13.

Quakers kept the commandment about intermarriage with heathens but ignored the preceding verse which ordered the Israelites to "smite them, and utterly destroy them; thou shalt make no covenant with them; nor shew mercy unto them."

54 Fox, *Works,* 7:180–81.

55 In 1738 Philadelphia Yearly Meeting reprinted the treatise and Rhode Island Monthly Meeting accepted 150 copies; in 1781 London Meeting for Sufferings authorized an edition of 1800 copies. Min. Philadelphia YM, 1 (7/18–22/1736): 393, 399, and (7/16–20/1738): 408; Min. Rhode Island MM, 2 (7/28/1736): 343. Min. London Meeting for Sufferings, 65 (6/22/1781): 141–42.

56 West, *A Treatise Concerning Marriage,* pp. 15–16, 30, 24, 26–27. See also David Hall, *Memoirs* (London, 1758), p. 134: Mary Leadbeater, *Memoirs and Letters of Richard and Elizabeth Shackleton* (London, 1822), pp. 35–36; Min. Philadelphia YM, 7/16–23/1721, p. 239.

57 An editorial comment made by a scribe making extracts from Abington minutes shows the difference between the 1720s and late 1740s. "Acknowledgments for outgoing in marriages, accompanied with . . . immoral conduct, were more readily rescinded, as well as those given for other offences, than acknowledgments in our time are, The great object appears to have been to *reclaim* the offender rather than *to cut them off.*" Min. Abington MM (Extracts), 1682–1746, p. 17. The same could be said in comparison of the 1740s and the 1760s.

58 Jack D. Marietta, "Ecclesiastical Discipline in the Society of Friends, 1682–1776," (Ph.D. diss., Stanford, 1968), p. 141; idem, "The Quaker Family as Sectarian Educator," Paper delivered at 1971 American Historical Association Convention, pp. 16–19. John Stephenson Rowntree, *Quakerism: Past and Present* (London, 1859), pp. 153–54.

59 Min. Philadelphia YM, 1 (7/16–20/1721): 239, and (7/15–19/1722): 245.

60 Min. Core Sound MM, 7/1/1786, p. 172; *BFHS* 51 (1962): 81; *JFHS* 10 (1913): 74; *PMHB* 17 (1893): 460; Abigail Pemberton to Israel Pemberton, 1 mo./1702, PP, 2: 180.

61 John Jay Smith, ed., *Letters of Doctor Richard Hill to his Children* (Philadelphia, 1854), pp. 88, 154; *Extracts from the Diary of Elizabeth Sandwich Drinker,* pp. 289–92. *PMHB* 18 (1894): 57.

62 George Howard, *History of Matrimonial Institutions* (Chicago, 1904), 2: 179–81. Peter Laslett, *The World We Have Lost,* pp. 141–42.

63 *Charter to William Penn, and Laws of the Province of Pennsylvania,* p. 110. *Statutes at Large of Pennsylvania,* 2: 8–9, 490–91.

64 Thomas Ellwood quoted in Philadelphia YM, Christian and Brotherly Advices, pp. 264–65, 206.

65 Philadelphia YM, "Additions to the Book of Discipline," 1734 and 1747, p. 40; New England YM, Discipline, 1708–38, pp. 10, 20–21: Min. Rhode Island MM, 2/30/1728, p. 257; Min. Philadelphia YM, 7/18/1725, p. 301.

66 George Brookes, *Friend Anthony Benezet* (Philadelphia, 1937), p. 372: Min. Philadelphia YM, 2 (9/2–10/1760): 141–42; Myers *Hannah Logan's Courtship,* 6/1/1748, p. 219.

67 Margaret Earle, *Customs and Fashions in Old New England* (New York, 1889), pp. 36, 45–57; Samuel Sewell, *Diary,* ed. Mark Van Doren (New York, 1963), pp. 237–41.

68 Fox, *Works,* 8: 230.

69 Min. Philadelphia MM, 5mo./1699; Min. Philadelphia YM, 7/14–18, p. 77.

70 Wells, "A Demographic Analysis of Some Middle Colony Quaker Families of the Eighteenth Century," pp. 18, 82.

71 Ann Whitall, "Diary," 7/22/1760, p. 29.

72 Edmund S. Morgan, *The Puritan Family* (New York, 1966), pp. 47–54.

73 Thomas Ellwood, *A Collection of Poems on Various Subjects* (London, 1700), pp. 22–25.

74 Joseph Sleigh, *Good Advice and Counsel Given forth by Joseph Sleigh of the City of Dublin* (London, 1696), p. 20.

75 Penn, *Works,* 1: 825, 900.

76 *PMHB* 15 (1891): 380; see also Thomas Richardson to Ann Newberry, 6/17/1703, Richardson Mss, NHS; James Logan to Sarah Read, 5/18/1714, Correspondence, 2: 112, Logan Papers; Joseph Pemberton to Israel Pemberton, 1/24/1767, PP, 19: 41.

77 Min. Symons Creek MM, 9/2/1749, 8/7/1766, 12/5/1746–47; Min. Rhode Island MM, 2 (1/29/1726): 236; London YM, *Epistles from the Yearly Meeting,* 1707, p. 106.

78 Israel Pemberton, Sr., to John Barton, 2/1/1738, PP, 3: 23–28. All the Pemberton brothers appear to have been Romeos. James Pemberton was so taken with Heddy Redwood that when he traveled to London at least three people described for him what she was doing, the people courting her, and their lack of results. John Pemberton courted Sarah Brown but broke off the romance so suddenly that her father wrote a strong letter reprimanding the young man. A favorite topic of gossip in Philadelphia involved who was courting whom. Here is William Logan's description: "Abraham Claypoole only Goes often as Usual to see her [Heddy Redwood], but It is thought by Some Without any Intention of Courtship. Harry Oxley went in the Winter to Barbadoes deeply Smitten with her, but She heartily despises him. Wil-

liam Fishbourne paid his Addresses to Sally Mifflin but she refused him, and since went a Journey to Bordens Town with G. Emlen, Jr. and is fallen in love with . . . Tallman, Sister to Jemmy Tallman, and Courts Strong but It is said His Success there is Likewise doubted." Afting citing a long list of weddings, Logan concluded with "Old John Petty about 75 to a Young Girl of 18." William Logan to James Pemberton, 1/14/1748–49, and 2/29/1749, PP, 5: 50, 72; Judah Foulke to James Pemberton, 9/19/1748, PP, 4: 160; Charles Read to James Pemberton, 2/28/1749, PP, 5: 71; William Brown to James Pemberton, 5/3/1761, QC.

79 John Smith, "Diary," vol. 2, 8/27/1746, and vol. 3, 2/10/1747.

80 Ibid., vol. 3, 8/30/1747, and vol. 4, 12/4–5/1747–48; Myers, *Hannah Logan's Courtship,* pp. 144, 147, 151.

81 John Smith, "Diary," vol. 4, 12/22/1747–48, 1/9/1748, 2/10/1748.

82 Myers, *Hannah Logan's Courtship,* p. 173.

83 Ibid., pp. 198, 201; John Smith, "Diary," vol. 5, 5/26/1748. Smith did visit Germantown meeting once and dined at Stenton with Hannah Logan during the month.

84 Richard Hill to Rachel Hill, 7/28/1758, Howland Mss, QC.

85 Ibid. Doctor Hill was not always consistent. When another daughter married secretly and out of unity with Friends, he was very critical. Harriet Scott to Richard Hill, 12/25/1755.

86 Richard Hill to Hannah Moore, 9/26/1756; Richard Hill to Rachel Hill, 7/29/1758.

87 Samuel Allinson to Elizabeth Smith, n.d., Allinson Mss, QC.

88 Elizabeth Drinker, "Diary," 7/13/1760. Extracts from the journal of Elizabeth Drinker, pp. 168, 146, 233. John Cresson, "Diary" 1 (3/30/1795), HSP. After the Revolution, Elizabeth Drinker allowed her son Henry, Jr., and daughter Sally to go out unchaperoned for sleigh rides, etc. with other young people.

89 John Ezell, ed., *The New Democracy in America: Travels of Francisco de Miranda into the United States, 1783–1784* (Norman, Oklahoma, 1963), p. 140. Louis B. Wright and Marion Tinlings, eds., *Quebec to Canada in 1785–1786: Being the Travel Diary and Observations of Robert Hunter, Jr., A Young Merchant of London* (San Marino, California, 1943), p. 173. Kenneth and Anna M. Roberts, eds., *Moreau de St. Méry's American Journey 1793–1798* (New York, 1947), p. 280.

90 Marquis de Chastellux, *Travels in North America,* trans. Howard C. Rice, Jr. (Chapel Hill, North Carolina, 1963), 1: 119–20, n. 47, p. 288. Gottlieb Mittelberger, *Journey to Pennsylvania* (Cambridge, Mass., 1960), pp. 69–72. *PMHB* 17 (1893): 448.

91 Albert C. Myers, ed., *Sally Wister's Journal* (Philadelphia, 1902), p. 203.

92 Ibid. 10/21/1779, p. 89; 12/11/1777, p. 123; 6/7/1778, p. 180.

93 Ibid., p. 198.

94 Courtly love has been a feature of Western civilization since the twelfth century. The troubadour's love, which could be sensual or ethereal, flourished outside marriage. In fact, marriage and love were incompatible. From the thirteenth to the eighteenth centuries the English wrote courtly love poetry, but the historian must be wary of using what may have been essentially a literary technique to indicate the way Englishmen actually felt. C. S. Lewis argues that the first poet to link courtly love to marriage was Edmund Spenser. In the *Amoretti* and *Epithalamion,* Spenser celebrated his love for his wife. A glorification of married love is found in some of Shakespeare's plays, Milton's *Paradise Lost* and divorce tracts, and a few of John Donne's lyrics. Denis de Rougement, *Love in the Western World* (New York, 1940); Morton Hunt, *The Natural History of Love* (New York, 1959), pp. 131–296; C. S. Lewis, *Allegory of Love* (Oxford, 1936), pp. 297–360.

95 Daniel Defoe, *History of The Plague of London* and *Religious Courtship* (New York, 1857). For Puritan ideas of love see William Haller, "Hail Wedded Love," *English Literary History* 13 (1946): 79–97; William Haller and Malleville Haller, "The Puritan Art of Love," *Huntington Library Quarterly* 5 (1942): 235–72; James Johnson, *A Society Ordained by God* (New York, 1970); John G. Halkett, *Milton and the Idea of Matrimony,* Yale Studies in English, no. 173 (New Haven, Conn., 1970).

96 Dietmar Rothermund, *The Layman's Progress* (Philadelphia, 1961), pp. 57–68, 128–31.

9 Quaker Marriage Customs

They were so one, that none could say,// Which of them rul'd or whether did obey.// He ruled, because she would obey; and she// In so obeying, rul'd as well as he.

Pennsylvania Chronicle, January 8, 1770

The Puritan critique of the Church of England had been particularly severe regarding such abuses as secret betrothals, child weddings, forced marriages, and hasty ceremonies. Since they could not reform the abuses of the clerical courts before 1640, the Puritans advocated giving the state jurisdiction over all areas of matrimonial law. While not denying the religious nature of wedlock, they objected to the sacramental nature of the ceremony and opposed such "pagan" customs as giving a ring or repeating such vows as "with my body I thee worship." Although a sermon could be preached at espousals in New England, the marriage took place under the authority of the magistrate and outside the church. Not until after the revocation of the charter of Massachusetts did clerics marry people in church, though by the time of the American Revolution ministers performed most ceremonies.[1] Friends had essentially the same objections as the Puritans to Anglican procedures, but the Quakers' solution was radically different, for they had the entire marriage procedure take place under the supervision of the meeting.

Pennsylvania laws were designed to correct the abuses of secret marriages, but they did not force all to practice Quaker customs; on the contrary, the laws sought to guarantee to every religious group the right to marry in its own way. A requirement that bans be posted at the courthouse or announced before the meeting or from the pulpit was designed to end unauthorized marriages of indentured servants or runaway young people. The Anglicans in Philadelphia at first refused to accept Pennsylvania's legislation, arguing that canonical oaths bound priests to marry anyone qualified. William Penn retorted that the laws strengthened canon law prohibitions while protecting property, in this case defined as white servants.[2]

The Society of Friends had established its marriage customs in England and their validity had been recognized before the end of the Interregnum. The practices were transferred intact to the New World. The man and woman first appeared at the women's meeting, and a female Friend introduced them to the men's meeting. There they declared that "with the Lord's permission and friends approbation they Intend to take each other In marriage."[3] This first step corresponded to the publication of bans by Puritans or Anglicans. If both parents were present, they gave their permission. Otherwise, written approval by the guardians or father and mother of each couple was required, even though the young people were normally of age. If either boy or girl lived within the "verge" of another meeting, he or she was required to bring a certificate of clearness from that meeting. Even when the persons had recently migrated from overseas, the meeting asked that they produce a certificate signifying parental permission and their clearness from others. Philadelphia Yearly Meeting's epistle to London in 1701 requested that such information not be omitted from certificates, for young people intending to wed "are very unwilling to wait for answers from England; and considering the uncertainty of Letters going and coming safe, we must confess it is a very hard case." Evidently, local meetings would not allow a marriage ceremony without some certification because the epistle mentioned that many couples refused to wait and so went to a priest. The providing of credentials served as a method of introducing a Friend in good standing to a meeting and also guarded against bigamy. The procedure was not always successful, however, since some men forged the documents.[4] Assuming that a man had or could get a valid certificate, the women and men's meetings appointed a committee to determine whether anyone had objections to the marriage, if there had been previous engagements, and if the couple were good Friends.

The man and his fiancée attended the next monthly meeting, again declared their intentions, and the overseers reported. Occasionally another man or women or a parent objected, claiming a previous promise. If such a betrothal could be substantiated, the marriage would not be permitted until the person made satisfaction to the injured party. Friends did not require a man to marry against his will, but they regarded the alienation of affections as a serious matter. Since the days of George Fox, Quakers had boasted that they made no contracts for marriage but that their promises were not broken. If the man had previously proposed or even seriously courted another without intending marriage, he was required by the meeting to confess his sin. At times a couple came to a meeting, requested permission to marry, and never came again. Friends required an explanation of such an occurrence, and that usually given was that either the boy or the girl had called off the whole affair.[5] If the certificates were in order and the parents gave permission, the meeting approved the marriage.

Most marriage requests received the approbation of Friends, because elders and preparative meetings warned people who could not pass before the meeting not to come. The two required appearances before the meeting often became social occasions, since the couple about to pass meeting would invite special acquaintances and have a supper afterwards. (In an attempt to reduce the cost of marriages, nineteenth-century Friends required just one trip to the monthly meeting.) Yearly meetings served notice that only close relatives of Friends were allowed to attend meetings for discipline, but the need of such advice showed that some brought too many of the world's people. Before the wedding the groom took invitations to special guests, and the day and time of the ceremony were announced at the conclusion of a first-day's meeting.[6]

The marriage was conducted much like a meeting for worship. The people entered quietly and sat in silence, perhaps hearing an exhortation by a ministering Friend. The couple stood and said their vows to each other. Although the Quaker protest against vain formalities did not allow a repeating of memorized words, certificates noted that the husband did "openly declare that he took her . . . to be his wife promising through the Lord's assistance to be unto her a loving and Faithful husband until death should separate them," and the wife made a similar statement.[7]

At the conclusion the couple and their guests signed a certificate. The document established the legal fact that the marriage had taken place and contained an identification of the parties, a notice that the marriage had been declared publicly, a certification of the freedom of the couple from other obligations, the approval of the meeting, the vows, and the signatures of at least twelve witnesses.[8] The form has not varied from that time to this.

During the eighteenth century, the meetings emphasized that marriages should be solemn religious observances. The Philadelphia discipline of 1704 contained a provision that two overseers be chosen to advise the parents before the marriage how to keep due moderation and to attend the ceremony and meal afterwards to ensure that everything done was a credit to Friends. Since by the end of the Colonial period the mother of the bride might request a certain person to serve as inspector, the attendance of such persons (who left relatively early after the supper) did not put too much of a damper on the proceedings.[9] Only infrequently did the overseers report that someone had misbehaved at a wedding.

Quaker marriage ceremonies could be either plain and simple or lavish affairs with several bridesmaids and great feasting. In 1690 George Fox suggested that the money spent on elaborate wedding meals be given to the poor; Thomas Chalkley repeatedly left before the meal, desiring to set an example by his disapproval.[10] Yearly meetings told members to refrain from ostentatious display and imitation of the world's wedding customs. All was to no avail. In 1703 James Logan wrote William Penn about the "splendor of entertainment" at weddings.[11] A succession of eighteenth-century travelers such as Peter Kalm, Gottlieb Mittelberger, and the Marquis de Barbé-Marbois commented on the elaborate wedding festivities of the colonists.[12] John Watson described the celebration of a late eighteenth-century wedding.

> The wedding entertainments in olden times were very expensive and harassing to the wedded. The house of the parent would be filled with company to dine. The same company would stay to tea and supper both. For two days punch was dealt out in profusion. The gentlemen visited the groom on the first floor, and then ascended to the second floor to see the bride in the presence of her maids, &c. Then every gentlemen, even to 150 in a day severally took his kiss—even the plain Friends submitted to these doings. I have heard of rich families among them which had 120 persons to dine.[13]

After the ceremony the newlyweds spent two weeks or more in the house of the bride's father. The bridesmaids and helpers of the groom might remain in attendance, and every day large numbers of persons would visit to pay their respects, eat cake, and drink tea or wine. At the end of the period of social calls the couple moved into their own home and were expected to begin repaying the visits. Failure to return a call meant that they did not wish to associate.

II

William Penn expressed what Friends thought should be the correct relationship between a man and wife. "Use all Means of true Endearment, that you may recommend and please one another; remembering your Relation and Union is the Figure of Christ's to the Church: Therefore let the Authority of Love only bear sway your whole life." The letters that husbands and wives wrote to each other brim with terms of affection. William Penn called his wife "the joy of my life; the most beloved, as well as the most worthy, of all my earthly comforts."[14] Phineas Pemberton addressed his wife Alice "in that endeared relation of Love and kindness that hath brought us together and united us in that oneness that makes us one where Love freely flows art thou very near and dear unto me." On her deathbed the wife of John Bevan reminded her husband that after 45 years of marriage "our love is rather more now towards one another than at the beginning." Elizabeth Allinson closed a letter to Samuel Allinson, "May Heaven continue to preserve the best of Husbands is the prayer of thy Affectionate."[15]

Domestic felicity did not come without proper care by both parties. A newly wedded person should not expect his partner to be a paragon of virtue and should make allowances for times of misunderstanding and weakness. Such passions as anger and jealousy were to be strictly avoided. Richard Hill warned his daughter against small trivial quarrels which often opened the way for major disagreements.

> A woman who must rise or fall by the good or ill conduct of her husband has a right to give her opinion in what concerns them both, but it's best policy in her to gain an influence over him by kindness, mildness and condescension and then it will be lasting.[16]

William Penn told his children to avoid all occasions of dispute and to "Never lie down with any Displeasure in your Minds."[17] Thomas Chalkley lived at home with his parents for 20 years, and heard only one quarrel—

> my father saying, I have been an indulgent husband unto thee, and my mother answered, I have not been one of the worst of wives to thee; which were the harshest words, and the greatest difference that I observed between them: for their life was a life of peace and love.[18]

If there were a serious disagreement between husband and wife, Friends, along with almost every one else in the eighteenth century, insisted on the subordination of the woman to the man. Eve sinned first and then led Adam into transgression. As a punishment for her disobedience, woman has since been considered weaker physically and mentally. While Penn used the metaphor in Ephesians 5:25 on loving a wife as Christ loved the church, George Fox also mentioned the preceding verse: "Therefore as the church is subject unto Christ, so let the wives be to their own husbands in every thing."[19] A consistent theme in Quaker writings about marriage was the necessity for a woman to be submissive to her husband. Thomas Gwin, whose writings were published early in the eighteenth century, told his daughter to study her husband's temper, "never to upbraid or provoke him; to be careful of his Concerns, prudent in your Carriage to his Relations; to love him with an entire

Affection." By such conduct she could so gain "the Command of his Heart" that he would "deny you nothing that is fit or convenient."[20] Jonathan Roberts praised his mother for her "condescension" in which she "almost made her husband's will, her own. It was virtue, and not inanity."[21] Frederick Smith, an English Friend who in 1810 wrote a tract entitled *On the Duty of a Wife,* was the strongest advocate of womanly weakness. In Smith's view, the way for a wife to retain the affection of her husband was to cater to his every whim. If he came home irritated, she should "by every soft and tender means, endeavour to bear with and sooth him by every little kind of attention, tho' at the expense of her own natural will and inclination." Smith approved of a woman who did not like black but dressed in that color because her husband preferred it. That same man wished to rearrange the pictures in the parlor " 'and though I was satisfied it would not correspond with the picture on the other side,' (of which I had full proof;) 'yet, as it was his wish, and he might feel disappointed, if it was not done, I therefore did not hesitate to make the alteration.' "[22] In Smith's pamphlet the husband was almost an outsider to the household, and the wife's duty was to create a place of happiness and comfort when he returned from the other world.

In an epistle written in 1676 George Fox defined the role of women. Most American Friends in 1776 would have agreed with him.

> First, to be sober; secondly, to love their husbands; thirdly, to love their children; fourthly, to be discreet; fifthly, to be chaste, and keepers at home, and good, obedient to their own husbands.[23]

Society prescribed that a woman's obligations were to her husband and family, and late eighteenth-century travelers contrasted the American maiden's freedom before marriage with the constriction in her life afterwards.[24]

Friends participated in the perennial battle of the sexes over the merits of male and female. They made jokes about women wearing the "breeches," the absurdity of reasoning with ladies whose minds were already made up, the female habits of talking, frequently changing their minds, being unable to keep a secret, and loving luxury—particularly Bohea tea. As late as 1796 a speech club staged a public debate on the question "Is [sic] the intellectual faculties of women, equal to those of men."[25] Ladies answered in kind by complaining how boring it was to be courted by men whose sole topics of conversation were domestic economy, religion, or politics. Maidens were advised to keep a list of promises that men made before marriage and to show them when they became less attentive afterwards. Women asserted that even if the male mind was "more strong and extensive," the female mind was "more ingenious and refined" with "strong retentive Faculties and quick discerning Spirits."[26] Jacob Taylor's almanacs carried on the battle for giving women their due:

> Well might a Man delight in woman take,
> For she, than he, is of a nobler make:
> She made of man, but man was made of Dust,
> The second work must needs exceed the first.

Taylor condemned the permanent bachelors who thought marriage too restrictive as wretches undeserving of the pleasures of matrimony. John Smith lauded women as "the finest part of God's visible creation."[27]

If Quaker women objected to their inferior social position, they did not often say so. In 1798 Priscilla Wakefield, an English Friend, wrote *Reflections on the Present Condition of the Female Sex.* Wakefield, whose interest was in expanding the education of girls so that they could play a larger role in society, failed to mention the inferiority of women in the household.[28] Elizabeth Drinker's comment on Mary Wollstonecraft's *The Rights of Women* (i.e., in "many of her sentiments, she . . . *speaks my mind*") was the first indication of the subsequent role that Quaker women were to play in the feminist movement in the nineteenth century.[29]

The wives of wealthy Philadelphians, who spent their leisure reading, visiting, and drinking tea, had time to reflect upon women's rights. Most women in colonial America spent their lives continually cleaning house, cooking for their families, and rearing children. If the family lived in the country, the wife might take care of the dairy and the poultry and sell eggs in the town market. Poorer Friends made their garments from homespun, and even William Penn's sons wore homemade shirts.[30] Any recreation time was usually spent attending meetings, and the yearly meeting served as a vacation for the women. Christopher Marshall, a Quaker disowned for his pro-American activities during the Revolutionary War, wrote a most appreciative description of his wife's work.

> To do her that justice which her services deserve by entering them minutely would take up most of my time, for this genuine reason how that, from early in the morning till late at night, she is constantly employed in the affairs of the family, which for some months has been very large, for besides the addition to our family in the house [is] a constant resort of comers and goers who seldom go away with dry lips and hungry bellies. This calls for her constant attendance not only to provide, but also to attend at getting prepared in the kitchen, baking our own bread and pies, meat, &c., but also on the table. Her cleanliness about the house, her attendance in the orchard, cutting and drying apples, of which several bushels have been procured, add to which her making of cider without tools, for the constant drink of the family, her seeing all our washing done, and her fine clothes and my shirts, all which are all smoothed by her, add to this her making of twenty large cheese, and that from one cow, and daily using milk and cream besides her sewing, knitting, &c. Thus she looketh well to the ways of her household, and eatheth not the bread of idleness, yea, she also stretched out her hand . . . to her needy friends and neighbors. I think she has not been above four times, since her residence has been here, to visit her neighbors, nor through mercy has she been sick for any time, but has at all times been ready, in any affliction to me or my family, as a faithful nurse and attendant, both day and night.[31]

The family was far wealthier than most Quakers, and the wife had the help of male and female servants. However, Marshall's description leaves no doubt that the servants did as little work as possible.

The only place where the Quaker woman had more freedom than her contemporaries was in the meeting. There was no inferiority in spiritual matters. Women could preach, serve as elders or overseers, and write tracts and pamphlets. The hierarchy of men's monthly, quarterly, and yearly meetings was paralleled by similar organizations for women. The women's meetings could not disown members, and they were often dependent upon the men's meetings for money, but, beyond this, they acted as autonomous agencies. Such eighteenth-century ministers as Rachel Wilson, Elizabeth Wilkinson, Rebecca Jones, Sophia Hume, and Sarah Morris crossed the Atlantic to preach to Friends. More frequently, women engaged in shorter journeys, though the danger of illness and the discomfort of accommodations made any travel an ordeal. Mary Pemberton assured her husband in 1751 that "it is no Pleasure to me to be Absent from thee and our Dear Children."[32] Among the heroes of colonial Quakerism are the husbands and wives who permitted their mates a year's travel in the ministry. The monthly meeting might consult with a wife before giving permission for the husband to take a missionary journey. If the husband kept his wife from a traveling ministry, he might be rebuked.[33]

Spiritual equality did not carry over into the rest of life, however. Legally, the Quaker housewife lost control of all her property upon marriage. The husband received title to her lands and money, and in return he was responsible for her debts and actions. Only through a contract made before the marriage could a young lady preserve control of her property.[34] The wife was guaranteed one-third of the husband's estate at his death; the rest was divided equally among all children except for the eldest son, who received a double share.[35] In 1718 the Pennsylvania Assembly passed a "feme sole" law designed to permit wives whose husbands were long absent to support themselves and their families by trading. Her property could not be used to pay the husband's debts, and he was not liable for her debts beyond the normal maintenance he was required by law to give.[36] This statute, which treated married women as if they were single, gave the same amount of economic freedom to women that they enjoyed in England.

Quaker women often helped their husbands in their trades, and since the ground floor of the house of an artisan or merchant could be used for business, wives and children tended the store when husbands were away. Benjamin Coole recommended choosing for a wife a prudent woman capable of supervising the shop. Alice Clark and Elizabeth Anthony Dexter have described the great variety of skills and occupations followed by English and American women, often as widows carrying on the business of their husbands. Sarah Fell kept the accounts of the estate at Swarthmore, managed a forge, and engaged in small-scale banking. One of her sisters made money from the salt business.[37] Hannah Penn managed William Penn's affairs during his final illness, acted as sole executrix of his will, and preserved the proprietary estates in Pennsylvania until her sons came of age. Tace Sowle, daughter of the Quaker printer Andrew Sowle, carried on the family business in London and published many books for Friends in the early eighteenth century. The wives of traveling ministers, including John Banks, William Edmundson, Thomas Chalkley, and Samuel Bownas, operated farms or shops while their husbands were absent. In the colonies, Phineas Pemberton entrusted to his wife, Alice, a variety of tasks concerning the management of his plantation. Elizabeth Sandwich (later Drinker) spent evenings checking accounts. Jane Hoskins, a traveling minister, carried trade goods on a journey to Philadelphia which she may have sold to defray the expenses of her trip. Deborah Morris, who was single, engaged in trade, purchased lands, and supervised the running of several farms.[38]

If the wife took the initiative and gave advice to her husband, she was wise to be diplomatic.

> I was a good deal affected at what thou wrote about A. D.—and hope my dear Billy will not think me too bold in saying I could wish thee would not distress the poor Creature by insisting (at present) on receiving the whole of thy demand on him. His affairs may perhaps take a more favourable turn, and if thee gets the half or more of what he owes thee—but I will not pretend to advise—forgive me if I've already said too much.[39]

Quaker men may have sometimes discussed business with their wives, but the ultimate responsibility for making decisions was a masculine one.

III

While Quakers frequently mentioned the spiritual aspects of marriage, they made few comments concerning the physical side. Before marriage, the person was warned to beware of permitting carnal desires or lusts to contaminate his motives, and he was advised to concentrate upon the religious unity between husband and wife. The ideal of connubial love was expressed by Richard Hunter, who stated that when he wed Elizabeth Atherton in 1654, he had "pure union with her in that which is pure and clean out of all and above all fleshly desire."[40] Innocent affection was viewed as completely separate from sexual desire, but the Society of Friends did not assert, as did the Shakers, that marriage and sex were evil. When Joseph Nicholson and his wife visited Salem, Massachusetts, as ministers in 1660, they found that the prevailing doctrine among Quakers was to oppose any physical relationship between husband and wife. Several couples had refrained from intercourse for a year or more and one couple for four years. Nicholson reported that "it went for a common report at Boston" that Quakers would have no children. Though the Salem Friends asserted that the Boston martyrs had advocated celibacy, Nicholson argued that an old couple from Rhode Island had first propagated it. The Nicholsons opposed the practice and brought a "large testimony" against it, for Mrs. Nicholson gave birth to a child while in New England.[41] Since early Friends believed that for all true Christians creation had been restored to its pristine purity, sexual relations within marriage were not evil. Children were a blessing from God and not an effect of sin. The normal marriage was both a physical and a spiritual union. Thomas Chalkley warned that long separations between man and wife were a dangerous practice. The couple should live together and sleep in the same bed. To sleep separately "is very unnatural, and often tends to lessen the love and affection they ought to have for each other."[42]

Young unmarried Quaker males made no pretence of denying their interest in the physical attractiveness of ladies. When James Pemberton traveled to England, Charles Read wrote that "Hetty [Redwood] is going to Rhode Island, If you can forget her Brilliant Eye, her ruby Lip, and Sprightly air, and Content yourself with an outside form that is Agreeable, and a disposition as any woman ever was possessed of, you may Supply your self in my neighbourhood."[43] In a letter asking permission to court, John Smith noted he believed that a "fair outside did not Constitute happiness," but after conversing with Hannah Logan, he realized "that though the Cabinet was Exquisitely framed, the mind lodged in it far Excelled." The danger from sexual attraction was the same as from any earthly device. Used with moderation and kept in place, procreation was a blessing from the Lord, but too much esteem brought idolatry, for man attempted to find happiness in temporal rather than eternal matters. Perhaps the need for disciplining his desires made John Smith read his father-in-law's two manuscript treatises on the passions just three days after wedding Hannah Logan.[44]

The absence of any mention of sex in private correspondence or pamphlets is striking, especially when one considers the frank disclosures of immorality in court and in meeting records. The few available facts indicate a streak of prudishness in Friends. In the private correspondence I read, there were only three letters that contained even mildly ribald comments.[45] Even a discussion of procreation was taboo. Quakers may have obtained some erotic stimulation from tales of pagan festivals or sensationalist stories about Roman Catholic priests that were printed in almanacs.[46] In the *Battle- Door* written in 1669, John Stubbs showed an almost Victorian sensitivity in condemning passages in schoolbooks that referred to the posteriors of men or animals: "Why doth a dog being to piss, hold up one leg?" "Sit, where the dogs sit . . . and Where do dogs sit . . . ? Upon their Buttock." "Where do Foxes fart? A little above their hams?" George Fox established women's meetings so the ladies could discuss matters that they could not, in "Modesty," talk about in the presence of men, though minutes give no insight into what those matters were. London Yearly Meeting in 1718 protested against that "Immodest Fashion of going with Naked Necks and Breasts." In 1763 John Smith, writing under the pseudonym of Atticus, castigated "indelicate double entendres" and "smutty tales." In the 1770s English Friends were shocked when a minister mentioned that God distinguished the sexes for the propagation of the species. In 1784 Samuel Shoemaker's wife refused to display a set of Wedgwood oval bas reliefs because the tiny figures were naked.[47]

After the Revolution such sensitivities were by no means confined to Friends. Moreau de St. Méry, a Frenchman who lived in exile in Philadelphia, wrote that American women described their bodies from head to waist as stomach and from there to the foot as ankles, and refused to mention specific parts of the body even to doctors. While Moreau gave Friends the credit for introducing the syringe into America and mentioned the Quaker women's fear of lecherous feelings, he did not believe that they were more prudish than other Americans. Some expectant mothers refused to have doctors attend them during childbirth, preferring to use midwives, and husbands were barred from the sight of a birth.[48]

Sexual relations outside marriage were a sin. Nevertheless, premarital intercourse was a rather frequent offense, even though involving only a small percentage of the total membership. Jack D. Marietta discovered that at least 70 percent of Pennsylvania Friends found guilty of fornication were found out when they married outside the Society and became parents too soon. The burden of proof in a paternity suit was definitely with the male, and if the mother accused him, he might be disowned whether or not he admitted the offense.[49] In England the precontract was viewed as a binding wedding and the marriage was often consummated that evening even though the church ceremony did not occur for some time.[50] Once a Quaker couple decided to marry, they had to attend at least two monthly meetings, after which the wedding day was set, invitations given, and all preparations made. Any woman who was pregnant at the time she married was forced to make public acknowledgment of the fact, and there was no shortage of people willing to check on couples by figuring the nine months. Quakers allowed no easing of restrictions just because the young people were engaged; rather, they viewed this as a time of special temptation, and any man who lived in the same household as his intended spouse was asked to move out. A couple who could not afford to wait two months because of advanced pregnancy might be married by a Quaker magistrate who, with twelve witnesses, constituted a legal but unofficial meeting.[51]

George Fox insisted that anyone who had carnal knowledge of a woman should marry her, no matter what the difference in outward rank or race.[52] The Pennsylvania law code of 1683 required that if a single man and woman were guilty of fornication, "he and she shall be punished, either by enjoining Marriage, or fine, or Corporal punishment, or all or any of these." The courts, which had discretionary powers, reduced penalties if one or both parties consented and the couple were married. Otherwise, the man and woman would be whipped and fined and the father forced to provide some sort of financial support for the child. The 1683 law enjoining marriage was reenacted in 1700, but the Crown disallowed it since "it may be unreasonable, where young men may be drawn in by lewd women."[53] The meetings applied Fox's doctrine with great latitude. There were even instances in which the young woman was asked if she wished to marry the man; if she refused, no action was taken.[54]

IV

Whether or not most Quaker marriages were happy is an intriguing question, which the historian unfortunately cannot answer. Meeting eulogies and personal correspondence stressed complete harmony. Marriages endured since there were no divorces and separations were rare. Quarrels that came to the attention of monthly meetings were few, but this could mean that the abuse was verbal or that neighbors did not know of physical fighting. Samuel Ogden's investigation of one relationship disclosed that

> while they lived together they were very unhappy often quarreling, which arose so high the last time he left home, she wished she might never see him more, and when he was brought home Dead, she little regarded it, more than if he had been an indifferent Person.[55]

The monthly meeting entered into marital affairs only if there were a serious problem, like fighting. Occasionally a husband was disciplined for nonsupport of his wife. If a man posted a bill declaring that he was no longer responsible for his wife's debts, the meeting was likely to intervene. Friends believed that living apart set a bad example, and they attempted to arbitrate disputes between estranged couples. Philadelphia Monthly Meeting spent nearly four years trying to persuade Thomas Fitzwater and his wife to dwell together. Success finally attended the meeting's efforts. Core Sound Meeting in North Carolina, after vainly trying to reconcile a couple, persuaded them to live together. If this proved unsatisfactory, she could live apart and he would provide an allowance; if she wished to move away, he would give her a reasonable dowry. In rare instances Quakers recognized that a man and woman could not live together in harmony, and thus they occasionally permitted a separation.[56]

Since the Church of England left the Roman Catholic church before the reforms of the Council of Trent, she entered the seventeenth century using the same complex canon law regulations on matrimony as had existed in medieval times. Legally, neither church nor state recognized a divorce *a vinculo matrimonii,* that is, with permission to remarry. For adultery, one obtained a divorce *a mensa et thoro,* which granted permission to be separated but did not allow remarriage, although in practice this restriction was ignored. But there was a long list of offenses that could result in annulments—such as degrees of kin, precontract, and some types of adultery.[57] The Puritans were extremely critical of the jurisdiction of the ecclesiastical courts in marriage cases, because practically anyone with enough money could find some legal technicality in order to gain an annulment.

Following the lead of the sixteenth-century German reformers, the Puritans in England and New England advocated giving divorces for a much greater number of offenses and allowing remarriage for the innocent party. William Perkins advised permitting divorce for desertion, malicious dealing with each other, long absence, and adultery.[58] John Milton insisted that since matrimony was to establish harmony, divorce should be allowed for incompatibility of temperament. In New England, Massachusetts refrained from making laws on the subject, but the General Court allowed divorce with remarriage for the wronged person in cases of adultery, desertion, and long absence. Connecticut defined the period for willful desertion as three years and that for providential absence as seven years. Total neglect of duty or nonsupport were also just causes for separation. Impotency, too close kinship with the other party, previous marriage, or fornication with a relative of the other party brought annulment.[59] The government not the church decided such matters.

Friends had little of the liberality that characterized the Puritan theories. In 1682 Pennsylvania permitted divorce (whether remarriage was allowed was not stated) for adultery if the husband or wife of the guilty party applied to the civil authorities within one year. The law was reenacted in 1693 and again in 1700 but voided by the Crown because English law permitted divorce only *a mensa et thoro.* When the assembly passed a new statute, divorce was limited to "board and bed" and gave no permission to remarry.[60] Thomas Chalkley noted that the only biblical basis for divorce was adultery, and he added that the Gospels did not allow for separation and remarriage. Any man who took a second wife while his first wife lived was an adulterer. Desertion and separation were not grounds for remarriage. Thomas Marle appealed to Philadelphia Yearly Meeting in 1687 saying that his wife had been absent for eight years and asked permission to remarry. The meeting answered, "he could not Take a Wife amongst Friends, If she should be yet Living." In 1748 a Philadelphia Friend was charged with adultery; his defense was that his wife had not been heard of for seven years. He was disowned.[61] If it was reasonably certain that a husband or wife was dead, the meeting allowed a Friend to re-marry.

V

Quakers attempted to bring the entire process of courting and marriage under the purview of the meeting. While the growing stress upon romance undermined the religious emphasis in courtship, there was no weakening of the meeting's control over the wedding. The couple appeared before the monthly meeting to state their intentions. After overseers or elders investigated to verify the parents' consent and see that the individuals were single Friends in good standing, the monthly meeting gave permission for the couple to wed. The actual ceremony took place at a special service for worship where the man and woman exchanged vows. Following the wedding, the bride and groom entertained guests at an elaborate feast.

Friends believed that a happy marriage could endure only through mutual concessions and advised husbands and wives to avoid quarrels and to make allowances for each other's weaknesses. If a serious dispute arose, Friends insisted on the subordination of the female. Although some husbands treated their wives as equals and consulted them on all matters of importance, most Quakers believed that a woman gained influence by being submissive. Beyond the assertion that a true marriage involved religious and physical unity, Friends remained silent on the subject of sex in marriage. The meeting intervened in marital affairs only if the couple fought openly or separated; in such cases, which were rare, arbitrators tried to restore harmony. Pennsylvania laws provided for divorce in cases of adultery, but no Quaker ever obtained a divorce. In an age when divorce was scandalous and the alternatives to married life unpalatable, the endurance of Quaker marriages should not be taken as an index of contentment. However, Friends did take divine commands seriously, and they believed that God desired a unity between husband and wife as perfect as the relationship between Christ and his church. Perhaps in their attempt to be obedient, Quakers created and maintained marriages based on love and respect. The documents describing happy marriages are not conclusive proof, but the historian should not presume to contradict his sources without persuasive evidence.

As previously noted, a few Quaker ladies in England and early America proved to be quite adept at managing plantations or businesses, but generally a married woman's role was restricted to laboring in the house and helping with farm chores. In the seventeenth century, Friends asserted the spiritual equality of male and female and approved when a woman wrote tracts, traveled on behalf of the meeting, and became a minister or an overseer. During the entire colonial period, however, no Quaker writer transferred the spiritual equality of women into other spheres.

Notes

1 George Howard, *A History of Matrimonial Institutions* (Chicago, 1904), 2: 127, 131, 140. Thomas Taylor, *Truth's Innocency and Simplicity* (London, 1689), p. 158.

2 Staughton George *et al*, eds., *Charter to William Penn and Laws of Pennsylvania* (Harrisburg, Penn., 1897), p. 151; J. T. Mitchell and S. Flanders, eds.., *Statutes at Large of Pennsylvania* (Harrisburg, Penn., 1908), 4: 153; Edward Beatty, *William Penn as a Social Philoso-*

pher (New York, 1939), pp. 254–55.

3 Min. Rhode Island MM, 2 (12/26/1722/3): 209.

4 London YM, Epistles Received, 1 (11/22/1686/7): 29–30; Min. Philadelphia MM, 9/29/1700, and 12/23/1710, p. 105; Min. Rhode Island MM, 2 (1/31/1729): 219. Albert Myers, ed., *Hannah Logan's Courtship* (Philadelphia, 1904), pp. 338–39.

5 Min. Philadelphia MM, 3 (10/30/1715): 11; (12/24/1715): 16; (10/21/1725): 130; Min. Rhode Island MM, 2 (8/30/1722): 203–05; Min. Perquimans MM, 2A (5/2/1759); George Fox, *Works,* 8: 242.

6 Philadelphia YM, Discipline, 1704–17; Christian and Brotherly Advices, 1755, p. 114.

7 Certificate of Thomas Mayburry and Rebecca Warder, 12/18/ 1766, Marriage Certificates, 2: 126, DP.

8 *BFHA* (1951): 71, 78.

9 Philadelphia YM, Discipline, 1704–17; Min. Goshen MM, 1 (1/5/1724–25): 37; Min. Philadelphia MM, 10/26/1707, pp. 40–41; Henry Biddle, ed., *Extracts from the Journal of Elizabeth Drinker* (Philadelphia, 1889) pp. 113, 115.

10 Fox, *Works,* 8: 309; Thomas Chalkley, *Works* (London, 1791), pp. 150–51.

11 Edward Armstrong, ed., *Correspondence Between William Penn and James Logan* (Philadelphia, 1870), 1: 196.

12 Peter Kalm, *Travels in North America* (New York, 1937), 2: 677; Gottlieb Mittelberger, *Journey to Pennsylvania* (Cambridge, Mass., 1960), pp. 69–70; *Moreau de St. Méry's American Journey* (Garden City, N.J., 1947), pp. 286–87; *BFHA* 17 (1928): 61.

13 John Watson, *Annals of Philadelphia* (Philadelphia, 1830), pp. 489–90. See also Dillwyn Mss, 1: 104, 118; *PMHB* 18 (1894): 59; 14 (1890): 370. John Smith, "Diary," 6 (10/8/1748).

14 William Penn, *Works* (London, 1726), 1: 900–01; idem, *A Letter from William Penn to his Wife and Children,* (London, 1761) p. 4.

15 Phineas Pemberton to Alice Pemberton 9/8/1700, PP, 2: 170; *A Collection of Memorials Concerning Divers Deceased Ministers and Others* (Philadelphia, 1787), p. 82; Elizabeth Allinson to Samuel Allinson, 12 mo./1767, QC.

16 Richard Hill to Rachel Wells, 2/22/1759, Howland Mss. QC.

17 Penn, *Works,* 1: 900–01.

18 Chalkley, *Journal,* p. 195.

19 Fox, *Works,* 7: 89; 8: 113.

20 Thomas Gwin, *The Will and Testament of Thomas Gwin* (London, n.d.), pp. 50–51.

21 Jonathan Roberts, "Memoirs," 1: 21, HSP.

22 Frederick Smith, *On the Duty of a Wife* (London, 1810), pp. 5–8.

23 Fox, *Works,* 8: 113.

24 *Moreau de St. Méry's American Journey,* pp. 287, 290; Marquis de Chastellux, *Travels in North America* (Chapel Hill, N.C.), 1: 120.

25 Richard Smith to John Smith, 2/3/1746, Smith Mss, 2: 237; Catherine Payton to John Smith, 8/1/1761, Smith Mss, 5: 232; Ezekial Edwards to Phineas Pemberton, 9/16/1768, PP, 20: 86; Jacob Taylor, *An Almanack for 1738* (Philadelphia, 1737); Roberts, *Memoirs,* 1: 88.

26 Betty Tell Truth to Atticus, Smith Mss, 7: 132–33.

27 Jacob Taylor, *Almanack for 1707* (Philadelphia, 1706); idem, *Almanack for 1726* (Philadelphia, 1725); "Atticus" [John Smith], *Pennsylvania Chronicle and Universal Advertiser,* 1, no. 37 (October 5–12, 1767): 152.

28 Priscilla Wakefield, *Reflections on the Present Condition of the Female Sex* (London, 1798), pp. 2–14.

29 *Extracts from the Journal of Elizabeth Drinker,* 4/22/1796, p. 285.

30 *PMHB* 21 (1897): 12; *Letters of Doctor Richard Hill and His Children* (Philadelphia, 1854), p. 201.

31 William Duane, ed., *Extracts from the Diary of Christopher Marshall* (Albany, 1877), pp. 157–58, 202–03, 223, 233, 258–59, 279–80.

32 Mary Pemberton to Israel Pemberton, Jr., 8/29/1751, PP, 7: 123.

33 Min. Falls MM, 2/5/1699, p. 91: David Ferris to Dobson Wheeler, 11/12/1772, Ferris Mss, FHL.

34 William Mather, *The Young Man's Companion* (London, 1723), p. 25; Richard B. Morris, *Studies in the History of American Law, with Special Reference to the Seventeenth and Eighteenth Century,* Columbia University Studies in History, no. 316 (New York, 1930), pp. 166–74.

35 Morris, *Studies in the History of American Law,* pp. 155–58. A generalization about inheritance patterns based upon surviving wills would not be very reliable. An impression is that sons received more than daughters and that boys received equal amounts. Some Friends continued to use primogeniture and entail. Few wills of Friends are available, and these often did not evaluate farm lands or town lots so that one cannot be certain whether the child who received a smaller tract did not receive an equivalent inheritance. Wills also did not itemize previously given stock in trade or farms or dowries. In this as in many other areas, historians should rely on New England, where documentation is more readily available. See also John Demos, *A Little Commonwealth: Family Life in Plymouth Colony* (New York, 1970), pp. 85–90.

36 *Statutes at Large of Pennsylvania,* 3: 157–59.

37 Alice Clark, *Working Life of Women in the Seventeenth Century* (London, 1919); Elizabeth Anthony Dexter, *Colonial Women of Affairs* (New York, 1931), pp. 18–57; Benjamin Coole, *Miscellanies* (London, 1712), p. 6; Isabel Ross, *Margaret Fell: Mother of Quakerism* (Plymouth, England, 1947), pp. 268–71, 279, 350.

38 Clark, *Working Life of Women,* pp. 17, 44–45, 199; Phineas Pemberton to Alice Pemberton, 9/9/1700, PP, 2: 171; Mary Pemberton to Samuel Carpenter, 2/5/1702, PP, 2: 181; Elizabeth Drinker, *Diary,* June 19, 1760, HSP; Morris Papers, Coates-Reynell Mss, HSP; *JFHS* 33 (1930): 32–33: John Reynell to Jane Hoskins, 4/27/1754, Letter-Book, 1752–54.

39 Margaret Morris to William Morris, ca. 1760s, Howland Mss, QC.

40 Richard Hunter to Margaret Fell, Autumn 1656, Swarthmore Mss, 1: 357; Transcripts 2: 645, FH.

41 Joseph Nicholson to Margaret Fell, 2/3/1660, Swarthmore Mss, 4: 107; Transcripts 2: 922–23; 5/10/1660, 4: 108; Transcripts 2: 928–29.

42 Chalkley, *Works,* pp. 583–84.

43 Charles Read to James Pemberton, 2/28/1749, PP, 5: 71.

44 Myers, *Hannah Logan's Courtship,* pp. 145, 261; John Smith, "Diary," 6 (10/10/1748, 10/18/1748). Smith experienced a religious depression just after his marriage.

45 Charles Norris to Isaac Norris, 2: 9/24/1733, Norris of Fairhill, Family Letters, 1: 12, HSP; Samuel Coates to William Logan, 9/26/1770, Coates-Reynell Mss, LC; James Logan to William Penn, Jr., 6/12/1706, Logan Mss, HSP; Henry Drinker to Joseph Smith, 7/9/1775, Henry Drinker Mss, HSP. Whether or not the latter is sexual depends upon the interpretation one gives to the Spanish custom referred to.

46 Taylor, *Almanack for 1726;* idem, *Almanack for 1739.* Friends could have purchased books by non-Quakers or enjoyed the tales printed in American and English newspapers.

47 George Fox, John Stubbs, and Benjamin Furly, *A Battle-Door for Teachers and Professors to Learn Singular and Plural* (London, 1669), pp. 2–4, 6–11; George Fox at house of Thomas Rouse, ca. 1672, Ancient Epistles, Minutes, and Advices, or Discipline, New England YM; Min. London YM, 5 (4/16/1718): 306; Atticus, *Pennsylvania Chronicle and Universal Advertiser,* June 6–13, 1763, p. 153; *PMHB* 17 (1893): 232; James Jenkins, "Records and Recollections," 1: 100, FH.

48 *Moreau de St. Méry's American Journey,* pp. 287–88, 312–14; Cecil Drinker, *Not So Long Ago* (New York, 1937).

49 Jack Mariotta, "Ecclesiastical Discipline in the Society of Friends" (Ph.D. diss., Stanford University, 1968), pp. 53–56.

50 Peter Laslett, *The World We Have Lost* (London, 1965), pp. 139–41.

51 William Shippen in 1706 and Samuel Rhoads and Molly Drinker in 1796 were married in this manner.

52 Fox, *Works,* 7: 338–39; Sermon at the home of Thomas Rouse, ca. 1672, Antient Epistles, Minutes, and Advices or Discipline, New England YM.

53 *Charter to William Penn, and Laws of the Province of Pennsylvania,* p. 145; *Statutes at Large of Pennsylvania,* 2: 490; *Records of the Courts of Bucks County Pennsylvania, 1684–1700,* pp. 21, 289, 292; West New Jersey's law on fornication, not passed until 1694, fined married people £10 and unmarried people £5. If the parties could not pay and both were married, they received twenty lashes each and could be sold into service for a certain time to pay their fines. Aaron Leaming and Jacob Spicer, eds., *The Grants, Concessions, and Original Constitutions of the Province of New Jersey* (Somerville, N.J., 1881), pp. 527–28.

54 Min. Rhode Island MM, 10/5/1773, pp. 6, 8.

55 Samuel Ogden to Samuel Allinson, 2/27/1789, Allinson Mss; Thomas Clarkson, *Portraiture of Quakerism* (London, 1807) 2: 4. Clarkson believed that most Quaker marriages were happy.

56 Min. Falls MM, 5/2/1684, p. 14; 5/3/1685, pp. 67–68; Min. Rhode Island MM, 12/28/1715, p. 126; 11/26/1754, p. 131; Min. Philadelphia MM, 1/29/1695, 8/30/1696, 11/29/1698, 12/24/1698; Min. Perquimans MM, 2A (9/3/1755); Min. Core Sound MM, 9mo./1750, p. 22; John Reynell to Mary Groth, 6/13/1753, Letter Book, 1754–56; H. C. Reed and G. J. Millers, eds., *Burlington Court Book* (Washington, D.C., 1944), pp. 163–64, 169.

57 George E. Howard, *History of Matrimonial Institutions,* 2: 60–102; Chilton Powell, *English Domestic Relations 1485–1653* (New York, 1917), pp. 64–74.

58 Powell, *English Domestic Relations,* p. 80.

59 Edmund S. Morgan, *The Puritan Family* (New York, 1966), pp. 34–38; Howard, *History of Matrimonial Institutions,* pp. 140–226.

60 George *Charter to William Penn, and Laws of the Province of Pennsylvania,* pp. 109–10; Mitchell and Flanders *Statutes at Large of Pennsylvania,* 2: 5–7, 180, 490. In 1682 for sodomy and bestiality a person was subjected to six months hard labor, a whipping, and forfeiture of one-third of his estate. In the 1700 law a mar-

ried man could be castrated and his wife granted a divorce. A single man could be confined to prison for life and whipped every three months. The Crown vetoed this act since the divorce was undefined and castration was "unreasonable especially in the case of a married man." When repassed in 1705 the sodomy law still contained a provision for divorce from "board and bed."

In the 1682 law the penalties were twice as heavy if the adultery occurred between two married persons rather than one single and one married individual. For a first offense the culprit was publicly whipped and suffered one year's imprisonment at hard labor. A second offense brought imprisonment for life. In the general revision of laws in 1700, the first offense was punished as before; a second conviction brought seven years' imprisonment and twenty-one lashes; for a third offense seven more years, whippings, and a branding with the letter A on the forehead. The distinction between married and unmarried people was dropped. The 1705 law reenacted the same penalties except that a fine of £50 could be paid in lieu of other punishment.

61 Chalkley, *Works,* p. 438. Min. Philadelphia YM, 1 (7/7/1687): 16; John Smith, "Diary," vol. 6, 7/20/1748 and 8/27/1748.

10 The Quaker Style of Life

Our desire is, that you may always outstrip and exceed the world, in virtue, in purity, in chastity, in godliness, and in holiness; and in modesty, civility, and in righteousness, and in love.

George Fox

The attempt to write the social history of a religious denomination is fraught with difficulties stemming from the varying degrees of loyalty of the individual members to the ideals of the entire body. One can no more easily stereotype an average Quaker than he can a typical Puritan church member. Contemporaries distinguished between city and country or "wet" and "strict" Friends, and the minutes of the various monthly meetings show hundreds of examples of persons who departed from proper behavior as specified by the disciplines. Most American Quakers were farmers; yet Friends dominated the artisan and merchant classes in Newport and Philadelphia. The Society encompassed middle-class people such as Thomas Chalkley, who worked as a ship's captain in order to support his family; poor people, who might end their days in the alms house in Philadelphia, and wealthy merchants and land speculators such as Samuel Carpenter, William Shippen, and Isaac Norris. There were Quaker gentlemen like William Penn, Robert Barclay, and John Archdale; intellectuals like James Logan or John Smith; and politicians such as David Lloyd or Isaac Norris II. A saintly John Woolman was balanced against an Abraham Redwood, Newport merchant and philanthropist, whose fortune in 1766 was amassed with the help of 230 slaves who toiled on his Antigua sugar plantation. The Friend could be an Anthony Benezet, who gave away much of his income and devoted his later years to teaching Negroes, or John Kinsey, lawyer, clerk of the yearly meeting, expert politician, and thief whose embezzling of public funds was not discovered until after his death. Even in the ministry there were contrasts between the wealth of John Pemberton, the scholarship of Thomas Story, and the scant education of John Churchman. Neither English nor southern Quakers had a significant voice in their political affairs, and in Virginia and North Carolina Friends were not members of the wealthy planter class. In Pennsylvania Quakers set the tone of society, maintained a majority in the assembly until 1756, and played a significant role in the government until the Revolution. Rhode Island and New Jersey Friends dominated the government at certain periods and constituted a powerful interest group at all times. The location of a Friend's residence, his occupation, his station in life, and the degree of his piety helped determine what he thought a Quaker should be—and there was as much variety in styles of living among

Quakers in 1690 as in 1780. When one writes about the plain style of life, he is describing only tendencies within a broad spectrum of behavior.

The diversities among the members do not mean that there were not also similarities. A Quaker merchant in Philadelphia did not live like his Anglican competitor, and a Quaker farmer in Rhode Island differed from his Baptist neighbor. The ways in which these Quakers diverged from their peers were similar and can be explained by the style of behavior demanded by the meeting. This is not to assert that all Friends thought or acted alike, however. But the sons of Quaker farmers in Rhode Island, Pennsylvania, and North Carolina read the same school books, catechisms, and theological tracts, heard local and traveling ministers inculcate the same virtues, worshiped in the same manner, watched the business of the meeting being transacted in the same way, and the conclusion that there was a distinctive Quaker culture seems inescapable. A Friend was expected to live balanced between moderation and asceticism. His use of food and clothing as well as his habits of speech, work, leisure and politics were influenced by his identification with Friends. The purpose of this chapter is to portray the various life patterns that could exist within the limits of Quaker beliefs.

Just as the theology of the Society of Friends was often similar to that of the Presbyterians or Puritans, so also were their ideals of social behavior.[1] Although recent scholarship has tended to play down direct Anabaptist influence, a few Quaker ethical attitudes (such as pacifism and refusing to swear) resembled the demands of Mennonites, Hutterites, and Amish for withdrawal from the world in order to preserve the purity of the sect. Eighteenth-century Quakerism was caught between the ideal of reforming the world and the desire to escape from the world to build a holy community. Generally, Quakers decided to work to reform the world at the risk of some degree of contamination. In Pennsylvania a few Friends debated from the very beginning whether they were equipped to govern the chosen few or the whole society, a conflict made particularly clear in time of war. Not until after the Revolution did all American Quakers adopt a sectarian policy of withdrawal from government.

Like the Puritans, Quakers believed in the beneficence of creation. George Fox preached that the Lord "hath created all things to his glory, and so to be used and spent." The fruits of the earth were given to man for "*Necessity, Convenience,* and lawful Delight, with this *Proviso* too, that the *Almighty was to be seen, and sensibly enjoy'd and reverenced, in every one of them.*" Robert Barclay thought that it was "beyond question, that whatever thing the creation affords is for the use of man, and the moderate use of them is lawful."[2] Like the deists, rational Christians, and Puritans, the Quakers believed that a correct study of the world pointed the way to its maker and they demanded a rational use of creation. "All Excess is ill." "If thou art clean and warm; it is sufficient; for more doth but rob the Poor, and please the Wanton." "In all things *Reason* should prevail."[3] John Woolman believed that God intended men to work for exercise and to provide for other physical needs, eat the produce of the earth for sustenance, and build homes to dwell in. "To provide things relative to our outward living in the Way of True Wisdom, is good, and the gift of Improving in things useful, is a good Gift."[4]

Friends condemned a monastic life because "that is a *lazy, rusty, unprofita-*

ble Self-Denial, burdensome to others to feed their Idleness." The true Christian was to be in the world and the only valid self-denial was in facing the world and then giving it up. "Christians should keep the Helm, and guide the Vessel to its Port; not meanly steal out at the Stern of the World, and leave those that are in it without a Pilot."[5] Imposing spiritual and inward discipline upon himself, a Friend existed in a sort of monastery all his life, but turtle-like he carried his true home with him into the world. Following Christ produced

> that mortification and abstraction from the love and cares of this world, who daily are conversing in the world (but inwardly redeemed out of it) both in wedlock, and in their lawful employments, which was judged could only be obtained by such as were shut up in cloisters and monastaries.[6]

While he believed that God made the world and "it was good," the Friend also knew that Adam fell because of an enticement that had resulted from the creation—an apple. His theology, which separated God and man, creator and creation, physical and spiritual, led the Friend to a distrust of the natural order. George Fox advised Quakers to be "as strangers to all things visible and created." Like Bunyan's famous Christian, the Quaker engaged upon a pilgrimage using physical entities "as though you did not possess them, and what you enjoy as though you did not."[7] Moderation in all lawful matters was qualified by the fear of being trapped or separated from God by physical creation. Christ said, "he that loveth Father or Mother, Son or Daughter, more than me, is not worthy of me," and "whosoever . . . forsaketh not all that he hath cannot be my disciple." One could interpret these verses to mean that pleasures should not be allowed to overshadow God; or they could mean that anything a person enjoyed was evil. "This Doctrine of *Self-Denial* is the Condition of Eternal Happiness."[8] George Fox rebuked a captain because he was too happy. Ann Whitall recorded in her journal, "O our dear Savior was never Seen to laugh but often Seen to weep." Samuel Allinson told his wife that whenever she was undecided between two courses of action, she should "*pursue that which is most in the Cross*—thus I believe duty and Mortification will go together." Anthony Benezet wrote to a Friend that everything of the flesh had a "tendency to hinder the work, by raising a dependence foreign to the matter," and in order to follow Christ he must avoid "everything which has a tendency to attach us to the world."[9] William Penn in his *Reflections and Maxims* represented the moderate Quaker's disciplined participation in the world; in his *No Cross, No Crown* he saw that even a golden mean could keep one from God. A good Friend's life was governed by a temperance that could easily become a desire for asceticism.

The Quaker's condition or need determined what part of the doctrine of creation he emphasized. If he were relaxing over a cup of tea, socializing at yearly meeting, eating a piece of roast beef, or exalting in the orderliness of nature, he could stress the need to use creation and praise God for his bounty. If he lost money in business, had a ship sink, experienced a bad harvest, or endured the death of a child or relative, he could reflect upon the vanity of all earthly delights and be thankful he had not prospered, for too much wealth cumbered the mind with trivia and a loss would make a person remember everlasting values.[10]

II

Friends experienced difficulties in defining and then staying within the limits of moderation in food, drink, housing, and furniture. Frederick B. Tolles' *Meeting House and Counting House* describes the conflicts in the merchant community in Philadelphia between the ideal of simplicity and the luxuries permitted by prosperity. Thomas J. Wertenbaker found a "Quaker Spirit in Brick and Stone," but more recent historians have discovered little, either in architecture or in furniture, to distinguish the homes of wealthy Quakers from those of Anglicans or Presbyterians.[11] Peter Kalm, a traveler from Finland, described the Quakers as "semi-Epicures," who enjoyed the best food in Philadelphia yet practiced restraint in drinking. A disapproving John Adams enumerated the formidable array of dishes served at a banquet held at the home of Miers Fisher, a plainly dressed Quaker lawyer, during the Continental Congress; such feasts were quite common among genteel Philadelphia Quakers.[12] In 1763 Elizabeth Wilkinson, an English Quaker minister, warned Anthony Morris and his children

> against pride. . . . My mind is grieved with Friends in this City in their endeavouring to outdo each other in the Grandeur of their Houses, Tables, Entertainments.

After attending a meeting in Newport, James Birkett was amazed to discover that Friends could not be distinguished "by their Language, dress, or behaviour."[13]

Some observers were less critical. Jacques Brissot de Warville enjoyed what he termed a "modest dinner" at the time of the yearly meeting. Crèvecoeur had an adequate repast at the home of the botanist and former Quaker John Bartram. The fare at Anthony Benezet's home was also simple. Rhoda Barber reminisced that in her father's home in rural Pennsylvania the first day's meal consisted of bread and butter, smoked beef, apples, and cider, and the women drank tea, which the men scorned as effeminate. While French observers tended to idealize Friends, one cannot discount Crèvecoeur's description of the Quaker settlers of Pennsylvania and Nantucket as people who engaged in hard work while keeping to modesty in dress and restraint in behavior.[14]

Although luxury may have been difficult for them to guard against, Friends refused to compromise their regulations forbidding what they termed "sinful customs." The Sermon on the Mount required Christians not to swear and to love their enemies. The prohibition of oaths was also defended on rational grounds: invoking the name of the Lord never forced anyone to tell the truth. No mouthing of formulas could make a lie into the truth or make a liar honest. If a person lived a sober life and was God-fearing, his declaration should be accepted as the truth.[15] For their refusal to take oaths to the king and the Church of England, Friends were severely persecuted in Restoration England. But suffering for this principle only burned the belief deeper into the consciousness of Friends. After the Glorious Revolution, Parliament in 1696 granted partial relief by allowing Friends to give an affirmation. Since the wording required the person to declare "before God and the world," the meetings, though officially accepting the form, did not approve of its contents, and some Quakers refused to use it. English Friends remained divided over the issue until a more tolerant code was enacted in 1722; this required the person to say, "I *A. B.* do sincerely declare and affirm."[16] In Pennsylvania, Quakers enacted in the first code of laws a proviso for an affirmation not mentioning the Lord's name, and, in spite of repeated vetoes by the Crown and several clashes with non-Quakers in the colony, they continued to reenact their statutes allowing for an affirmation until 1724. In that year the assembly passed a law bringing its requirements into line with those in England. Since Quaker judges generally were not allowed by the meeting to administer oaths, it became customary to have at least one justice per court who was not a Friend.[17] While literally complying with the biblical command, the Quakers' protest against the usefulness of swearing became *pro forma,* since a solemn affirmation was in fact an oath in everything except the naming of God.

Friends' testimony in favor of religious toleration and against a hireling priesthood and a state church led them to oppose tithes or parish rates. Friends' system of relief, which duplicated in most respects the methods of the English poor law, sought to aid poor members and to justify Quakers' refusal to pay parish rates. Throughout the colonial period, however, in England, New England, and the South, Quaker families suffered periodic requisitions by the authorities for money, livestock, or household goods as tithes. In Rhode Island, Pennsylvania, and New Jersey, Quakers were exempted from this form of taxation.

The "peace testimony" was not firmly established until the Restoration period,[18] but from 1660 until the present Quakers have refused to kill, fight, or serve in the military and have attempted to influence goverments by passive resistance. (Although the criminal code of Pennsylvania had far fewer capital crimes than were specified in English law, Friends always gave the civil magistrate the power to take life. The revisions of criminal law in 1700 and 1719 increased the severity of penalties and the number of capital offenses.[19]) Friends objected to war because they did not see how one could "love your enemy" and still try to kill him. Legislation in Pennsylvania, Rhode Island, and New Jersey provided that no conscientious objector need serve in the militia. Non-Quaker political opponents in Pennsylvania used pacifism as an argument against the Friends' control of the assembly, but legislators did vote funds to be used by the English government for war. Under William Penn, the appointed governors had always been non-Friends, and a militia was formed shortly after 1702.[20] In Rhode Island Quakers served as governors during King Philip's War and the Seven Years War. English Quakers had consistently maintained the duty of paying taxes even in wartime; but during the French and Indian War, Friends in New Jersey, Pennsylvania, and New England could not agree on a set policy. Some paid the war levies and others did not, and the issue continued to divide Quakers until after the Revolution. Before Pennsylvania Friends finally surrendered control of their assembly in 1756, English Quakers had worked out a compromise with the Crown specifying that some Friends would withdraw so that the sect would not hold a majority in the assembly during wartime. In return the ministry agreed to ignore the demands of Anglicans and Presbyterians in Pennsylvania to bar Friends from all governmental positions by requiring officeholders to take an oath.[21] The withdrawal salved the consciences of those Friends who were distressed by the vigor with which some Quakers in the assembly supported the war. A few

Friends who thought defense permissible remained in the assembly throughout the war. But in spite of compromises made by Friends in the legislature, no Quaker was forced to enter the militia, and meetings expelled anyone who fought. In the southern colonies Friends often suffered for refusing to join in military training.

The religious testimonies on oaths, tithes, and peace did not normally affect daily life, but the peculiar customs of social honor, speech, and dress reminded the member every day of his religious principles. Quakers refused to doff their hats or bow to any man either as a mark of respect or for any other reason, and Friends wore their hats and stood straight even in the presence of the king. Bowing and removing of hats were formalities; correct social behavior was not a matter of outward proprieties or conduct that could be taught by a dancing master. Friends carried their protest against vain customs into the ale houses and refused to offer toasts, because drinking to someone's health was a false form of honor and frequently led to overindulgence in alcohol. By refusing to bow, remove their hats, use fancy titles, or drink toasts, Quakers protested against the pride of men in their own persons. "All these titles and styles of honour are to be rejected by Christians because they are to seek the honour that comes from above, and not that honour that is from below."[22]

Friends never addressed a single person as "you," never signed a letter "your humble servant" or "yours truly," never addressed a man as "mister," "sir," "your excellency," "your highness," "your Grace," or "your holiness." They kept the plain style of speech because it was scripturally based, grammatically correct, honest, and a rebuke to false pride. In the Bible the Lord God was addressed as "thou," and "thee" and "thou" were consistently used to refer to single individuals. Although in the north of England, where the Quaker movement began, the "thou" and "thee" forms of speech may have been the normal practice, most English Quakers adopted the archaic form as a religious testimony.[23] At first, addressing a superior as "thou" had a touch of the leveler spirit.

> For amongst the Great and Rich ones of the earth, they will *Thou* or *You* one another, if they be equal in Degree . . . but if a man of low Degree . . . come to speak to any of them, he must *You,* the Rich Man, but the Rich man will *Thou* him.[24]

Any social radicalism was soon dropped, and the custom became a purely religious testimony against pride, a "sore cut to proud flesh, and them that sought self-honour, who, though they would say it to God and Christ, could not endure to have it said to themselves."[25] Quaker writers maintained that the separation of singular and plural in the second person was found in all other languages and that consistent grammar demanded their usage. The plain style of speech stood as a shibboleth and defined the limits of membership. Anyone who became a Quaker or wished to remain one used the "thee" and "thou."

The demand for consistency, truth, and spiritual equality appeared in other customs of speech. A man might sign a letter "your humble servant" when he was neither humble nor in the service of the receiver. Such an address was dishonest. Since men were created alike, the only true worth was spiritual and only spiritual qualities should be honored.[26] Those to whom such flattering appellations were attached often inherited their positions and made no pretense to the qualities described. All persons should be called simply "Friend" or addressed by the complete name with no adjectives attached. True respect came from service through actions, not from meaningless titles.

Any protest against social formality risks the danger of becoming pretentious. The Swarthmore manuscripts show that the salutations of the early Quakers could be very ornate. An example that raises intriguing questions as to why Friends employed such vivid language only in religious metaphors is the greeting to Margaret Fell by Walter Somers in 1658:

> Dear dear dearly beloved who hath been and is unto me more than a sister in the travail of thy soul, for the deliverance of thine own in me, which is now through the truth which is pure and precious . . . whosoever lift their hand against thee shall not prosper. Dear one, let me speak for my life is open unto thee having been refreshed in thy bowels and with thy travail I have found deliverance and have as it were sat on thy knee and been suckled at thy Breast and nourished by thy side.[27]

An adulation written to George Fox by John Audland began, "Dear and precious one in whom my life is bound up and my strength in thee stands, by thy breathings I am nourished and refreshed: and by thee my strength is renewed; blessed art thou for Ever more."[28] Though the sender might claim that such effusions were the truth, Fox crossed out certain hyperbolic salutations. Eighteenth-century Friends were more subdued, but the simple "Dear Friend" was often replaced by "Esteemed," or "Loving," or "Respected." The need to publish tracts explaining to outsiders the reasons for the Quaker customs served to keep Friends aware of the dangers of flattering address.

The desire for complete honesty and abstention from excess in speech led to a certain slowness and carefulness in Friends' discourse. "In Conversation, mark well what others say or do, and hide your own Mind, at least till last; and then open it sparingly as the Matter will let you." "It is safer to Learn, than teach; and who conceals his Opinion, has nothing to answer for." Meetings told Friends to keep their words "few and savoury." Quakers were to avoid disputes if possible but to strive for truth rather than victory in a debate. Opponents ascribed their habits of speech to evasiveness; Friends maintained that their caution came from a desire for complete truthfulness.[29]

Friends also opposed pagan elements in the culture. Like the Puritans, they refused to celebrate Christmas or other holy days as popish or pagan relics. While Pennsylvania and New Jersey laws required rest upon the Sabbath, Friends justified these statutes because some day of rest was needed—not because Sunday was a more hallowed day than any other.[30] The Quaker bore his testimony against the pagan origins of the names of the days of the week and of the months. Sunday derived its name from the worship of the sun, Monday from the god of the moon. The Lord designated days in Genesis according to number and so Friends called Sunday "First day," Monday was "Second day," and so on. The names of the months were also of heathen origin: March honored Mars; April, Venus; May, Maia; June, Juno. Friends used the common names for September through December since they were of numerical origin. After the calendar reform in 1752 these names were no longer accurate, and so September became "Nineth Month," etc.[31] The letter books of Quaker merchants show that eighteenth-century Friends often deviated from the practice of numerical listing.

III

The history of Quaker attitudes toward clothing illustrates the conflict between moderation and asceticism. During the Civil War and Interregnum, Puritans and Friends—with ample biblical precedent—opposed indulgence in finery. Penn argued that men's clothes had been used originally "to cover their Shame [after the fall], therefore *Plain and Modest;* Next, *To fence out Cold,* therefore Substantial; Lastly, To declare Sexes; therefore Distinguishing." While dress had once been functional, it had become—due to men's pride—something to be seen.[32]

The early Friends adopted as correct dress a simplified form of whatever was customary at the time. Their protest was against luxuries and superfluities such as ribbons, gold ornaments, and fancy silver shoe buckles. George Fox defended William Penn's wearing a wig, because Penn was bald and a plain modest wig kept his head warm. But Friends opposed large and ornamental wigs and the cutting of hair so that one could wear a wig.[33] Like rationalists of all ages, Friends objected to the tyranny of changing fashions. In 1667 George Fox preached:

> Keep out of the vain fashions of the world; let not your eyes, and minds, and spirits run after every fashion [in apparel]. . . . And Friends that see the world so often alter their fashions, if you follow them, and run into them, in that ye cannot judge the world, but the world will rather judge you. Therefore, keep all in modesty and plainness.[34]

The testimony against changing fashions became more important when styles of dress altered. After young Quakers adopted a new style of hat or bonnet, the meetings deduced they were guilty of pride in appearance and were trying to look attractive by conforming to the standards of the rest of the world. To guard against such practices Friends regularly, from 1680 until after the American Revolution, opposed any change of costume. It was not so much that one type of dress was holy as that any change was unholy, though in practice this distinction proved difficult to maintain, and ancient Friends tended to sanctify the garb they were wearing. The regulations contained in the Philadelphia discipline of 1704 were duplicated in minutes throughout America, England, and Ireland.

> If any men wear longlapp'd sleeves, or Coats folded at the sides, Superfluous buttons, Broad ribbons about the hat, or gaudy, flower'd or strip'd Stuffs, or any sort of perriwigs unless necessitated, and if any are necessitated, that then it be as near in Colour as may be to their own and in other respects resembling as much as may be, a sufficient natural head of hair without the vain customs being long behind or mounting on the forehead. Also, if any women that profess the Truth wear or suffer their children to wear their Gowns not plain or open at the breast with gaudy Stomachers, needless rolls at the Sleeves or with their Mantuas or Bonnets with gaudy colours, or cut their hair and leave it out on the brow, or dress their heads high, or to wear hoods with long lapps, or long Scarfs open before, or their Capps or pinners plaited or gathered on the brow or double hemm'd or pinch'd. . . . It being not agreeable to that Shamefac'dness, plainness and modesty which people professing Godliness with good works ought to be found in.[35]

The extent and limits of the meetings' power over individuals show in the result of these cautions. From 1660 until 1800 there was no established Quaker costume. In a study of the evolution of Quaker dress, Amelia Gummere concluded:

> It may be set down as a safe rule, in seeking for a Quaker style or custom at any given time, to take the worldly fashion or habit of the period preceding. When the mode changes, and a style is dropped, the Quaker will be found just ready to adopt it, having by that time become habituated to its use.[36]

Members accepted the right of meetings to legislate on fashions, and while the desire for normal attire was too strong to be blotted out, a Quaker gentleman's or lady's clothing always remained distinctive.

As in other of the peculiar testimonies, one could keep the letter of the law and ignore the spirit. The diary that Sally Wister kept during the Revolutionary War reveals that one could take considerable interest in fashion and pride in dress and still remain a plain Friend. "I was dressed in my chintz, and look'd smarter than the night before." "I left my chamber between eight and nine, breakfasted, went up to dress, put on a new purple and white striped Persian, white petticoat, muslin apron, gauze cap, and handkerchief. Thus array'd, Miss Norris, I ask your opinion."[37] At times a legality of regulations overwhelmed the testimony, as when Deborah Hill told her son that he could "wear plain gold or silver buckles or buttons but not wrought." Peter Kalm noticed that, although Quaker women censured all adornment, "I have seen them wear just as gaudy shoes as other English women." Some Friends undoubtedly kept the letter and spirit of the testimony. Jacques Brissot de Warville noted that at the Philadelphia Yearly Meeting in 1788, 90 percent of the 1,500 people present wore homespun.[38]

The Friends defended their singularities with many arguments. They found scriptural precedents to justify the forbidding of luxuries, the granting of false honors, the making of war, and the swearing of oaths. These practices were not trivial matters to be engaged in as one saw fit. The Holy Spirit led the first professors into the truth, and Friends ever since had concurred in their testimony. Even those who felt that the practices were indifferent matters had to realize the effect of not bearing a testimony.[39] If a person believed that he could keep to moderation, he should set an example to those who were weaker than himself. The Christian should not weigh his actions according to "private Satisfaction" but "Publick Good." If all the money spent on ornaments and needless luxuries such as jewels, feasts, gambling, fine houses, and laces could be collected for a public fund, "there might be *Reparation* to the broken Tenants, Work-Houses for the Able, and *Alms-Houses* for the Aged and Impotent."[40]

Friends denied that they made an idolatry of clothes or speech. True holiness did not consist in dress, speech, or social customs. But because there was an appearance of evil in these practices, Quakers abstained from them.

> But upon Supposition they were of that indifferent Nature, as some imagine they are, is it not Better to cross our Wills in such Things, because we see they have a tendency to Unlawful, than by giving them the Reins, to suffer them to run beyond

> the just Bounds? Is it not a Point of Wisdom to restrain our selves in some lawful Things, and teach our Appetites to submit to Reason.[41]

The testimonies served as a barrier between a Friend and evil. They reminded the Quaker of the principles for which he stood: complete honesty, plain speech, spiritual equality, moderation, and peace. Outsiders could identify Friends and easily detect both their rightful acts and their wrongdoings. Just as a clerical collar helps remind a clergyman of his ministry, so did the plain style of dress remind the Friend to act as a Christian. The Quaker customs tended to cut Friends off from outsiders and to foster a sectarian consciousness. By so doing they probably were important in keeping the church alive, but at the same time they hindered the growth of the Society. The desire for seclusion in upbringing was strengthened by the need to convince children of the necessity of keeping the testimonies. Youth exposed to non-Quakers would probably drop the "thou" and want to know why Friends dressed so strangely. The climate of eighteenth-century America and England was not conducive to unusual religious behavior, and the peculiar customs struck many people as an odd form of piety. The religious danger in such customs was that form replaced thought. By keeping to the letter of the regulations one could ignore the spirit of the protest.

IV

The peculiar customs of dress and speech emphasized the sectarian nature of Quakerism, but of equal significance in the lives of the members were the difficulties in applying ethical standards to wealth, work, politics, and leisure. Quakers denied that their principles of conduct had any connection with social leveling and insisted that addressing a person according to his name rather than flattering him with fanciful and often untrue appellations did not result in any radicalism. Like most English dissenters after 1660, Quakers did not question the rights of private property or the prerogatives of high social status. The rank of a Friend influenced the requirements of the plain style of life. A gentleman with an income of £1,000 was not expected to live the same as an artisan or a yeoman farmer. "We say not . . . that no man may use the creation more or less than another: for we know, that as it hath pleased God to dispense it diversely, giving to some more, and some less, so they may use it accordingly." A man whose estate was ample and who was accustomed to eating beef, drinking good wine, and dressing in the finest wool could continue to do so after becoming a Friend. His constitution was adjusted to the amenities of life; to subject him to frugal fare would be unreasonable, perhaps even detrimental to his health.

> And if a man be clothed soberly and without superfluity, though finer than that which his servant is clothed with, we shall not blame him for it: the abstaining from superfluities, which his condition and education have accustomed him to, may be in him a greater act of mortification than the abstaining from finer clothes in the servant, who never was accustomed to them.

If a man lived moderately according to his station and could afford silk stockings or velvet breeches, he should have them. As long as he picked merchandise not for luxury but for "need and conveniency," he was not violating the plain style of living.[42]

English and American Friends continued to justify and practice differences in styles of life for the rich and poor throughout the eighteenth century.[43] Some historians have used the increasing wealth of Philadelphia Quakers, reflected in dwellings, furniture, and dress, as a sign of decline. This is an oversimplification. The meetings demanded that men live within their incomes and plainly, not abstemiously. Even when he was nearly bankrupt, Penn lived according to the standards of a gentleman. Why could not prospering Isaac Norris, John Smith, or Israel Pemberton, Jr., do the same? Quaker laments about increasing worldliness should be approached with the same caution as Puritan jeremiads. Such dirges tell more about Quaker ancestor veneration than about the ancestors.[44]

If some found in the heritage a justification for genteel plainness, others discovered a prophetic voice that condemned such easy living. A few Friends in both England and America condemned any unnecessary wealth and adopted very austere habits of life as a reaction to the love of comforts that they saw all around them. John Woolman refused to drink from a silver goblet and made clear his opposition to the use of silver dishes. Like George Fox, Woolman was disturbed by the luxury of the few and the poverty of the many. (Woolman was also influenced by his belief that the Indians and slaves working the silver mines in Mexico were subjected to intolerable hardships.) Anthony Benezet contrasted the fortune of £60,000 that Israel Pemberton, Jr., reportedly left "for the corruption of his offspring" with the dire conditions of the poor in Philadelphia.

The attitude of Friends toward social rank was always ambivalent. Like the Puritans, they saw God's hand in most events and accepted the divine origin of gradations in society. God placed the poor and the rich, and each person should seek to serve in his position. About the only consolation given to the destitute was that Jesus associated with the very poor and promised them rewards in heaven. Quakers were aware that society was not static and that men ascended and descended the social scale. William Penn condemned pride in ancestry since it was based upon the length of the family tree rather than the virtue of the forebears. A noble family that did not improve itself by education and discipline would soon be replaced in the social hierarchy. While making no plea for social equality, Penn insisted that virtue was no respecter of persons.[46]

Quakers did not assign just one cause to poverty. People became poor from indolence, because the wealthy suppressed them, and from being placed in a lower rank by God. Charity was not a dole but the provision of a means of support so that the poor could raise themselves. Fox made clear that beggars were to be set to work and taught "how to labour in the creation" so that there would be "no beggars in Israel." The poverty-stricken, through hard work, honesty, virtue, and the blessings of God, could rise. When a Quaker merchant gained wealth, the meeting approved. Fox noted with pleasure the increase in prosperity of many early Friends. Advices given to young people and apprentices commended hard work and honesty as a means of improving social station.[47] While accepting with the Puritans the belief that the blessing of God came to the virtuous, Friends did not confuse saintliness with wealth. The providences of the Lord were too inscrutable to be simplified into a virtue-plus-diligence-equals-riches belief. The Old Testament bore witness to the prosperity of the righteous, but the Book of Ecclesiastes prophesied, "One Event cometh to the righteous, and to the Wicked."[48] A prudent businessman's ship could sink just as easily in a storm as that of a dishonest prodigal.

The Quaker's attitude toward money varied between the ideal of moderate use and the fear of being corrupted by filthy lucre. William Penn reflected the moderate attitude.

> Let your industry and parsimony go no farther than for a sufficiency for life, and to make a provision for your children. . . . I charge you help the poor and needy; let the Lord have a voluntary share of your income, for the good of the poor, both in our society and others.[49]

Money was a blessing, but the end to which it was put determined whether or not its effect was good. Like other Protestants, Friends believed in stewardship. God had given money on trust and would demand an accounting of how it was used. London Yearly Meeting advised in 1741 that "the principal, if not only satisfaction a man of truly Christian disposition can have, in the affluence and increase of things of this world, must arise from the greater advantages and opportunities put into his hands of doing good therewith." The main advantage in being a rich man was the increased opportunity for doing charitable works.[50]

Some of the strongest sections in *No Cross, No Crown* were directed against covetousness.

> Tis plain that most People strive not for *Substance,* but *Wealth.* Some there be that love it strongly, and spend it liberally, when they have got it. Though this be sinful, yet more commendable, than *to love Money for Money's Sake,* That is one of the basest Passions the Mind of Man can be captivated with: A Perfect Lust: and a greater, and more Soul-defiling one there is not in the whole Catalogue of *Concupiscence.*[51]

Friends attempted to guard against the enticements of wealth in many ways. When Robert Barrow feared worldly concern, he turned his business over to his son with the proviso that he be given an annual stipend. Upon his conversion to Quakerism in 1773, Moses Brown announced his retirement from business. John Woolman, who several times thought himself in danger of being corrupted by money, changed his occupation. Christopher Wilson, a minister who went bankrupt in trade, recommended that "a low station best suits a minister of Christ, to eat sparingly clothed just decently and have the mind free from cumber."[52] Ministering Friends could curtail their money-earning power by going on religious journeys. Howard Brinton has discovered that one stage in the spiritual development of many Quaker journalists was to take steps to curtail their involvement in business.[53]

In the eighteenth century some Friends and many outsiders thought that too many Quakers pursued money without due moderation. William Edmundson noted the mercenary spirit in Irish Friends in 1699, and before 1710 anti-Quaker polemics in England and America condemned a money-seeking spirit in Friends. The epistles of London and Philadelphia Yearly meetings regularly opposed "Hastening to be Rich" as a "Pernicious and Growing

Evil." At the beginning of the nineteenth century, Thomas Clarkson found the "money-getting spirit" to be a weakness in the Society.[54]

The frequent admonitions against money-grubbing remind one of the similar complaints issued by the clergy in New England. Friends were caught in the same dilemma as the Puritans and for many of the same reasons. Both religious groups detested idleness and thought a man should spend most of his time in work or in religious service. (Quakerism probably took much more time from business life than did Puritanism since Quakers had no paid clergy.) The virtues of the Puritan and the Quaker were identical: self-control, moderation in desire, frugality, hard work. Both groups applied the Reformation doctrine of a "calling" not only to religious life but also to a secular vocation, and they criticized the Roman Catholics for regarding a secluded life as more virtuous than active participation in any occupation. The essential similarity in their attitudes toward work and wealth is shown by the debate over whether Benjamin Franklin's advices on business were those of a secularized Quaker or of a Puritan. New England Puritans strove for economic success as evidence of virtue, and they tended to have a static view of the social hierarchy. Some, but by no means all, Quakers had the same beliefs.[55] Neither religious organization was able to solve the contradiction in prescribing hard work but proscribing the results of prosperity.

A man had three duties: to take care of his family, to be diligent in his calling, and to improve the opportunities that God was pleased to grant him. The danger was that the care sometimes became immoderate, the diligence often turned into slavery, and the opportunities were apt to be used to the detriment of the neighbors.[56] Perhaps the clearest exposition of the Quaker doctrine of work was provided by Thomas Chalkley.

> We have liberty from God . . . lawfully, and for accomodation's sake, to work or seek for food or raiment; though that ought to be a work of indifference, compared to the great work of salvation. Our Saviour saith, "Labour not for the meat which perisheth, but for that which endureth for ever, or to eternal life"; by which we do not undersand, that Christians must neglect their necessary occasions, and their outward trades and callings; but that their chief labour, and greatest concern ought to be for their future well-being in his glorious kingdom. . . . It is also written, "That he that will not work shall not eat." By this . . . it appears that we are to understand, that it is our duty so to do. The farmer, the tradesman, and the merchant, do not understand by our Lord's doctrine, that they must neglect their calling, or grow idle in their business.[57]

George Fox's *Journal* and his *Epistles* were filled with fiery denunciations of contemporary business practices. "In fairs, also, and in markets, I was made to declare against their deceitful merchandise, cheating, and cozening." His most famous epistle on commerce was entitled, "The line of righteousness and justice stretched forth over all merchants, & c," and his most characteristic expression—directed to merchants, housewives, and husbandmen—was, "Do rightly; that is the word of the Lord God to you all."[58] Neither Fox nor later Friends ever laid down precise formulations on how much profit was allowable; nor did they define what constituted correct trading practices. Friends were concerned with the attitude of the shop-keeper, and what they wanted was very close to the medieval "just price." The merchant was to deal fairly with the consumer; he was to be scrupulously honest neither under- nor over-valuating his produce.

To end oppression by the rich and dishonesty in selling, early Friends began a policy of setting a fair price and refusing to bargain. Haggling was time-consuming, noisy, created passions, and took place in an atmosphere of "deceit and guile."[59] Friends charged what they regarded as a just amount, a practice that put the full responsibility upon the merchant's integrity. At first people refused to accept this new way of doing business, and Friends lost money, but later the just price became a way of attracting customers. Quakers sometimes violated their testimony, but observers in England and Pennsylvania commented upon the new custom.[60] Account books of eighteenth-century merchants in Newport and Philadelphia show that supply and demand determined the importers' charges. The level of profit is impossible to establish since a merchant's estimate might omit freight, insurance, and duties and list only the difference between buying and selling prices.[61] Trading was a difficult profession since the importer was dependent upon the financial acumen of distant correspondents who sent goods of uneven quality to unpredictable markets. In America the goods might be sold on credit to farmers whose ability to pay depended upon an export trade. James Logan advised a prospective immigrant that he could make a living by working hard upon a farm, but that real prosperity could come only by living in a town and trading.[62] Being a merchant was the most rapid path to financial security, particularly if trading was combined with shrewd land speculation.

The Pennsylvania assembly set the maximum interest rate there at 8 percent in 1700 and lowered it to 6 percent in 1723. Bucks Quarterly Meeting decreed that any rate of interest above the legal rate was usury, but meetings never disciplined anyone for charging too much interest. Thomas Richardson, clerk of New England Yearly Meeting, complained in 1718 when receiving 6 percent that he was accustomed to obtaining 10 percent.[63] By the 1760s Philadelphia merchants were paying 6 percent on outstanding debts. The rate could be reduced to 5 percent as a special favor. The Pennsylvania assembly did regulate the price of beer, bread, and a meal or a night's lodging, but most of these regulations were designed to control quality, not profit rates. William Penn sent to the assembly a bill proposing to fix the wages of laborers, but after a long discussion the matter was suspended over the practical problem of deciding who should receive how much.[64] Quaker beliefs were not the basis for this sort of legal interference, since justices in England and New England had long been accustomed to setting the price of labor, beer, and bread.

The monthly meetings generally restricted their intervention in economic matters to the issuance of cautions and the arbitration of disputes. Since Friends were forbidden legal disputes with each other, any intrasect argument was settled by a group of arbitrators appointed by the meeting and the parties involved. These Friends heard both sides and came to a decision. Usually the disputants would accept the verdict; should someone refuse, the other person was given permission to take the case to court. But refusing to accept a decision by mediators was a disownable offense, and the meetings did not hesitate to tell the courts of the decision they had reached. In a rural meeting, such as Perquimans in North Carolina, most of the arbitrations were over land disputes, but in Philadelphia and Newport there was much greater variety, and arbitrations could involve wills, wages, or business contracts. If one were a successful merchant such as Henry Drinker or John Reynell of Philadelphia, he might spend a considerable amount of time as a mediator. The success of the Quakers in settling differences was shown by the Burlington Court records from 1680 to 1709. There were almost no instances of Quaker opposing Quaker. But, since Friends were not forbidden to engage in lawsuits against outsiders, Quakers appeared in many cases involving nonmembers.[65] The early courts in West New Jersey and Pennsylvania often appointed arbitrators, but the custom disappeared after New Jersey became a royal colony; and the Pennsylvania law permitting court-appointed referees was not renewed after 1693.

In 1720 Rhode Island Monthly Meeting entered a dispute, charging that W. C. had begun a court case intending to defraud a non-Friend. W. C. was ordered to drop the proceedings immediately or be disowned and have Friends' decision presented as evidence. He submitted. A Newport elder was disciplined for selling a bushel of apples that did not contain a full measure; a North Carolina Quaker was told not to build a pond that would draw off the water from another Friend's millpond.[66] Normal trading procedures, however, did not come under the meeting's scrutiny. There was no Quaker case similar to the disciplining of Robert Keayne in Massachusetts for charging what the Puritans thought was too high a price for an item.

An economic situation in which the monthly meetings became regularly involved was bankruptcy. The epistles recommended an annual accounting in order to determine if one were living within his income. Elders might warn a person to take an accounting or to curtail his standard of living before it was too late. (The only time that a court case between members could occur was when a Quaker feared his debtor was going bankrupt and might flee the province.) Sometimes the meeting would intervene on request of creditors, ask for an evaluation of goods, and perhaps, through arbitrators, arrange some kind of settlement. The meeting tried to distinguish between a failure due to circumstances beyond control and one in which a Friend was guilty of defrauding his creditors. If a man lost his money because of speculation, imprudent management, taking too great a risk, or living extravagantly, he was disowned. Even if a man made a settlement with his creditors, Friends held that he was morally responsible for paying back his entire debt and refused to allow any person in this circumstance to speak in a meeting for business or contribute funds.[67] A man who went bankrupt was guilty of at least three offenses: dishonesty, failure to support his family, and the bringing of dishonor upon Friends. There was no condemnation of the man because God had shown through worldly events that he was a sinner.

The queries of yearly meetings asked if anyone had defrauded the king of his customs. Whether this testimony dissuaded Quakers from smuggling depends upon whose evidence one accepts. The meetings found no violation of the query. While Penn and his supporters played down the amount of illegal trading, Edward Randolph, Robert Quary, and other opponents of the proprietary government tried to magnify transgressions.[68] James Claypoole, one of the early migrants to Pennsylvania, as an English merchant falsified accounts to avoid or lower customs duties. James Logan imported Dutch wire as madeira wine and shipped tobacco to Newfoundland under the guise of bread. He defended the latter as "not very Justifiable though common." In 1749 George Mifflin, Jr., had a cargo seized for trading in the French West Indies.[69] Theodore Thayer, the biographer of Israel Pemberton, Jr., concluded that Pemberton normally did not engage in smuggling but that he did give orders to unload molasses out of the reach of Philadelphia customs officials. During wartime, Pemberton traded with the Dutch islands, using them as a neutral depot from which to supply the French. John Reynell refused to participate in this trade. When he feared that an embargo on shipping was imminent during the French and Indian War, Reynell took the precaution of having his papers cleared early and then sent his ship out at night to evade the blockade. When John Smith had a ship come into New York harbor, he attempted to register it in New Jersey to avoid paying New York duties. Customs officials forced him to bring the ship to Perth Amboy for registration, but he then sailed back to New York City to unload.[70] Quaker Samuel Galloway of Maryland engaged in illegal direct trade with the French in wartime and after peace came in 1763 continued to smuggle sugar and molasses. Thirteen merchants from Rhode Island, including several prominent Quakers, asserted the right of Americans to trade in the Spanish and French islands even during wartime. In instructing Pennyslvania's colonial agent to keep out of the controversy over contraband, Isaac Norris II insisted that few Philadelphia merchants traded with the French and Spanish islands and that Pennsylvania would not serve as a "catspaw" in Rhode Island's squabbles.[71] In England as in America the amount of smuggling seems to have depended upon where one lived. London Yearly Meeting in the 1750s attempted to stop Friends in Cornwall, Scarborough, and Bridlington from smuggling. In America illegal trading by Friends was more common in Rhode Island than Pennsylvania, though Friends in all colonies engaged in some questionable activities. If the letter books of Quaker merchants were candid, one should conclude that Friends normally engaged only in legal trade.

Friends interpreted their peace testimony to mean that they could not arm ships, engage in privateering, or buy prize goods; but there was less agreement on whether they could sell goods to be used for military purposes. When the British fleet anchored off Rhode Island in 1745, Quaker Whitney Lovell rejoiced that "Whatever Philadelphia Saints may think . . . we are well pleased with the Arm of Flesh especially if we had more Fresh provisions to give them." As a member of the assembly in 1755, James Pemberton supervised the buying of grain destined for use by the British troops.[72] After the Quaker withdrawal from the assembly in 1756, Friends' consciences became more tender on such issues. Both British and American merchants attempted to send their ships in convoy during wartime, ostensibly because the insurance rates were lower. A few Friends were disowned for having part ownership in privateers, and many merchants tried to avoid dealing in prize goods.[73] Israel Pemberton, Jr., wrote a scathing letter to John Hunt, an English Quaker merchant and minister, charging him with buying a prize, arming it with cannon, and permitting his captain to allow a female indentured servant stay in his cabin on the voyage over and back. Hunt answered that he did not know when he had purchased the vessel, that it was indeed a prize, and that the few cannon on board were not for defense. The captain's explanation regarding the woman was that she did not like the climate in America and so had returned to England. Hunt argued that whether the captain were honest or not, a merchant could not be completely responsible for the conduct of his sailors.[74]

Friend and foe commented unfavorably on the avariciousness of Quaker merchants. The libelous *News from Pennsylvania* (1703) charged: "Their way of Trade and Commerce, is in outward appearance, Sir, as even as your Two Eyes; but they will be sure to overreach you in Contracts and Bargains, if possible." Indignant at the emerging pattern of Pennsylvania society, a disowned Friend charged in 1715 that Quakers did not discipline for their two "Epidemical sins, viz. *Covetousness* and *Extortion.*"[75] James Logan in 1721 and again in 1741 asserted that Friends' pursuit of wealth was not in keeping with their holy profession. Anthony Benezet complained that a person who attempted to regulate his business practice by "right reason" would be taken advantage of by others claiming the "necessities of Trade."[76] Quaker mercantile practice during the Revolution brought a host of complaints from patriots against the "stiff Rumps" in plain coats whose only God was "gain." Thomas Clarkson quoted an English apothegm that Friends pursued wealth "with a step as steady as time, and as keen as death."[77] How justifiable was this reputation?

If Friends followed the advice they gave their children and apprentices, they must have been very shrewd, close-mouthed, and difficult to do business with. Penn's maxims showed no optimism about human nature. "Trust no Man with the main Chance, and avoid to be trusted." "Only trust thy self, and another shall not betray thee."[78] When Elias Bland began trading, John Reynell, his former master, gave liberal doses of advice.

> Keep thy Business to thyself, and don't let it be known, who thou dost Business for, or what sorts of Goods thou Ships off. Some will want to know both, perhaps, with a Design to Circumvent Thee. Endeavour to know what Prices other People give for Goods, but Say nothing of what thou gives thy self, or where thou Buys; its very Probable some will Tell thee, they give more for a thing than they did on Purpose To make thee buy dear. . . . If thou finds out a Place where they Sell cheap, keep it to thy Self, for if thou Ships off Goods cheaper than others, it will increase Business. . . . Now to Conclude, do justly to every man and Endeavour after a Circumspect Walking before God.[79]

The Quaker businessman was to be cautious, but he was not to be a shyster. Benjamin Coole warned against gaining a reputation for slickness and recommended doing no business with an untrustworthy person. The Friend was not to be a "Sharp and Witty" trader nor so "Easie and Tame, as to suffer People to Impose" upon his good nature.[80]

The most accurate evaluation of the Quakers as merchants was obtained by Jacques Brissot de Warville. After repeatedly hearing Quaker merchants charged with dishonesty, he investigated by questioning English, American, and French traders who had had dealings with Friends. Quakers were noted as being "shrewd dealers" who bought cheap and sold dear. "I have not heard of a single instance of dishonesty. They limited themselves to saying that Quakers are in general sharp, strict, and inflexible, and that they do favors only for members of their own sect."[81]

Although believing that no man was to be trusted too far, the Quakers relied on members of their denomination more than on outsiders. Peter Kalm found in 1749 that "they cling together very close now, and the more well-to-do employ only Quaker artisans if they can be found. If a skilled workman, laborer or someone else of their faith backslides and joins another church, they have nothing more to do with him."[82] John Kelsall in Wales recorded that when a Quaker collier and a maid went to a priest to be married, both were dismissed by their Quaker employers. The New York discipline of 1800 recommended that any Friend entering into a partnership for trade "keep in view the propriety and great safety of confining their prospects to those who are in membership with us."[83]

The existence of an international Quaker community of merchants tended to bind the whole Society together. Quakers, trading with their coreligionists, formed a network of merchants residing in England, New York, New England, Virginia, the West Indies. English Friends had a near monopoly of the trade of American Friends, partially because meetings on both sides of the ocean tried to ensure business rectitude. Businessmen in America preferred to trade with any Quaker, however distantly related, whom they could term "kinsman." Thomas Richardson of Newport traded with relatives in Boston, Long Island, New York, and Barbados. John Reynell did business with his cousins in England and Jamaica as well as with leading London Quakers. Jonathan Dickinson had "brothers" (or brothers-in-law) in England and Jamaica and a cousin in Newport. He once debated opening a correspondence with a man who had married the daughter of a widow whose sister was married to his brother Caleb.[84] When James Pemberton began business, John Reynell advised George Laurence, a Madeira wine merchant, that "he is a young Man just going Into Trade, and Perhaps it may be worth while to Endeavour to Please him, not only on his own, but on his fathers and Brothers Account." When Cadwalader Evans visited Jamaica in 1748 he lost his letter of introduction, but before leaving he met the Quakers living there. Although most of the merchants had ceased to be practicing Friends, "I loved them much Better than other folks in common Notwithstanding." Thomas Gawthrop, a soldier-turned-Quaker, used a religious visit to Philadelphia to establish a business arrangement with the Pembertons.[85] Thomas Chalkley regularly combined his trade as a ship's captain with religious visits. Merchants sent their sons on trading voyages to enable them to establish some kind of personal relationship with Quaker merchants in London, Newport, or Jamaica.

The great prosperity of Quaker merchants in London and America showed the effectiveness of their trading practices. The English and Pennsylvania iron industries became virtual Quaker monopolies. In English banking circles such Quaker names as Barclay and Lloyd are still prominent. In Philadelphia the wealthy Quaker families constituted a financial aristocracy bound together by religion and kinship. By the Revolution the Morrises, Norrises, Logans, Pembertons, Emlens, Powells, Lloyds, Zanes, Dickinsons, and Smiths were related.

The wealth and style of life of the prominent families of Philadelphia, London, or Newport are not indicative of the lives of all Quakers. In order to show how city Friends' wealth compared with that of the general population, the 1754 Philadelphia tax list was compared with the earliest membership list of Philadelphia Monthly Meeting (dated 1759–62) and a list of Friends visited by Daniel Stanton and James Pemberton between 1757 and 1760.[86] (Such family visits usually involved every member of the meeting.) Of the 559 names on the tax list, 139 were identified as Friends. The lowest classification was £12 taxable estate, which was referred to as "poor." Fourteen percent of Friends were evaluated at £12, 34 percent had taxable wealth worth less than £20, 54 percent less than £40, 67 percent less than £60. There were nine men evaluated at over £100.

Assessed Wealth in 1754	*Total Population*	*Quakers*
10–19	50	34
20–29	15	15
30–39	21	22
40–49	7	7
50–59	3	4
60–79	3	5
80–99	2	6
100–	4	6

The second Philadelphia membership list, which begins in 1773, was compared with the tax list for Philadelphia for 1774. Two hundred fifty-six Quaker households were located (31 of which were not found in the 1774 list but were mentioned in the city tax list for 1769 or the constable's returns for 1775).[87] The 1774 list provided a better sample because persons with no property or with less than £10 worth were mentioned. Twenty-six percent of Friends were classified as having no taxable property and 17 percent as having property worth less than £10. In spite of the discrepancy between the lowest evaluation in the two tax lists, the 1754 list assessed 61 percent of Friends as worth less than £40, and the 1774 list so assessed 63 percent. The figures for the general population below the £40 level are 86 percent and 88 percent. Quakers were significantly fewer than the general population at the lowest rank on both tax lists, while between this and the £50 level, Quakers and the general population were nearly equivalent. Only when one gets to the higher amounts of property does the clear-cut Quaker superiority to the entire population appear.

Assessed Wealth in 1774	*Total Population*	*Quakers*
0	53	26
1– 9	17	17
10– 19	9	8
20– 29	5	6
30– 39	4	6
40– 49	2	2
50– 59	2	6
60– 79	3	6
80– 99	2	6
100–149	3	5
150–199	1	2
200–	3	8

A note of caution is required in interpreting these figures. It is assumed that the same kinds of wealth were being assessed in the same way for all individuals. But it is impossible to know what percentage of the total property was being evaluated. For example, in 1760 James Pemberton assessed his real property as worth £9000, not including stock in trade, but in 1754 he was evaluated at £170 and in 1769 at £432. The wills of John Pemberton and John Reynell, both of whom died after the Revolution, showed that each was worth over £10,000, but their assessed valuations in 1774 were £433 and £211, respectively. Israel Pemberton, Jr., was assessed at £974 in 1774, but he was worth £60,000 at his death in 1779. The Philadelphia tax figures are not a reliable index for total wealth; all they provide is a comparative standard regarding the place a man occupied in relation to his fellows.

In addition, of the total entries in the two Quaker membership roles, over two-thirds of the names in 1759 and nearly one-half in 1773 could not be located on the tax lists. Most of the unidentified individuals were inmates in another person's house, women who may have been single or whose husbands' names were not mentioned in the membership list, or children. (Tax lists never gave names of married women; the membership roles did not provide the ages of children and listed single individuals under their parents' names until they married.) Since the wealthy members that the historian recognizes are invariably found on the tax lists, any distortion of statistics resulting from the missing names would most likely effect the lower ranks. A sociologist working with contemporary America probably would not generalize from such an incomplete sample, but the historian may allow himself more latitude, even though he should be very careful about drawing strong conclusions from fragmentary data.

Both tax lists support the established conclusion that Philadelphia Quakers included some of the richest men of the town and comprised a greater number of wealthy families than their numerical proportion of the population would warrant. The tax tables show that Friends occupied the middling ranks of Philadelphia in almost the same percentages as the total population and also encompassed a sizable number of the poor. An hypothesis defining late eighteenth-century Philadelphia Friends as predominately of one class cannot be validated. Friends' ethical standards and religious beliefs attracted rich, poor, and in-between. Unfortunately, there are no comparable membership lists for anywhere else in America before the Revolution so that it is impossible to determine whether Philadelphia Quakers were typical.[89]

Just as many city Friends were not wealthy, so also many country Friends were not destitute. James Lemon's investigation of Chester and Lancaster counties in Pennsylvania disclosed that Quakers and Mennonites "dominated the top tax brackets in the most productive areas." Even in the poorer areas of the two counties, Quakers were the leading taxpayers. Because the lands owned by the sectaries were not appreciably different in quality from the lands of others, social factors such as the attitudes toward work and wealth must have been responsible for the prosperity. (The number of poor Friends might be underrepresented in these calculations, which are based upon a comparison of tax lists, township records, and genealogies rather than membership lists.) Lemon's description of the wealth of rural Quakers, the involvement of farmers in commercial agriculture from an early date, and the amount of contact between city and country folk should make historians ponder the accuracy of the traditional distinction between rich and worldly city Friends and their poor and pious country cousins.[90]

V

Since life was a pilgrimage and Christians would be called to account for every idle moment, Quakers opposed recreations that might detract from the true purpose of man. How could any person remember God while dancing, playing cards, attending plays, or reading novels? These activities were "diversions" in the worst sense of the word, for they "naturally tend to draw men from God's fear," and "to foster lust, vanity, and wantonness." As a moral and rational man's being, aim should be to improve his character, but amusements degraded him. Playing cards or racing brought forth "every perverse passion" including avarice, hard heartedness, and dishonesty. Dancing resulted in a lustful, wanton, emulative spirit hardly conducive to a quiet waiting on God.[91]

Even instrumental music raised up a "*light, airy, frothy, wanton* Mind." The lyrics of songs celebrating martial exploits, bacchanalian revels, unchastity, or the cruelty of the hunt were considered morally degrading. Music brought no intellectual improvement, corrupted pure thoughts, and diverted mankind from God. Unlike the Puritans, the Quakers allowed no formal singing in their meetings. Occasionally, a person sang an extemporaneous hymn to the Lord, but congregational singing led to all sorts of lies. "The daily Feaster, whose Legs can scarce bear about his corpulent body, he sings, *My Knees are weak thro' Fasting, and my Flesh faileth of Fatness.*"[92]

Hunting for sport or pleasure excited a cruel exaltation in the sufferings of a poor fox or a timid hare. No person had the "right to make a pleasure of that which occasions pain and death to animal-creation." Friends were not generally vegetarians and allowed hunting or killing of animals for food but, "if the death of animals is to be made serviceable to men, the least they can do in return is to mitigate their sufferings while they expire."[93]

Plays were nothing but a "studied complex of idle and lying words." Actors uttered the most scandalous sentiments against all religion and virtue. Novelists played upon the emotions to excite a "romantic spirit, a sort of wonder-loving imagination, and a disposition towards enthusiastic flights of fancy." Those who were addicted to reading fiction frequently became boastful of their knowledge and lived in a world of fantasy. Like both Anglicans and Nonconformists, Friends feared the effect of reading novels on females, whose minds were weaker and more susceptible to day dreaming and romanticism than were the minds of men. The qualities that novels fostered in the mind of a woman were the opposite of the prudence and virtue needed to be a good wife and mother.[94]

Friends forbade amusements that diverted time from more profitable tasks. In a passage that sounds much like Cotton Mather's *Essays to do Good,* William Penn wrote that the "*Best Recreation is to do Good.*" If a man were diligent in his calling, frequent in attendance at worship, a visitor of good neighbors for edification and bad neighbors for the purpose of reforming them, careful in the raising of children, exemplary in treating servants, willing to relieve the poor, ready to help the sick, always ready to visit those in prison, and interested in studying such profitable subjects as husbandry, geometry, gardening, and medicine—then how could he have time to play cards, attend plays, gamble, or drink and feast throughout the night? Even if a person did not believe in God, Christ, heaven, hell, or the need to live a Christian life, "yet would *Charity to the poor, Help to the Needy, Peace amongst Neighbours, Visits to the Sick, Care of the Widow and Fatherless* . . . be a Nobler Employment, and much more worthy of your Expense and Pains" than frivolous pastimes.[95]

Although Friends separated church and state in Pennsylvania (a task made imperative by the fear that Penn might surrender the government to the Crown), unlike the Puritans in New England they did not deny political office to ministers. Penn, as weighty Friend and proprietor, mingled religious and political responsibility, and since all Quaker ministers were laymen pursuing a secular calling, Friends saw no incongruity in their serving as justices of the peace or assemblymen. John Smith calculated that twenty-seven Quaker ministers served in the council or the assembly. With some justification the adherents of George Keith charged in 1697 that ministers and elders used their governmental positions to prosecute the Keith people for religious differences.[96] So long as yearly meeting occurred just before election day and Quakers maintained a majority in the assembly, opponents suspected that the yearly meeting meddled in politics. For example, within a four-month period John Smith, at age twenty-eight, was named to the governing board of Penn Charter School, became an overseer of the meeting, was selected to run for the assembly at a meeting held at the Pembertons, and was elected.[97] Documents showing how the meeting influenced politics are rare, but prominent elders serving in the council or the assembly (such as John Kinsey, who was the clerk of yearly meeting and speaker of the Pennsylvania assembly) dramatized the linkage.

Since the meeting endorsed no theory of government except obedience to lawful superiors where conscience did not conflict, the exigencies of the colonial situation had more impact upon political ideology than religion. As Friends, the assemblymen felt a responsibility to insure that there would be no established church, no tithes, no compulsory military training, and no required oaths or legal impediments to Quakers' governing. They did not believe that the distinctive tenets of one religious body should be imposed upon all, but they expected the government to foster goodness and suppress wickedness.

In order to discourage the licentious from immigrating and protect the righteous from the wrath of God, the Pennsylvania assembly proscribed what Quakers defined as moral evils. The list of illegal sports, for example, was long, although the assembly did not forbid the reading of novels or singing or hunting for pleasure. The "Great Law" of 1682 prohibited "such rude and riotous sports and practices as Prizes, Stage-plays, Masques, Revels, Bull-baitings and Cock-fightings." Violators received ten days' imprisonment or a 20s. fine. A person earned five days imprisonment or 5s. fine for "playing at Cards, Dice, Lotteries, or such like enticing, vain, and evil Sports and Games." After these laws were reenacted in 1700, the Crown repealed them because they forbade "some innocent sports" and were vaguely drawn. In a law passed in 1705 the assembly again prohibited plays, revels, bull-baiting, cockfights, or being "a party in any riotous sport or play whatsoever." This law, which survived the Crown's scrutiny, regulated taverns by forbidding fourteen different games including cards, dice, "shovel-board," billiards, ninepins, and "any other kind of game whatsoever, now invented or hereafter to be invented."[98] As the Quaker percentage of the population dwindled, the meetings cooperated with Presbyterians and other political opponents to obtain legislation on moral issues. Since after 1756 Friends could no longer legislate for the entire colony, the meetings increasingly relied on the power of petitions to persuade the assembly to outlaw plays and other so-called moral evils.

Owing to their minority status, Friends in England and most parts of America could not enact blue laws. Thus, Quakers felt themselves clear of evil if they petitioned or testified against an idle diversion. In England John Kelsall saw a group of young people dancing around a maypole. He bore his witness against this pagan custom and then went away. In New Jersey John Woolman heard about a magician performing shows. He went to the place of diversion and told the spectators why he opposed such amusements. After staying for about an hour, he concluded that he had done his duty and left.[99] Before the Revolution, Friends tried to persuade recalcitrant members that slavery was evil. If all else failed, slaveowners were disowned. After cleansing their own membership Quakers joined with others to lobby for antislavery legislation.

While Friends opposed recreation designed for enjoyment alone, a useful pastime was always allowed. Since no one could be exclusively attentive to work, he could vary his tasks. Robert Barclay distinguished between "innocent diversions" and those practices that were evil in themselves or that brought harmful results. A lawful recreation was analogous to moderate working, eating, and drinking. Barclay believed that conversation with Christians, reading history, visiting acquaintances, and using geometrical or mathematical instruments were useful, harmless, and even godly diversions.[100] A person who gardened could see the handiwork of God in nature, create a place of beauty, and receive needed exercise. Running a race, however, which provided physical training, was taboo because its by-product was stimulation of evil desires to gamble and excel. Even the excitement of watching such a contest was not conducive to quiet, disciplined living.

What individual Quakers practiced as recreation depended upon a variety of factors including their degree of piety, education, and social status. The first Friends condemned the reading of fiction and poetry but permitted "useful" reading. Yet, long before 1700 devout Quakers in England and America read and wrote poetry, and versification was taught in some eighteenth-century schools. Even though cosmopolitan Friends stretched useful reading to include every kind of book, the staples remained devotional and theological tracts, and some who read romances felt guilty. Elizabeth Drinker was mortified at having to keep the Library Company's copy of Rabelais in her home overnight, and Samuel Morris greeted a gift of a Rousseau treatise with, "he's a fine writer, I wish he was as much a Christian."[101] Interest in botany and science was so widespread among American Friends that Howard Brinton concluded—with some exaggeration—that "almost every Quaker had a scientific hobby."[102]

The diaries of Sally Wister, John Smith, and Elizabeth Drinker give no impression of undue strictness on the subject of recreation. Having people in for tea and conversation was a daily occurrence among prosperous Quakers. Ice skating, sleighing, fishing, hunting, and gardening were common. John Churchman gave up music when he was converted and even refused to whistle, but Sally Wister sang and Henry S. Drinker played a flute. Painting was officially forbidden, but Friends had no testimony against creating with scissors and dark paper a cutout profile of a prominent person.[103] When Benjamin West, the son of a rural Quaker, wished to become a painter, the monthly meeting held a special session. John Williamson arose and stated, "God has bestowed on the youth a genius for the art, and can we believe the Omniscience bestows His gifts but for great purposes? What God has given, who shall dare to throw away?" Though Friends could not decipher the reason for the Lord's bestowing such a talent, the meeting approved of West's studying painting.[104] Edward Hicks, whose many versions of the *Peaceable Kingdom* are esteemed as fine examples of American primitivism, was a Quaker minister and painter, though he had some difficulty reconciling both his callings.

Early Friends left no records of any sense of humor, though they could thrust barbed witticisms deep into theological rivals. In all periods jokes were unusual in personal correspondence, but later generations relaxed more and appreciated conviviality. Thomas Clarkson commented on the pleasant conversation in Quaker homes, John Churchman's memorial read: "His disposition being cheerful, he sometimes discovered a turn of pleasantry in conversation." Joseph Fry, an English minister, was described as having a "rich fund of anecdote" which both "instructed and entertained."[105]

The Philadelphia discipline disapproved of smoking "except privately and moderately," and William Logan, John Smith, Thomas Lightfoot, George Churchman, and Hannah Pemberton smoked pipes. When Charity Cook of Bush River, South Carolina, visited London in 1797, she scandalized English Friends by strolling around the town with a pipe in her mouth.[106]

If the prohibition against idleness produced intensive introspection and morbidity as evidenced by Dr. John Rutty's complaints about overeating and having indulged himself, for others it did little more than produce feelings of guilt after a frivolous evening. In his bachelor days John Smith attended a gathering of young people. He complained in his diary of the unedifying nature of the conversation, but the next day he returned to the same house, talked with the same people, and escorted the same young lady home.[107] Throughout the colonial period the meetings did not compromise their testimonies against dancing, playing cards, attending the theater, and running races. But "wet Quakers," who attended meetings for worship but refrained from participating in meetings for business, engaged in many of these officially forbidden pleasures.

VI

Quakers expected their theological tenets to guide conduct, but often differed as to how their beliefs on plainness, simplicity, moderation, honesty, and hard work should be interpreted. All desired a disciplined use of creaturely comforts, but members could interpret this to mean either living moderately according to their station or ascetically in order to wean themselves from worldliness. The meeting wanted no compromise of the God-given commandments on plain speaking, oaths, tithes, and peace. All these testimonies, particularly the distinctive dress and the thee and thou speech, stood to Friends and outsiders as badges of the faith and served to separate the faithful from the worldly. In the same manner as the family was to seclude the child from evil ways, the peculiar customs were to erect a barrier between adults and the sinful world.

In the colonial period Friends did not often question their guiding principles, but found many perplexities in applying them in mundane existence. They agreed on the necessity to be pacifists, but could not agree whether pacifism required nonpayment of war taxes, refusal to trade in war supplies, and abdication of positions of authority in a government at war. Scripture outlawed oaths, but at what point did an affirmation become an oath? Dress should be moderate and simple but did the gospel require a particular fashion? A man should not cater to pride by using empty titles, but when did everyday speech cease to be candid and become a formality? Leisure was designed for doing good for oneself and others, but the meeting found it impractical to regulate what was permissible.

Ethical standards for godly business practice were also clear: honesty, hard work, obedience to the law, fair dealing. But how in practice could a merchant determine exactly what was a just price? How could a farmer be certain that he enjoyed working hard because he was faithful to his calling? Was he instead engaged in an inordinate pursuit of wealth? Poverty could result from an artisan's personal failure or the inscrutable providence of God. Was it possible to be faithful to God, obedient to the law, fair to the customer, honest with fellow traders and still make a living?

When every member faced such perplexities, it is easy to see why Friends sometimes equivocated. But those who compromised or betrayed the testimonies could at any time meet a Quaker willing to point out their inconsistencies. Weighty Friends were under a divine obligation to ferret out error, and those whose faith compelled them to minister far away from home were not likely to be deterred by the wealth or prominence of the offender. In local, quarterly, and yearly meetings merchants, farmers, schoolmasters, artisans, slave owners, abolitionists, the sophisticated and the rustic encountered each other. Because Quakers were a family sharing a common faith, they met together to reaffirm their beliefs and to discuss their dilemmas. Close-knit because they were different from their neighbors, Friends preserved a distinctive culture wherever they lived.

Notes

1 Frederick Tolles, *Meeting House and Counting House* (New York, 1963), pp. 52–53.
2 George Fox, *Works,* (Philadelphia, 1831), 7: 73; William Penn, *Works,* (London, 1726), 1: 367; Robert Barclay, *Apology for the True Christian Divinity,* (Manchester, England, 1869), prop. 15, pg. 2: 327.
3 Penn, *Works,* 1: 824, 851, 911.
4 John Woolman, *Journal,* (New York, 1922), pp. 202, 227–28.
5 Penn, *Works,* 1: 295–96
6 Barclay, *Apology,* prop. 15, pg. 2: 328.
7 Fox, *Works,* 8: 18.
8 Matthew 10:37; Penn, *Works,* 1: 287.
9 George Fox, *Journal,* (New York, 1963), p. 236: John Smith to E. B., 9 mo./1739, entitled "Concerning the Narrow Way," in "A Collection of Sundry Writings on Diverse Occasions," p. 35, LC; Ann Whitall, "Diary," 5/12/1760, p. 10 QC; Samuel Allinson to Martha Allinson, 4/9/1776 QC; Anthony Benezet to George Dillwyn, 9/15/1779, in *Friend Anthony Benezet,* (New York, 1937), p. 338.
10 John Pemberton to James Pemberton, 4/7/1749, PP, 5: 107; John Smith, "Diary," vol. 3, 12/21/1746.

11 Thomas Jefferson Wertenbarker, *The Founding of American Civilization: The Middle Colonies* (New York, 1938), pp. 231–55; Tolles, *Meeting House and Counting House,* pp. 127–28, n. 46.

12 *BFHA,* 32 (1942): 31; *PMHB* 17 (1893): 460, and 18 (1894): 55, 63; John Adams, *Diary,* ed. L. H. Butterfield, *The Adams Papers* (Cambridge, Mass., 1961), 2: 126–27. The meal consisted of "Ducks, Hams, Chickens, Beef, Pigg, Tarts, Creams, Custards, Gellies, fools, Trifles, floating Islands, Beer, Porter, Punch, Wine and a long &c." Ann Whitall confessed to her diary in 11 mo./1762, "What a terrible thing this eating of too much is, and has been to me many times. I think I can say of a truth it is the worst sin that ever I did. I do believe it is as bad as drinking too much."

13 Elizabeth Wilkinson, "Journal of a Religious Visit in America, 1761–1763," 1/11/1763, pp. 115–16, QC: *JFHS* 20 (1923): 139.

14 Jacques Brissot de Warville, *New Travels in the United States,* (Cambridge, Mass., 1964), p. 303; Benjamin Ferris to Robert Vaux, 7/28/1816, in *Friend Anthony Benezet,* p. 465; J. Hector St. John Crèvecoeur, *Letters from an American Farmer* (New York, 1904), letters 8, 11, pp. 156–58, 202–04; Rhoda Barber, "Journal," HSP.

15 Fox, *Journal,* pp. 416, 446; Penn, *Works,* 1: 868.

16 Min. London YM, 5 (3/21/1714) and (3/25/1715): 16–21. When London Yearly Meeting tried to decide whether it should support a renewal of the law defining the allowable affirmation, Friends engaged in an acrimonious debate. No general sense of the meeting could be obtained by normal procedures. Finally, a poll of the delegations of each quarterly meeting determined that twenty-one quarterly meetings were for renewing the present affirmation; six counties unanimously opposed renewal; two counties were equally divided; ten counties had more delegates favoring renewal than opposing it; four counties had more against renewal than favoring it. In an advice directed to New Jersey Friends, Philadelphia Yearly Meeting in 1710 gave permission to use or not to use the affirmation as the New Jerseyites saw fit.

17 The dispute between Pennsylvania Friends and the English government over the affirmation lasted from 1693, when Governor Fletcher required an oath of all officeholders, until 1725, when the Pennsylvania act was approved by the Crown. In the first English act an affirmation was not permitted in criminal cases, for juries, or as a test for office. The Anglicans in Pennsylvania wanted the English law extened to the colony as a way of barring Friends from governing. Quakers used a variety of methods to circumvent the English law.

18 Francis Gawler to George Fox, 1/26/1659, Swarthmore Mss, 4: 219: "Transcripts" 2: 259, FH.

19 Lawrence H. Gipson, "Crime and Its Punishment in Provincial Pennsylvania," *Pennsylvania History* 2 (1935): 3–16; H. Clay Reed, ed. *Burlington Court Book* (Washington, D.C., 1944), pp. xlviii–xlix; *PMHB* 60 (1936): 242–69.

20 Edward Armstrong, ed., *Correspondence Between William Penn and James Logan* (Philadelphia, 1870), pp. 124, 287; Robert Davidson, *War Comes to Quaker Pennsylvania 1682–1756* (New York, 1957), p. 5. Herman Wellenreuther and Jack Marietta have made significant contributions to the understanding of Quaker pacifism and the crisis of 1755 in recent articles. *PMHB* (1970): 135–172 and 95 (1971): 3–27. Richard Bauman, *For the Reputation of Truth* (Baltimore, 1972) discusses Quaker politics from 1750–1800.

21 Min. Philadelphia YM 2 (9/1724/1757): 107–10; PP, 10: 75 and 11: 20–22. For an account of how economic advantage through war contracts and trading relationships influenced London Quakers to persuade their Philadelphia brethren to withdraw from government, see A. G. Gary "Political and Economic Relations of English and American Quakers 1750–85," (Ph.D. diss. St. Hugh's College, Oxford, 1935), pp. 60–95.

22 Penn, *Works* 1: 871; Thomas Chalkley, *Works* (London, 1791), pp. 87–88; Barclay, *Apology,* Prop. 15, pp: 111, 330; Staughton George *et al.,* eds., *Charter to William Penn, and Laws of the Province of Pennsylvania* (Harrisburg, Penn., 1896), p. 111.

23 Fox, *Works,* 3: 410–11, 416; Penn, *Works,* 1: 869; Barclay, *Apology,* prop. 15, pp. iv. 332; Hugh Barbour, *Quakers in Puritan England,* (New Haven, Conn., 1964), pp. 164–65.

24 James Parnell quoted in Barbour, *Quakers in Puritan England,* p. 164.

25 Fox, *Journal,* pp. 381–82.

26 Barclay, *Apology,* prop. 15, pp. iv, 330.

27 Walter Somer to Margaret Fell, 6/25/1658, Swarthmore Mss, 1: 186; Transcript 4: 335.

28 Charles Leslie, *Snake in the Grass,* in *Works,* (London, 1792), 2: 169; *JFHS* 26 (1929): 41–42.

29 Penn, *Works,* 1: 850, 897; Susanna Dillwyn to George Dillwyn, 4/6/1791, Dillwyn Mss, vol. 1; Marquis de Chastellux, *Travels in North America,* (Chapel Hill, North Carolina, 1963), 1: 166–67; Thomas Clarkson, *Portraiture of Quakerism,* (London, 1806), p. 365.

30 John Willsford, *A Brief Exhortation,* (Philadelphia, 1691), pp. 5–6; Peter Kalm, *Travels in North America,* (New York, 1937), 2: 676; Simon Addam, *Concerning the Observation of the First Day to be Kept Above Any Other Day* (1663), p. 1; George Keith, *Presbyterian and Independent Churches* (Philadelphia, 1689), pp. 193–96; Staughton George *et al.*, eds., *Charter to William Penn, and Laws of the Province of Pennsylvania* p. 108; J. T. Mitchell and S. Flanders, eds., *Statutes at Large of Pennsylvania* (Harrisburg, Penn., 1896), 2: 175–77. Friends seem to have observed Sunday by shutting their shops if it were customary but keeping them open otherwise. Governor Belcher complained that the Burlington, New Jersey, shops were open on the Sabbath. A.C. Myers, ed., *Hannah Logan's Courtship,* (Philadelphia, 1904), n. 34.

31 George Fox, *Instructions for Right Spelling,* (Philadelphia, 1702), p. 52; London YM, Christian and Brotherly Advices, 1751, p. 341; Henry J. Cadbury, "Heathen Names for Days of the Week and Months," *BFHA* 17 (1928): 55–58; *Charter to William Penn, and Laws of the Province of Pennsylvania,* p. 116. Early laws of Pennsylvania required the numerical naming of the days of the week and month.

32 Penn, *Works,* 1: 350; Barclay, *Apology,* prop. 15, pg. vii, 338.

33 John Mulliner, *A Testimony Against Periwigs and Periwig Making* (1677), pp. 8–9; Ambrose Rigge, *A Faithful Testimony Against Extravagant and Unnecessary Wiggs* (London, 1699). By 1750 Quaker men quite often wore wigs whether they were bald or not.

34 Fox, *Works,* 7: 300.

35 Philadelphia YM, Discipline, 1704–17.

36 Amelia Gummere, *The Quaker Costume* (Philadelphia, 1901), p. 183.

37 *Sally Wister's Journal,* A.C. Myers, ed., (Philadelphia, 1902), 10/20/1777, p. 87 and 6/7/1778, p. 179.

38 Deborah Hill to Hannah Moore, 5/25/1745, Howland Mss, QC; *BFHA* 31 (1942): pp. 30–31; Brissot de Warville, *New Travels,* pp. 300–01.

39 David Hall, *Some Brief Memoirs,* (London, 1758), pp. 92–93; Min. Philadelphia YM, 7/20–24/1729, p. 343.

40 Penn, *Works,* 1: 370, 373.

41 Richard Claridge, *Life and Posthumous Works* (London, 1726), pp. 522–23.

42 Barclay, *Apology,* prop. 15, pg. vii, 11, 326, 337.

43 Hall, *Some Brief Memoirs,* p. 90; Charlotte Rees, *Parental Instruction in Familiar Dialogues,* (Bristol, England, 1811), pp. 23–24; Isaac Norris to Joseph Pike, 12/15/1707, *Penn-Logan Correspondence,* 2: 259; Jonathan Roberts, "Memoirs," 1: 6, HSP.

44 In the period between 1672 and 1770, I have discovered little basic change in Quaker thought or behavior patterns. William Penn had been ambiguous on the relation of the inward light to reason or conscience, and so were a few eighteenth-century Friends. The strengthening of discipline weeded out many lukewarm members, but gentility or poverty did not disqualify a person from membership at any period. From the beginning Friends wavered between general counsels and those addressed only to believers. Fox, Penn, and John Bellars condemned the evils of English society and advocated reforms in much the same way that John Woolman and Anthony Benezet spoke out against slavery. Quakers never restricted their influence on Pennsylvania to those who held official positions. When Pennsylvania Friends were forced out of government, which occurred only during the Revolution, their situation became analogous to that of Friends in England. Major changes came to Pennsylvania Quakers between 1770 and 1790, and although the roots of their eventual adjustment came in earlier times, the fruition came in response to external factors. For differing views, see Sydney James, *People Among Peoples* (Cambridge, Mass., 1963), and Richard Bauman, *For the Reputation of Truth.*

45 Woolman, *Journal,* pp. 98, 113–14, 309–10; George Brookes, *Friend Anthony Benezet,* pp. 392, 337.

46 Philadelphia YM, *A General Epistle* (Philadelphia, 1688), p. 12; Penn, *Works,* 1: 323, 332–33; *PMHB* 13 (1889): 436.

47 Fox, *Works,* 7: 93–94; idem, *Journal,* pp. 197–98; Ambrose Rigge, *A Brief and Serious Warning to such as are Concerned in Trade* (1678).

48 Min. Philadelphia MM, "Testimonial to Thomas Chalkley," 4 (2/20/1769): 36. Thomas Sharp, "Sentiments Respecting the Dispensations of Providence," in Thomas Scattergood Mss Notebooks, no. 2, 9, DP. "The Lord is all the wise Disposer of Events, he maketh Rich and maketh poor . . . yet I am forc'd to confess—that with regard to his outward—as well as inward administrations, of prosperity and adversity—his judgments are unsearchable and his ways past finding out. It is obvious I own that trouble is often the result of our own perverseness and arises from the determi nation of an unsanctified Will—the Imprudence of our undertakings and folly of our Choice. But then I think it equally obvious that they sometime Arise from a different source, and must necessarily be resolv'd into the inerringly Wise & Inscrutable Providence of God."

49 William Penn, *A Letter from William*

Penn to his Wife and Children (London, 1761), p. 11.

50 Sophia Hume, *An Exhortation to the Inhabitants of South Carolina,* (Bristol, England, 1751), p. 15; London YM, Epistles from the Yearly Meeting, 1744, p. 209; Penn, *Works,* 1: 333.

51 Penn, *Works,* 1: 341, 344.

52 London YM, Epistles Received, 1697, 1: 262; Woolman, *Journal,* pp. 164, 183; Christopher Wilson, Testimony, 6/30/1759, Letters of American Friends, QC. Philadelphia Yearly Meeting warned in 1734 that a person might be a just businessman and give generously to charities and still have succumbed to an inordinate desire for wealth.

53 Howard Brinton, "Stages in Spiritual Developments as Recorded in Quaker Journals," in Children of Light (New York, 1938), pp. 403–05.

54 William Edmundson quoted in John S. Rowntree, *Quakerism, Past and Present,* (London, 1859), p. 95; Clarkson, *Portraiture of Quakerism,* 3: 255, 260.

55 Chalkley, *Works,* pp. 378–79; see also n. 47.

56 Stephen Crisp quoted in Isabel Grubb, *Quakerism and Industry before 1800* (London, 1930), p. 37.

57 Chalkley, *Works,* pp. 99–100.

58 Fox, *Journal,* p. 107; idem, *Works,* 4: 160–61, and 7: 192–93. Most Quaker business advice for the next hundred years appears in this epistle. In 1710 London Yearly Meeting recommended that all shopkeepers read Fox's advices at least once a year.

59 William Smith, "Universal Love," in *Balm From Gilead* (1675) pp. 14–18.

60 Grubb, *Quakerism and Industry,* pp. 146–147; *PMHB* 84 (1960): 208.

61 Thomas Richardson of Newport and James Logan expected 150 percent gains, and Isaac Norris I found profits ranging from 100 to 200 percent. Richardson did not wish to engage in a trade that made only 50 percent, but John Reynell thought a narrow profit was from 10 to 15 percent. James Logan to John Askew, 5/4/1712, Letter Book 1712–15, p. 34; Thomas Richardson to Richard Partridge, 11/7/1716 and Thomas Richardson to I. Bayard, Letterbook, 1715–19, p. 69, NHS; Isaac Norris to Rip Vandem and Walter Thong, 5/8/1699 and Isaac Norris to Jeffery Pinnell, 4/12/1699, Letter Books, 1: 34, 5, HSP; John Reynell to Elias Bland, 11/3/1758, John Reynell to Thomas Sanders, 12/19/1754 and John Reynell to Michael Lee Dicker, 8/3/1733 all in Reynell Letter Book, 1756–59, 1754–56, and 1733–35.

62 James Logan to Daniel Flexney, 3/4/1715, Logan Letterbook, 1712–15, p. 286.

63 *Charter to William Penn, and Laws of Pennsylvania,* p. 180; *Statutes at Large of Pennsylvania,* 2: 17 and 3: 338–39; Bucks Quarterly Meeting, Extracts of Minutes, 12/22/1704, p. 25; Thomas Richardson to Moses Austell, 3/23/1718, Letterbook, 1715–19.

64 *Charter to William Penn, and Laws of the Province of Pennsylvania,* pp. 135, 139, 169, 478. *Statutes at Large of Pennsylvania,* 2: 61, 84, 88, 95, 221–22, and 3: 259, 263, 288–91, and 4: 73–77.

65 Reed, *Burlington Court Book,* pp. xi-xii.

66 Min. Rhode Island MM, 2 (3/31/1720, 6/30/1720): 176–77, 180, 182–83, and 2 (12/29/1729): 277; Min. Perquimans MM, 2A (9/6/1758).

67 London YM, Epistles Received, 1702, 1: 379; Minutes, 1759 Epistle, 2: 498; Philadelphia YM, Epistle, 1701, Clarkson, *Portraiture of Quakerism,* 2: 59–60; Philadelphia MM, Original Certificates, 1714–29, pp. 188, 246; Baltimore YM, *Discipline of the Yearly Meeting of Friends* (Baltimore, 1806), pp. 40–41.

68 Min. Philadelphia YM, 1 (7/17–21/1743): 434; London YM, *Epistles from the Yearly Meeting* (1719), p. 137; *PMHB* 25 (1901): 282–83, and 24 (1900): 70, 78; Gary Nash, *Quakers and Politics 1681–1726* (Princeton, N. J., 1968), pp. 187–98.

69 Marion Balderston, ed., *James Claypoole's Letter Book* (San Marino, California, 1967), pp. 49, 143, 180; James Logan to Theodorus Hodshon, 1/12/1725, and James Logan to William Keen, 3/4/1723, Letterbook 1717–30, pp. 315, 409; Samuel Emlen, Jr., to James Pemberton, 3/31/1749, PP, 5: 97, 101.

70 Theodore Thayer, *Israel Pemberton: King of the Quakers,* pp. 14–17. Israel Pemberton, Sr., to James Pemberton, 3/31/1749, 3/11/1749, 5: 101, 68; John Reynell to John Barrell, Jr., April 22, 17 —, Reynell Letter Book, 1756–59; John Smith, "Diary," vol. 5, 5/18/1747-5/20/1748.

71 A. T. Gary, "Political and Economic Relations of English and American Quakers 1750–85," Ph.D. Diss. (St. Hugh's College, Oxford, 1935), pp. 262–77; Isaac Norris to Richard Partridge, 7/6/1751, 9/7/1751, Norris Letter Book, "Wallpaper" Book, Logan Mss. pp. 66, 67, HSP; Rhode Island Historical Society, Mss, 4: 139

72 London YM, *Epistles from the Yearly Meeting* (1757), p. 266; John Reynell to Elias Bland, 11/3/1758 and 12/11/1744, Letter Book 1744–45 and 1756–59; Whitney Lovell to Abraham Redwood, 10/23/1745, Abraham Redwood Letters, 2: 32, NHS; PP, 10: 108, 111, 114, 117; A. T. Gary, "Political and Economic Relations of English and American Quakers," pp. 101–183.

73 Elias Bland to Israel Pemberton,

1/14/1744, PP, 3: 158; John Reynell to Elias Bland, 10/27/1747, 10/10/1745, 12/10/1745, and John Reynell to Daniel Flexney, 6/13/1742, Letter Books, 1741–47. Philadelphia merchants such as Pemberton and Reynell attempted to avoid paying insurance as long as possible by sending the company notification as late as possible and on as slow a ship as they could find. The rebate received for shipping by convoy during wartime was 5 gn. one per 100-pound policy.

74 John Hunt to Israel Pemberton, 8/8/1748, 4/9/1748, PP, 4: 120, 140. John Reynell sent a parcel of pistols to Elias Bland on a forty-gun ship. John Reynell to Elias Bland, 12/14/1745, Letter Book, 1745–47.

75 *News from Pensilvania* (London, 1703), p. 28; Philalethes, *Tribute to Caesar* (1715), p. 22.

76 James Logan to Simon Clements, 2/20/1721, Letter Book 1717–30, p. 181; *PMHB* 6 (1882): 408; Anthony Benezet to John Smith, 1/8/1765, Smith Mss. 6: 199.

77 *PMHB* 22 (1898): 138, and 21 (1897): 127: Gérard de Rayneval to Court de Vergennes, 9/18/1779, in *Friend Anthony Benezet,* pp. 449–50; Clarkson, *Portraiture of Quakerism,* 3: 253.

78 Penn, *Works,* 1: 828, 898, 827.

79 John Reynell to Elias Bland, 4/22/1743, and 8/2/1743, Letter Book, 1741–43.

80 Benjamin Coole, *Miscellanies* (London, 1712), p. 6; Hall, *Memoirs,* p. 75; Richard Hill to Henry Hill, 7/30/1757, and Richard Hill to Samuel Moore, 10/26/1741, Howland Mss, QC.

81 Brissot de Warville, *New Travels,* p. 314.

82 *BFHA* 32 (1942), p. 31.

83 John Kelsall, "Diary Extracts," 2: 106, F.H.; New York YM, *Rules of Discipline, and Christian Advices, of the Yearly Meeting of Friends for the State of New York and Parts Adjacent* (New York, 1800), p. 62.

84 A. G. Gary, "Political and Economic Relations of English and American Quakers," pp. 228–38; Jonathan Dickinson to Isaac Gale, 6/11/1716, Letter Book, 1714–21, p. 85.

85 John Reynell to George Laurence, 3/29/1745, Letter Book, 1744–45; Cadwalader Evans to James Pemberton, 8/13/1748, PP, 5: 1; John Hunt and Isaac Greenleaf to James Pemberton 2/26/1748, PP, 4: 110.

86 Two Penny Tax for Philadelphia, 1754, HSP; List of Members, Philadelphia Monthly Meeting, 1759–62, DR: "A Directory of Friends in Philadelphia, 1757–1760," PMHB 16 (1892): 219–38.

87 List of Members, Philadelphia Monthly Meeting, 1773, DR; Constable Returns for the City of Philadelphia, 1775, Dept. of Archives, City Hall, Philadelphia; W. H. Egle, ed., *Proprietary, Supply, and State Tax Lists of the City and County of Philadelphia, For the Years 1769, 1774, 1779,* in *Pennsylvania Archives,* 3d ser. 14 (Harrisburg, Penn., 1897).

88 PP, 13: 149, and 29: 121; Register of Wills, no. 11, vol. T, pp. 18–22, and vol. X, pp. 267–82. Part of the discrepancy in wills and estimates of property and tax lists comes from the fact that property owned outside of the city would not be listed in the Philadelphia taxes. However, in 1760 James Pemberton possessed £4600 worth of city property. The total value of the wills of John Pemberton and John Reynell was impossible to determine since the figures were listed in both currency and sterling and no evaluation was given for lands or annuities. The figure of £10,000 probably underestimates the total property of each individual.

89 Quaker membership lists tend to be arranged by family and to span several generations. To determine from them who was living in an area at a given time would be extraordinarily difficult.

90 James T. Lemon, *The Best Poor Man's Country,* (Baltimore, 1972), pp. 19–22, 60–64, 189–92, 199. Prosperous Chester County farmers could have lived in greater conformity to the plain style than city Friends, but it is also possible that the compromises of the merchants are better known because of their prominence and the quantity of manuscripts concerning traders. I suspect that wealthy Friends in the country had far less riches than the Quaker grandees; however, a comparison of the tax list of Philadelphia in 1754 with that of Chester County in 1760 showed farmers to be far more prosperous than city dwellers. James Lemon and Gary Nash, "Distribution of Wealth in Eighteenth-Century America," *Journal of Social History* 2 (1968): 1–24.

91 Barclay, *Apology,* prop. 15, pp. viii, ix, 340, 343; Clarkson, *Portraiture of Quakerism,* 1: 24, 27, 33, 37–38.

92 John Kelsall, *A Testimony Against Gaming, Musick, Dancing, Singing, Swearing, and Peoples calling upon GOD to DAMN them* (London, 1682), broadside; Fox, *Journal,* p. 107; Hume, p. 28; Solomon Eccles, *A Musick-Lector* (London, 1667).

93 Clarkson, *Portraiture of Quakerism,* 1: 138–39, 141; Woolman, *Journal,* pp. 156–57.

94 Barclay, *Apology,* prop. 15, pg. viii, 341; London YM, *Epistles from the Yearly Meeting* (1720), p. 141; Clarkson, *Portraiture of Quakerism,* 1: 123–29.

95 Penn, *Works,* 1: 355, 388.

96 Smith Mss, 1: 131; Daniel Leeds, *News of a Trumpet Sounding in the Wilderness*

(New York, 1697), pp. 91–97; *PMHB,* 11 (1887): 157–59.

97 John Smith, "Diary," 4/28/1750, 6/31/1750, 7/27/1750, 8/2/1750.

98 *Charter to William Penn, and Laws of the Province of Pennsylvania,* p. 114; *Statutes at Large of Pennsylvania,* 2: 5, 186, 350, 489–90; *PMHB* 6 (1882): 322, and 20 (1896): 287, 298.

99 John Kelsall, "Diary Extracts," 2 (4/23/1721): 35–36 FH.; Woolman, *Journal,* p. 266.

100 Barclay, *Apology,* prop. 15, pp. ix, 342.

101 *PMHB* 15 (1891): 379; Elizabeth Drinker, *Extracts from the Journal of Elizabeth Drinker,* (Philadelphia, 1889), pp. 364, 366, 280; Tolles, *Meeting House and Counting House,* pp. 146–47.

102 Howard Brinton, "The Quaker Contribution to Higher Education in Colonial America," *Pennsylvania History* 25 (1958): 245–46.

103 John Churchman, *Journal,* in *Friends' Library,* eds. William Evans and Thomas Evans (Philadelphia, 1842) 6: 178–79; Drinker, *Extracts from the Journal,* p. 232. *BFHA* 19 (1940): 7–16. Isaac Norris I sent to England in 1722 for a landscape painting to decorate his house, and James Logan, Isaac Norris II and his wife, and Mary Lloyd Norris had their portraits painted.

104 John Galt, *The Life and Studies of Benjamin West* (London, 1816), pp. 51–56. For the dispute as to the reliability of this biography, see *PMHB* 33 (1909): 3, 375–77, 382, and 45 (1921): 306, and 50 (1926): 134.

105 Clarkson, *Portraiture of Quakerism,* 1: 365, 375, 300, and 2: 300–02; John Churchman, *Journal,* 6: 177; James Jenkins, "Records and Recollections," 1: 265, F.H.

106 Philadelphia YM, Discipline 1704–17. *BFHA* 19 (1930): 83.

107 John Rutty, *Spiritual Diary and Soliloquies* (London, 1796). John Smith, "Diary," vol. 2, 1/27/1745–46.

11 Conclusions

The paradoxical elements in Quaker thought and activities have often led to a misunderstanding of the Friends. They have been called Puritanical, mystical, evangelistic, quietistic, anti-intellectual, worldly, and complacent. American Friends were criticized for making a "dogma of the absence of dogma," which resulted in theological insecurity and an inability to adjust to new world conditions.[1] These labels ignore the complexity of the religion. Quakers could be intellectuals and yet anti-intellectual, social activists and mystics, evangelical and quietistic, complacent and insecure, intent on making money and anxious to avoid being wealthy, dogmatic and nontheological, tolerant and strict. Friends were a sect and a church, a chosen people and a mixed multitude.

The Society of Friends can be best understood as a product of, and a reaction to, English Puritanism. William Penn and Richard Baxter could have agreed upon ultimate goals: a purified church, the necessity of church discipline, the centrality of the quest for salvation, the need for doctrinal uniformity within the church, the fear of contamination by the worldly, and the desire for a disciplined life. The Friends were Calvinistic in aims while remaining anti-Calvinist in specific doctrines. Quakers often took particular Puritan doctrines and applied them in radical ways. Puritanism changed greatly between 1650 and 1770. The essential elements of Quakerism remained the same between the time of William Penn and that of John Woolman.

The central difference between early and eighteenth-century Friends was the growing realization that the truth would not sweep over the entire world. Quakers had to adjust to the fact that they were only a small sect. Since the survival of the meeting rested less upon converting others and more upon sons and daughters accepting the faith of their fathers, Quakers made the religious instruction of children a major preoccupation. In order to justify remaining within their meetings, Friends emphasized strongly the theological and ethical differences among themselves and other Protestant denominations. Quakers continued to believe that they alone possessed the true Christianity, and they insisted upon preserving intact the faith of the founders. The movement toward defining and maintaining Quaker orthodoxy began before 1700 and continued throughout the colonial period.

While there was never a Quaker character, there were types of behavior fostered by the religion. In general, Friends were a devout people. The faith demanded too much to command the loyalties of the indifferent. For the lukewarm it was easier to conform to the customs of the world in speech and fashion and to escape from the control of the meeting. Quaker worship was not exciting or colorful, and certainly there was as much prestige—if not more—attached to the Anglican church.

The religion heightened the tendency to superstition. At some point the supernatural joined the natural man, and Friends expected communications from God. When one is attuned to "feelings" as a guide to action, he is very likely susceptible to other manifestations of cosmic significance. The meetings opposed astrology, but in early Pennsylvania almanacs contained the signs of the zodiac and described the influences of the stars. Many Quaker journalists and influential members recorded dreams and interpreted events in light of them.

Nearly all visitors to Pennsylvania commented upon the Quakers' business acumen and hard work. Favorable viewers believed they were diligent, frugal, and honest in their callings. Opponents charged that Friends were shrewd, evasive, and covetous. These negative characteristics were usually ascribed to the merchant class, a powerful group but one which composed no more than 10 percent of the Society of Friends.

The Quakers' ideal of living required restraint and composure. The child learned patience, self-control, and moderation from early life. Attending a meeting for a two-hour period, during which silence was broken only by a prayer or sermon, must have instilled an ability to sit quietly and meditate.

Compared to New England Puritans, American Quakers were a benevolent people. Since they saw the divine potential in every man, they asserted that one must treat his neighbor as a Friend. Certainly their pacifism was a strong factor in leading them toward a humanitarian position. No matter what one believes about the justice of New Englanders toward the Indians, the fact remains that the Puritans fought two major wars within fifty years and repeatedly threatened the use of force. Until the conflicts between England and France spilled over into Pennsylvania some seventy years after the first settlements, the Friends used neither threats nor force to keep peace on the frontier. When fighting did come, Quakers vigorously debated whether to pay war taxes and strongly resisted making extermination of the Indians and expulsion of the French into holy causes. The Quakers' protest against slavery was the primary extension of their religious testimony in the eighteenth century. The concern of a few individuals became a general policy by obtaining the consent of the entire body of Friends. The meetings' opposition to slavery was arrived at only through a compassionate concern for the welfare of both the Negro and the slaveholder. Many Friends reacted very sensitively to the mistreatment of domestic animals or to killing for pleasure. Textbooks telling pupils not to torture a fly or prolong the agony of a worm when baiting a hook testify to the gentleness of Friends.

The Society of Friends was characterized by conservatism and moral harshness. One could be disowned as quickly for marrying a Presbyterian as for committing adultery. The concern for discipline was often so strong that monthly meetings did little besides oversee marriages and censure individuals. The stress upon peculiar customs allowed legality to overcome the spirit of the original protest.

The Society became ingrown. The early sectarian ideal of being a chosen people whose bond of unity was an experience of God was replaced by a policy of birthright membership. While the goal of evangelism toward outsiders never faded, the meeting became tribalistic. For social and business activities, Friends associated mainly with members of their own denomination. The education of children proceeded from the premise that exposure to the world resulted in contamination. Home, school, and meeting combined to mold the child into a virtuous person. A man became religious not only by the grace of God but from the force of habit. At the end of the seventeenth century, the dwindling number of outsiders joining the meeting prompted Friends to emphasize the family. Pious parents would guarantee the survival of the faith by implanting religious norms in the next generation.

Quaker beliefs about the functions of the family show an extraordinary continuity in the century preceding the American Revolution. The roles of husbands, wives, children, apprentices, and schools altered very little. In all periods the nuclear family had the primary role in the children's maintenance and in their religious and secular training but it shared responsibility with the school (if one were available) and the meeting (which often included kin). The changes that did occur indicate no consistent pattern of either decline or increased importance of the family. Differences in ideas and practices resulted partially from modifications within the meeting but mainly from the transformation of American and English society. After 1760, the Quaker emphasis upon the distinct personalities of infants suggests an increasing significance of family ties, particularly those involving mother and child. However, like other Americans in the late eighteenth century, Friends began to place more importance on schools and thereby reduced the time the child spent at home. The example of English Friends and post-Revolutionary sectarian isolation contributed to the impulse to create family-like boarding schools. The family retained a role in imparting occupational training. Boys and girls learned a vocation not in a classroom (though their education was in a broad sense utilitarian) but by apprenticeship or by helping in the home or on their fathers' farm or in his trade. Seventeenth-century Friends, by demanding religious unity, cautioning against marriage contracts or mercenary matches, and bestowing upon young people a veto over any proposed match, weakened parental power over matrimony. Eighteenth-century marriage narratives show that some Friends married for religious unity, some for dowries, and some for love. In the middle and upper classes a romantic, sentimental view of courtship prevailed. The meeting continued to insist upon religious unity and parental consent, but the number of disownments shows that acquiescence was far from universal. Romantic marriage need not have resulted in any great change in the relationship between husband and wife, since early Quakers assumed that godly love bound a man and women in holy wedlock. In the colonial period a Quaker wife experienced neither a pronounced rise nor a decline in status. She enjoyed spiritual equality in the meeting, had more freedom than the law prescribed, and acquiesced in her position as a member of the weaker sex.

An attempt to assess the impact of Quakerism upon colonial America is fraught with difficulty. Friends originated some elements in American life and strengthened attitudes that others arrived at independently. Because of their numerical weakness, Quaker influence was dependent upon other peoples' acceptance of their ideas. The Friends either were or rapidly became a minority wherever they lived. Unlike Puritan New England, there is no area that could be labeled as distinctively Quaker. Eastern Pennsylvania and western New Jersey came closest, but even there it would be impossible to determine what was a product of Quakerism and what came from other Protestant churches.

Religious toleration stands as the Friends' primary political contribution.

Pennsylvania served as a testing ground to prove that separation of church and state and religious diversity did not lead to governmental weakness. The Quaker tenet of pacifism, though never becoming a dominant characteristic of Americans, has remained a persistent practice of dissent. Friends' attitudes toward work and wealth certainly served to strengthen those elements in American thought that were later termed the "Puritan or Protestant ethic." Conversely, John Woolman symbolizes the long tradition of American thinkers who vigorously denounced a pervasive materialism. Abolitionist sentiments rested upon Quaker and English evangelical origins. In the nineteenth century Friends, along with other Protestants, became involved in a whole spectrum of reforms ranging from women's rights to temperance.

Many American attitudes concerning religion are far closer to those of the Quakers than to those of the Puritans. American churches have long remained dogmatic while refusing to be theological. The Friends denigrated systematic theology and refused to view the exposition of their beliefs as theology. Many American sects have accepted the political implications of toleration while refusing to deny their monopoly of truth. The Friends advocated toleration but refused to concede that this belief required non-denominationalism, the belief that all approaches to Christianity are equally valid. Most often Quaker religious and social attitudes served to reinforce the same ideas held by the Puritans. Both groups were characterized by a great deal of moral rigidity, and both assumed that a true church could not envelop all men as members.

Historians are fond of discussing the Puritan impact upon American life, but they almost never comment upon Quaker influences. The recent revival of interest in American Puritanism has not led to a complete reexamination of the Friends. Perhaps this neglect results from the failure of Friends to become one of the main-line denominations or to found prominent universities. The Friends did not become "the American church" because they refused to jettison the doctrines and practices that had made them distinctive. If the criterion for the success of a denomination is numerical, then the Quakers can be found wanting. If the measure of a church is the preservation of what the members hold most holy, the Quakers can be judged at least partially successful. The sect did survive, and it did manage to preserve much of the original witness. The endurance of the Society of Friends in a world hostile or apathetic to Quaker beliefs is a testimonial to the Quaker family's accomplishment in inculcating those beliefs in succeeding generations.

Notes

1 Daniel J. Boorstin, *The Americans: The Colonial Experience* (New York, 1964), p. 69.

Appendices

APPENDIX A An Account of all the Yearly, Quarterly, Monthly, and Particular Meetings of Friends in America, 1772, MS, QC

Rhode Island (New England) Yearly Meeting
13 monthly meetings
47 particular meetings
Flushing (New York) Yearly Meeting
4 monthly meetings
20 particular meetings
Pennsylvania and New Jersey Yearly Meeting
35 monthly meetings
103 particular meetings
Maryland Yearly Meeting
4 monthly meetings
20 particular meetings
Virginia Yearly Meeting
5 monthly meetings
26 particular meetings
North Carolina Yearly Meetings
7 monthly meetings
23 particular meetings

APPENDIX B Unity of Thought in Eighteenth-Century Quakerism: A Note on Sources

The three sources most important to understanding the established position of the meeting on theological and ethical matters are epistles, disciplines, and printed pamphlets. The epistles from the yearly meetings discussed religion in practical terms, giving advice on rearing children, controlling servants, educating youth, getting married, and conducting business. They contained much repetition and quoting of each other's advice, and once a counsel was included, it reappeared at frequent intervals. Matters not discussed in the epistles were not very important in the religious life of Friends. Regardless of where the epistles originated there was little or no variation in their content. These epistles are an authoritative source concerning Quaker beliefs on most religious and social questions.

The official statement of the yearly meeting's position on most "concerns" was contained in the disciplines and compilations of advices. The disciplines (documents usually drawn up at one time but composed of the decisions of previous meetings) served as a constitution. They prescribed the proper procedures to follow in marriage, in dress, in giving to the poor, in disownment, and in appealing a decision. The first book used as a discipline in the colonies was a collection of epistles and sermons that George Fox delivered in 1672 in Newport. Formal disciplines were drawn up by Philadelphia in 1704 and 1719, New England in 1708, and London in 1738.[1] The "Christian and Brotherly Advices" were assemblages of what the yearly meeting had said about significant problems over the years. For example, the book might list what the discipline, the epistles, or the yearly meeting had concluded about education in 1690, 1719, 1760, and 1778. Volumes of the discipline and advices were owned by monthly, quarterly, and yearly meetings, and often yearly meetings possessed copies of those of both London and Philadelphia. Throughout the colonial period these books existed only in manuscript form. London Yearly Meeting printed its revised discipline in 1783; and, typical of the consecutive course of Quaker meetings, New England published one in 1785, Pennsylvania and New Jersey in 1799, New York in 1800, and Maryland in 1806.

In theory the overseers of the press examined every manuscript written by a Friend before publication. A group of men from Philadelphia Monthly Meeting supervised the press there until 1709 when a committee appointed by the Yearly Meeting replaced it. In England the Morning Meeting of Ministers and Elders in London read manuscripts, and New England Yearly Meeting appointed special committees for this task. After the Keithan schism, Philadelphia exercised strict control of the only press in Pennsylvania and in 1705 rebuked Jacob Taylor for not having submitted his almanac for perusal.[2] There are no extant minutes of the committee in Philadelphia that reviewed books, but the records of the Morning Meeting in London show that generally only those books on religious subjects were read. The committee could decide to print the manuscript at the meeting's expense or it might tell the author to pay to have it published. The committee could recommend circulation in manuscript, advise publication under the author's name but separately from the Society of Friends, or refuse to let the work appear at all.[3] Failure to abide by the committee's determination was a disownable offense.

The diary of John Smith of Burlington contained a full description of how a tract was published. When Gilbert Tennent's sermon on the lawfulness of war appeared in print on January 1, 1747, Smith read it and decided to write an answer. He spent the next few days composing his tract. When it was completed, he gave the manuscript to Israel Pemberton, Jr., who read it, approved, and suggested a few additions. Smith agreed to the changes and rewrote his answer to Tennent. He then sent his manuscript to the overseers of the press. Later he allowed Friends in the assembly in New Jersey, and John Kinsey, clerk of yearly meeting and speaker in the Pennsylvania assembly, to see it. When Kinsey returned it, Smith and the overseers of the press went over the manuscript again. The committee asked that the pamphlet be published in an edition of 1,000 copies, 500 to be sold and 500 to be given away. Exactly thirty days after Tennent's sermon was printed, Smith's answer was published and distributed.[4]

From the beginning of their religious movement, Friends insisted on a wide dissemination of their tracts in order to make converts and to counteract pamphlets written against them. London Yearly Meeting as early as 1672 resolved to send two copies of each book it published to every quarterly and monthly meeting, and this regulation, reenacted in 1695, remained standard procedure throughout the eighteenth century.[5] In 1690 Philadelphia Yearly Meeting asked for six copies of every book printed by Friends in England. In 1691 Philadelphia Yearly Meeting decided to print 200 copies of every book it approved and to send copies to each monthly meeting. In an effort to keep each other informed of controversies, Philadelphia and London Yearly Meetings agreed in 1702 to send each other copies of every book defending or critical of Friends.[6] This policy, which may have been neglected occasionally during the first half of the century, was renewed in 1757. What was done with these books when they reached America is unknown, but probably the committees in charge of the press read them. Each meeting gave permission for the other to reprint anything of use.

English Friends sent many books and tracts overseas as a means of propagating Quaker beliefs. The assembly in Virginia complained about the spread of such literature as early as 1660. Before 1700 London Meeting for Sufferings sent shipments of books, some of which were gifts and others paid for by the recipients, to Friends in New England, Maryland, Pennsylvania, and New Jersey. In 1700, for example, New England received 250 books of thirty-four varieties while Maryland got 900. The Yearly Meeting in London in 1701 sent a catalogue of all Quaker books in existence to Friends in Rhode Island and Maryland to aid them in deciding what to buy. In 1721 London shipped 126 books of six kinds to Charlestown, South Carolina.[7] Virginia in 1704, North Carolina in 1707, Rhode Island in 1713, and Maryland in 1715 all received books. London generally regarded its role as that of supplier for new or weak meetings. In 1733 eighty-five books went to Connecticut; in 1744 seventy-three books went to Cape Fear, and in 1745, 113 books were sent to South Carolina. After 1750 English Friends increased the number of their shipments of many kinds of books to all the colonies. In 1758 the London Meeting for Sufferings authorized the sending of over 900 tracts by such esteemed Quakers as William Penn, Robert Barclay, Stephen Crisp, Benjamin Holme, and Robert Claridge; most of these books went to Virginia, Maryland, and North Carolina.[8] Books in "High and Low Dutch" were given to Pennsylvania and New England. After 1750, Philadelphia Yearly Meeting began to send books to meetings elsewhere in America and by the time of the Revolution was sending almost as many as London.

While printings of the folio volumes of the collected works of famous Friends usually occurred only in England, American Quakers printed and purchased an impressive number of books. Pennsylvania had a press by 1685 and Newport by 1727. The number of copies of a tract varied considerably, depending upon whether it was given away, sold for a few pennies, or delivered by subscription. In 1691 Philadelphia Yearly Meeting's standard edition was 200 copies; in 1718 the meeting authorized printing 1,500 cautions against pride and giving each family a copy. By 1759 tracts could be issued in editions as small as 500 or as large as 4,000 copies. New England Quakers, sometimes passed over in discussions of eighteenth-century Friends, printed books in editions of 1,000 copies or more and purchased 1,600 copies of a popular work like Job Scott's *Journal.* In 1728 Rhode Island Quakers subscribed to 500 copies of Robert Barclay's *Apology,* a volume of 500 pages costing 16s. per copy. In 1774 New England Yearly Meeting ordered 600 more copies of the *Apology.* Friends in New England, New York, North Carolina, and Pennsylvania purchased or were given copies of Fox's *Journal* and *Doctrinals* and Penn's *Works,* which were printed in England.[9] Because of the frequent sending of epistles, disciplines, and tracts and the close relationship between Friends in England and America in the eighteenth century, books written in England can be used as sources for Quaker thought everywhere.

Notes to Appendix B

1 Ancient Epistles, Minutes, and Advices, or Discipline, New England YM Archives, John Carter Brown Library; Min. Rhode Island MM, 1/28/1682, p. 22. At the beginning of the North Carolina Yearly Meeting minutes, a statement is found indicating that the meeting revised the discipline made "by the yearly meeting of 1704." Since no North Carolina discipline of that date has been found, this may refer to the Philadelphia discipline. The volumes containing "Christian and Brotherly Advices" are sometimes labeled "Early Meeting Advices" or "Yearly Meeting Advices." The first term has been used in footnotes to refer to these books.

2 Min. Philadelphia MM, 2 (8/26/1705): 6. In 1687 the meeting condemned Daniel Leeds's almanac for certain expressions deemed derogatory to Friends.

3 Arnold Lloyd, *Quaker Social History* (London, 1950), p. 151; Luella Wright, *Literary Life of the Early Friends,* (New York, 1932) pp. 97–109.

4 John Smith, *Diary,* 4 (11/1/1747–11/30/1747); Smith Mss, 3: 17, 19, LC. For Smith's editing of Thomas Chalkley's *Journal,* see Smith's "Diary," 11/5–8/1745. For the controversy in the editing of Job Scott's *Journal* in 1797, see Edmund Prior to Moses Brown 3/7/1797 and 4/14/1797, and Brown's answer of 4/21/1797, Austin Collection, Moses Brown Papers.

5 Min. London YM, 1 (3/30/1672): 3; London YM, Christian and Brotherly Advices (1695), p. 27, and (1697), p. 28.

6 Min. Philadelphia YM, 7/19/1690, pp. 23–26, and 7/15/1695; London YM, Epistles Sent 1: 339–40; Min. London Morning Meeting, 3 (6/21/1704): 182, and (11/29/1704): 192. In 1691 Philadelphia distributed books as follows: Bucks 16, Philadelphia 64, Chester 30, New Castle 10, Shrewsberry 20, Falls 15, Burlington 20, Gloucester 10, Salem 15. I am indebted to Willman Spawn for this information.

7 London YM, Epistles Sent, 1: 343, 369, 373; Min. Charlestown MM, 11/3/1721. The minutes of the London Meeting for Sufferings show that few books were sent between 1715 and 1730, at least as compared with other decades. The books listed above are a small sample of the total number sent to America.

8 Min. London Meeting for Sufferings, 25 (12/22/1733): 356, and 27 (4/15/1744 and 4/21/1745): 430–37, 524, 530, and 30 (7/16/1756 and 11/15/1758): 10–11, 244–45. The books sent to a newly begun meeting at Cape Fear included George Fox, *Epistles,* Robert Barclay, *Apology* and *Catechism,* William Penn, *No Cross, No Crown* and *Rise and Progress of the People Called Quakers,* plus works by Crooks, Pugh, Jeffry, Crisp, and Pyott.

9 Min. Philadelphia MM, 9/28/1718; Min. Philadelphia Meeting for Sufferings, 11/15/1759; Min. New England YM, pp. 118, 131, 151, 160, 183, 211, 222, 305; Moses Brown to James Pemberton, 4/5/1797, Moses Brown Papers, Austin Collection, no. 13, New England Yearly Meeting Archives; Moses Brown Papers, Letters, pp. 728, 746, 762, 801, 927, Rhode Island Historical Society; Min. North Carolina YM, 1 (10/26–28/1764): 84, Guilford College; George Brooks, *Friend Anthony Benezet* (Philadelphia, 1937), pp. 236–37, 267, 282. London Yearly Meeting in 1700 had 7,000 copies of Barclay's *Apology* printed in English and 1,500 in French. London YM, Epistles Sent, 1: 362–63.

APPENDIX C An Account of Ministering Friends from Europe Who Visited America, 1656–1842, MS, QC, and from Pennsylvania and New Jersey who went to England and Ireland, 1693–1844, MS, QC

EUROPE TO AMERICA		AMERICA TO EUROPE	
1651–1660	7	1693–1700	4
1661–1670	13	1701–1710	6
1671–1680	21	1711–1720	4
1681–1690	7	1721–1730	5
1691–1700	23	1731–1740	7
1701–1710	10	1741–1750	9
1711–1720	12	1751–1760	13
1721–1730	11	1761–1770	4
1731–1740	16	1771–1780	4
1741–1750	7	1781–1790	11
1751–1760	16	1791–1800	22
1761–1770	11		
1771–1780	4		
1781–1790	5		
1791–1800	8		
Total	171	Total	89

APPENDIX D Returns of the Number of Deaths of Quaker Ministers as Recorded in London Yearly Meeting, Minutes 1690–1789, vols. 1–20, and as Compiled by Charles Hoyland

LONDON YM DATA

Year	Average Deaths Per Year	Number of Men	Percentage of Men
1690–1694	14.4	*	*
1695–1699	15.8		
1700–1704	24.2		
1705–1709	22.2		
1710–1714	24.4	17.6	72
1715–1719	29	20.6	73
1720–1724	33	21.4	65
1725–1729	27.6	18	65
1730–1734	29.6	18.6	63
1735–1739	23.4	15.8	63
1740–1744	28.8	17.4	60
1745–1749	22.6	13.6	60
1750–1754	22.6	11.6	51
1755–1759	23.2	12.8	55
1760–1764	23	12.6	55
1765–1769	18.8	9.2	49
1770–1774	22.2	11.6	52
1775–1779	15.4	7	46
1780–1784	16.8	8.6	51
1785–1789	14	7	50

CHARLES HOYLAND DATA

Years	Men	Women	Total
1700–1709	144	43	187
1710–1719	192	73	265
1720–1729	205	108	313
1730–1739	159	88	247
1740–1749	155	102	257
1750–1759	116	102	218
1760–1769	123	95	218
1770–1779	80	95	188
1780–1789	80	73	153
1790–1799	51	55	106
1800–1809	47	47	94
1810–1819	33	61	94

*During the early years certain quarterly meetings recorded the number rather than the names of deceased ministers.

*APPENDIX E Number of Ministers in Philadelphia Yearly Meeting**

1680–1689	5
1690–1699	4*+18*
1700–1709	6
1710–1719	7**+24*
1720–1729	31
1730–1739	32*+6*
1740–1749	43
1750–1759	38
1760–1762	12
1762–1763	no data available
1764–1769	28
1770–1779	65

*Figures for the period until 1762 are derived from John Smith, *Lives of Ministers Among Friends,* 3 vols., MS, QC. In 1764 Philadelphia Yearly Meeting began to record the deaths of ministers. Minutes, vol. 2, 1764–79.

Bibliography

The historian of Quakers is fortunate in having a number of valuable bibliographic aids. Joseph Smith's *Descriptive Catalogue of Friends' Books* (London, 1859), *Supplement to a Descriptive Catalogue of Friends' Books* (London, 1893) and *Bibliotheca anti-quakeriana* (London, 1873) list all editions of books written by or against Friends. While Smith's information was more complete for England than for America, the Quaker libraries at Haverford, Swarthmore, and Friends' House, London, have records of additional materials. Practically every book listed in Smith can be found at one of these libraries. Excellent annotated bibliographies for American Quakers are provided in Frederick Tolles, *Meeting House and Counting House* (Chapel Hill, North Carolina, 1948) and Sydney V. James, *A People Among Peoples: Quaker Benevolence in Eighteenth-Century America* (Cambridge, Massachusetts, 1963). Tolles concentrates on the Philadelphia Friends while James provides information about the various types of meeting records and includes all the colonies. *The Guide to the Manuscript Collections of the Historical Society of Pennsylvania,* 2d ed. (Philadelphia, 1949) and Norman Wilkinson, ed., *Bibliography of Pennsylvania History* (Harrisburg, 1957) are valuable guides to the primary and secondary materials available. *Quaker History* lists articles about Friends appearing in other periodicals or books.

MANUSCRIPTS

Historical Society of Pennsylvania (including Mss owned by the Library Company of Philadelphia)

Account of Servants Bound and Assigned before James Hamilton, Mayor of Philadelphia, 1745–46.
Barber, Rhoda. Journal, 1726–82.
Barnard, Richard. Diary, 1774–91.
Cresson, John Elliott. Diary, 1795–96.
Coates, Samuel. Cyphering Book, 1724.
Dickinson, Jonathan. Letterbook, 1698–1701. Maria Dickinson Logan Family Papers.
______. Letterbook, 1715–21. Logan Papers.
Dillwyn Papers, vol. 1.
Drinker, Elizabeth. Diary.
Dyers, _____. Journal, 1763–1805.
Indentures of Apprentices, 1677–1849.
James, Abel. Diary, 1766–68.
Logan, James. Letterbooks and Correspondence. Logan Papers.
Logan, Maria Dickinson. Family Papers.
Mifflin, Thomas. Abridgement of Metaphysics.
Morris, Deborah. Account Book, 1759–86.
______. Papers. Coates-Reynell Papers.
Morris, Susanna. Travels, 1729–54.
Norris, Isaac. Letterbook, 1735–55. Logan Papers.
Norris, Isaac of Fairhill. Papers. Letterbook, 1730–52. Family Letters, vols. 1–2. Student newspapers and school books from Penn Charter School. Norris Papers.
Oxley, Joseph. Joseph's Offering to his Children.
Pastorius, Francis Daniel. Papers.
Pemberton Papers.
Pemberton Papers. Etting Collection.

Pennsylvania Chronicle. January 1767-August 1770.
Philadelphia Two Penny Tax, 1754.
Powel, Samuel. Notebook, 1757. Powel Papers.
Proud, Robert. Collection.
Reynell, John. Letterbooks and Correspondence. Coates-Reynell Papers.
Roberts, Jonathan. Memoirs.
Smith, John. Diary and Correspondence. John Jay Smith.
Transcript of the Fifteenth Eighteen Penny Provincial Tax Assessed 13 March 1772 for Philadelphia City and County.
Willis, Robert. Journal, 1770–89.

Quaker Collection, Haverford College

Allinson Family Papers.
An Account of all the Yearly, Quarterly, Monthly, and Particular Meetings of Friends in America, 1772.
An Account of Ministering Friends from Europe who Visited America, 1656–1843.
Book of Meetings, ca. 1763.
Cooper, David. Diary.
Churchman, George. Journal, 1759–88.
Farmer, John. Autobiography.
Howland, Guliema M. Collection.
Letters of America Friends.
New England Yearly Meeting. Discipline, 1708–38.
New England Yearly Meeting. Discipline, 1760.
Overseers of Penn Charter School. Minutes.
Morris-Sansom Papers.
Pemberton Papers.
Smith, John. Lives of the Ministers of the Gospel among the People called Quakers.
Wilkinson. Elizabeth. Journal of a Religious Visit to Friends in America, 1761–63.
Whitall, Ann Cooper. Diary, 1760–62.

Friends' Historical Library, Swarthmore College

Abington Monthly Meeting, Extracts of Minutes, 1682–1746.
Biddle Manuscripts.
Buckingham Monthly Meeting. Extracts of Minutes, 1720–63.
Bucks Quarterly Meeting. Extracts of Minutes, 1684–1805.
Burlington Monthly Meeting. Births and Deaths, 1682–1800.
______. Certificates of Removal, 1675–1749.
______. Marriages, 1680–1728.
Burlington Quarterly Meeting. Extracts of Minutes, 1686–1770.
Cecil (Maryland) Monthly Meeting. Marriages, 1698–1784.
Cedar Creek (Virginia) Monthly Meeting. Minutes, ·1739–73.
Concord Monthly Meeting. Minutes, 1684–1795.
Falls Monthly Meeting. Minutes, 1683–1730.
______. Marriages, 1704–1843.
Ferris Manuscripts.
Greenwich (Rhode Island) Monthly Meeting. Births, Deaths, Marriages, 1704–1883.
Goshen Monthly Meeting. Minutes, 1722–36.
Haddonfield Monthly Meeting. Marriages, 1686–1836.
Perquimans (North Carolina) Monthly Meeting. Minutes, 1734–74.
Philadelphia Monthly Meeting. Minutes, 1682–1771.
______. Marriages, 1682–1779.
Philadelphia Yearly Meeting. Minutes, 1681–1779.
Rich Square (North Carolina) Monthly Meeting. Marriages, 1760–1826.
Rhode Island Monthly Meeting. Births, 1683–1812. Marriages, 1643–1888.
______. Minutes, 1676–1773.

Philadelphia Yearly Meeting, Departments of Records

Bradford Monthly Meeting. Miscellaneous Papers, 1760–69.
Charlestown (South Carolina) Monthly Meeting, Minutes, 1719–59.
Philadelphia Monthly Meeting. Original Certificates, 1686–1729.
———. Membership Role, 1759–62.
———. List of Members, 1773.
Philadelphia Yearly Meeting. A Collection of Christian and Brotherly Advices Given forth, from Time to Time by the Yearly Meeting of Friends for Pennsylvania and New Jersey, 1682–1777.
———. Discipline, 1704.
———. Discipline, 1719.
———. Discipline, 1747.
Scattergood, Thomas. Notebooks.

Quaker Collection, Guilford College, North Carolina

Coresound Monthly Meeting. Minutes, 1733–91.
London Yearly Meeting. Book of Discipline, 1768.
North Carolina Yearly Meeting. Minutes, 1704–93.
———. Minutes of Standing Committee, 1757–1832.
Symons Creek (Pasquotank) Monthly Meeting. Minutes, 1699–1785.
Symons Creek Women's Meeting. Minutes, 1717–68.

Archives of New England Yearly Meeting, at the John Carter Brown Library, Providence, Rhode Island

Antient Epistles, Minutes and Advices, or Discipline, 1672–1735.
Brown, Moses. Papers. Austin Collection.
East Greenwich Monthly Meeting. Marriage Certificates, Births and Deaths, 1708–1883.
East Greenwich Women's Meeting. Minutes, 1704–90.
New England Women's Yearly Meeting. Minutes, 1764–76.
New England Yearly Meeting. Minutes, 1683–1787.
New England Yearly Meeting. Minutes and Extracts about the Yearly Meeting School which was opened on 2d. day the 8th of 11th Mo. 1784. Austin Collection.
New England Yearly Meeting for Ministers and Elders. Minutes, 1707–97.
Pembroke Monthly Meeting. Minutes, 1702–1741, 1801–1830.
———. Births, Deaths, Marriages, 1676–1876.
Pembroke Quarterly Meeting. Minutes, 1686–1780.
Rhode Island Women's Quarterly Meeting. Minutes, 1706–83.
Salem (Massachusetts) Monthly Meeting. Minutes, 1676–1778.
———. Marriage Certificates 1683–1800.
Scott, Job. Some Brief Remarks on the Nature of Salvation by Christ. Moses Brown Papers. Austin Collection.

Friends' Reference Library, Friends' House, London, England

Ackworth Reports, 1780–1826.
Jenkins, James. The Records, and Recollections of James Jenkins Respecting himself, and others from 1761 to 1821 being a period of sixty years with Additions tending to illustrate the whole. Typewritten transcript, compiled by Mildred Campbell.
Jermym, Emily. Transcripts of the Swarthmore Manuscripts.
Kelsall, John. Diary.
London Yearly Meeting. Christian and Brotherly Advices Given Forth from time to time by the Yearly Meetings in London.
———. Epistles Sent, 1682–1738.
———. Epistles Received, 1683–1758.
———. Minutes, 1668–1773.
London Yearly Meeting of Ministers and Elders. Minutes, 1757–66.

London Morning Meeting. Minutes, 1692–1734.
London Meeting for Sufferings. Minutes, 1675–1783.
Nuttall, Geoffrey F. Early Quaker Letters from the Swarthmore Mss to 1660 Calendared, Indexed, and Annotated. 1952.
Southwark Monthly Meeting. List of Members, 1737, 1762, 1782, 1795.
______. Miscellaneous Manuscripts.

Newport Historical Society

Redwood, Abraham. Letterbooks 1–4.
Rhode Island Monthly Meeting. Marriages, 1648–1776.
Richardson, Thomas. Letterbook, 1715–19.
Rotch, William. Account of Nantucket During the Revolution, 1814.

Rhode Island Historical Society

Brown, Moses. Papers, vols. 1–4. Miscellaneous Mss.
Rhode Island Historical Society Manuscripts, Boxes 1–7, 13.
______. Bound Volumes 1, 2, 5, 6, 8, 9–13.
______. Broadsides, 1721–70.

Chester County Historical Society

Brinton, John H. Notes and Reminiscences of Chester County.
Budd, Rebecca. Diary of Weston School.
Hawley, Benjamin. Diary, 1761–63.

Miscellaneous

Clerkenwell School. Minute Book, 1721–31. Friends' School, Saffron Walden, England.
Constable Returns of the City of Philadelphia, 1775. Department of Archives, City Hall, Philadelphia.
Diary, 1752–1754 (once attributed to Thomas Butts). Duke University.
Flushing Monthly, Quarterly, and Yearly Meetings, vol. 1, 1671–1703. New York Yearly Meeting Archives.
Hutton, Richard. Commonplace Book. Friends' School. Saffron Walden, England.
Newport Mercury, nos. 1–222. John Carter Brown Library.
Peckover, Edmond. Journal, May 6, 1742–April 5, 1743. New York Public Library.
Register of Wills, City Hall Annex, Philadelphia.
Shoemaker, Samuel. Diary, November 7, 1783–October 5, 1785. New York Historical Society.
Thompson, James. Papers, 1775–93. Duke University.
Westtown Archives. Boxes 1–3. Westtown, Pennsylvania.

PUBLISHED PRIMARY SOURCES

Adam, Simon. *Concerning the Observation of the First Day to be Kept above any Other Day, which is the Worlds old Idol, wherein they satisfie their Lusts in Pride and Idleness.* 1663.
Adams, John. *Diary and Autobiography of John Adams. The Adams Papers.* Edited by L. H. Butterfield. Vols. 1 and 2. Cambridge, Mass., 1961.
An Account of the Rise, Progress, and Present State, of the School and Work-house Maintain'd by the People Called Quakers at Clerkenwell. London, 1746.
An Address To Those who have the Care of Children. Also, The Universal Rule of Equity. Philadelphia, 1819.
Advice to ______ on his Quitting Friends School and Workhouse at Clerkenwell. London, 1780?
Antrobus, Benjamin. *Some Buds and Blossoms of Piety, Also, Some Fruit of the Spirit of Love, Which Directs to Divine Wisdom.* London, 1684.
Arscot, Alexander. *Some Considerations Relating to the Present State of the Christian Religion, Wherein the Nature, End and Design of Christianity, as well as the Principal Evidence of*

the Truth of it, are explained and recommended out of the Holy Scripture; with a general appeal to The experience of all Men for Confirmation thereof. Philadelphia, 1752.
Banks, John. *A Journal of the Life, Labours, Travels, and Sufferings (In and for the Gospel,) of that Ancient Servant, and Faithful Minister of Jesus Christ, John Banks, With a Collection of his Epistles, and Papers.* London, 1712.
———. *A Rebuke to Unfaithful Parents and a Rod for Stubborn Children.* London, 1749.
Barclay, David. *Advice to Servants.* n.d.
Barclay, Robert. *An Apology for the True Christian Divinity, as the Same is Held Forth and Preached by the People, in Scorn, Called Quakers.* 13th ed. Manchester, England, 1869.
———. *The Antient Testimony of the People called Quakers, Reviv'd.* Philadelphia, 1723.
———. *A Catechism and Confession of Faith, Approved.* Philadelphia, 1726.
———. *Truth Triumphant, through the Spiritual Warfare, Christian labours, and writings of . . . Robert Barclay. To which is prefixed, an account of his life and writings. . . .* From the octavo edition of 1718, collated with the folio edition of 1692. Philadelphia, 1831.
———; Penington, Isaac; and Penn, William. *A Treatise on Church Discipline, taken, principally, from the writings of Robert Barclay, William Penn, and Isaac Penington.* Compiled by Job Scott. New Bedford, 1805.
Baxter, Richard. *One Sheet Against the Quakers.* London, 1657.
Bellers, John. *To the Criminals in Prison.* n.d.
Benezet, Anthony. *A First Book for Children.* Philadelphia, 1779.
———. *The Pennsylvania Spelling Book.* Philadelphia, 1779.
———. *Remarks on the Nature and Bad Effects of Spirituous Liquors.* n.d.
———. *Some Serious and Awful Considerations, Recommended to all, particularly to the Youth in a Representation of the Uncertainty of a Death-Bed Repentence.* Philadelphia, 1769.
Bevans, John. *A Brief View of the Doctrines of the Christian Religion.* Philadelphia, 1810.
Biddle, Owen. *A Plan for a School On an Establishment similar to that at Ackworth.* Philadelphia, 1790.
Bockett, Richard, Jr. *Fruits of Early Piety, Consisting of Several Christian Experiences, Meditations and Admonitions.* London, 1722.
The Books of Discipline Agreed on by the Yearly Meeting of Friends for New-England. Providence, 1785.
Bowles, George. *A Tender Exhortation, In the Love of Christ, To the Youth Amongst the People called Quakers.* London, 1720.
Bownas, Samuel. *A Description of the Qualifications Necessary to a Gospel Minister.* London, 1750.
Brief Memorials of the Virtuous Lives, and dying Sayings of Several of the People called Quakers, particularly Young Persons. Extracted from eight volumes, entitled *Piety Promoted.* London, 1781.
Budd, Thomas. *Good Order Established in Pennsilvania and New Jersey in America.* Philadelphia, 1685.
Bugg, Francis. *De Christiana Libertate, Or Liberty of Conscience Upon It's true and proper grounds Asserted & Vindicated. And the Mischief of Impositions amongst the People called Quakers, Made Manifest.* London, 1682.
———. *The Pilgrim's Progress, from Quakerism to Christianity.* London, 1698.
———. *Seventy Queries to Seventy Quakers.* London, 1698.
Burnaby, Andrew. *Burnaby's Travels Through North America.* New York, 1904.
Burnyeat, John. *An Epistle from John Burnyeat to Friends in Pensilvania.* Philadelphia, 1686.
Caton, William. *An Abridgement of Eusebius Pamphilius' Ecclesiastical History.* London, 1698.
Chalkley, Thomas. *The Works of Thomas Chalkley.* London, 1791.
Chastellux, Marquis de. *Travels in North America in the Years 1780, 1781, and 1782.* Translated by Howard C. Rice, Jr. Chapel Hill, N.C., 1963.
Chateaubriand. *Voyage en Amérique.* Edited by Richard Switzer. Vol. 1. Paris, 1964.
Claridge, Richard. *Carmen Spirituale: or Christian Counsel to Youth.* London, 1716.
———. *The Life and Posthumous Works of Richard Claridge, Being Memoirs and Manuscripts Relating to His Experiences and Progress in Religion: His Changes in Opinion, and Reasons for them. With Essays in Defence of several Principles and Practices of the People call'd Quakers.* Edited by Joseph Besse. London, 1726.
Clark, Joseph. *A Collection of Religious Tracts, Recommended to the Serious Attention of Mankind Generally, Particularly the Youth.* Philadelphia, 1804.
Clarkson, Thomas. *A Portraiture of Quakerism, as taken from a View of the Moral Education,*

Discipline, Peculiar Customs, Religious Principles, Political and Civil Economy, and Character of the Society of Friends. 3 vols. (Vol. 1, 2d ed., vols. 2 and 3, 3rd ed.) London, 1806–07.

Claypoole, James. *James Claypoole's Letter Book: London and Philadelphia 1681–1684.* Edited by Marion Balderston. The Huntington Library, San Marino, Calif., 1967.

Coar, Thomas. *An Essay Towards an English Grammar for Ackworth School.* York, England, 1800.

A Collection of Memorials Concerning Divers Deceased Ministers and others of the People called Quakers, in Pennsylvania, New-Jersey, and Parts adjacent, from nearly the first Settlement thereof the Year 1787. Philadelphia, 1787.

The Concurrence & Unanimity of the People Called Quakers in Owning and Asserting the Principal Doctrines of the Christian Religion. London, 1694.

Coole, Benjamin. *Miscellanies, or Sundry Discourses Concerning Trade, Conversation, and Religion: Being the Advice of a Father, to his Children, on those Subjects.* London, 1712.

Correspondence Between William Penn and James Logan, And Others. 1700–50. Edited by Edward Armstrong. Notes, Mrs. Deborah Logan. Memoirs of the Historical Society of Pennsylvania, vols. 9 and 10. Philadelphia, 1870, 1872.

Cotton, John. *Spiritual Milk for Boston Babes in Either England.* Cambridge, Mass., 1656.

Crèvecoeur, J. Hector St. John. *Letters from an American Farmer.* New York, 1904.

Crisp. Stephen. *A New Book for Children to Learn In.* London, 1706.

———. *A Short History of a Long Travel, from Babylon to Bethel.* London, 1777.

Crook, John. *The Design of Christianity, Testified in the Books, Epistles and Manuscripts, of that Ancient Faithful Servant of Christ Jesus, John Crook.* London, 1701.

Cross, Paul. *Some Tender Advise, of a Sober Youth.* London, 1704.

Dalton, John. *Elements of English Grammar: Or a New System of Grammatical Instruction, for the Use of Schools and Academies.* London, 1801.

Darby, Abiah. *An Exhortation in Christian Love, To All Who Frequent Horse-Racing, Cock-Fighting, Throwing at Cocks, Gaming, Plays, Dancing, Musical Entertainments, or Any other Vain Diversions.* Shrewsbury, England, 1769.

———. *Useful Instruction for Children, by Way of Question and Answer.* London, 1763.

Dickinson, Jonathan. *A Brief Illustration and Confirmation of the Divine Right of Infant Baptism; In a plain and familiar Dialogue Between a Minister and one of his Parishioners.* Providence, 1763.

———. *God's Protecting Providence, Man's Surest Help and Defence, In Times of the Greatest Difficulty, and Most Eminent Danger.* London, 1700.

Dilworth, Thomas. *A New Guide to the English Tongue.* Philadelphia, 1770.

———. *The Schoolmasters Assistant: Being a Compendium of Arithmetic, Both Practical and Theoretical.* Philadelphia, 1781.

Discipline of the Yearly Meeting of Friends. Baltimore, 1806.

Dover, William. *Reasons for Erecting an Additional Number of Schools, For the Better Education of Youth in Learning and Virtue, and for giving Greater Encouragement to Well Qualified Masters and Mistresses to Conduct the Same.* London, 1752.

Drinker, Elizabeth. *Extracts from the Journal of Elizabeth Drinker.* Edited by Henry Biddle. Philadelphia, 1889.

Early Christian Instruction, in the form of a Dialogue between a Mother and a Child, written at the Desire of the Society of Friends. London, 1807.

"Early Minutes of Philadelphia Monthly Meeting of Friends, 1682–1775," *Publications of the Genealogical Society of Pennsylvania* 1–2, 4, 6–15 (1898–1945).

Eccles, Solomon. *A Musick-Lector, or the Art of Musick (that is so much vindicated in Christendome) Discoursed of, by way of Dialogue between three men of several Judgments.* London, 1667.

Edwards, Christopher. *A Tender Salutation of Love Unto all the Young-Convinced.* London, 1674.

Edmundson, William. *A Journal of the Life, Travels, Suffering, and Labour of Love in the Work of the Ministry, of that Worthy Elder, and Faithful Servant of Jesus Christ, William Edmundson.* Dublin, 1715.

———. *An Epistle Containing Wholesome Advice and Councel to all Friends, Grounded upon Antient Examples, Recorded in Scriptures of Truth.* 1701.

Eliot Papers. Edited by Eliot Howard. London, 1895.

Ellwood, Thomas. *A Collection of Poems on Various Subjects.* London, 1700.

Elson, Mary. *A Tender and Christian Testimony to Young People and others, whom it may concern in this present day, who walk with us under Profession of the blessed Truth.* 1685.

Epistles from the Yearly Meeting of the People called Quakers, Held in London To the Quarterly and Monthly Meetings in Great Britain, Ireland, and Elsewhere, From the Year 1675, to 1759, inclusive. London, 1760.

Evans, Joshua. *A Journal of Joshua Evans.* Byberry, Pa. 1837.

Extracts from the Minutes and Advices of the Yearly Meeting of Friends Held in London. London, 1783.

Ferris, David. *Memoirs of the Life of David Ferris, An Approved Minister of the Society of Friends.* Philadelphia, 1825.

Field, John, and Scoryer, Richard. *Friendly Advice in the Spirit of Love Unto Believing Parents, And Their tender Off-Spring in Relation to their Christian Education.* London, 1688.

Forster, Josiah. *A Quaker's Reasons for Opening his Shop on that called Christmas-Day.* London, 1780.

Fothergill, John, *A letter to a friend in the Country, Relative to the Intended School, at Ackworth, in Yorkshire.* London, 1779.

———, ed. *A Short Account of the Several Books of the New Testament, from Dr. Percy's Key. For the Use of Ackworth-School.* London, 1780.

Fothergill, Samuel. *Memoirs of Samuel Fothergill.* Edited by George Crosfield. New York, 1845.

———. *The Prayer of Agur, Illustrated in a Funeral Discourse: and the Advantages resulting from An Early and steadfast piety.* Newport, 1773.

———. *A Sermon Publicly Delivered at a Meeting of People Called Quakers.* Newport, 1773.

———. *Two Discourses and a Prayer, Publickly Delivered on Sunday the 17th and Tuesday the 19th Days of May, 1767, at the Quakers Yearly Meeting, at the Fryers, in Bristol.* New York, 1768.

Fox, George. *A Collection of Many Select and Christian Epistles, Letters and Testimonies. Written on sundry Occasions, by that Ancient, Eminent, Faithful Friend and Minister of Christ Jesus, George Fox.* Vol. 2. London, 1698.

———. *Gospel Family Order, Being a Short Discourse Concerning the Ordering of Families, Both of Whites, Blacks, and Indians.* Philadelphia, 1701.

———. *Instructions for Right-Spelling, and Plain Directions for Reading and Writing True English.* Philadelphia, 1702.

———. *Journal.* Edited by Rufus Jones. New York, 1963.

———. *The Works of George Fox.* Vols. 3–8. Philadelphia, 1831.

———; Stubbs, John; and Furly, Benjamin. *A Battle-Door for Teachers & Professors to Learn Singular & Plural.* London, 1669.

Fox, George the Younger. *A Collection of the Several Books and Writings, given forth by that Faithful Servant of God and his People, George Fox, the Younger.* London, 1662.

Franklin, Benjamin. *The Autobiography and Other Writings.* Edited by L. J. Lemisch. New York, 1961.

Freame, John. *Scripture Instruction; Digested into Several Sections, By Way of Question and Answer. In Order to Promote Piety and Virtue, and Discourage Vice and Immorality.* London, 1713.

———, and Purver, Anthony. *Counsel to Friends' Children on Education.* London, 1799.

Friends' Library comprising journals, doctrinal treatises and other writings of the members of the religious Society of Friends. Edited by William Evans and Thomas Evans. 14 vols. 1837–50.

Friends' Miscellany. Edited by John Comly and Isaac Comly. Vols. 1-12. 1831–59.

Fry, John. *An Essay on Conduct and Education.* London, 1738.

Fuller, Samuel. *Some Principles and Precepts of the Christian Religion.* Leeds, England, 1737.

Gawler, Francis, and Watkins, Morgan. *The Children of Abraham's Faith, Who are Blessed, Being found in Abraham's Practice of Burying their Dead in their own Purchased Burying-Places, Are not to be Reproved; But therein are justified in the sight of God, and the practice of Holy Men in former Ages.* 1663.

George, Staughton; Nead, Benjamin M.; and McCamant, Thomas, eds. *Charter to William Penn, and Laws of the Province of Pennsylvania, Passed between the Years 1682 and 1700, Preceded by the Duke of York's Laws in Force from the Year 1676 to the Year 1682, With an Appendix.* Harrisburg, Penn., 1879.

Gough, James, and Gough, John. *A Practical Grammar of the English Tongue.* 1764.

———. *Memoirs or The Life, Religious Experiences, and Labours in the Gospel, of James Gough, Late of the City of Dublin, deceased.* Compiled by John Gough. 1802.

Gough, John. *Practical Arithmetick in Four Books.* London, 1773.

Gratton, John. *A Journal of the Life of That Ancient Servant of Christ, John Gratton.* London, 1720.

Greenway, Robert. *Short Sentences, worthy of Serious Consideration, and a Good Application. Being the Meditations of R. G. when at Sea.* March 9, 1678–79.

Greenwood, James. *An Essay Towards a Practical English Grammar.* London, 1753.

Griffith, John. *A Journal of the Life, Travels, and Labours in the Work of the Ministry, of John Griffith.* Philadelphia, 1780.

______. *Some Brief Remarks upon Sundry Important Subjects, Necessary to be Understood and Attended to By all Professing the Christian Religion.* London, 1764.

Griscom, John. *Considerations Relative to an Establishment for Perfecting the Education of Young Men Within the Society of Friends.* New York, 1815.

Grubb, Sarah. *Some Account of the Life and Religious Labours of Sarah Grubb.* With an Appendix Containing an Account of Ackworth School, Observations on Christian Discipline, and Extracts from Many of Her Letters. Dublin, 1792.

______. *Some Remarks on Christian Discipline, as it Respects the Education of Youth.* London, 1798.

Gwin, Thomas. *A Memorial of Anne Gwin. A Prudent and Virtuous Maiden, who departed this Life, at Falmouth, the 15th Day of the 2nd month, called April, 1715, in the 23rd year of her age.* London, 1715.

______. *A Salutation of Love, To Those who are Entered as a Spiritual Travel; with Cautions against Sundry Dangers which may attend them in the Way.* London, 1713.

______. *The Will and Testament of Thomas Gwin, of Falmouth; Being some Religious and Serious Considerations, which He recommends to his Children and Friends, and such as may remain after his Decease.* London, n.d.

Hack, Maria. *First Lessons in English Grammar, Adapted to the Capacities of Children, from Six to Ten Years Old.* London, 1813.

Hall, David. *Some Brief Memoirs of the Life of David Hall; with an Account of the Life of his Father John Hall.* To which are added Divers of his Epistles to Friends, on various Occasions. London, 1758.

______. *An Epistle to Friends in Great-Britain, or elsewhere, containing Advice and Consolation, particularly address'd to those who are under Tribulation.* London, 1754.

______. *An Essay on Intemperance, Particularly Hard-Drinking.* 1742.

Hannah Logan's Courtship. Edited by Albert Cook Myers. Philadelphia, 1904.

Hamilton, Alexander. *Gentleman's Progress: The Itinerarium of Dr. Alexander Hamilton, 1744.* Edited by Carl Bridenbaugh. Chapel Hill, N.C., 1948.

Hands, John. *A Seasonable Epistle to Believing Parents, and their Children.* 1705.

Harrison, George. *Education Respectfully Proposed and Recommended, As the Surest Means, within the Power of Government, To Diminish the Frequency of Crimes.* London, 1810.

______. *Practical Advice to Housekeepers, And Others who may be in Straitened Circumstances.* London, n.d.

______. *Some Remarks Relative to the Present State of Education, in the Society of the People Called Quakers.* London, 1802.

Hartshorne, Richard, et al. *A Further Account of New Jersey, In an Abstract of Letters Lately Writ from Thence.* 1676.

Hatt, Francis. *Friendly Advice to Children and All Mankind in General, Professors and others, of what Name or Country soever.* London[?], 1765.

Hayes, Alice. *A Legacy, or Widow's Mite; Left by Alice Hayes, To Her Children and others. With an Account of Some of Her Dying Sayings.* London, 1723.

Hayler, James. *Observations and Remarks on the Present Mode of Apprenticing out poor Children and on Unprotected and Unprovided for Situations of Many Poor in this Nation: Pointing out the Defects therein, with Plans annexed for remedying them.* London, 1794.

Hazard, Thomas. *Nailer Tom's Diary, Otherwise the Journal of Thomas B. Hazard of Kingstown Rhode Island 1778–1840.* Edited by Caroline Hazard. Boston, 1930.

Hepburn, John. *The American Defence of the Christian Golden Rule, or an Essay to Prove the Unlawfulness of Making Slaves of Men.* Philadelphia, 1714?

Hewetson, Isaac. *Reading Made Easy; or, A Step in the Ladder to Learning: Whereby, the Young Student Is led gradually on, from the easiest Words, To Those of Two and Three Syllables.* London, 1800.

Hill, Hannah. *A Legacy For Children, Being some of the Last Expressions, and Dying Sayings of Hannah Hill, Junr.* Philadelphia, 1717.

Hill, Richard. *Letters of Doctor Richard Hill and His Children: Or, The History of a Family.* Philadelphia, 1854.

Holme, Benjamin. *An Epistle of Tender Counsel to Parents, School-Masters, and School-Mistresses; and Likewise to the Youth.* London, 1749.

How, Samuel. *The Sufficiency of the Spirit's Teaching Without Humane Learning: or a Treatise Tending to prove Human Learning to be No Help to the Spiritual Understanding of the Word of God.* Wilmington, Del. 1763.

Hull, Henry. *An Address to the Youth of the Society of Friends, In Great Britain and Ireland, Especially Those who Attended the Yearly Meeting in London, in 1812.* New York, 1812.

Hume, Sophia. *An Exhortation to the Inhabitants of the Province of South-Carolina, To bring their Deeds to the Light of Christ, in their own Consciences.* Bristol, England, 1751.

"Sophia Hume's Answers to the Queries." "Relics of the Past, No. 20." *The Friend* 17 (6th mo. 8. 1844): 295.

Hunt, Samuel. *Instructions for Children and Others: By Way of Question and Answer. Demonstrating to them, How they may come to know God and Jesus Christ, whom to know is Life Eternal.* London, 1711.

Hunter, Robert. *Quebec to Canada in 1785–1786: Being the Travel Diary of Robert Hunter, Jr., A Young Merchant of London.* Edited by Louis B. Wright and Marion Tinling. San Marino, California, 1943.

Incestuous Marriage, or Relations of Consanguinity and Affinity hindering and dissolving Marriage, as making all Marriages within such Relations to be Incestuous, and all Children begotten of such Marriages to be Illegitimate, or Bastards to all intents and purposes. London, 1677/78.

Jacob, Elizabeth. *An Epistle in True Love Containing, A Farewell Exhortation to Friends Families.* London, 1719.

Jaffary, Alexander. *Diary of Alexander Jaffary . . . To Which are Added, Particulars of His Subsequent Life, Given in Connexion with Memoirs of the Rise, Progress, and Persecutions, of the People Called Quakers, In the North of Scotland.* London, 1834.

Jones, George. *Observations on plainness, and simplicity in conduct and conversations,* n.d.

Kalm, Peter. *Peter Kalm's Travels in North America: The America of 1750.* 2 vols. Translated by Adolph B. Benson. New York, 1937.

Keith, George, trans. *An Account of the Oriental Philosophy, Shewing the Wisdom of some Renowned Men of the East; and particularly, the profound Wisdom of Hai Ebn Yokdan, both in Natural and Divine things.* 1674.

———. *The Deism of William Penn, and his Brethren, Destructive to the Christian Religion, Exposed and plainly laid open.* London, 1699.

———. *A Journal of Travels from New-Hampshire to Caratuck on the Continent of North-America.* London, 1706.

———. *Immediate Revelation, (or Jesus Christ the Eternal Son of God).* 2d ed. London, 1675.

———. *The Presbyterian and Independent Visible Churches in New-England and else-where Brought to the Test, and Examined According to the Doctrine of the Holy Scriptures, in their Doctrine, Ministry, Worship, Constitution, Government, Sacraments and Sabbath-Day.* Philadelphia, 1689.

———. *A Refutation of Three Opposers of Truth, by plain Evidence of the Holy Scriptures, viz.* I. *Of Pardon Tillinghast, who pleadeth for Water Baptism . . . II. Of B. Keech, in his Book called, Tutor for Children . . . III. Of Cotton Mather, . . . in his Appendix to his Book, called Memorable Providences, relating to Witchcrafts, &c.* Philadelphia, 1690.

———. *A Serious Appeal to all the more Sober, Impartial & Judicious People in New-England . . . Whether Cotton Mather in his late Address, &c. hath not extremely failed in proving the People call'd Quakers guilty of manifold Heresies, Blasphemies and Strong Delusions.* Philadelphia, 1692.

———. *Some of the Fundamental Truths of Christianity . . . by way of Question and Answer.* Philadelphia, 1692.

———. *Truth Advanced in the Correction of Many Gross & hurtful Errors; Wherein is occasionally opened & explained many great and peculiar Mysteries and Doctrines of the Christian Religion.* New York, 1694.

———. *The Way to the City of God Described, or A Plain Declaration . . .* including *"The Way to Discern the Convictions, Motions, &c. of the Spirit of God, and Divine Principle in us, from those of a man's own Natural Reason, &c.*" London[?], 1678.

Kelsall, John. *A Testimony Against Gaming, Musick, Dancing, Singing, Swearing, and Peoples calling upon God to Damn them.* London, n.d.

Kendall, John. *Remarks on the Prevailing Custom of Attending Stage Entertainments; Also on the Present Taste for Reading Romances and Novels; and on Some Other Customs.* London, 1796.

———. *Some Principles and Precepts of the Christian Religion Explained, By Way of Question and Answer, For the Use of Children.* London, 1785.

Kersey, Jesse. *A Narrative of the Early Life, Travels, and Gospel Labours of Jesse Kersey, Late of Chester County, Pennsylvania.* Philadelphia, 1851.

Lawrence, Thomas. *The Streight Gate and Narrow Way, Manifest in Seven Treatises.* ca. 1673.

———, and Fox, George. *Concerning Marriage: A Letter Sent to G. F. And with it, A Copy of an Answer to a Friend's Letter Concerning marriage.* And some Queries, and his Reply to the answer and Queries, and an additional to G. F.'s Reply, containing 13 Queries, concerning Marriage; Also the manner how the parties intending Marriage are to go together. Published . . . by the consent and advice of Friends, 1663.

Lawson, Thomas. *Dagon's Fall Before the Ark. Or, The Smoak of the Bottomless Pit scoured away, by the breath of the Lord's mouth, and by the brightness of his coming.* London, 1679.

———. *A Mite into the Treasury, Being a Word to Artists, especially to Heptetechnists, the Professors of the Seven Liberal Arts, so called, Grammar, Logick, Rheterick, Musick, Arithmetick, Geometry, Astronomy.* London, 1680.

———. *A Serious Remembrancer to Live Well, Written Primarily to Children and Young People, Secondarily to Parents, Useful (I hope) for All.* London, 1684.

Leadbeater, Mary. *Extracts and Original Anecdotes; for the Improvement of Youth.* Dublin, 1794.

———. *Annals of Ballitore. Leadbeater Papers.* London, 1862.

———. *Memoirs and Letters of Richard and Elizabeth Shackleton, Late of Ballitore, Ireland.* London, 1822.

Leaming, Aaron, and Spicer, Jacob, ed. *The Grants, Concessions, and Original Constitutions of the Province of New Jersey. The Acts Passed during the Proprietary Governments, and other material Transactions before the Surrender thereof to Queen Anne.* Somerville, N.J., 1881.

Leeds, Daniel. *News of a Trumpet Sounding in the Wilderness.* New York, 1697.

Leslie, Charles. *The Snake in the Grass: or, Satan Transform'd into an Angel of Light* in *The Theological Works of the Reverend Mr. Charles Leslie.* London, 1721. Pp. 1–172.

Lessons for Youth Selected for the Use of Ackworth and Other Schools. London, 1795.

Letchwork, Thomas. *Discourse As Delivered at a Meeting (Supposed at Canterbury) of the People called Quakers, In the Year 1768.* Cork, 1776.

Lingard, Richard. *A Letter of Advice to a Young Gentleman Leaving the University Concerning His Behavior and Conversation in the World.* New York, 1696.

Loughton, William. *A Practical Grammar of the English Tongue: Or a Rational and Easy Introduction to Speaking and Writing English Correctly and Properly.* London, 1740.

Love, John. *An Epistle to all Young Convinced Friends, Whom the Lord hath reached by His mighty Power, and separated from the World, and turned their Hearts, so as to forsake Father, and Mother, Wife, and Children, for his Name sake.* London, 1696.

Lucas, Margaret. *An Account of the Convincement and Call to the Ministry of Margaret Lucas.* London, 1797.

Lumpkin, William, ed. *Baptist Confessions of Faith.* Chicago, 1959.

Marriage-Portion Fund. London, 1797.

Marshall, Christopher. *Extracts from the Diary of Christopher Marshall, Kept in Philadelphia and Lancaster, During the American Revolution 1774–1781.* Edited by William Duane. Albany, 1877.

Martin, Joseph. *Remarks on a Poem, Intitled, The Fair Quakers. In a Conference between Hilary and Theophilus.* London, 1714.

Massey, William. *Musa Paraenetica; or a Tractate of Christian Epistles, on Sundry Occasions, in Verse.* London, 1746.

———. *Instructions for a Boarding-School.* n.d.

Mather, William. *The Young Man's Companion: Or, Arithmetick made Easy.* London, 1723.

Maule, Thomas. *An Abstract of a Letter to Cotton Mather, of Boston in New-England.* New York, 1701.

———. *New-England's Present Sufferings under their Cruel Neighbouring Indians.* London, 1675.

[———?] *Tribute to Caesar, How paid by the Best Christians, and to What Purpose. With Some Remarks on the Late Vigorous Expedition Against Canada.* Philadelphia, 1712?

———. *Truth held Forth and Maintained According to the Testimony of the holy Prophets, Christ and his Apostles recorded in the holy Scriptures.* New York, 1695.

Mirando, Francisco de. *The New Democracy in America: Travels of Francisco de Mirando in the United States, 1783–1784.* Translated by Judson P. Wood, and edited by John S. Ezell. Norman, Okla., n.d.

Miscellanies, Moral and Instructive, in Prose and Verse; Collected from Various Authors, For the Use of Schools, and Improvement of Young People of both Sexes. Philadelphia, 1787.

Mitchell, J. T., and Flanders, S., eds. *Statutes at Large of Pennsylvania, 1700–1759.* Vols. 2–5. Harrisburg, Penn., 1896–1908.

Mitchell, Mary. *A Short Account of the Early Part of the Life of Mary Mitchell, Late of Nantucket, Deceased.* New Bedford, 1812.

Mittelberger, Gottlieb. *Journey to Pennsylvania.* Edited by Oscar Handlin, and translated by John Clive. Cambridge, Mass., 1960.

Moon, John. *Observations and Quotations on obtaining Church-Membership by a Natural Birth and Education; with some Remarks on a Part of our Discipline: Being an Address to the People Called Quakers.* Stokesley, England, 1815.

———. *A Second Address to the People Called Quakers; containing some further Quotations and Expostulations.* Stokesley, England, 1815.

Morris, Margaret. *Margaret Morris: Her Journal with Biographical Sketch and Notes.* Edited by John W. Jackson. Philadelphia, 1949.

Morton, John Latimer. *A Letter to a Friend, Concerning the School at Ackworth, in Yorkshire.* London, 1782.

Mott, Abigail. *Observations on the Importance of Female Education and Maternal Instruction; with their Beneficial Influence on Society.* York, England, 1825.

Mott, James. *Observations on the Education of Children: and Hints to Young People on the Duties of Civil Life.* New York, 1816.

Muchlow, William. *The Spirit of the Hat: Or, the Government of the Quakers Among Themselves, As it hath been Exercised of late years by George Fox, and other Leading-Men, in their Monday, or Second-days Meeting at Devonshire-House, brought to Light.* London, 1673.

Muhlenburg, Henry Melchior. *Journals of Henry Melchior Muhlenburg.* Translated by Theodore Tappert and John Doberstein. 3 vols. Philadelphia, 1943.

Mulliner, John. *A Testimony Against Periwigs and Periwig-Making, and Playing on Instruments of Musick among Christians, or any other in the days of the Gospel.* 1677.

Murray, Lindley. *A Compendium of Religious Faith and Practice Designed for Young Persons of the Society of Friends.* York, England, 1815.

———. *English Exercises Adapted to Murray's English Grammar.* Philadelphia, 1800.

———. *The English Reader: or, Pieces in Prose and Poetry, Selected from the Best Writers, Designed to Assist Young Persons to Read with Propriety and Effect; To Improve their Language and Sentiments; And to Inculcate Some of the Most Important Principles of Piety and Virtue.* Philadelphia, 1803.

———. *Introduction to the English Reader.* Philadelphia, 1814.

Narratives of Early Pennsylvania West New Jersey and Delaware. Original Narratives of Early American History. Edited by Albert Cook Myers. General Editor, J. Franklin Jameson. New York, 1912.

New England Meeting for Suffering. *From the Meeting for Sufferings for New-England, to the several Quarterly and Monthly-Meetings belonging to the Yearly Meeting.* Providence, 1782.

News from Pensilvania: Or a Brief Narrative of Several Remarkable Passages in the Government of the Quakers, In that Province. Touching their Proceedings in their Pretended Courts of Justice; their Way of Trade and Commerce; with Remarks and Observations upon the whole. London, 1703.

Nixon, Barnaby. *Extracts from the Manuscript Writings of Barnaby Nixon, Deceased.* Richmond, Va., 1814.

Norris, Isaac. *Friendly Advice to the Inhabitants of Pensilvania.* Philadelphia, 1710.

Pastorius, Francis Daniel. *A New Primer or Methodical Directions to Attain the True Spelling, Reading and Writing of English. Whereto are added, some things Necessary and Useful both for the Young of the Province, and Likewise For Those, Who from Foreign Countries and Nations Come to Settled Amongst Us.* New York, 1698.

Payne, Isaac. *Outlines of a Plan of Education.* London, 1805.

Penington, Isaac. *Letters of Isaac Penington.* Compiled by John Barclay. London, 1828.

______. *Selections from the Works of Isaac Penington.* New Bedford, 1818.

______. *The Works of Isaac Penington, A Minister of the Gospel in the Society of Friends.* Vols. 2, 4. Sherwoods, N.Y., 1837?

Penn, William. *Collection of the Works of William Penn.* 2 vols. London, 1726.

______. *A Further Account of the Province of Pennsylvania and Its Improvements.* London, 1685.

______. *A Letter from William Penn to His Wife and Children.* London, 1761.

______, et al. *Gospel-Times, Or Oaths Forbidden Under the Gospel.* Philadelphia, 1712.

Phipps, Joseph. *To the Young of Norwich Meeting.* 1775.

Portsmouth, Henry. *An Essay on the Simplicity of Truth; Being an Attempt to Ascertain the Use and Extent of Discipline, in the Church of Christ; to which is added a Postscript on Tithes.* Particularly Addressed to the People Called Quakers; by Catholicus, A Peaceable member of that Society. London, 1779.

Prittle Prattle or a Familiar Discourse on the Persons I, Thou, He or She, We, Ye or You, and They. London, 1752.

Proud, Robert. *The History of Pennsylvania in North America, from the Original Institution and Settlement of that Province, under the first Proprietor and Governor William Penn, in 1681, till after the Year 1742.* 2 vols. Philadelphia, 1797–98.

The Provincial Bounty or a Plan for the Encouragement for Female Servants, Who have lived three Years in Friends' Families, In the Province of and have Preserved good Characters. Dublin, 1781.

Pugh, Ellis. *A Salutation to the Britains.* Philadelphia, 1727.

Purver, Anthony. *Counsel to Friends' Children.* London, 1801.

A Quaker Post-Bag: Letters to Sir John Rodes of Barlbrough Hall, in the County of Derby, Baronet, and to John Gratton of Monyash, 1693–1742. Compiled by Mrs. Godfry Locker Lampson. London, 1910.

Rack, Edmund. *Mentor's Letters, Addressed to Youth.* Bath, England, 1778.

Rawes, William, Jr., comp. *Examples for Youth in Remarkable Instances of Early Piety.* London, 1797.

"Record of Indentures of Individuals Bound Out as Apprentices, Servants, Etc. and of German and Other Redemptioners in the Office of the Mayor of the City of Philadelphia, October 3, 1771-October 5, 1773." *Proceedings and Addresses of the Pennsylvania-German Society* 16 (1905): 1–325.

Reed, H.C. and Miller, G.J., eds. *The Burlington Court Book.* Washington, D.C., 1944.

Rees, Charlotte. *Parental Instruction in Familiar Dialogues: Intended Principally for Children of the Society of Friends.* Bristol, England, 1811.

Rigge, Ambrose. *A Brief and Serious Warning to such as are Concerned in Commerce and Trading, who go under the Profession of Truth, to Keep within the Bounds thereof, in Righteousness, Justice and Honesty towards all men.* 1678.

______. *A Scripture Catechism for Children.* London, 1702.

______. *A Faithful Testimony Against Extravagant and Unnecessary Wiggs.* London, 1699.

Robinson, Ann. *An Epistle of Tender Caution and Advise to Friends Especially the Youth.* London, 1751.

Rules and Orders for the Government of Friends School and Workhouse at Clerkenwell. London, 1780.

Rules for the Government of Ackworth School, Established for the Education of Children Who are Members of the Society and Whose Parents are not in Affluent Circumstances. London, 1790.

Rules of Discipline of the Religious Society of Friends with Advices: Being Extracts from the Minutes and Epistles of their Yearly Meeting, Held in London, From Its First Institution. London, 1834.

Rules of Discipline and Christian Advices, of the Yearly Meeting of Friends for the State of New-York and Parts Adjacent. New York, 1800.

Rules of Discipline and Christian Advices of the Yearly Meeting of Friends for Pennsylvania and New Jersey. Philadelphia, 1797.

Rutty, John. *Spiritual Diary and Soliloquies.* London, 1796.

St. Méry, Moreau de. *Moreau de St. Méry's American Journey, 1793–1798.* Translated and edited by Kenneth and Anna M. Roberts. Garden City, N.Y. 1947.

Salt, William. *The Light, the Way, that Children ought to be trained up in, wherein the Holy Men of God Walked.* London, 1660.

Sanford, Peleg. *The Letter Book of Peleg Sanford of Newport, Merchant (later Governor of Rhode Island) 1666–1668.* Transcribed by Howard Preston. Providence, 1938.

Savery, William. *A Journal of the Life, Travels, and Religious Labours of William Savery.* Compiled by Jonathan Evans. Philadelphia, n.d.

Scott, Job. *Journal of the Life, Travels and Gospel Labours of that Faithful Servant and Minister of Christ Job Scott.* New York, 1797.

A Seasonable Account of the Christian and Dying-Words, of Some Young Men; Fit for the Considerations of All: But Especially of the Youth of This Generation . . . Published For Instruction and Caution to the Youth Among Friends, called Quakers. Philadelphia, 1700.

Sewall, Samuel. *Diary.* Edited by Mark Van Doren. New York, 1963.

Shewen, William. *A Brief Testimony Against Tale-Bearers, Whisperers, and Back-Biters, Shewing That where they are given ear unto amongst Friends, Neighbours, and Relations, or in any Christian Society, such can never Live in Peace, Concord and Unity.* Philadelphia, 1701.

Simpson, William. *Going Naked a Sign.* London, 1660.

Sleigh, Joseph. *Good Advice and Counsel Given forth by Joseph Sleigh of the City of Dublin, In the Time of his Sickness, to his Children.* London, 1696.

Smith, Frederick. *On the Duty of a Wife.* London, 1810.

______. *A Letter to Parents and Others Who Have the Care of Youth in the Society of Friends.* London, 1806.

______. *A Letter to the Children and Youth of the Society of Friends.* London, 1806.

Smith, Humphrey. *To All Parents of Children upon the Face of the whole Earth.* London, 1660.

Smith, William. *Balm from Gilead. A Collection of the Living Divine Testimonies. Written by the Faithful Servant of the Lord, William Smith.* 1675.

Some Advice to Teachers, Particularly Recommended to the Attentive Perusal of Governors and Governesses of Boarding Schools. Dublin, 1794.

A Spelling Book For the Use of Ackworth School. London, 1790.

Stanton, Daniel. *A Journal of the Life, Travels, and Gospel Labours of a Faithful Minister of Jesus Christ, Daniel Stanton.* Philadelphia, 1772.

Stidston, George. *An Epistle of Love to Friends, Especially to the Youth, By Way of Tender Advice and Caution.* London, 1717.

Stiles, Ezra. *Extracts from the Itineraries and other Miscellanies of Ezra Stiles, D.D., LL.D., 1755–1794 with a Selection from his Correspondence.* New Haven, Conn., 1916.

Story, Thomas. *A Journal of the Life of Thomas Story: Containing, an Account of his Remarkable Convincement of, and Embracing the Principles of Truth, as held by the People called Quakers; and also, of his Travels and Labours in the Service of the Gospel: with many other occurrences and Observations.* Newcastle, England, 1747.

______. *Sermons on the following Subjects: I. Salvation by Christ; and the Universality of it asserted. II. Nature and Necessity, with the Benefit and advantage of Silence considered.* Leeds, England, 1739.

Sutcliff, Robert. *Travels in Some Parts of North America, In the Years 1804, 1805, and 1806.* York, England, 1815.

Tatham, Joseph. *Rules and Instructions, For the Regular Management of the Seminary, Kept by Joseph Tatham, Leeds.* Leeds, England, 1806.

Taylor, Christopher. *Institutiones Pietatis, In quibus Saluberrima vitae Praecepta, et alias res notatu dignissimae, continetur. Primum a G. F. et E. H. Anglice editae, nunc autem in usum Christianae Juventutis Scholasticae Latine redditae, &c. Instructions of Godliness. . . .* 1676.

______. *Compendium Trium Linguarum Latinae, Graecae, & Hebraicae, In usum Studiosae & Christianae Juventutis, Brevi & Facili Methodo dispositum & exhibitum. A Compendium or Abridgement of Three Languages The Latin, Greek, and Hebrew, Couched and exhibited in a short and easie Method, For the use of the Studious and Christian youth.* London, 1679.

______, et al. *A Testimony to the Lord's Power and Blessed Appearance In and Amongst Children: wherein is expressed the great Love of God to them, who, as Young and Tender, have Tasted for his Good Word and Heavenly Life.* 1679.

Taylor, Jacob. *An Almanack for the Year 1705, 1706, 1707, 1709, 1711, 1712, 1713, 1719, 1720, 1723, 1726, 1737, 1738, 1739, 1740, 1741, 1742, 1743, 1744, 1745, 1746.* Philadelphia, 1704–46.

Taylor, Thomas. *A Few Necessary Questions and Conclusions for Present Parish Teachers,* 1670.

______. *Truth's Innocency and Simplicity Shining Through the Conversion, Gospel-Ministry, La-*

bours, Epistles of Love, Testimonies and Warnings to Professors and Profane, (with the Long and Patient Sufferings) of that Ancient and Faithful Minister and Servant of Jesus Christ, Thomas Taylor, Who finish's his Course in the Year MDCLXXXI. London, 1697.

The Testimony and Caution to such as do make Profession of Truth, Who are in Scorn called Quakers, and more especially such who profess to be Ministers of the Gospel of Peace, That they should not be Concerned in Worldly Government. Philadelphia, 1693.

Tompkins, Anthony, and Needham, R. *A Few Words of Counsel and Advice to All the Sons and Daughters of Men; More Especially to the Children of Believers, from the Motion of Gods Spirit upon my Heart, in the Love of God that they may come to lead the course of their Lives in this World; so as to lay down their Heads in Peace with the Lord, when time in this World shall be no more.* London, 1687.

Thompson, William. *The Care of Parents, Is a Happiness to Children: or the Duty of Parents to their Children, and of Children to their Parents.* London, 1710.

______. *The Child's Guide to the English Tongue: Or, A New Spelling-Book.* London, 1711.

______. *Some Fruits of Solitude: In Reflections and Maxims Relating to the Conduct of Humane Life.* London, 1705.

Thomson, Thomas. *A Salutation of Love to Friends and their Children.* 1704.

Trafford, Rebeckah. *A Brief Account of the Innocent Example, and Pious Sayings of Rebeckah Toovey, Aged Nine Years, Recommended unto Children for their serious Perusal.* London, 1715.

Wagstaffe, John. *An Elegy Written in a Quakers Burial Ground to which is added the Country Quaker.* London, 1764.

Wakefield, Priscilla. *Reflections on the Present Condition of the Female Sex; with Suggestions for Its Improvement.* London, 1798.

Walker, Williston. *The Creeds and Platforms of Congregationalism.* Boston, 1960.

Ward, Samuel. *Correspondence of Governor Samuel Ward, May 1775-March 1776 . . . and Genealogy of the Ward Family.* Rhode Island Historical Society. Providence, 1952.

Waring, Mary. *A Diary of the Religious Experience of Mary Waring.* London, 1805.

Watson, John. *An Alarming Portraiture of the Pernicious Effects of the Customary Use of Distilled Spirituous Liquors.* Philadelphia, 1813.

West, Moses. *A Treatise Concerning Marriage, Wherein the Unlawfulness of Mixt-Marriages is laid open from the Scriptures of Truth.* London, 1726.

Wigham, John. *Christian Instruction in a Discourse as Between a Mother and her Daughter.* London, 1815.

Willsford, John. *A Brief Exhortation to All Who Profess the Truth, To Come Clear Out of Babylon, and not to Joyn with any Hurtful or Unseemly Practice, Nor Make Marriages with Unbelievers, but be a Separate People from Every Unclear Thing, that God may receive you.* Philadelphia, 1691.

Wilson, Rachel. *A Discourse, Delivered on Saturday The 10th Day of August 1769.* New York, 1769.

Wister, Sally. *Sally Wister's Journal.* Edited by Albert C. Myers. Philadelphia, 1902.

Woolman, John. *A First Book for Children.* Philadelphia, 1774.

______. *The Journal and Essays of John Woolman.* Edited by Amelia M. Gummere. New York, 1922.

SECONDARY SOURCES

Adamson, J. W. "The Extent of Literacy in England in the Fifteenth and Sixteenth Centuries: Notes and Conjectures," *The Library,* 4th Ser., 10 (1930): 163–93.

Aries, Philippe. *Centuries of Childhood.* Translated by Robert Baldick. New York, 1962.

Arnold, Samuel Greene. *History of the State of Rhode Island and Providence Plantation.* 2 vols. Providence, 1894.

Bailyn, Bernard. *Education in the Forming of American Society.* Chapel Hill, N. C., 1960.

Barbour, Hugh. *The Quakers in Puritan England.* New Haven, Conn., 1964.

Barclay, Robert. *Inner Life of the Religious Societies of the Commonwealth.* London, 1876.

Bauman, Richard. *For the Reputation of Truth.* Baltimore, 1972.

Beamish, Lucia Katharine. "The Quaker Understanding of the Ministerial Vocation with special reference to the Eighteenth Century." Bachelor of Letters thesis, Oxford University, 1965.

Beatty, Edward C. O. *William Penn as a Social Philosopher.* New York, 1939.
Benson, Mary Sumner. *Women in Eighteenth Century America: A Study of Opinion and Social Usage.* Columbia University Studies in History, no. 405. New York, 1935.
Braithwaite, William C. *The Beginnings of Quakerism.* 2d. ed. Prepared by Henry J. Cadbury. Cambridge, 1955.
———. *The Second Period of Quakerism.* 2d. ed. Prepared by Henry J. Cadbury. Cambridge, 1961.
Brayshaw, A.Neave. *The Quakers: Their Story and Message.* New York, 1938.
Bridenbaugh, Carl. *Cities in Revolt.* New York, 1955.
———. *Cities in the Wilderness.* New York, 1938.
———. *The Colonial Craftsman.* New York, 1950.
———, and Bridenbaugh, Jessica. *Rebels and Gentlemen: Philadelphia in the Age of Franklin.* New York, 1942.
Brinton, Anna, ed. *Then and Now: Quaker Essays, Historical and Contemporary.* Philadelphia, 1960.
Brinton, Howard. "Dreams of Quaker Journalists," *Byways in Quaker History.* Wallingford, Pa., 1944. Pp. 209–32.
———, ed. *Children of Light.* New York, 1938.
———. *Friends for 300 Years.* New York, 1952.
Bronner, Edwin B. *William Penn's Holy Experiment.* New York, 1962.
Brookes, George S. *Friend Anthony Benezet.* Philadelphia, 1937.
Bullock, Thomas K. "Schools and Schooling in Eighteenth Century Virginia." Ed.D. dissertation, Duke University, 1961.
Burrage, Champlin. *The Early English Dissenters 1550–1641.* Cambridge, 1912.
Cady, Edwin H. *John Woolman: The Mind of the Quaker Saint.* New York, 1966.
Caley, Percy B. "Child Life in Colonial Western Pennsylvania," *Western Pennsylvania Historical Magazine* 9 (1926): 33–49, 104–21, 188–201.
Calhoun, Arthur W. *A Social History of the American Family.* Vol. 1. New York, 1960.
Carroll, Kenneth L. "Quakerism in the Eastern Shore of Virginia," *Virginia Magazine of History and Biography* 75 (1966).
Clark, Alice. *Working Life of Women in the Seventeenth Century.* London, 1919.
Creasey, Maurice A. "The Theology of Robert Barclay." Bachelor of Divinity thesis, University of Leeds, 1951.
Cremin, Lawrence A. *American Education: The Colonial Experience.* New York, 1970.
Davidson, Robert L. *War Comes to Quaker Pennsylvania 1682–1756.* New York, 1957.
Davis, W. W. H. *The History of Bucks County.* Doylestown, Penn., 1876.
Delaware History. Vols. 1–12. 1946–67.
Demos, John. *A Little Commonwealth: Family Life in Plymouth Colony.* New York, 1970.
Dewess, Watson, and Dewess, Sarah. *History of Westtown Boarding School.* Philadelphia, 1899.
Dexter, Elisabeth Anthony. *Colonial Women of Affairs.* New York, 1931.
Doherty, Robert W. *The Hicksite Separation.* New Brunswick, N. J., 1967.
Doncaster, Leonard Hugh. *Quaker Organisation and Business Meetings.* London, 1958.
Douglas, Paul H. *American Apprenticeship and Industrial Education.* Columbia University Studies in History, Economics, and Public Law, vol. 95. New York, 1921.
Drake, Thomas E. "Patterns of Influence in Anglo-American Quakerism." Supplement no. 28 to the *Journal of the Friends' Historical Society.* London, 1958.
———. *Quakers and Slavery in America.* New Haven, Conn., 1950.
Drinker, Cecil K. *Not So Long Ago.* New York, 1937.
Dunlap, William C. *Quaker Education in Baltimore and Virginia Yearly Meetings with an Account of Certain Meetings of Delaware and the Eastern Shore Affiliated with Philadelphia.* Philadelphia, 1936.
Dunn, Mary M. *William Penn: Politics and Conscience.* Princeton, N. J., 1967.
Earle, Alice Morse. *Child Life in Colonial Days,* New York, 1929.
———. *Colonial Dames and Good Wives.* New York, 1913.
———. *Customs and Fashions in Old New England.* New York, 1889.
———. *Home Life in Colonial Days.* New York, 1913.
Eeg-Olofsson, Leif. *Conception of Inner Light in Robert Barclay's Theology.* Lund, Norway, 1954.
Endy, Melvin B., Jr. "William Penn and Early Quakerism: A Theological Study." Ph.D. dissertation, Yale University, 1969.
Erikson, Erik. *Childhood and Society.* New York, 1963.

Eversley, D. E. C., and Glass, D. V., eds. *Population in History: Essays in Historical Demography.* London, 1965.

______. "The Demography of Irish Quakers: Evaluation of Family Data Relating to a Religious Sect in Ireland in the Seventeenth and Eighteenth Centuries." Paper presented to the Colloquium in Historical Demography, September 23–26, 1965, at Eotvos Lorand University, Budapest.

Field, Edward. *State of Rhode Island and Providence Plantations at the End of the Century: A History.* Vol. 1. Boston, 1902.

Fletcher, Stevenson W. *Pennsylvania Agriculture and Country Life 1640–1840.* Harrisburg, Pa., 1950.

Ford, Paul Leicester. *The New England Primer.* New York, 1897.

Freiday, Dean, ed. *Barclay's Apology in Modern English.* Alburtis, Pa., 1967.

Friends' Historical Association, Journal (London). Vols. 1–63. 1903–70.

Friends' Historical Association, Bulletin (Philadelphia). Vols. 1–59. 1906–70. In 1962 the name of this publication was changed to *Quaker History.*

Friends in Wilmington 1738–1938. Wilmington, Del., 1937.

Fry, A. Ruth. *John Bellers 1654–1725.* London, 1935.

Galt, John. *The Life and Studies of Benjamin West, Esq.* London, 1816.

Geiser, K. P. *Redemptioners and Indentured Servants in the Colony and Commonwealth of Pennsylvania.* (Supplement to *Yale Review* 10 [1902].) New Haven, Conn., 1901.

Gilbey, Walter, and Cuming, E. D. *George Morland.* London, 1907.

Gorn, Janice L. "John Locke's Educational Theory and Some Evidences thereof in Pennsylvania." Ed.D. dissertation, New York University, 1963.

Greven, Philip J., Jr. *Four Generations: Population, Land, and Family in Colonial Andover, Massachusetts.* Ithaca, N. Y., 1970.

______. "Historical Demography and Colonial America: A Review Article." *William and Mary Quarterly,* 3rd Ser. 29 (1967): 438–54.

Grubb, Isabel. *Quakerism and Industry before 1800.* London, 1930.

Gummere, Amelia Mott. *The Quaker: A Study in Costume.* Philadelphia, 1901.

Hazard, Caroline. *The Narragansett Friends' Meeting in the Eighteenth Century.* Boston, 1899.

Heartman, Charles F. *American Primers, Indian Primers, Royal Primers, and thirty-seven other types of Non-New England Primers issued prior to 1830.* Highland Park, N.J., 1935.

Herrick, Chessman A. *White Servitude in Pennsylvania: Indentured and Redemption Labor in Colony and Commonwealth.* Philadelphia, 1926.

Hinshaw, William Wade. *Encyclopedia of American Quaker Genealogy.* Vols. 1–3. Ann Arbor, Mich., 1938.

Hole, Helen G. *Westtown Through the Years 1799–1942.* Westtown, Pa., 1942.

Homan, Walter Joseph. *Children and Quakerism.* Berkeley, Calif., 1939.

Home, G. J. N. Logan. *History of the Logan Family.* Edinburgh, Scotland, 1934.

Howard, George Eliott. *A History of Matrimonial Institutions,* Vols. 1–3. Chicago, 1904.

Hubbard. Dorothy G. B. "Early Quaker Education." Master's thesis, University of London, 1940.

Hull, William. *Benjamin Furly and Quakerism in Rotterdam.* Lancaster, Penn., 1941.

Hunt, David. *Parents and Children in History.* New York, 1970.

James, Sydney V. *A People Among Peoples: Quaker Benevolence in Eighteenth-Century America.* Cambridge, Mass., 1963.

______. "The Impact of the American Revolution on Quakers' Ideas About their Sect." *William and Mary Quarterly,* 3rd Ser. 19 (1962): 360–82.

Jernegun, Marcus Wilson. *Laboring and Dependent Classes in Colonial America, 1607–1783.* Chicago, 1931.

Jones, Mary Hoxie. *The Standard of the Lord Lifted Up: A History of Friends in New England 1656–1700.* 1961.

Jones, Matt Bushnell. "Thomas Maule, The Salem Quakers and Free Speech in Massachusetts Bay." *Essex Institute Historical Collections* 72 (1936): 1–42.

Jones, Rufus M. *The Later Periods of Quakerism.* Vols. 1–2. London, 1921.

______; Sharpless, Isaac; and Gummere, Amelia. *The Quakers in the American Colonies.* New York, 1966.

Kelsey, Rayner W. *Centennial History of Moses Brown School 1819–1919.* Providence, 1919.

Kiefer, Monica. *American Children Through Their Books, 1700–1835.* Philadelphia, 1948.

King, Rachel. *George Fox and the Light Within.* Philadelphia, 1940.

Kirby, Ethyn Williams. *George Keith.* New York, 1942.

Klain, Zora. *Educational Activities of New England Quakers.* Philadelphia, 1928.
———. *Quaker Contributions to Education in North Carolina.* Philadelphia, 1924.
Knox, Ronald A. *Enthusiasm: A Chapter in the History of Religion.* New York, 1961.
Kobrin, David. "Saving Remnant: Intellectual Sources of Change and Decline in Colonial Quakerism, 1690–1810." Ph.D. dissertation, University of Pennsylvania, 1968.
Laslett, Peter. *The World We Have Lost.* London, 1965.
Leach, Frank Willing. "Old Philadelphia Families." *North American.* Philadelphia, 1908–12.
Learned, Marion Dexter. *Life of Francis Daniel Pastorius.* Philadelphia, 1908.
Lemon, James T. *The Best Poor Man's Country.* Baltimore, 1972.
———, and Nash, Gary. "The Distribution of Wealth in Eighteenth Century America: A Century of Change in Chester County, Pennsylvania, 1693–1802." *Journal of Social History* 2 (1968): 1–24.
Littlefield, George Emery. *Early Schools and School-Books of New England.* Boston, 1904.
Lloyd, Arnold. *Quaker Social History, 1669–1738.* New York, 1950.
Lockridge, Kenneth A. *A New England Town: The First Hundred Years.* New York, 1970.
Lokken, Roy N. *David Lloyd, Colonial Lawmaker.* Seattle, 1959.
Lotka, A. J. "The Size of American Families in the Eighteenth Century." *Journal of American Statistical Association* 22 (1927): 154–70.
Marietta, Jack D. "Ecclesiastical Discipline in the Society of Friends, 1682–1776." Ph.D. dissertation, Stanford University, 1968.
Memorials of Rebecca Jones. Compiled by William J. Allinson. Philadelphia, 1849.
The Mennonite Encyclopedia. Vols. 1–4. Scottsdale, Pa., 1955.
Middlekauff, Robert. *Ancients and Axioms: Secondary Education in Eighteenth-Century New England.* New Haven, Conn., 1963.
Miller, Perry. *Errand into the Wilderness.* Cambridge, Mass., 1956.
———. *The New England Mind: The Seventeenth Century and From Colony to Province.* Cambridge, Mass., 1953, 1954.
Moller, Herbert. "Sex Composition and Correlated Culture Patterns of Colonial America." *William and Mary Quarterly,* 3rd Ser. 2 (1945): 113–53.
Morgan, Edmund. *The Puritan Family.* New York, 1966.
———. *Virginians at Home: Family Life in the Eighteenth Century.* Williamsburg, Va., 1952.
Morris, Richard B. *Government and Labor in Early America.* New York, 1965.
———. *Studies in the History of American Law, with Special Reference to the Seventeenth and Eighteenth Centuries.* Columbia University Studies in History, Economics, and Public Law, vol. 316. New York, 1930.
Nash, Gary. *Quakers and Politics: Pennsylvania, 1681–1726* Princeton, N.J., 1968.
New, John F. N. *Anglican and Puritan: The Basis of Their Opposition.* Stanford, Calif., 1964.
Nutall, Geoffrey F. *The Holy Spirit In Puritan Faith and Experience.* Oxford, England, 1946.
Oberholtzer, Ellis P. *Philadelphia: A History of the City and its People.* Vol. 1. Philadelphia, 1914.
Peare, Catherine Owens. *William Penn.* Ann Arbor, Mich., 1966.
Pearson, Lu Emily. *Elizabethans at Home.* Stanford, Calif., 1967.
Pennsylvania Archives. 3rd Ser., vol. 14. Harrisburg, 1897.
Pennsylvania History. Vols. 1–35. 1934–69.
Pennsylvania Magazine of History and Biography. Vols. 1–93. 1877–1969.
Pettit, Norman. *The Heart Prepared: Grace and Conversion in Puritan Spiritual Life.* New Haven, Conn., 1966.
Pinchbeck, Ivy, and Hewitt, Margaret. *Children in English Society.* Vol. 1. London, 1969.
Pinn, Fritz M. J. "Parental Views on Education with Special Reference to Ackworth School 1782–1825." Thesis for Teacher's Certificate, University of London, 1953.
Pomfret, John E. *The Province of West New Jersey, 1609–1702.* Princeton, N.J., 1956.
Powell, Chilton L. *English Domestic Relations 1487–1653.* New York, 1917.
Pumphrey, Thomas. *The History of Ackworth School.* Ackworth, England, 1835.
Raistrick, Arthur. *Quakers in Science and Industry.* New York, 1950.
Rhode Island Historical Society Collections. Vols. 1–34. 1907–41.
Rhode Island History. Vols. 1–27. 1941–68.
Rhode Island Historical Society, Publications. Vols. 1–8. 1893–1901.
Ross, Isabel. *Margaret Fell: Mother of Quakerism.* Plymouth, England, 1949.
Rowntree, John Stephenson. *Quakerism, Past and Present: Being an Inquiry into the Causes of its decline in Great Britain and Ireland.* London, 1859.

———. "Membership in the Society of Friends." *Friends' Quarterly Examiner* 6 (1872): 249–73.
Russell, Elbert. *History of Quakerism.* New York, 1943.
Schaff, Philip. *Creeds of Christendom.* Vol. 3. New York, 1919.
Sharpless, Isaac. *The Quaker Experiment in Government.* Philadelphia, 1902.
Shea, Daniel B., Jr. *Spiritual Autobiography in Early America.* Princeton, N.J., 1968.
Smith, Joseph. *A Descriptive Catalogue of Friends' Books.* 2 vols. London, 1867.
Stone, Lawrence. "Literacy and Education in England, 1640–1900." *Past and Present.* No. 42 (1969): 69–139.
———. *The Crisis of the Aristocracy.* New York, 1967.
Stroud, L. John. "The History of Quaker Education in England." Master's thesis, University of Leeds, 1944.
Taylor, William R. "Domesticity in England and America, 1770–1840." Paper submitted to the Committee on the Role of Education in American History, Symposium on the Role of Education in Nineteenth-Century America, Chatham, Mass., June 1964.
Thayer, Theodore. *Israel Pemberton: King of the Quakers.* Philadelphia, 1943.
———. *Pennsylvania Politics and the Growth of Democracy, 1740–76.* Harrisburg, Pa., 1953.
Thompson, Mack. *Moses Brown, Reluctant Reformer.* Chapel Hill, N.C., 1962.
Thorne, Dorothy Gilbert. "New Data from Minutes of Perquimans Monthly Meeting (Quaker), 1729–1736." *The North Carolinian,* 3 (1957): 3, 327–34.
———. "North Carolina Friends and the Revolution." *North Carolina Historical Review* 38 (1961): 323–40.
Tolles, Frederick B. *James Logan and the Culture of Provincial America.* Boston, 1957.
———. *George Logan of Philadelphia.* New York, 1953.
———. *Meeting House and Counting House: The Quaker Merchants of Colonial Philadelphia 1682–1763.* New York, 1963.
———. *Quakers and the Atlantic Culture.* New York, 1960.
Trotter, Eleanor. *Seventeenth Century Life in the Country Parish.* Cambridge, England, 1919.
Trueblood, David Elton. *Robert Barclay.* New York, 1968.
Two Hundred Fifty Years of Quakerism at Birmingham, 1690–1940. West Chester, Penn., 1940.
Two Hundred and twenty-fifth Anniversary of Concord Monthly Meeting of Friends, 1686–1911. Philadelphia, ca. 1911.
Upton, Dell. "History of the Quakers in Dutchess County, New York." B.A. thesis, Cornell University, 1970.
Vipont, Elfrida. *Ackworth School.* London, 1959.
Walzer, Michael. *The Revolution of the Saints: A Study in the Origins of Radical Politics.* Cambridge, Mass., 1965.
Waterhouse, Ellis. *Painting in Britain 1530–1790.* London, 1962.
———. *Gainsborough.* London, 1958.
———. *Reynolds.* London, 1941.
Watson, John. *Annals of Philadelphia, Being a Collection of Memoirs, Anecdotes, and Incidents of the City and its Inhabitants.* Philadelphia, 1830.
Watters, R. E. "Biographical Technique in Cotton Mather's Magnalia." *William and Mary Quarterly,* 3rd Ser. 2 (1945): 155–63.
Webb, Maria. *The Penns and Peningtons of the Seventeenth Century.* London, 1867.
Wells, Robert Vale. "A Demographic Analysis of Some Middle Colony Quaker Families of the Eighteenth Century." Ph.D. dissertation, Princeton University, 1969.
Wertenbaker, Thomas J. *The Founding of American Civilization: The Middle Colonies.* New York, 1938.
Whitney, Janet. *John Woolman: American Quaker.* Boston, 1962.
Wickersham, James Pyle. *The History of Education in Pennsylvania.* Lancaster, Pa., 1886.
Woody, Thomas. *Early Quaker Education in Pennsylvania.* New York, 1920.
———. *Quaker Education in the Colony and State of New Jersey.* Philadelphia, 1923.
Worrall, Arthur. "New England Quakerism, 1656–1830." Ph.D. dissertation, Indiana University, 1969.
Wright, Luella M. *The Literary Life of the Early Friends.* New York, 1932.
Vann, Richard T. *Social Development of English Quakerism 1655–1755.* Cambridge, Mass., 1969.
———. "Quakers and the Social Structure in the Interregnum." *Past and Present.* No. 43 (1969): 71–91.
———, and Jones, Hurwich. "Social Origins of Early Quakers: Debate." *Past and Present.* No. 48 (1970): 156–64.

Index

Allinson, Elizabeth (Smith), 42, 165, 175
Allinson, Samuel, 43, 85, 121, 137, 165, 175
Anglicans, 11, 48–49, 56, 60, 65, 66, 94, 97, 133, 138, 150–151, 156, 158–159, 172–173, 182, 188, 190, 191, 207–208, 217
Apprentices, 40, 52, 54, 56, 64–65, 74, 95, 127, 136–147, 219
Apology for the True Christian Divinity, 11, 24, 26, 51, 224
Artisans, 1, 121, 136–138, 145–146, 187, 196, 203

Bailyn, Bernard, 75, 98, 101, 144–145
Baptist, 61, 65, 97, 167, 188
Banks, John, 38, 77, 78, 80, 139, 178
Barbados, 65, 113, 134, 141, 204
Barclay, Robert, 6, 10, 13–14, 17, 18, 20–21, 24–27, 30–31, 45–48, 51–52, 66–67, 83, 128–129, 152, 187, 209, 224
Benezet, Anthony, 35, 50, 67, 81, 94, 103, 105, 108–112, 114–116, 118–119, 121, 123, 127–128, 161, 163, 187, 189–190, 197, 203, 213
Birth-rate, 69–70, 89. *See also* Demography
Bland, Elias, 52, 82, 142–143, 157, 203
Brinton, Howard, 30–31, 32, 40, 198, 209
Brown, Moses, 99, 103, 115, 121, 128, 139, 198
Business, 1, 19, 35, 56–57, 136, 141–144, 151, 198–204, 218

Chalkley, Thomas, 32, 69, 71, 80, 81, 121, 123, 140, 141, 145, 156, 174–175, 178–179, 182, 187, 199
Charity, 4, 24, 50, 59, 64–65, 97, 208: apprenticeship, 142–147
Children, 1, 2, 7, 12, 31–34, 37, 41, 42, 54, 56, 59, 64–92, 93–98, 102–105, 109, 112–118, 133–136, 140–142, 145, 150: church membership, 67–69, 87–88; examples for, 76, 151; games and fun, 81–83, 103–104, 138; plain style in dress, 78; seclusion from evil, 74–75, 93, 133, 147, 218–219; sentimentalization of, 71, 85–88, 219; status of infant, 65–69, 88
Churchman, George, 40, 128, 210
Churchman, John, 40, 100, 143, 187, 209, 210
Clarkson, Thomas, 37, 60, 78, 82, 98, 128, 133, 199, 203, 210
Classics, 100, 112, 118–121, 126
Clothing, 35, 56, 103, 104, 194–197, 211, 222
Connecticut, 2, 182, 223
Coole, Benjamin, 45, 77, 82, 178, 203
Country Friends, 1, 99, 110, 187, 206
Covenant theology, 14, 16, 52. *See also* Reformed theology
Crisp, Stephen, 15, 113, 223

Death, 33, 37, 41–44, 67, 70–71, 80–81, 90
Demography, 70–71, 90, 151–152
Dickinson, Jonathan, 124, 128, 139, 141, 144, 204
Dillwyn, William, 67, 71, 86, 126, 128
Drinker Elizabeth (Sandwich), 71–72, 144, 165, 177, 178, 209
Drinker, Henry, 140, 165, 201, 209

Earle, Alice Morse, 67, 73, 83
Edmundson, William, 71, 178, 198
Education, 2, 93–105, 109–129, 138, 144–146, 218–219. *See also* Children; Apprentices; Latin: Ackworth School, 102–103, 115, 116, 123; ambiguity in terminology, 93–94; curriculum, 94–95, 96, 103, 104, 110–111; English school, 111–112, 116–118, 121, 123, 136; daily life in schools, 121–127; family school, 102–105, 107; girls' education, 121, 125–127; schoolbooks, 93, 100, 112–118, 129; student newspapers, 124–126; teachers, 96–112; William Penn Charter School, 96–97, 101, 108, 112, 115, 121, 129
Edwards, Jonathan, 10, 16, 58
Ellwood, Thomas, 51, 135, 162
Emlen, Samuel Powell, 141, 157
England, 1, 4, 5, 11, 19, 39, 41, 43, 48, 58, 65, 95, 98, 101, 102, 108, 110, 117, 120, 128, 133, 135, 140, 142, 158, 172–173, 178, 180, 190–191, 195, 196–197, 198, 200, 202, 204, 209, 219, 225
Erikson, Erik, 7, 74, 90

Family, 1, 7, 8, 31, 53–54, 60, 64–65, 69–70, 73, 76–77, 79, 99, 102–105, 109, 136, 139, 140–142, 145–147, 150, 159, 177–178, 199, 201, 211, 219–220
Farmers, 1, 7, 188–189, 196, 215
Fell, Margaret, 72, 150, 156, 193
Ferris, David, 51, 127, 153–154
First Publishers of Truth, 10, 51, 74
Fox, George, 3, 6, 11, 14, 17, 20–21, 23–24, 30, 45, 50–52, 64, 66, 74, 84, 111–113, 115, 127–128, 145, 150, 152–153, 158, 159, 161, 173, 176, 180, 181, 188, 189, 193, 194, 197, 199, 222, 224

Girls, 93, 102–104, 111, 121, 122–127, 129, 137, 144–145, 209. *See also* Women
Griffith, John, 33–35, 40, 51, 59, 157
Great Awakening, 45, 58, 100
Greek, 94, 112, 120–121. *See also* Classics

Hill, Hannah, 43, 67, 81

Hill, Richard, 72, 156, 160, 164–165, 175
Hume, Sophia, 38, 72, 178

Inheritance, 135, 169, 184
Ireland, 4, 71, 115, 141, 194, 198

Jenkins, James, 31, 40, 60, 128
Jones, Rebecca, 111, 118, 178
Journals, 30–35, 38, 40, 44, 52, 78, 80, 110, 199

Kalm, Peter, 36, 174, 190, 195, 203
Keith, George, 10–11, 14, 17, 20–21, 28, 40, 48, 50, 56–57, 66–67, 68, 88, 110, 128, 208, 222
Kelsall, John, 34, 36, 79, 81, 153, 204, 209

Latin, 10, 94, 100, 110, 112, 113, 119–125. *See also* Classics
Logan, Hannah, 155, 157, 163–164, 180
Logan, James, 60, 71, 73, 98, 100, 120, 124, 126, 135, 143–144, 155, 157, 164, 174, 187, 200, 201, 203
Logan, William, 120, 126, 142, 143, 144, 146, 163–164, 170–171, 210
London Yearly Meeting, 4–5, 8, 10, 38, 39, 50, 53, 64, 69, 76, 78, 93, 96, 100–101, 105, 109–110, 120, 140, 156, 198, 222–223, 226: Meeting for Sufferings, 5, 39, 101, 120; Morning Meeting of Ministers and Elders, 5, 6, 222

Marietta, Jack D., 57, 159, 180
Marriage, 49, 66, 150–183, 219, 222: age at marriage, 151–152; betrothal, 173, 181; celibacy, 150; divorce, 181–183, 186; dowries, 157–158; duration of marriages, 151–152; inward light, 152–153; love, 77, 151–152, 154, 162–168, 171, 175–176, 183, 219; parental role, 154–156; prohibition to near kin, 160–161; remarriage, 152, 161–162; wealth as a factor in, 156–158, 167; wedding customs, 172–174; without Friends' approval, 24, 55–57, 155, 158–160, 218; wives, 175–179
Maryland, 4, 6, 8, 64, 97, 99, 223
Massachusetts, 2, 97, 140, 182, 201
Mather, Cotton, 30, 41, 79, 139, 207
Merchants, 1, 129, 136, 142, 144, 157, 188, 197, 199, 201, 204, 218
Milton, John, 100, 126, 150, 182
Morgan, Edmund S., 19, 73, 144, 162
Morris, Sarah, 38, 42, 178
Mothers, 72–73, 76–78, 84–86

Negro, 57, 79, 140, 144, 218
New England, 4–6, 8–9, 11, 36, 39, 53, 56, 58, 69, 95–97, 99, 102, 103, 112, 113, 116, 128, 144, 172, 182, 191, 204
New England Puritans, 12, 15, 19, 36, 67–68, 73, 97, 108, 112, 120, 127, 135, 144, 150, 168, 199, 208, 218–219. *See also* Puritans
New England Yearly Meeting, 4, 69, 96, 97, 103, 161, 200, 222
New Jersey, 4, 8, 96, 99, 105, 137, 187, 191, 193, 201–202, 212–213, 219, 223, 225
Newport, Rhode Island, 4, 143, 146, 190, 200–201, 204, 223
New York, 6, 103, 139, 204, 224
No Cross, No Crown, 41, 110, 189, 198

Norris, Isaac I, 67, 187, 197, 214
Norris, Isaac II, 67, 71, 100, 143, 157, 187, 202
North Carolina, 4, 5, 8, 35, 53, 56, 58, 69, 97, 99, 113, 188, 224

Oaths, 17, 24, 35, 190–191, 195, 208, 211

Pacifism, 191–192, 202, 211, 218. *See also* War
Parents, 2, 7, 16, 64–66, 74–81, 85, 94, 99, 133–140, 152, 154–156, 219
Pastorius, Francis D., 100, 110, 112–113, 115, 122–123, 126
Pemberton, Hannah, 67, 157, 210
Pemberton, Israel, Jr., 42, 87, 109, 134, 143, 144, 146, 163, 197, 202
Pemberton, Israel, Sr., 41, 100, 123, 126, 139, 141, 143, 144
Pemberton, James, 67, 82, 86, 141, 157, 160, 171, 179, 202, 204–205, 215
Pemberton, John, 86, 141, 157, 170, 187, 206, 215
Pemberton, Joseph, 134, 144
Pemberton, Phineas, 71, 122–123, 126, 154, 175, 178
Pembertons, 128, 144, 146, 208
Penington, Isaac, 51, 128, 156
Penn, William, 6, 10–11, 14, 17, 23, 28, 30, 41, 45, 51, 58–59, 67, 68, 73, 77, 83, 94–96, 98, 118, 127–128, 134–136, 144, 152, 155, 157, 162, 172, 175, 178, 187, 189, 194, 197–198, 201, 207, 217, 223
Pennsylvania, 2–4, 8, 53–54, 57, 68, 75, 95–96, 99, 105, 114, 140, 155, 172, 180–181, 187–188, 190, 191, 193, 200–203, 208, 212, 219, 225
Philadelphia, 7, 36, 38–39, 44, 83, 97, 99–101, 109–110, 116, 120, 127, 129, 137, 139, 145–146, 161, 172, 200–202, 205
Philadelphia Monthly Meeting, 39, 43, 53, 57, 79, 96, 100, 121, 154, 181, 204, 224
Philadelphia Yearly Meeting, 4–5, 8, 39, 64, 69, 96, 100–101, 109, 139, 140, 173, 182, 195, 198, 212, 223–224, 227
Piety Promoted, 41, 43, 44, 67
Poverty, 197–198, 211, 222. *See also* Charity
Presbyterians, 11–12, 25, 26, 48–49, 56, 68, 98, 100, 159, 188, 190, 191, 218
Proud, Robert, 110, 112, 121–122
Puritans, 1, 2, 10, 12–13, 25, 38, 48, 52, 60, 66–68, 78, 81, 87, 94, 96, 139, 150, 152, 156, 158, 160, 162, 167, 172, 182, 188, 193, 194, 197, 199, 207–208, 217, 220

Quaker catechisms, 83–85
Quaker customs: affirmations, 190–191, 212; asceticism, 188–190, 196; moderation, 44, 188–190, 196, 210; numerical listing of days and months, 193; oaths, 17, 24, 35, 190–191, 195, 208, 211–212; pacifism, 191–192, 202, 211, 218; payments of ministers (tithes), 191–192, 210; plain dress, 35, 56, 103, 104, 137, 194–196, 211, 222; plain speech, 35, 56, 192–193, 196, 211; social honor, 192
Quaker government, 2–3, 54, 58–60, 135–136, 187, 191–192, 208–209
Quaker organization: birthright membership,

Quaker organization (*Continued*)
68–69, 89, 100; books, 6, 56, 110, 223–224; church discipline, 48–61, 101, 135, 159, 202, 218; disciplines, 4–5, 135, 174, 222; disownment, 54–55, 159–160, 202, 222; elders, 3, 36, 39–40, 51, 53, 54, 173, 201, 208; epistles, 4, 8, 93, 221; family visits, 53–54; libraries, 6; meetings for sufferings, 5; meetings for worship, 35–40, 54; ministers, 5, 31, 35–40, 51, 53–55, 58, 188, 199, 208, 225, 227; monthly meeting, 3–4, 53, 159, 173, 222, 223; overseers, 3, 53, 173–174; preparative meetings, 3, 173, 222; press, 223; quarterly meetings, 4, 8, 55, 100, 161, 221, 222; queries, 4, 56–57, 59, 201; oligarchy of meeting, 60; sense of the meeting, 4; sermons, 37–40, 44–45, 78, 80; yearly meetings, 4, 55, 173, 208, 212, 222–223
Quaker theology, 16, 25: assurance, 19–20, 42; conversion, 32–34, 69, 88; discerning states of men, 38, 51; heathens, 17; inward light, 14–19, 22–23, 25–26, 40, 44, 51, 76, 113, 127, 129, 152–153, 214; irresistibility of grace, 17; justification, 19, 33–34; liberty of conscience, 50; limited atonement, 13; ministry, 3, 35, 119, 127, 173, 191, 196, 208; original sin, 12; perfection, 20–21, 32; predestination, 13–14, 66; reason, 13, 22, 51–52; sacraments, 24–25, 66; sanctification, 19, 33; Scripture, 21–25, 52, 84–85, 96, 113, 115, 127; seed, 15–16

Rank, Quaker attitude to, 192–193, 196–197, 218
Recreations, Quaker attitude to, 207–211
Redwood, Abraham, 141, 142, 144, 146, 187
Reformed theology: assurance, 19; irresistibility of grace, 12, 17; justification, 19; limited atonement, 12, 13, 17; original sin, 12; perfection, 20; perseverance of the saints, 12, 20; predestination, 13, 17, 66; sanctification, 19; Savoy Declaration, 11; Scripture, 21–23; Synod of Dort, 11, 12
Religious toleration, 2, 49, 93, 191, 208, 219–220
Reynell, John, 42, 82, 100, 143–144, 146, 155, 201–204, 206, 214–215
Rhode Island, 3, 6, 8, 33, 97, 111, 179, 188, 191, 201–202
Rhode Island Monthly Meeting, 58, 97, 99, 137, 161, 201
Richardson, Thomas, 200, 204, 214
Roberts, Jonathan II, 110, 143, 176
Roman Catholics, 10, 41, 66, 88, 97, 140, 150, 158–159, 167, 180, 182, 199

Schools, 1, 2, 4, 56, 60, 74, 80, 83, 94–132, 139, 145, 219. *See also* Education
Scott, Job, 33, 59, 80, 224
Servants, 54, 76, 78, 136, 140–141, 172, 177. *See also* Apprentices
Sewall, Samuel, 73, 79, 161
Sex, 54–56, 66, 70–71, 138, 179–181, 185–186
Slavery, 5, 51, 57, 58, 78, 209, 218
Smith, John, 35, 38–39, 52, 71, 73, 82, 86, 100, 144, 155, 157, 163–164, 176, 180, 187, 197, 208, 209–210, 222
Smith, William, 66–67, 153, 156
Speech, Quaker attitude to, 35, 56, 192–193, 196, 211
St. Méry, Moreau de, 165, 180
Stanton, Daniel, 38, 137, 204
Story, Thomas, 30–31, 33–34, 128, 157, 187
Symons Creek Monthly Meeting, 58, 99, 162

Taylor, Christopher, 113, 116, 119
Tolles, Frederick, 5, 45, 99–100, 112, 190

Virginia, 4–5, 8, 35, 39, 97, 102, 103, 134, 204

War, 24, 53, 56–57, 137, 188, 191–192, 195, 202–203, 218
Warville, Jacques Pierre Brissot de, 158, 190, 195, 203
Wealth, 197–206, 220
Wells, Robert V., 69, 150, 164, 168
Westminster Confession, 11, 17, 20, 22, 26
Whitall, Ann Cooper, 36–37, 40–41, 60, 162, 189
Wister, Sally, 125, 165–166, 195, 209
Women, 1, 37–38, 54–55, 72, 77, 78, 85–87, 125, 137, 142, 152, 170, 173–179, 181–182, 207, 219
Woolman, John, 31–32, 34, 50, 59, 64–65, 67, 79, 82, 108–109, 122, 123, 137–138, 187–188, 209, 214, 217, 220

Youth, 32–34, 37, 74–75, 82, 108, 132–147, 196

1 2 3 4 5 6 7 8 9 10 11 12 13 14 15 88 87 86 85 84 83 82 81 80 79 78 77 76 75 74 73